PEER HEALTH EDUCATION

Concepts and Content

Written by

Luoluo Hong

THE UNIVERSITY OF HAWAII AT HILO

Edited by

Jason Robertson and Julie Catanzarite

THE UNIVERSITY OF NORTH CAROLINA AT GREENSBORO

and

Lindsay Walker McCall

CECIL G. SHEPS CENTER FOR HEALTH SERVICES RESEARCH,

THE UNIVERSITY OF NORTH CAROLINA AT CHAPEL HILL

University Readers™
San Diego, CA

First published in the United States of America in 2011 by University Readers, Inc.

Trademark Notice: Product or corporate names may be trademarks or registered trademarks, and are used only for identification and explanation without intent to infringe.

15 14 13 12 11   1 2 3 4 5

Printed in the United States of America

ISBN: 978-1-60927-888-5

University Readers™
800.200.3908 | www.universityreaders.com

CONTENTS

Chapter 1

Campus Peer Health Education

By Luoluo Hong and Jason Robertson

Health Education: The Context for Peer Education

Regardless of the changes for higher education, as long as we believe that education has something to do with helping individuals achieve their maximum potential for self-development, the development of connection to others, and effective contribution to a lively democracy and its institutions, *we cannot achieve the mission of higher education without dealing in some way with health.* If we believe we can, we do so at the risk of ignoring major personal, environmental, and political dimensions of education (Burns 1990).

The health of college students is essential to their academic success during their undergraduate years. Health habits and lifestyle practices learned and adopted in college most likely will endure for a lifetime, and impact quality of life and longevity. Throughout the twentieth century, campus health services have played a major role in caring for students' health and well-being. They have succeeded in providing quality care at an affordable cost. Professional health educators have been integral members of the health care team for college students for several decades. Now, peer health educators have joined that team.

The work of campus health educators, both peers and professionals, falls under the rubric of public health. **Public health** is the science and art of preventing disease, prolonging life, and promoting health through organized community efforts focused on the sanitation of the environment, control of communicable infections, education in personal hygiene, organization of medical services, and the development of the social system to ensure everyone a standard of living adequate for maintenance of health. Public health focuses primarily on the health of populations, communities, and organizations rather than on individuals, and is committed to social responsibility. Usually public health is concerned with a health problem, based on the assumption that the social, physical, and political environments play major roles in the amelioration of the problem (Modesto 1996).

Specifically, **health education** is an educational process concerned with providing a combination of approaches to lifestyle change that can assist individuals, families, and communities in making informed decisions on matters affecting restoration, achievement, and maintenance of health. It is a deliberately structured discipline or profession that provides learning opportunities about health through interactions between educators and learners using a variety of learning experiences. This process of learning can enable people to voluntarily change conditions or modify behavior. Health education is more than factual information. It includes those experiences that affect the way people think and feel about their health, and it motivates them to put information into practice (Modesto 1996).

In contrast, **health enhancement** refers to that dimension of health promotion pertaining to the aim of reaching higher levels of wellness beyond the mere absence of disease and infirmity. Health enhancement begins with people who are basically healthy, but is not limited to the well population. Everyone, including those with chronic health conditions, can improve their level of health.

Similarly, **prevention** refers to the process whereby specific action is taken to prevent or reduce the possibility of a health problem or condition development and to minimize any damage that may have resulted from a previous condition. There are three levels of prevention:

- **Primary:** stopping the health problem or condition before it occurs;
- **Secondary:** early detection and prompt treatment to deter further decay; and
- **Tertiary:** interventions to limit further disability and early death.

Finally, **health promotion** uses a combination of health education and specific interventions, such as anti-smoking campaigns, at the primary level of prevention designed to facilitate behavioral and environmental changes conducive to health enhancement. Health promotion aims at helping people change their lifestyle through public participation in a combination of efforts to enhance awareness, and create environments that support positive health practices that may result in reducing health risks in a population.

Health promotion involves three levels of attempts to improve and maintain health: disease prevention, health enhancement, and medical care. Tasks include needs assessment, problem identification, development of appropriate goals and objectives, creation of interventions, implementation of interventions, and the evaluation of outcomes or results. Benefits of health promotion may include changes in attitude, increased awareness and knowledge, lower risk for certain health problems, better health status, decreased morbidity and mortality, and improved quality of life.

Defining Peer Education

Peer education consists of instruction by or guidance from equals (Gould and Lomax 1993)—individuals who have some similarity with those they are teaching. Variables such as age, gender, race, religion, sexual orientation, socioeconomic status, and life experience or group affiliation may be used by target audiences to determine who is perceived as being "equal" or having similar lives. Thus, diversity in the student population requires a corresponding diversity of peer education staff. Ultimately, whether the audience perceives the educator as a peer or not is the determining factor in the effectiveness of the interventions (Gould and Lomax 1993). University campuses are not the only locations for peer education programs. Peer education models have been adapted in a variety of settings—schools, prisons, and churches—to impact a variety of human behaviors (health, crime, career, etc.). For example, many prisons have instituted peer education interventions in which inmates teach fellow inmates about HIV prevention and drug abuse.

On university campuses peer education programs have taken many forms. Some are incorporated as part of residential living (e.g., resident assistants); academic advising programs frequently use peers; orientation programs may use ambassadors to provide new students with support and assistance; athletic departments may rely on mentoring programs to ensure retention of student-athletes. The vast majority of campus peer education programs are based in the student health center or health education department and used to provide health and wellness information to the student population.

Activities implemented by peer health educators vary from campus to campus and take place in one-on-one and group settings, ranging from individual consultations, small-group presentations/discussions, role plays, theater/skits, games, mass media campaigns, and campus-wide awareness weeks. Outreach educational programs are targeted to student living areas or for target student populations. Peers may also develop, produce, and disseminate public service announcements in video and other formats. Some peers serve on student health center advisory boards. Still others staff hotlines, resource centers, or outreach offices where students can access health information and participate in self-assessments. Additionally, peer educators on many campuses act in theater troupes (Gould and Lomax 1993; Sloane and Zimmer 1993).

Keeling and Engstrom (1993) have identified ten earmarks of what they call an enhanced peer education program. Such a program:

1. possesses an ability to sense, monitor, and react to change—a quality that makes programs durable, popular, and indispensable;
2. is frequently and carefully evaluated, in the context of an ongoing appraisal of campus needs in health education and health promotion;
3. has the ability to match the talents, skills, and preparation of peer educators to the most appropriate tasks, activities, and programs;
4. recruits people with specific talents that match the program's needs;
5. recruits students who are broadly representative of the diversity of students on campus;
6. conducts highly targeted, carefully designed, frequently evaluated training activities, which are specifically tailored to the needs of each group of trainees;
7. exhibits an awareness of and responsiveness to the diversity of learning styles among students and their focus on visual learning;
8. displays a commitment to inclusive programming;
9. possesses flexibility; and
10. focuses on effective marketing for maximum visibility.

History of Peer Health Education

Peter Finn (1981,13) has noted that peer education takes place "constantly among youngsters and adults, regardless of instructional efforts to promote the use of more 'reliable' sources of information and advice." He continues, "It is essential that we seek, through formal training, to put the inevitable peer education that will take place to positive use, rather than leave it to the vagaries of chance."

It is not reported in the literature when and where the first college peer health educators emerged. One of the earliest recorded examples of a peer education intervention was at the University of Nebraska in Lincoln; student health aides were recruited in response to a 1957 epidemic of Asian flu (Helm, Knipmeyer, and Martin 1972). In rural New England, a small group of college students initiated their own campus reproductive-health peer education program in 1971. At that time, abortions and abortion counseling were illegal; contraceptives were not available on campus, and the nearest Planned Parenthood was forty miles away. The students traveled to Washington, DC, to receive training, then returned to campus to recruit and train other students to help them. These students distributed a Canadian handbook on birth control, hosted peer education sessions about contraception, and assisted women in raising funds and identifying resources for safe abortions. Furious, college administrators threatened to suspend the academic privileges of the group's leaders until the mother of one of the peer educators—an alumna—openly supported both the group's efforts and her daughter's participation. She reminded the administrators of a student from her graduating class of 1949 who died after an illegal abortion. By the 1973 commencement ceremonies, birth control services were available to students, and the peer education program was funded by the college (Zapka 1981).

The University of Massachusetts at Amherst pioneered campus-based peer education programs in 1970, providing a national model for substance abuse and sexuality peer education (Edelstein and Gonyer 1993). Now, over four decades later, the number of peer health education programs at colleges and universities across the US is burgeoning. Estimates are that nearly 80% of colleges and universities use some form of peer education or peer counseling to disseminate health information (Salovey and D'Andrea 1984). Several regional and national conferences now exist on peer health education, and the number of research articles investigating peer health education is gradually increasing.

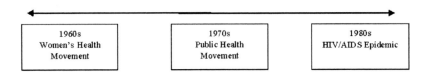

Figure 1: *Events that Shaped Campus-Based Peer Health Education. This diagram shows major moments in health that helped to inform and develop peer education programs.*

The **Women's Health Movement (1960s)** fostered greater emphasis on self-care and self-empowerment of the patient. Priority was placed on disseminating accurate information regarding birth control to women of all walks of life. Women demanded that patient and provider be regarded as more equal partners in health care. There was a demand to demystify medicine and a similar move to make health care more accessible to the layperson, thus debunking the monopoly of the professional health care provider as a purveyor of health information. Alternative modalities of treatment began to gain popularity.

When the **Public Health Movement (1970s)** resurged, large-scale epidemiological studies revealed that many instances of morbidity and mortality in the US were due to controllable lifestyle factors (rather than genetic traits or unavoidable infectious agents). Educational strategies could be used to change these behavioral factors. At the same time, university campuses saw an upsurge in enrollment, requiring additional resources and services.

The **HIV/AIDS Epidemic (1980s)** signified the emergence of a fatal disease for which there is no cure, and shifted emphasis from treatment (medical model) to prevention (public health/community health model). Educational campaigns using gay men to reach their peers were launched in cities such as San Francisco and New York; these programs were successful in curbing the rate of HIV infection among gay men, thus demonstrating the effectiveness of peer education.

Structure of Peer Education Organizations. While most peer health educators are supervised by a student health center or health education unit, occasionally some have been advised by an academic unit (Medical School, Nursing School, Allied Health & Life Sciences, College of Education, Department of Kinesiology, etc.) or some other student affairs/services department (e.g., residential life, dean of students, counseling center, campus activities, student health services, and health promotion).

Depending on the campus's financial and staffing resources, peer health educators may be unpaid volunteers; receive course credit (1–6 hours) for their training, service, or both; or are paid as student employees (work-study, financial aid, etc.). The selection process for peer educators varies by school and by organization, as well. Some organizations may have no membership requirement (i.e., open membership). Many institute an application/screening process to ensure quality among their candidates. At some institutions, targeted recruitment for members (e.g., student-athletes, Greek leaders, minority students, non-traditional students) takes place (Gould and Lomax 1993).

Training received by peer health educators also differs across campuses and may take the form of weekend retreats; weekly/biweekly in-service meetings; non-credit course(s); for-credit course(s); attendance at local, regional, and national conferences; or a combination of the above (Gould and Lomax 1993).

Motivations of Peer Educators. Klein, Sondag, and Drolet (1994) examined the factors that motivate individuals to volunteer for a peer health education program. Based on data from five focus groups with nineteen subjects ranging in age from 17 to 34 years (four men, fifteen women), the researchers identified numerous reasons students became volunteer peer educators, many of which overlapped.

Many of the peer educators attributed their motivation to join to family experiences, some positive but many negative (e.g., father was alcoholic, mother was manic-depressive). Some respondents indicated that the experiences of friends (e.g., unplanned pregnancy, date rape) provided the impetus for volunteering. Still other subjects reported that personal circumstances, such as past risk-taking or strong religious values prompted them to serve as peer educators. Some respondents were motivated to become volunteers after observing other peer educators during presentations. Some subjects joined peer health education programs out of a desire to help or serve others—to improve the health of their peers. Finally, a group of respondents became volunteers to gain job or public speaking experience, to simply meet people with similar interests, or to gain health information for personal benefit.

Pros and Cons of Peer Health Education. Here are some of the common arguments about the advantages and strengths of peer health education:

- In times of shrinking health care costs from which colleges are not immune, peer educators are cost-effective and cost-efficient (Gould and Lomax 1993; Sawyer, Pinciaro, and Bedwell 1997; Sloane and Zimmer 1993).
- Peers are the best venues for conveying health information of a sensitive or value-laden nature (especially sexual health, and alcohol and other drugs); they can be regarded as non-threatening authorities who "speak their language." Students are most likely to open up to a peer educator (Sawyer, Pinciaro, and Bedwell 1997; Sloane and Zimmer 1993; Wessel 1993).
- Students (particularly traditional-aged) are most likely to turn to their peers for health-related information; peers are readily accessible in terms of location and time—they live with the students (Sloane and Zimmer 1993).
- Peers (especially leaders of social groups) can effectively model healthful attitudes and behaviors and are credible role models (Sloane and Zimmer 1993).
- Some health information may be easier for a student to grasp if it is explained by a peer (Damon 1984).
- Peer education, through the leadership and service opportunities it provides, trains future professionals in health and human services (Klein, Sondag, and Drolet 1994; Drellishak 1997).

Several drawbacks and weaknesses of peer health education have also been pointed out:
- Evaluation efforts have been skimpy at best (Fennell 1993; Haines 1993; Keeling and Engstrom 1993).
- The input by professional staff to train, supervise, and motivate peers far exceeds output of peers (Haines 1993; Lindsey 1997).
- The quality of programs (e.g., informational accuracy) provided is not as good as those provided by professionals, and students are less likely to perceive peers as credible sources of information

(Lindsey 1997). The greatest gain and impact is accrued by the peer educators themselves; the impact on others is questionable, short-term, and minimal at best (Kelley 1993).

- Use of peer health educators may reduce the commitment of a university to invest more resources into health education efforts and staffing (Wessel 1993; Lindsey 1997).
- Many advisors also agreed that the majority of campus peer education programs fail to recruit or retain student staff from a diverse range of backgrounds reflective of the campus population; for example, the majority of peer educators at many large, public university campuses are white females of traditional college age (18–23 years).

Evaluation of Peer Education Programs. Peer health education bears particular quality assurance issues that can be measured by both process and outcome evaluation techniques. **Process evaluation**, some types of which are frequently referred to as quality assurance review, is the most commonly used method by those campus peer health education programs that do conduct evaluation. This type of evaluation requires that standards of performance be identified and applied before the effects of programs are measured. The evaluation process then documents what is occurring in any given program or workshop and analyzes its structural elements (Green and Lewis 1986). In most college health services, process evaluations constitute the "customer satisfaction" aspect of assessment.

Outcome evaluation measures how effective an intervention is in producing changes in knowledge, attitudes, beliefs, and behavior (Green and Lewis 1986). Because it requires the identification of clear and accurate outcome measures, this is the most challenging form of evaluation for health educators (Croll, Jurs, and Kennedy 1993). Only four such studies exist in the literature. Furthermore, researchers have long argued about whether or not the short-term, one-shot program interventions typical of health education have any long-term impact in changing behavior.

Sawyer, Pinciaro, and Bedwell (1997) conducted a study documenting the effects on behavior change of a long-term intervention. They examined the effect that year-long service in a peer sexuality education program had on sixty-five peer educators from ten universities in the US. While quantitative analysis comparing pre- and post-test results on three instruments (Rosenberg Self-Esteem Scale, Personal Development Inventory, and Safe Sex Behavior Questionnaire) yielded a positive change that was statistically insignificant, qualitative data described increased levels of self-reported self-esteem, confidence in public speaking, and practice of safer-sex behaviors among study participants. In addition, 20% of respondents changed their future career interests to health education or public health as a result of their service as a peer educator.

Peer Education: A Contrast in Paradigms

There exist two predominant models of peer health education; they differ both in their administrative characteristics and in their educational goals. The **traditional health education model** has been in existence on many college campuses since the 1960s and is the model adopted by most peer health education programs. The community action model (also known as the **system leadership** model or **service-learning model**) is a relatively new way of conceptualizing campus peer health education programs.

Based on her extensive work with peer educators, Pat Fabiano (1994), a health educator at Western Washington State University, has compared the two peer health education models, examining differences in philosophy, training, recruitment, activities, and goals.

Philosophy. In the traditional model, individuals are largely responsible for their health by virtue of the choices they make, i.e., personal decisions regarding lifestyle and behavior. People can reduce their health risks and improve their health status largely through personal decision to change. Health-enhancing behavior can be increased by providing students with sufficient information about risk, teaching new skills, and increasing their sense of self-esteem.

In contrast, the community action model regards health as a process that occurs within the dynamic interaction between the individual and the environment in which he or she lives. Health is neither achieved nor compromised in isolation. An individual's health and the health of his or her environment and society are inextricably interrelated. Health decisions, therefore, are made and sustained within the whole context of a person's life. The basis of "health" is more than a medical issue. Rather, it is an issue of sufficient food, shelter, safety, affiliation, work, and community. The focus of health education must encompass and exceed working with individuals one by one to make changes in the way they live. It must also include working with social, cultural, and political systems to enhance the capacities of communities to help the individuals who live in them solve problems and make healthier choices.

Training. Training curriculum is largely health-content-oriented in the traditional model. The content may either be general health issues (wellness, health risks, health objectives) or specific topic-based issues (HIV/AIDS, alcohol and other drugs, etc.). Training may also include (1) process skills necessary for peers to present effective programs (e.g., presentation skills, active listening, role playing) and (2) value clarification for peers to assess their attitudes and beliefs before presenting programs.

In the community action model, preparation includes traditional health content areas and exceeds them. Students are trained to become aware of interconnectedness of "personal health problems" and "public health issues." All specific health content topics are presented from a systems model emphasizing the interdependence of individuals and the environments in which they live. Students are challenged to see health issues in the context of society and culture.

Recruitment. In the traditional model, a small number of highly qualified students are selected through an application and interview process. Students are trained to "do programs" and provide service largely confined to the campus community. In programs guided by the community action model, large numbers of students are recruited and registered for peer education training courses. The goal is to train sufficiently large numbers of students on a campus to approach a "critical mass," empowered to speak from experience about the reality of making and sustaining healthy lifestyles. Students who come into the program who are themselves "wounded" or recovering from specific health concerns are seen as resources. Supervision shifts to a model of mentoring.

Activities. Information and skills-based programs are usually offered within the context of the college campus (e.g., residence halls, health fairs, displays in the student health center, targeted classrooms) in traditional peer education models. Programs may include planning and implementing health promotion campaigns, such as those for National Collegiate Alcohol Awareness Week, National Condom Week, Sexual Assault Awareness Month, and World AIDS Day.

However, in the community action model, students are offered a variety of service levels for participation. Some students present traditional health information and skills-building programs in the college residence halls or in classrooms. Other students are encouraged to apply what they have learned in community service sites where they gain hands-on experience regarding the complexity and interconnectedness of solving personal and public health problems. A third group of students takes its place as "health opinion leaders," willing to assert its opinions regarding thorny health issues at the natural teachable moments in normal social life and interaction. Health opinion leaders are the keystone of the social action approach. Their work redefines the context of "program" to everyday natural interactions students have with each other.

Goals. Programs under the traditional model aim to increase the health literacy of the students and to decrease students' risk for illness and injury while they are in college and in the future. Goals may also include providing peer health educators with valuable, hands-on, paraprofessional experience in a health-related field. In contrast, the focus of community action-based programs and curricula is to facilitate students' understanding of the connections between their personal health and the health of their communities (Fabiano 1994).

Figure 2: *Comparison of Traditional Health Education and Community Action Models*

Adapted from Montana State University, Peer Health Education Program. Program presented at 1994 American College Health Association Annual Meeting, Atlanta, GA.

Traditional Health Education Model	Community Action Model
1. **Health Educators** Focus on education of individuals by providing information.	1. **Health Leaders** Focus on changing campus environment through organizational development.
2. **Centralized** Program based in and operates out of a student health center.	2. **Decentralized** Programs, staff, and leaders are spread throughout the campus community.
3. **Content Focused** Ninety percent of program energies are devoted to providing information in creative ways.	3. **Process Focused** Ninety percent of energies are devoted to developing and changing campus organization.
4. **Steep Organizational Hierarchy** Proper information goes from health educator to specialized staff to student presenters. Pyramid shaped.	4. **Circular Organizational Structure** Large numbers of students and staff with accountability to each and mentors, rather than a director. Wheel shaped.
5. **Individual Change Model** Efforts devoted to influencing the campus by affecting the beliefs and behaviors of individual students.	5. **Social Change Model** Efforts devoted to influencing the campus through reshaping social and organizational norms.
6. **Deficit Reduction** View students as lacking knowledge, skills, or attributes. Peer educators need to attend training before contributing.	6. **Asset Building** View students and the campus as resource rich. Students are encouraged to jump in and learn while contributing.
7. **Students as Prevention Receptacles** Staff-driven programs reach the student body through student programs.	7. **Students as Prevention Partners** Staff and students interact as partners in the process of reshaping campus culture.
8. **Inadequate Support** Program does not receive necessary administrative and financial resources. Support from one source.	8. **Priority Support** Central to the campus mission, program receives noticeable financial and administrative support from many sources.
9. **Reactive Management** Works within the current system to impact students without challenging the system.	9. **Proactive Management** Challenges current system through organizational change and political activism.
10. **Sole Source** Health educators function as gatekeepers of campus health information.	10. **Multiple Resources** Health educators work themselves out of jobs by empowering others and the system.

Suggestions for Further Reading

Glanz, K., Lewis, F. M., & Rimer, B. K. (Eds.). (1990). Health behavior and health education: Theory, research and practice. San Francisco: Jossey-Bass Publishers.

Newton, F.B. & Ender, S.C. (2010). Students helping students: A guide for peer educators on college campuses. San Francisco: Jossey-Bass.

Patrick, K. (Ed.). (1992). Principles and practices of student health: Volume three, college health. Oakland, CA: Third Party Publishing Company.

Questions to Consider

1. How do you see yourself fitting into the peer education program?
2. Why is a peer education program important on the campus?
3. In what ways do you view peer education as being beneficial to you? To your peers?
4. How does peer education fit into the community action model?
5. What events have influenced peer education today? (e.g., Women's movement)

References

Burns, W. D. (1990). Health education in higher education's future. *Journal of American College Health, 39,* p. *103–108.*

Croll, N., Jurs, E., & Kennedy, S. (1993). *Total quality assurance and peer education. Journal of American College Health,* 41, p. 247–249.

Damon, W. (1984). Peer Education: The Untapped Potential. *Journal of Applied Developmental Psychology* 5(4), p. 331–334.

Drellishak, R. (1997). The merits of peer education programs [Letter to the editor]. *Journal of American College Health,* 45, p. 218.

Edelstein, M. E. & Gonyer, P. (1993). Planning for the future of peer education. *Journal of American College Health,* 41, p. 255–257.

Fabiano, P. M. (1994). From personal health into community action: Another step forward in peer health education. *Journal of American College Health,* 43, p. 115–121.

Fennell, R. (1993). A review of evaluations of peer education programs. *Journal of American College Health,* 41, p. 251–253.

Finn, P. (1981). Teaching students to be lifelong peer educators. *Journal of Health Education* 12 (5), 13–16.

Gould, J. M., & Lomax, A. R. (1993). The evolution of peer education: Where do we go from here? *Journal of American College Health,* 41, p. 235–240.

Green, L.W., & Lewis, F. M. (1986). *Measurement and evaluation in health education and health promotion. Palo Alto,* CA: Mayfield Publishers.

Haines, M. (1993). Professionals' experiences of peer education: Four experts speak. *Journal of American College Health,* 41, p. 300–301.

Helm, C.J., Knipmeyer, C., & Martin, M. R. (1972). Student involvement in a university health center program. *Journal of American College Health Association* 20(4), p. 248–251.

Keeling, R. P., & Engstrom, E. L. (1993). Refining your peer education program. *Journal of American College Health,* 41, p. 259–263.

Kelley, S. (1993). *Professionals' experiences of peer education: Four experts speak. Journal of American College Health,* 41, p. 300–301.

Klein, N. A., Sondag, K. A., & Drolet, J. C. (1994). Understanding volunteer peer health educators' motivations: Applying social learning theory. *Journal of American College Health,* 43, p. 126–130.

Lindsey, B. J. (1997). Peer education: A viewpoint and critique. *Journal of American College Health,* 45, p. 187–189.

Modesto, N. (1996). *Dictionary of public health and education terms and concepts.* Thousand Oaks, CA: Sage Publications.

Salovey, P., & D'Andrea, V. J. (1984). *A survey of campus peer counseling activities. Journal of American College Health* 32(6), p. 262–265.

Sawyer, R., Pinciaro, P., & Bedwell, D. (1997). How peer education changed peer sexuality educators' self-esteem, personal development, and sexual behavior. *Journal of American College Health, 45,* p. 211–217.

Sloane, B. C., & Zimmer, C. G. (1993). The power of peer health education. *Journal of American College Health, 41,* p. 241–245.

Wessel, L. (1993). Professionals' experiences of peer education: Four experts speak. *Journal of American College Health, 41,* p. 300–301.

Zapka, J. M. (1981). *Health education in college health service.* Atlanta, GA: American Hospital Association/Centers for Disease Control.

Chapter 2

How Behavior Can Be Changed

By Luoluo Hong and Jason Robertson

Individual Level Theories and Models

Stimulus Response Theory (Skinner 1953). Learning results from temporally associated consequences that either increase or decrease the likelihood that a particular behavior will occur. Consequences of behavior can either be reinforcement or punishment. **Reinforcement** is any event following a behavior that increases the probability of that same behavior being repeated in the future. Behavior is most likely to recur if (1) reinforcement is frequent, and (2) reinforcement is immediate. **Punishment** is any event following a behavior that decreases the probability of that same behavior's reoccurrence. Both reinforcement and punishment can be either positive (adding stimuli to an event) or negative (removing stimuli from an event).

2 x 2 Table of the Stimulus Response Theory

Behavior	Consequences	
	Positive (adding to)	*Negative (taking away)*
Increase in frequency	Positive reinforcement	Negative reinforcement
Decrease in frequency	Positive Punishment	Negative punishment

Social Cognitive Theory, or Social Learning Theory (Rotter 1954; Bandura 1986).

While reinforcement is an integral part of learning, various cognitive constructs (synthesized thoughts or key concepts) also play a role. Behavior becomes a function of the subjective value of an outcome and the subjective probability (or expectation) that a particular action will achieve that outcome; such formulations are known as value-expectancy theories.

Frequently used constructs of social cognitive theory include:

1. **Reinforcement.** Responses to behavior that increase the chances of its recurrence. Responses can occur (1) directly, (b) vicariously, or (c) through self-management.
2. **Behavioral Capability.** Knowledge and skills necessary to perform a behavior.
3. **Outcome Expectations.** Beliefs that the likely outcomes of certain behaviors will be positive rather than negative.
4. **Expectancies.** The values that individuals place on an expected outcome; if a person values an expected outcome, s/he is more likely to perform the necessary behavior to yield that outcome.
5. **Self-Control or Self-Regulation.** Gaining control over one's own behavior through monitoring and adjusting it.
6. **Self-Efficacy or Efficacy Expectations.** Refers to the internal state that an individual experiences as "competence" to perform a certain desired task or function. This state is situational. Individuals

become self-efficacious in four ways: (a) through performance attainments (personal mastery of a task); (b) through vicarious experience (observing the performance of others); (c) as a result of verbal persuasion (receiving encouragement from others); and (d) through emotional arousal (interpreting one's emotional state).

7. **Reciprocal determinism.** Behavior changes result from an interaction between the person and the environment; change is bidirectional.

8. **Locus of control.** Refers to a person's belief about whether or not his or her own actions lead to certain reinforcements.

9. **Emotional coping response.** For people to learn, they must be able to deal with the sources of anxiety that surround a behavior.

Theory of Reasoned Action (Fishbein and Ajzen 1975)

An individual's intention to perform a given behavior is a function of his/her intention to perform the behavior, his/her attitude toward performing the behavior, and normative beliefs about what relevant others (individual or groups) think s/he should do, weighted by motivation to comply with those others. These normative beliefs are frequently referred to as the **subjective norm**.

Theory of Planned Behavior (Ajzen 1988)

Like Theory of Reasoned Action, this theory includes attitudes toward the behavior and subjective norm as determinants of behavior and adds the concept of perceived **behavior control**—the perceived ease or difficulty of performing the behavior, based on experiences as well as anticipated impediments and obstacles. In general, the more favorable the attitude and subjective norm with respect to a behavior and the greater the perceived behavior control, the stronger should be the individual's intention to perform the desired health behavior.

Theory of Freeing (Freire 1973)

This theory is aimed at empowering education, where **empowerment** refers to the process by which individuals, organizations, and communities acquire the ability to control their own lives and effect change. An underlying concept of this theory is that **critical consciousness** is determined by the reciprocal interaction with one's culture. Oppressed people are "of the world"; that is, their consciousness is a product of the culture, and they are unable to perceive, respond, and act with power to change concrete reality. Free people are "in the world"; their consciousness is a creator of culture. Interactive, iterative education based on dialogue between teachers and participants is the key to becoming critically conscious.

There are three stages in this theory. **Stage 1** is the listening stage, in which members of the target population have an opportunity to share thoughts, identify problems and needs, and establish their own priorities. **Stage 2** entails dialogue revolving around a code—any concrete, tangible physical representation of an identified community issue. Group facilitators help move the target population from a personal to a social analysis and action level with five statements: (1) Describe what you see and feel; (2) As a group, define the many levels of the problem; (3) Share similar experiences from your lives; (4) Question why this problem exists; and (5) Develop action plans to address the problem. **Stage 3** is the collective action stage, in which members of the target population try out the plans outlined in Stage 2, reflect on their experiences, and refine the plan.

Health Belief Model, or HBM (Rosenstock et al. 1988)

This model hypothesizes that health-related actions depend upon the simultaneous occurrence of three classes of factors:

1. The existence of sufficient motivation (or health concern) to make health issues salient or relevant.

2. The individual perception that one is susceptible (vulnerable) to a serious health problem (**perceived susceptibility**) or to the sequelae of that illness or condition (**perceived seriousness, or severity**). This is often perceived as **perceived threat**. Factors that modify perceived threat include:
   a. **Demographic variables** (sex, age, race, ethnicity, and social class);
   b. **Sociopsychological variables** (personality, and peer and reference group pressure;
   c. **Structural variables** (knowledge about and prior contact with the disease); and
   d. **Cues to action** (mass media campaigns, advice from others, reminder postcards from health care provider, and illness of family member or friend).

3. The belief that following a particular preventive behavior would be beneficial in reducing the perceived threat (**perceived benefits**), and at a subjectively acceptable cost. Cost refers to the **perceived barriers**—both financial and otherwise—that must be overcome in order to implement a particular health recommendation. When perceived benefits exceed perceived barriers, the likelihood of taking recommended preventive health action is increased.

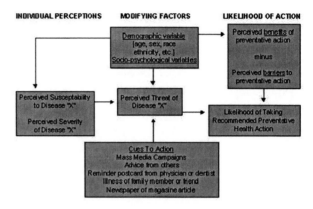

Figure 3: *Health Belief Model. This is a graphic representation of the core tenants of the Health Belief Model.* (*Source:* Communication and Community Development for Health Information: Constructs and Models for Evaluation *by John E. Bowes. Review prepared for the National Network of Libraries of Medicine, Pacific Northwest Region, Seattle, December 1997.*

Transtheoretical Model, or Stages of Change (Prochaska 1979)

This model describes the cyclical change pattern that the majority of individuals experience as they attempt to alter their health behavior over time. Movement through these stages is not linear; rather, most people will relapse and return to the precontemplation or contemplation stage before eventually succeeding in maintaining the desired behavior.

STAGE	TIMEFRAME
Precontemplation	Not seriously thinking about changing their behavior during the next six months; unaware or underaware of their health status.
Contemplation	Aware that a health problem exists, seriously thinking about change in the next six months, but have not yet made a commitment to take action.
Preparation	Intending to take action within the next month, actively planning change, taking some small steps toward action.
Action	Overtly making changes in behavior, experiences, or environment to overcome health problem.
Maintenance	Taking steps to sustain change and resist temptation to relapse.

Relapse Prevention Model (Marlatt 1982)

This refers to a self-control program designed to teach individuals who are trying to change behavior how to anticipate and cope with relapse. Relapse is triggered by *high-risk situations* (intrapersonal or interpersonal)—situations that threaten the individual's sense of control. Individuals who possess the coping skills to deal with high-risk situations have a much greater chance of preventing relapse than those do not. A complete application of the relapse prevention model includes both specific and global strategies for self-control. **Specific** intervention procedures help the individual anticipate and cope with the relapse episode itself, while **global** intervention procedures are designed to modify the early antecedents of relapse, including restructuring of the individual's lifestyle.

Social Level Theories and Models

Diffusion Theory (Rogers 1983)

This socioanthropological model of cultural change explains the diffusion of new ideas, techniques, behaviors, and programs within a target population. When people become "consumers" of an innovation, they are referred to as adopters; adopters can be categorized by when they adopt the innovation, and the rate at which people become adopters is represented by the bell-shaped curve. **Innovators** (less than 3% of the population) are the first to adopt the innovation. **Early adopters** (14%) are very interested in the innovation but do not want to be the first involved; they are typically respected and regarded as opinion leaders in their social networks. The early majority (34%) is composed of people who may be interested in the innovation but require external motivation to get involved. People who are skeptical and will not adopt the innovation until most people in the social system have done so represent the late majority (34%). The **laggards** (16%) will be the last group to adopt an innovation, if at all.

Leadership-Focused Model (Academy for Educational Development 1996)

This model combines aspects of diffusion theory and community organizing theory. Naturally emerging leaders—not just formal leaders—within a community are encouraged to exhibit and communicate an innovation to their peers. Because these innovations may be different from the community's established behaviors or social norms, this model focuses on how risk-reduction strategies become the norm within a social structure. Key steps in implementing this model include locating relevant leaders, enlisting their support, motivating them to take on the work and risk of advocating for an innovation, and preparing them for this task (education, support, materials). The effectiveness of the leadership-focused model depends on the level of resistance to change among powerful segments of the community, the lifespan of the social network involved, and the duration of influence of the leaders who are communicating the innovation.

Social Network Theory (Academy for Educational Development 1996)

This describes relationships or interactions between two or more people. Networks are matrices linked by family relationships, friendships, or commercial relationships—referred to as ties—that generate a special or unique feeling: need, concern, loyalty, frustration, power, affection, obligation, etc. Researchers characterize social networks either in terms of the individual and his/her relationship to others, or in terms of any set of linkages among people in a given group or network. Additionally, an individual may serve as a link between two seemingly unconnected networks. From a health-promotion perspective, when people are "networking," they are looking for relationships that are useful in helping them with their concerns, such as problem solving, program development, and resource identification.

Social Movement/Community Mobilization Theory (Goldstein 1992)

This is a description of how a community's culture, institutions, experiences, or characteristics can be changed to improve the health of that community by members of that community. Existing or emerging local leaders usually initiate and maintain social movements, but they can also occur as the result of outside interventions.

Social movements represent loosely organized collections of social activities, either in protest or for promotion, that exhibit some continuity over time and are based on a core of moral ideas. Local popular involvement and mobilization in the civil rights movement, the women's movement, and the gay rights movement have given rise to more formal, national collectives that lend visibility and provide leadership to the values they advocate.

Misperceived Norms Model (Perkins and Berkowitz 1986)

This model posits that health promotion interventions focusing exclusively on health problems and draw attention to their negative consequences may inadvertently create a perception that the campus population is less healthy than it really is. Perkins and Berkowitz (1986) cite statistics from studies of alcohol abuse and cigarette use that find that substantial numbers of students who hold moderate views about drinking and smoking incorrectly perceive their peers as being more permissive. Students who experience themselves as deviating from this false norm increase their consumption of alcohol or cigarettes over time in order to more closely conform to their peers' purported behavior. Research shows that student leaders, staff, faculty, and administrators are all prone to these kinds of misperceptions. Therefore, efforts to correct misperceptions and focus on healthful, positive behaviors can serve as a method of alleviating perceived peer pressure to use alcohol and other drugs, or of delaying the onset of use.

Social Marketing

Social Marketing is the adaptation of commercial marketing technologies to programs designed to influence the voluntary behavior of target audiences in order to improve their personal welfare and that of the society of which they are a part. "Social marketing brings to the challenge of [prevention] three important features: a focus on understanding how and why individuals behave as they do; creation of beneficial exchange relationships to influence those behaviors; and a tool for strategic program management", (CDC 1995).

Social marketing can be divided into a series of sequenced steps, each reinforcing and expanding the other. Information gathered during one step can influence a previous step. For example, data gathered as you segment audiences may cause you to revisit your definition of the problem, or you may change your marketplace assessment as you determine gaps.

Step 1: Define the Problem. At the heart of any health problem, you will always find human behavior. Epidemiology helps pinpoint who's at risk and what they do that puts them at risk. But it isn't the whole story. Epidemiology doesn't give program planners the necessary insight into a target audience's perspectives on behaviors, especially the causes or "determinants" of behaviors: external factors like low income and isolation from services, and internal factors like perceptions of self-efficacy (the individual's belief that he or she can do the desired behavior), social norms, barriers to performing lifesaving behaviors, and benefits of adopting lifesaving behaviors. This information is critical to understanding how an audience sees and reacts to a specific behavior you want to promote. To get it, you need behavioral science for insights into the target audience's current knowledge, skills, attitudes, beliefs and behaviors, and marketing data about consumers' buying behaviors and the external and internal forces that prompt them.

Step 2: Assess the Marketplace. This stage is commonly called needs assessment. It includes "environmental scanning" to get a picture of the community in which you will be working: its politics, its consumers and their habits (what they buy, what they do for fun, etc.), what its media have reported on, and other characteristics. During this step, program planners should:
- identify and consult with relevant community groups;
- analyze what they know about the audience and what they need to know to design an audience-centered prevention program;

- assess local health promotion and disease prevention programs—Who do programs serve? What are their services? What are the gaps in service? What resources are available to address those gaps?

Step 3: Segment Audiences. Demographics are an obvious way to define groups—for example, along racial/ethnic lines, by sexual activity, by gender, or by age. But demographics don't provide the whole picture of a given audience. Within a community, within age groups, within sexes, within socioeconomic rungs, different people share different values, are affected by different pressures, and receive information through different channels. Social marketing defines groups according to these various lifestyle factors, and spotlights likenesses and dissimilarities within and across groups. For example, even across race, ethnicity, sexual orientation, and socioeconomic status, research shows that young adults aged 18–25 are more alike than they are dissimilar. It makes sense to create messages that capitalize on that similarity.

But even people who share lifestyle factors may be at different levels of readiness for new behaviors. In a single peer group, one college student might be committed to abstaining from sex, another might be sexually active but willing to try condoms, and another might reject the idea that he or she is at risk for sexually transmitted infections, including HIV infection. Behavior science helps program planners determine which perceptions, attitudes, and beliefs are important to specific audiences.

Step 4: Plan a Program with Specific Behavioral Goals. Armed with extensive audience research, social marketers define audience segments and set measurable, realistic, and prioritized goals for each segment. Proposed interventions aim to influence specific beliefs, develop specific skills, enhance specific knowledge, and change or maintain specific behaviors.

The program plan should outline specific strategies and methods for delivering messages and an evaluation plan that includes both process and outcome measures to monitor the impact of your messages.

Step 5: Develop and Pretest Strategies and Materials. Design and test strategies and materials for effectiveness—delivery effectiveness, communication effectiveness, and effectiveness in influencing audience behaviors. Adapt strategies and materials based on audience feedback.

Step 6: Determine the Marketing Mix. A program's *marketing mix*—or the *"four Ps"* of **product, price, promotion,** and **place**—is central to its success. These four elements balance the audience's perceptions and feelings about a given health behavior to create optimum appeal. This is where formative research with the target audience is invaluable, because that research reveals what the audience believes about your product, what they are willing to do (or not do) to get your product, how you can best position the product to appeal to them, where and how they can get the product, and so forth.

Product. In commercial marketing, "product" usually means a thing to sell to consumers—an item, a service, sometimes an idea. In social marketing, the product is typically the desired attitude or behavior that will be exchanged for another attitude or behavior. To be successful, a product must offer a benefit people want. For example, extra-strength deodorant "offers" better body odor. What does safer sex or low-risk drinking "offer" that people want—and want enough to exchange unsafe sex or high-risk drinking for?

Price. The old saying, "Everything has its price," couldn't be more true in social marketing. But the price usually isn't merely the actual monetary cost. In this context, the "price" is the monetary, physical, and/or emotional cost to the consumer to buy or use the product. The highest costs are often social, psychological, or emotional. For example, research with people at high risk for HIV infection often reveals that they fear losing their partner if they insist on using condoms—a high, and seemingly unaffordable, cost to them.

Prevention program planners must understand and appreciate the costs their targeted audiences will pay in exchanging behaviors. At the very least, it is essential to know that changing behavior is seldom, if ever, easy. And difficulties are increased monumentally when people's self-esteem, safety, comfort, and other central ego supports are involved. This is compounded when they don't get immediate benefits that they care about after paying what to them may be very high costs.

Appreciating how students perceive costs helps you identify a desired behavior that has benefits that make the costs worth it. Only then can you position the desired behavior and its benefits and realistically ask people to change.

It's important to remember that messages may not center on lowering the cost, but on increasing the value of the product. For example, your audience might appreciate the benefits of latex condom use (protection from HIV and other STDs, peace of mind, greater staying power, etc.), making the costs of using condoms (less skin-to-skin contact, loss of sensation, or perceived lack of spontaneity, etc.) seem reasonable and affordable. Or they might value the benefits of complete abstinence (no need to worry about infections or pregnancy, feeling good about being an individual and not going along with the crowd, knowing your partner cares for you and not just for sex), making the costs of abstaining (such as being perceived as a prude, not being like your peers, foregoing pleasure, losing love) seem less consequential.

Promotion. Promotion is about messages and the channels that deliver them. A comprehensive promotion plan takes into consideration the full range of communication tools—such as social advertising, public and media relations, media advocacy, entertainment media, personal selling, community-based programs, direct marketing, special events, and live entertainment. Messages should be clear, break through the clutter of other messages, and be memorable, persuasive, accurate, and widely recognized. Promotion is designed to prompt a decision to practice the target behavior. That decision is then acted on in various places.

Again, the student's needs, lifestyle, and other factors must take precedence. Just because administrators, program planners, or others may be personally influenced by editorial coverage in newspapers and magazines doesn't mean that students will be. The targeted audience may not regularly read newspapers or magazines. Or if they do, they may not find these sources of information to be credible.

Place. In commercial marketing, "place" refers to the location a product is offered. The optimal place is the most convenient outlet to consumers that is *also* the outlet that offers the most emotional benefits. For example, a product (e.g., perfume) with a high price ($65 an ounce) could be placed in a variety of retail locations ranging from discount stores to department stores. Discount stores would likely be the most convenient place for potential consumers, but would they offer consumers an emotional benefit? Consumer research would probably show that people would not expect to purchase expensive perfume in those locations and would not want to think of themselves as discount shoppers for this item. On the other hand, large department stores might be less convenient to get to, but shoppers would be more likely to expect to purchase a high-ticket item in them, and consumers would feel good buying in such stores.

In social marketing, when the product is usually a behavior, the analysis of convenience and emotional benefits is equally important, but the goals are different. Analyzing place is really analyzing the locational constraints on behavior. It takes into account that people may have made a previous decision—for example, to say no to sex or to always practice safer sex—and then examines how a particular place, such as a bar, might affect that previously made decision. The analysis asks, "What can I do to make the place where people act on their decisions more likely to prompt the target behavior?"

A key question to ask in thinking about place is: What has the audience told us about this? Where do the consumers spend the majority of their time? Or, what various "lifepoints"—buildings, streets, stores, restaurants, libraries, classrooms, etc.—do they cross daily? Do you know how these locations affect their behavior? Sometimes, there is relatively little that can be done to make a place more likely to elicit the desired behavior, but other times your creative analysis of place will pinpoint some avenues for change.

Step 7: Deliver the Program. Put the program to work with the target audience. Distribute materials and messages, and generate support. Ensure all linked organizations and campus departments—academic units, student services, student government, student organizations, etc.—work together to reinforce the program and its behavioral goals.

Step 8: Evaluate and Alter As Needed. Monitor the program. Change strategies, messages, materials, and channels as necessary to meet evolving needs. Social marketing programs are not unchanging, static programs. They change as audiences change—constantly!

Evaluate the total program. Use both process criteria and outcome criteria. How many people did you reach? Whom did you reach? When? Where? How often? Who responded? How? What changes occurred? Based on what you learn, ask: "What do we need to change to move closer to our program goals?"

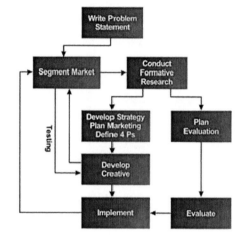

The Evidence-Based Social Marketing Model

Figure 4: *Social Marketing Model. This depicts the steps in the Social Marketing process graphically. (Source: www.metrix-marketing.com/services.htm)*

Figure 5: *Comparison of Individual and Social Level Prevention Strategies.*

Individual Wellness (Individual-Level Approaches)	Community Well-Being (Social-Level Approaches)
• Health is viewed as the result of personal decisions regarding lifestyle and behavior. • People reduce health risks and improve health status via personal decisions to change. • Health-enhancing behavior increased by providing information about risk, teaching new skills, and increasing self-esteem. • Focus on changing individual attitudes, beliefs, and values. • Focus on the relationship between the individual and health problems. • Short-term in scope. • Individual is the audience. • Professionals and "experts" make the decisions.	• Health is viewed as an on-going process that results from interaction between an individual and the environment and culture in which s/he lives. • Health decisions are made within the whole context of a person's life. • Health-enhancing behavior increased by working with social, cultural, economic, and political systems to enhance the abilities of communities to help individuals who live in them solve problems and make healthier choices. • Focus on policy development and changing cultural and peer group norms. • Focus on individuals gaining power by acting collectively. • Long-term in scope. • Individual is the advocate. • Professionals help create avenues for students to develop and express their power.

Source: The Marin Institute for the Prevention of Alcohol and Other Drug Problems (1994).

Questions to Consider

1. Why is it important for peer educators to understand behavior change theory?
2. Name two theories you find most interesting? How can you see these being useful?
3. Why is it important to use theory to inform the work you do as a peer educator?
4. Think of a health issue affecting college students. Create a brief social marketing plan.

References

Academy for Educational Development. (1996). *What intervention studies say about effectiveness.* Atlanta, GA: Centers for Disease Control and Prevention.

Ajzen, I. (1988). *Attitudes, personality and behavior.* Chicago: Dorsey Press.

Bandura, A. (1986). *Social foundations of thought and action.* Englewood Cliffs, NJ: Prentice-Hall.

Centers for Disease Control and Prevention. (1995). *The Prevention marketing initiative.* Retrieved from http://www.cdc.gov/

Fishbein, M., & Ajzen, I. (1975). *Belief, attitude, intention and behavior: An introduction to theory and research.* Reading, MA: Addison-Wesley.

Freire, P. (1973). *Education: The practice of freedom. London:* Writer's and Reader's Publishing.

Goldstein, M. S. (1992). *The health movement: Promoting fitness in America.* New York: Twayne.

Marlatt, G. A. (1982). Relapse prevention: A self-control program for treatment of addictive behaviors. In R. B. Stuart (Ed.). *Adherence, compliance and generalization in behavioral medicine.* New York: Brunner/Mazel.

Perkins, H. W., & Berkowitz, A. D. (1986). Perceiving the community norms of alcohol use among students: Some research implications for campus alcohol education programming. *International Journal of Addiction,* 21, p. 961–976.

Prochaska, J. O. (1979). *Systems of psychotherapy: A transtheoretical analysis.* Homewood, IL: Dorsey Press.

Skinner, B. F. (1953). *Science and human behavior.* New York: Free Press.

Roger, E. M. (1983). *Diffusion of Innovations* (3rd ed.). New York: Free Press.

Rosenstock, I.M., Strecher, V. J., & Becker, M. H. (1988). Social learning theory and the health belief model. *Health Education Quarterly,* 15(2), p. 175–183.

Rotter, J. B. (1954). *Social learning and clinical psychology.* New York: Prentice-Hall.

Chapter 3

Planning Effective Educational Programs

By Luoluo Hong and Julie Catanzarite

The PRECEDE Model for Health Education Planning

Green et al. (1980) offered the following model for planning health education interventions. This model is frequently followed by professional health educators, and serves as a basis for peer health educators.

Step 1: Social Diagnosis. Assess the quality of life in the target population, as well as the major problems that concern that group. Individuals are more motivated to change if the issue is relevant to them. Subjectively define problems of individuals or communities. Social indicators: illegitimacy, population, welfare, unemployment, absenteeism, alienation, hostility, discrimination, votes, riots, crime, crowding, etc.

Step 2: Epidemiological Diagnosis. Identify the major causes of morbidity and mortality in this population. Allocate scarce resources to more serious health problems. Account for nonhealth factors, e.g., natural disasters, weather. Vital indicators: morbidity, mortality, fertility, disability, etc. Dimensions: incidence, prevalence, distribution, intensity, duration, etc.

Step 3: Behavioral Diagnosis. Identify the specific behaviors related to major health problems. Prioritize these behaviors. Account for nonbehavioral causes, e.g., genetic, environmental, economic. Behavioral indicators: utilization, preventive actions, consumption patterns, compliance, self-care, etc. Dimensions: earliness, frequency, quality, range, persistence, etc.

Step 4: Educational Diagnosis. Describe the following three factors: (1) "predisposing factors," which increase or decrease the motivation for change, including cognitive variables such as attitudes, beliefs, knowledge, perceptions, and values; (2) "enabling factors," the barriers to change created by societal forces and systems, including availability of resources, accessibility, referrals, and skills; and (3) "reinforcing factors," social feedback that encourages or discourages behavior change, including attitudes and behavior of health and other personnel, peers, parents, employers, etc. Decide which factors will be the focus of the intervention.

For example, an educational diagnosis applied to campus alcohol abuse might yield the following predisposing, enabling, and reinforcing factors:

Predisposing factors:

- Myths and misconceptions about the effects/physiology of alcohol abuse;
- Binge drinking;
- Drinking as a rite of passage (Butler 1993);
- Drinking as a form of "liquid bonding" (Kuh and Arnold 1993);
- Drinking as a recreational activity unto itself;
- Drinking as a "social lubricant";
- Drinking as a coping strategy; and
- Sexual victimization (acquaintance rape, childhood sexual assault, sexual harassment, etc.)

Enabling factors:

- Lack of university-wide coordination of prevention efforts;
- Failure of teachers, physicians, law enforcement, etc. to refer students for intervention after alcohol-related incidents;
- Lack of skills in appropriate intervention by peers;
- Lack of political support and understanding of the problem;
- Paucity of financial resources allocated for alcohol abuse prevention, relative to other investments;
- Media advertising (radio, television, campus newspaper, local bars);
- Issue of confidentiality for treatment services;
- Presence of hard-to-reach populations (e.g., men, Greeks, etc.); and
- Competition from promotional efforts of alcohol distributors.

Reinforcing factors:

- Peer pressure and false perception that everyone drinks;
- Parents and other mentors sanction drinking;
- Alcohol allowed at many community events, including athletics, social, theater, music, and academic;
- Campus leaders are limited in their knowledge of alcohol use/abuse and their impact on academic performance quality of life;
- Campus/opinion leaders oftentimes model alcohol abuse;
- Medical professionals do not recognize seriousness of alcohol-related incidents;
- Legal loopholes in the State underage drinking statutes; and
- Problem of law enforcement (inconsistencies in application of law).

Step 5: Administrative Diagnosis. Assess resources, time constraints, and abilities. Only intervention components with highest priority can be implemented with limited resources. Components of a health education program should include: (1) direct communication to the public, patients, etc.; (2) training for community organizations; and (3) indirect communication in the form of staff development, training, supervision, consultation, and feedback.

Step 6: Evaluation. Assess intervention impact and effectiveness on a continuous and ongoing basis.

Behind the Scenes: Eight Steps to a Successful Program

Step 1: Receive Your Assignment. You and your co-facilitator(s) will receive a program assignment from your advisor or the health education department administrator, depending on who schedules the programs. You should generally have 2–3 weeks' notice. This assignment should include the following information:

- time, date, and location of the workshop
- organization or residence hall requesting the workshop
- number of people expected to attend
- demographic profile (sex, age, etc.)
- special topic requests (if any)
- name and phone number of contact person

Step	Content
1	Receive your assignment
2	Confirm your assignment
3	Develop an outline
4	Prepare and practice
5	Reconfirm and practice
6	Set up
7	Evaluate the workshop
8	Debrief with your co-facilitators

Figure 6: *The eight steps to a successful program. A quick reference to getting ready for a program.*

Step 2: Confirm the Assignment. This is very important from both a public relations perspective and a logistical one. Designate one co-facilitator to verify the above information with the contact person as soon as you receive an assignment. Discuss refreshments (what and when) and advertising (content, who is responsible). Also consider what resources the audience might be able to use prior to the event. Send any questions, surveys, or articles to the contact person to help frontload participants. Always research your audience as thoroughly as possible. Be sure to ask important questions such as:

- What motivated the contact person to make this request? Did an incident occur recently? Is she concerned about an individual in the hall or group?
- Who is being invited and what are the circumstances? Is attendance mandatory or voluntary? Are audience members close friends or casual acquaintances?

The answers to these questions can have ramifications on how you plan and deliver your program.

Step 3: Develop an Outline. Always do this, even if you've already done a similar program on the same content area. A well-written, thorough outline is the single most important thing you can do to have a successful program. It can also serve as a valuable tool in your preparation and planning. In addition, many peer education organizations maintain a notebook of outlines from past workshops to assist new members in program development.

Clearly delineate on the outline who is responsible for each item. Record the approximate time allotted for each section; a timekeeper may be assigned. Most importantly, make decisions about which material is absolutely essential to cover, and indicate which material can be discarded in the event that discussion runs over or you run out of time. Conversely, be familiar enough with your content information to expand on areas the audience may express particular interest in. Make sure each co-facilitator has his/her own copy.

In general, for a one-hour workshop, plan programming and activities for forty-five minutes; this builds in an automatic fifteen-minute time cushion for questions and answers, discussion, or unexpected delays. Whichever format you select, all peer education programs should have the following structure:

I. **Introduction.** Establishing credibility and legitimacy early in the program is important, as is establishing a nonjudgmental, comfortable tone.
   A. **Introduce yourself.** Say more than just a name or major; perhaps share why you became a peer educator, your favorite health fact, etc. This is an opportunity for the audience to start getting to know you and for you to establish rapport and trust.
   B. **Briefly discuss the purpose of your peer education organization.** This means you need to be familiar with the history, mission, and activities of your organization.
   C. **Talk about the Student Health Center.** Describe all three units: Medical Clinic, Mental Health Service, and Wellness Education Department. Be sure to have pamphlets available; provide appropriate phone numbers.
   D. **Outline the agenda for the program.** A useful strategy is to highlight the two or three main points of your program. Negotiate with the audience: Does this meet their needs? What are their expectations? Are there any questions to begin with?
   E. **Establish ground rules.** Examples of relevant ground rules might be confidentiality, respectful listening, negotiation of terms/language that are acceptable to the audience, etc. Post or write these ground rules on a board or easel if possible.

II. **Mini-Lecture.** Improving health and wellness typically involves a combination of increasing knowledge, assessing values, and changing behavior. Some information is best understood when delivered in a straightforward manner using layperson's terms. This is an opportunity to include basic information regarding statistics, definitions, etc. Try to limit this section to no longer than 10–15 minutes.

III. **Discussion or Interactive Activity/Game.** Students learn best when they are required to share their viewpoints and ideas about the particular topic. Don't be afraid to "give up control" and let the audience do some self-exploration.
   A. Discussion topics should focus on an issue that is open-ended, generates a lot of emotions, lends itself to multiple perspectives (i.e., not a "black or white" issue), or is perhaps even controversial. To enhance audience participation, try to maintain the role of a moderator (by restating audience views, asking questions to clarify), and refrain from sharing your views until the end. Also, don't be afraid of silences; those are crucial for thinking! (Try the five-count: one one-thousand, two one-thousand, etc., before jumping in.)
   B. For interactive activities and games, use those you've picked up during your training, but also feel free to design something on your own. Possibilities include quizzes, game shows, values clarification exercises, board games, brainstorms, etc. Be sure that humor associated with the activity doesn't contradict your message or hurt people inadvertently. Sarcasm should be avoided.

IV. **Closure.** Some programs may have aroused strong emotions for students. The program may have been thought-provoking. Challenge students to continue learning with each other, perhaps by asking what they intend to do after attending this program.
   A. Summarize your two or three key points.
   B. Provide the appropriate on- and off-campus resources for referral.
   C. Answer questions. If you don't know the answer to a question, don't be afraid to say so. Offer to follow up; arrange for a way to get in touch with the student.
   D. Thank the group for attending and participating.
   E. Distribute and collect evaluations.

What follows are two examples of program outlines. The mistake that most peer educators make is to write an outline that is too sparse. Remember, for the outline to be helpful, it must be dense with information. Err on the side of putting too much in the outline rather than too little. A guideline for developing an outline is to ask yourself, "Could another peer educator reproduce my workshop just from reading my outline?" If not, then you've probably done an insufficient job on the outline. However, remember that you will not be referring to the outline directly during the workshop. Doing so erodes your credibility and makes you appear as though you have not practiced. If you wish to have notes to refer to during the workshop, jot them down on index cards no larger than 3″ x 5″ in size.

Sample Outline #1 for Educational Program

Topic or Title: Sex in the Age of AIDS

I. **Introduction**
   A. Each group member introduce him- or herself
   B. Talk about Sexual Health Advocates (peer education organization)
   C. Discuss the Student Health Center, Counseling Center, Wellness/Health Promotion Office
   D. Set up ground rules:

1. Humor okay
2. Please ask questions
3. Respect audience members' confidentiality (this is a potentially touchy subject)

II. **Brief Lecture on HIV/AIDS**
A. History
B. Statistics
   1. As of 2008, one in 1,500 college students are HIV-positive
   2. Half of all HIV infections are among people under the age of 30
   3. In terms of geographical areas, the region with the highest rates of persons living with AIDS are in the south (40%), followed by the west (20%), northeast (29%), and midwest (11%) (CDC 2007).
   4. AIDS isn't a gay disease: over 75% of AIDS cases worldwide are among heterosexuals
   5. Women are four times more likely to contract HIV from their male partner than vice-versa
C. Modes of Trasmission
   1. Blood (sharing unclean needles for steroids, illegal drugs, ear piercing, etc.)
   2. Semen (unprotected vaginal or anal intercourse, oral sex on a man
   3. Vaginal secretions (unprotected vaginal intercourse, oral sex on a woman)
   4. Mother-to-child
   5. Not transmitted through tears, kissing, toilet seats, mosquito bites
D. Risk Reduction
   1. Discuss how to reduce risks
   2. Abstinence
   3. Safer sex
E. Importance of honest communication

III. **Interactive Activity: Condom Cards** (To teach about safer sex)
A. Distribute condoms cards randomly to members of the audience; each lists a step in putting on a condom:
   1. Lots of hugging, touching, and kissing
   2. Talking about sex
   3. Clothes drop to the floor
   4. Couples becomes aroused
   5. Erection
   6. Condom package is ripped open (slowly, of course, so the condom won't be ripped)
   7. Pinch the tip of the condom to leave room for what "comes" later
   8. Partner places condom over the tip of the erect penis
   9. Condom rolled down over the penis
   10. Partner smooths out any air bubbles in the condom
   11. Partner puts on lots of water-based lubricant all over the condom
   12. Insert spermicide containing Nonoxynol-9 into vagina or anus
   13. Intercourse
   14. Orgasm
   15. Man holds onto the base of the condom as penis is slowly withdrawn
   16. Throw out the condom
   17. Savor the moments of the afterglow of love

18. Fall asleep
   B. Have volunteers from audience line up in to correct order for correctly putting on a condom; other audience members can assist by "editing" the volunteers' work; demonstrate the steps with penis model as audience members read the cards out loud
   C. Discuss: what are some barriers to condom use? how can we overcome them?
      1. Embarrassment
      2. Don't have a condom
      3. Partner gets offended
      4. Doesn't feel as good
      5. Ruins the moment
      6. Others?

IV. **Conclusion**
   A. Emphasize importance of abstinence as only 100% method of protection
   B. Emphasize importance of using condoms with spermicide to reduce risk of HIV infection if the choice is to be sexually active
   C. Talk about HIV antibody testing sites for students
   D. Answer any questions
   E. Distribute evaluation forms
   F. Pass out brochures

Sample Outline #2 for Educational Program

Topic or Title: Sexual Assault Prevention for Men

I. **Introduction**
   A. Each facilitator introduces himself
   B. History and purpose of Men Against Violence
   C. Describe services at your Student Health Center
   D. Set up ground rules
      1. Confidentiality—what's said in this room stays in this room
      2. Active participation enhances your learning
      3. Please respect each other's opinions
      4. Informal atmosphere—please ask questions

II. **Discussion: Fact or Fiction?** (Note that all statements are *fiction!*)
   A. If she really didn't want it, she would have fought back harder. (The "You Can't Thread a Moving Needle" Theory)
   B. When she says "no," she really means "yes" but is playing hard to get. (The "No Means I Want to be Seduced" Theory)
   C. The majority of women secretly fantasize about being raped. (The "She Really Wanted It" Theory)
   D. Most women who accuse a man of rape are doing it to "get back at him" if he doesn't call or go out with her. (The Vindictive Woman Theory)

    E. It's highly unlikely that a woman who has had a lot of sex partners could be raped. (The Virgin-Whore Theory)

    F. It's not fair for a woman to sexually tease a man, for example, give him a blow job, and then expect him to stop when it comes to intercourse. (The Blue Balls Theory, or the Point of No Return)

    G. Men who rape are generally those who do not have ready access to a steady sexual partner.

III. Legal Definitions of Rape, Aggravated Rape, Forcible Rape, Simple Rape, and Sexual Battery in State of Louisiana.

    A. Rape is the act of anal or vaginal sexual intercourse with a male or female person committed without the person's lawful consent. Emission is not necessary and any sexual penetration, vaginal or anal, however slight is sufficient to complete the crime *(La. R.S. 14:41)*.

    B. Aggravated rape is rape committed under any one or more of the following circumstances: (1) the victim is overcome by use of force or threat of force or bodily harm: (2) the offender is armed with a dangerous weapon; (3) the victim is under the age of twelve; or (4) two or more offenders participate in the act *(La. R.S. 14:42)*.

    C. Forcible rape is rape committed in which the victim is prevented from resisting by force or threats of physical violence under circumstances where the victim reasonably believes that such resistance would not prevent the rape *(La. R.S. 14:42.1)*.

    D. Simple rape occurs when a victim who is not the spouse of the offender is incapable of resisting or understanding the nature of the act due to any one or more of the following circumstances: (1) diminished mental capacity produced by an intoxicating, narcotic or anesthetic agent; (2) in a stupor or is unconscious; (3) temporary or permanent unsoundness of mind and the offender knew or should have known about the victim's incapacity; or (4) false belief that the offender is a spouse, and this belief is intentionally induced by any artifice, pretense or concealment practiced by the offender *(La. R.S. 14:43)*.

    E. Sexual battery is the touching of the anus or genitals of the victim by the offender using any object or any body part of the offender, or the touching of the anus or genitals of the offender by the victim using any object or any body part of the victim, where the offender acts without the consent of the victim, or where the victim is not yet 15 years old and at least three years younger than the offender *(La. R.S. 14:43.1)*.

    NOTE: These are specific to the State of Louisiana. Peer Educators would need to research their state law and add that information here.

IV. Solutions: How Men Can Prevent Rape

    A. No man ever thinks to himself, "I'm a rapist." It's not enough to be "against rape." Take an active stand.

    B. Never assume; learn to ask straightforward but respectful questions about intent, sexual boundaries, and desire, e.g., "Do you want to have sex with me now?" Forget about being embarrassed or offensive. If you think you're ready to have sex, then you should be comfortable dealing with open, honest communication—even if it means you get rejected.

    C. Refrain from coercive, pressuring techniques; if she wants to play mind games, too bad for her. You can always find a mature woman who does know her mind. No sex is worth an accusation of sexual assault.

    D. Realize that men and women interpret non-verbal signals, dress, and behavior in different ways. Men, in general, tend to interpret cues as signs of sexual interest when women see them as merely being friendly or flirtatious (e.g., going up to a guy's room, revealing clothing, etc.). ***Take everything except a verbal, audible, and sober "yes" from your partner as a "no."***

E. Don't use her alcohol consumption or yours as justification for why you ended up having sex. We're not saying you can't drink; just realize that you are always responsible for your actions. It's best to not mix drinking and sexual activity.

F. It's true; many college women are confused about their sexuality: do they want it or not? But it's not your job to make the decision for them.

G. Realize that the way men are brought up has a lot to do with how men think about sexual relationships and about women. We understand the pressure you are under to prove your masculinity. Remember that true masculinity arises from being the best that you can be; don't use women to prove your masculinity.

H. Greek men and student-athletes are not ordinary men; they consciously choose to hold themselves to higher standards. Make sure that you remember the values you chose to follow.

Step 4: Prepare and Practice. There are a variety of formats that a peer education program can take. Peer educator teams can range from two to six individuals, and activities can include interactive games, video viewing, discussion, debate, role playing, and theater presentations. The key to a successful peer education program is selecting a format and style that feels comfortable and natural to you and your co-facilitator(s). In addition, deliberately select co-facilitators who have different strengths and experiences from yours to enhance the effectiveness of your peer education team, as well as increase the likelihood that your audience will relate and respond to you.

Co-facilitators should always meet and discuss who is responsible for content areas, activities, etc. Discuss any possible concerns or potential obstacles with your advisor. Decide what handouts and props you will use, and designate a co-facilitator who will be responsible for picking them up. If possible, visit the location at which you will be giving the workshop to familiarize yourself with the lighting, space, acoustics, microphone, AV equipment, etc., as necessary.

If you require any equipment that is not available, make arrangements with your advisor or the program contact person as soon as possible. You need to know early what you will have available so that you can make adjustments to your program accordingly. With the burgeoning technology available to college students, be sure that your workshop environment will be able to accommodate your audiovisual needs. For example, it probably won't be feasible to plan a PowerPoint presentation using your laptop computer for a residence hall program, as you will be unable to attain the appropriate data projector.

Remember, preparation is the key to a successful, effective program. Run through the entire program at least twice; don't just "talk through" the outline. That way, you'll have a better sense of the flow and timing, and have an opportunity to work out kinks. Audiences can detect if you are unfamiliar with your topic, or if you did not care enough to practice, thus eroding your credibility. The one mistake made most often by peer educators is to assume that they know the material or that "everything will fall into place when we do it." Don't just write out the scripts for role plays and skits: actually rehearse them. Similarly, rehearse any new game or activity. If you will be using audiovisual equipment, practice their handling and operation prior to the workshop so you don't appear incompetent.

Practice speaking in front of a mirror or in front of friends. Look for and minimize distracting facial expressions, unnecessary body movements, or poor posture. Listen for and get rid of monotonic delivery, mumbling, and speech fillers such as "and, uh," and "you know." It's always illuminating to videotape yourself and watch!

Step 5: Reconfirm the Assignment. The day before the workshop, confirm with the contact person once again. At least one day before the workshop, a co-facilitator should pick up the pamphlets, evaluation forms, supplies, visual aids, videos, equipment, etc. needed for the workshop from your health promotion/health education office.

Step 6: Set Up. Arrive a half hour before the workshop to set up the room. Discuss any final glitches that may need to be ironed out. Be sure to pay attention to such things as noise level, lighting, room temperature, and visibility of visual aids.

Step 7: Evaluate the Workshop. After the workshop, be sure to distribute and collect evaluations from the audience. Time for this activity should be allocated in your outline. These evaluations are to be submitted to the advisor for reviews. Plan to remain an extra 10–15 minutes to answer questions or to make referrals.

There is no need to be afraid of the evaluation process. This is an opportunity to learn your strengths, as well as receive feedback about areas that you can improve. In addition, evaluations help ensure quality in peer education programs, and are the building blocks for expanding and improving your services.

Step 8: Debrief with Your Co-Facilitators. You should never plan anything to take place immediately after your scheduled workshop time. Co-facilitators should always meet for an additional 10–15 minutes immediately after the program to discuss the strengths and challenges during the workshop. An understanding of what worked well, what didn't work and why, will enhance skills for future workshops. Each facilitator should complete a written evaluation of his or her own performance to be submitted to the advisor. If necessary, schedule an appointment with the advisor to discuss any problems encountered, receive feedback, and incorporate suggestions.

Questions to Consider

1. Choose a topic, other than alcohol, and determine its predisposing, enabling, and reinforcing factors.
2. Using the eight steps of a successful program, as well as the topic used in question one, create an outline for a successful program.

References

Butler, E.R. (1993). Alcohol use by college students: A rite of passage ritual. *NASPA Journal*, 31(1), p. 48–55.

Green, L.W., Kreuter, M. W., Deeds, S. G., & Partridge, K. D. (1980). Health education planning: A diagnostic approach. Mountain View, CA: Mayfield Publishing.

Kuh, G. D., & Arnold, J. C. (1993). Liquid bonding: A cultural analysis of the role of alcohol in fraternity pledgeship. *Journal of College Student Development, 34*(5), p. 327–334.

Chapter 4

Effective Facilitation Skills for the Peer Educator

By Luoluo Hong and Julie Catanzarite

Understanding Facilitation

The first step toward becoming an effective facilitator is to understand what a facilitator does. Facilitators need to have strong speaking abilities, but having good speaking abilities does not make you a good facilitator. Speakers concentrate on delivering information alone. In contrast, a facilitator promotes learning; that is, he or she makes it easier for learning to take place within a group environment. A facilitator accomplishes this by using various tools to help a group discuss and resolve an issue. S/he generates and moderates group discussion, enabling the individuals within the group to use their own acquired skills and resources in arriving at their own new insights. The group's skills and resources are enhanced by your training and specialized knowledge.

Remember, a facilitator is not a lecturer in the traditional sense; the primary goal is not the delivery of facts or opinions. Rather, a facilitator tries to foster an environment in which group process and problem-solving can effectively and constructively occur. One metaphor to use for understanding good facilitation is to regard the group members as pieces of a puzzle and the facilitator as the glue to put the puzzle together.

Your role as a facilitator of peer education programs includes: (1) being a role model for the group; (2) making the group as comfortable as possible for the participants by being nonjudgmental, redirecting disruptive behavior, challenging comments that are disrespectful or uncivil to others, and mediating conflict and tension; (3) generating discussion by guiding dialogue and involving audience members who are being left out; (4) clarifying (or restating) and summarizing participants' thoughts, ideas, and impressions; (5) challenging audience members to move beyond simply not being part of the problem to being active participants in seeking a solution; and (6) being a reliable source of information and referral. Note that you are not there to debate or "prove your point." In fact, injecting too many of your own views and opinions may have the adverse effect of isolating audience members and reducing your credibility as an objective, nonjudgmental facilitator.

Before you become a peer educator, it is important to evaluate your own readiness. Facilitating workshops on topics such as sexual health, violence, substance abuse, or diversity are especially challenging—and rewarding—for peer educators. The topics themselves are inherently emotion-laden, and typically arouse strong feelings and opinions. It may be uncomfortable to you at first to handle groups that become passionately inflamed by the discussion. Oftentimes, individuals in the audience will say things that contradict and challenge your own views. Your job is to carefully balance the need for honest, open dialogue with the need to create a safe forum for civil, controlled discourse.

If a member of your family of origin is a recovering alcoholic, conducting programs on alcohol abuse can be healing, but it can also arouse discomfort and anger. Similarly, if you are a survivor of sexual assault, conducting education on rape prevention can be empowering, but you may overly identify with the survivor and be unable to deliver prevention information to both men and women in a manner that does not accuse or "bash men." If you have struggled with an eating disorder, you may be eager to conduct educational programming and "get the word out" to help stop others from developing such a disorder; however, it would be important to have a mental health professional evaluate you and determine that you are indeed well down the road to recovery. In other words, peer education work is deeply personal work; you cannot separate your feelings or your experiences from education. It is therefore important to acknowledge and accommodate those feelings and experience. A discussion with your advisor can guide you in clarifying these things.

Workshops are designed to foster participants' learning; your needs will need to be temporarily subverted when you are in the role of facilitator. Therefore, be sure to evaluate your own level of cultural competency. If you have not resolved key issues with regard to your own cultural background or health-related experiences, or develop acute feelings of guilt, anger, or frustration related to the topic at hand, you may want to explore these issues before facilitating a workshop. These feelings will interfere with your ability to be an effective facilitator.

As you facilitate workshops, be aware that communication occurs on many levels, both explicit and implicit. Remember that all communication consists of three components: (1) the messenger, that is, the one who intends to send information, values, or opinions; (2) the message, or the content and tone of the information, values, opinion, or perspective; and (3) the listener, or receiver—the intended target for the message. For effective communication to take place, the intended message sent by the messenger must be the same message heard and understood by the listener. The only way to do that is by "checking in," using both overt and covert responses.

The interesting thing about facilitation is that the roles of messenger and receiver are revolving. You as the facilitator will be the messenger for the majority of the program; however, your effectiveness as a facilitator will be dependent on your ability to accurately and correctly receive messages from your audience. You must therefore have both excellent "messaging" skills and good listening skills.

Students will sometimes approach you either immediately following an educational program or at other occasions on and around campus because of your role as a peer educator. In these instances, as when facilitating a program, good communication skills are essential for effectively understanding the student's concern, helping them to problem-solve, and making appropriate referrals for further assistance, if necessary.

Basic Active Listening Skills

Asking Relevant Questions. Don't bombard the person with questions. He or she will give you the information they want you to know. Ask questions to help the person, not to satisfy your curiosity. If a questions is necessary, ask open-ended questions that cannot be answered with simply "yes" or "no"; "yes" or "no" questions are known as closed questions. Also avoid "why" questions; they are judgmental, and may cause the person to become defensive without knowing why. Listen carefully to the answers given and analyze their content before asking the next questions; this will help you avoid asking unnecessary questions.

Paraphrasing. Occasionally summarize what the student is saying so that s/he knows you are listening. This will also give the student a chance to determine whether or not you are accurately hearing what s/he is saying. Whenever possible, use the same language or words used by the student to describe their experience or response.

Reflecting Feelings. This means listening to and responding to the feelings of a student. Be empathetic, not sympathetic. Communicate basic understanding of what the person is feeling and the experiences/behaviors underlying these feelings (content). You are trying to "get inside" the other person's world.

Avoid the urge to start solving a student's problem as soon as s/he starts to describe it. Taking time to "tune in" to feelings and emotions, e.g., fear, anger, sadness, or happiness demonstrate caring and patience. Try to identify the most basic, predominant feeling that you hear being expressed. Be sure you don't confuse cognitions (e.g., confused) with emotions (e.g., scared). All feelings can be classified into one of these four: anger, sadness, happiness, and fear.

Examples of feeling words include angry, frustrated, hurt, excited, and relieved—not "good" or "bad," or some other vague terms; example of feeling phrases include "I feel down in the dumps," "I feel ready to bust";

finally, examples of feeling expressed by the word "like" with both experiences and behaviors might be, "I feel like giving up," or "I feel like the world has collapsed on me."

The following is an example of feeling and content together. A friend says: "I don't find any kind of challenge in school. The courses don't offer much. The instructors are really cold. I sit around class twiddling my thumbs. I'm not really motivated to do much outside class." You respond with: "It's all very boring for you. School, teachers, courses—none of these seems to have much to offer." This response recognizes your friend's feelings (boredom) and what he or she sees as giving rise to the feelings (school, teachers, courses that aren't challenging). Notice that this kind of response doesn't take sides. It doesn't suggest that either your friend or the school is to blame or not to blame.

A helpful starting point? Until you get used to communicating the understanding of feeling and content, you may want to use the phrase: "It sounds to me as though you're feeling [feeling word or phrase] because [experience/behaviors that underlie the feeling]."

Summarizing. This skill requires condensation and clarification of what the student has said. Identify the primary feeling conveyed by the student, and use one sentence to describe the key problem confronting the student. Check in with the student to make sure you understand him or her correctly: "Is that what you meant?" or "Did I hear you correctly?"

Interpreting. This response includes explaining, summarizing, and adding data from your frame of reference. Essentially, you are offering your perspective on what the student has shared with you. It may involve your clarifying some points or naming some feelings that the student did not explicitly state. For example, "Even though you didn't say this, I'm picking up that you're feeling …"

Other Hints. There are many other helpful listening hints, as well. Listen for voice-related behaviors that go beyond just the speaker's words; these include voice level, intensity, spacing of words, emphasized words, and silence. Keep calm even when you don't feel calm. Don't allow yourself to feel guilt about what's happening—don't personalize, even if the person might be attacking you.

Furthermore, don't minimize what the person is saying, e.g., "There's no reason to be anxious about that." Similarly, be swift to hear and slow to speak, or, as leadership guru Stephen Covey (1989) has put so well, "Seek first to understand, then to be understood." As such, the goal of listening is to understand, not to agree: eliminate internal and external variables. You can also disagree with an individual's perceptions or opinions without invalidating them. Don't label someone's experience or understanding of an issue as "invalid," "illogical," "irrational," or "unfounded."

Always consciously engage in unconditional positive regard for the student. Refrain from making judgments. Become acutely aware of your own views and values, and when someone is "pushing your buttons."

Examples of poor listening skills	Examples of better listening skills
• Not listening to various cues, signals. • Butting in. • Making assumptions, "knowing" answers, putting words into the other's mouth. • Over-influencing. Trying to provide own solution, manipulative. • Asks leading or closed questions, and asks two at one time. • Threatening, heavy-handed, devaluing and defensive; pressuring, and sarcastic. • Lack of empathy, not able to acknowledge the true feelings. • Offers unrealistic promises/choices. • Speaks too much, too hurriedly, not allowing time for answers. • Critical and shocked.	• Listening carefully. Taking up issues. • Allowing space, and some pauses. • Seeking the individual's answers. • Shaping the interview, but encouraging person to come to own solution. • Asks open questions that draw out more information. Avoids yes/no questions. • Friendly, gentle, sincere, encouraging, and genuinely interested. • Strong empathy and compassion. • Realistic and rational assessment of genuine choices. • Slows the interview down. Takes time. • Positive even if feeling surprised.

Egan (1990)

Finally, be aware of the following barriers to good listening. If you really want to hear what others are saying, make sure you're not a:

- **Mind reader.** You'll hear little or nothing if you suspect the speaker has an ulterior motive and you're asking, "What is this person really thinking or feeling?"
- **Fortune teller.** You think you already know what the person is going to say before they say it.
- **Rehearser.** Your mental run-through about what you'll say next tunes out the speaker.
- **Filterer.** Some call this selective listening—hearing only what you want to hear.
- **Dreamer.** Thinking about what you have to do this weekend or drifting off while a person is speaking can lead to an embarrassing, "What did you say?" or, "Could you repeat that?"
- **Identifier.** If you interpret everything you hear in the context of your own experience, you probably didn't really hear what was said.
- **Comparer.** When you get sidetracked assessing the messenger, you're sure to miss or misunderstand the message.
- **Derailer.** Changing the subject too quickly soon tells others you're not interested in anything they have to say.
- **Sparrer.** You hear what's said but quickly belittle it, discount it, or argue about it. That puts you in the same class as the derailer.
- **Placater.** Agreeing with everything you hear just to be nice or to avoid conflict does not mean you're a good listener or an assertive one.

Setting Boundaries. Ultimately, the workshop or one-on-one session is not about you, so you can choose not to share personal information. Avoid voluntarily sharing your own personal experiences unless there is a strong educational purpose for doing so. Sharing your own "stuff" places the listener in the position of having to respond to your needs, which is not his/her role.

If you are asked to reveal personal information during a workshop or one-on-one consultation such as, "Are you sexually active?", "Do you drink?", or "Have you been raped?", it is your personal decision whether or not to answer directly. However, don't be evasive. For example, you can respond, "It doesn't matter whether or not I'm sexually active; what's important is that we all need to take responsibility for our behaviors." An alternative is to try understanding the true question that underlies the explicit question. A question such as "Do you drink?" may really be the student's way of asking, "Why should I listen to you and change my drinking habits if you drink, too?" Knowing this, you can answer the student's implicit question in this way: "You're probably wondering whether or not I go out and get smashed. I do choose to drink, but what matters is that I also role model low-risk drinking."

Always decide before conducting a program your comfort level in answering such questions, as well as what you will provide as an answer. Remind the listener(s) that information you share should be treated as confidential.

Another goal of boundary-setting is to **avoid getting yourself into a position where you end up giving advice or attempting to solve problems for others.** That's not your role, and doing so disempowers the listener. If a student asks you "What should I do?", "Give me your advice," or "Tell me what you think," respond by:

- **Reflecting.** For example: "You really wish I would tell you what to do right now," or, "You're feeling so confused right now that you don't think you can make a good decision."
- **Leveling with them.** For example: "I hear you asking me to tell you what to do and I'm not sure I can do that. I think this is something you are going to have to decide," or, "I'm not supposed to give advice, but I'll help you look at some alternatives."
- **Helping the person explore alternatives.** For example: "What are some things you think you can do?" "What do you want to happen?" "What could you do to make that happen?" "What help do you need from others?" "As I see it, from what you have said, you have these choices ..." and "Let's brainstorm how you could handle this." (Then lead person through the decision-making process.)

Improving Your "Messaging" Skills

Be Aware of Your Non-Verbal Cues. Body posture, tone, facial expressions, and style of dress are crucial non-verbal cues. You should be aware of what your body is communicating to the group; this non-verbal communication should be consistent with what you are saying.

- Use *direct eye contact,* and be sure to scan the entire audience. You don't necessarily have to look right into students' eyes; you can scan objects on the wall behind the audience, just above their eye level.
- Be sure that your *tone of voice* projects sufficiently, and vary the volume level appropriately. A monotonic voice can put your audience to sleep.
- Use appropriate *hand gestures* and movements to emphasize your points and to project your personality into a larger audience. However, refrain from having your hands in front of your face, and don't move your hands excessively or else they become a distraction. Don't fiddle with hair; long or bothersome hair should be tied back or pinned with a barrette out of the way. Women who touch their hair frequently when speaking are perceived as flirting and therefore as less credible.
- Your *body posture* should convey ease and openness (e.g., don't fold your arms across your chest or shove both hands in your front pockets). Sit or stand in a poised manner, and don't wiggle or rock. If you sit, do so at the front edge of the chair, balance your weight on one foot and cross the other

leg underneath at the knee. If you stand, plant your feet apart in line with your hips to give you stability and balance. If you feel uncomfortable with your hands at your side, try holding a pen or index card notes.

- Be sure that your *facial expression* doesn't inadvertently express disapproval, disgust, etc., or contradict your verbal communication.

Dress Appropriately. Clothing is one of the major nonverbal cues through which we send our messages. While your dress does not have to a three-piece suit and tie—in fact, dressing that formally defeats the purpose of using peers—it should reflect an understated level of professionalism and convey respect for self and for your work. (Exceptions are professional conferences; for those, you may want to choose a more distinctly professional style of dress; discuss with your advisor.) Obviously, be sure to shower and practice good hygiene before conducting a workshop. Jeans without holes in them are acceptable for men and women, particularly if worn with the shirt from your peer education organization (jean cut-offs are not acceptable).

If you haven't gotten around to the laundry and don't have a clean shirt from your organization, there are alternatives. Ideal for men would be khaki pants with a polo shirt; women can wear a casual one-piece dress or casual skirt/slacks and shirt. Choose clothing that is more conservative, rather than outfits that scream out your extreme individualism. Let your personality define your individualism, rather than have the audience automatically shut you out because they don't approve of the way you dress.

Keep jewelry to a minimum, and avoid jewelry that clangs or otherwise distracts the audience. Finally, **never wear a hat or sunglasses** to a presentation; they cover your eyes and make a poor statement about how you see your paraprofessional role.

Establish Rapport. Most audiences decide within the first two to three minutes whether or not they like or will listen to a speaker. You must connect with the audience immediately. Once you lose them in the beginning, it becomes difficult to get them back. Introduce yourself. Always begin by thanking the group for inviting you. Remain open to questions and individual concerns. One way to demonstrate your openness is to begin a workshop by asking if anyone has any questions.

Research your audience demographics before you arrive. What characterizes the group? Know what is important to them, as well as what they expect from you. Has anything happened in the recent past that might affect their reactions to the topic or to you? Then, personalize the information to your audience.

Use appropriate humor, i.e., not offensive humor, if you are comfortable doing so to relax the audience. It must be natural, not forced. If you are not a funny person, don't try this strategy—it will backfire! Most importantly, be yourself. You may try at first to pattern your speaking or teaching style on someone you admire, but it is essential to quickly develop your own style. There is nothing like insincerity or a superficiality to turn off an audience.

Establish Credibility. Be aware of the audience's level of knowledge—don't "talk down" to them or use a patronizing tone. Keep your message simple. Deliver information succinctly and clearly. Use transitions. Incorporate differing opinions from the group without undermining your own message. For example, if a student makes a point that you don't agree with or that you know contradicts the facts, say, "You do have a valid (or interesting) point. Just remember that …"

Be prepared. If you use notes, write them on 3" x 5" index cards and refer to them as minimally as possible. It conveys a lack of professionalism and a lack of caring on your part. Using notes for specific statistics, e.g., numbers and rates, will not undermine credibility. However, be sure to always have the source notated in case a student asks for a citation.

It is okay not to know an answer. If you cannot answer a question, apologize and say you do not know the answer but you will consult a source that does and follow up with them. Don't make up an answer! Make sure you do this! Or, refer the student to an appropriate resource in the campus or community.

Finally, avoid "scare tactics." Examples of scare tactics include showing a crashed car to teach students about the dangers of drinking and driving, or displaying pictures of sexually transmitted disease so students won't ever want to have sex again. They are obvious efforts at grabbing attention, and that is about all they do. Your goal is to change behavior, and research in health behavior change demonstrates emphatically that scare tactics don't work.

Foster open-mindedness and tolerance. Be sensitive and nonjudgmental. Avoid making uninformed or unqualified generalizations, particularly across sex, race, religion, or sexual orientation. Acknowledge other views, lifestyles, decisions. Never "put someone on the spot." For example, don't force an individual to share their own experiences if they don't want to. Be aware that some members of the audience may not want to be there, as they may have been mandated to attend. Try to encourage them to participate and change their feelings about the workshop.

Generate Discussion. "Gray" issues with no right or wrong answers are much more conducive to generating discussion. Because you are working in content areas that are value-laden and have room for opinion in many instances, you have this as an advantage. Therefore, limit the amount of facts and statistics you give accordingly. Characteristics of a successful discussion topic that fosters a lot of dialogue are

- it is controversial with no simple, single "right answer";
- it requires a minimal amount of details—just enough to get "the facts";
- it addresses a moral or emotional issue;
- it is somewhat distanced from audience members (not personally threatening);
- it is one that most individuals would typically already have some kind of opinion about.

In addition, the most successful and lively discussions occur when the facilitator refrains from sharing his or her opinion. This way, audience members do not feel that you are biased toward one side or another.

What follows are additional suggestions for getting your audience members more involved.
- Ask open-ended questions, i.e., not "yes" or "no" questions, to elicit participation.
- Avoid calling on the same people or people who came to the workshop together.
- Give information as succinctly as possible, thus allowing more time for audience members to respond.
- Don't be judgmental or put anyone down for his/her values or views; this is the quickest way to curtail audience participation. Always validate opinions offered by audience members, even if they aren't the same as yours. Never say "You're wrong!" when someone doesn't give the correct answer.
- Avoid asking direct, personal questions in front of the entire group that put someone on the spot. An obvious example of such a blunder would be "Are you gay?"
- Address the group, not an individual, when you are asking a question, then call on an individual to respond.
- Present information in the form of questions rather than providing it up front, e.g., ask, "Does anyone have a definition for multiculturalism?" or "What would you consider to be signs and symptoms of an eating disorder?" Always reaffirm and repeat a correct answer, i.e., positive

reinforcement. If a wrong answer is given, acknowledge the effort and then give the correct answer. If nobody answers within a minute, tell the group the answer.

• Briefly summarize information at the end of each section. Use a logical transition to the next topic.
• If you get a question that you cannot answer, ask if anyone in the group can help you out. This creates a feeling of group efficacy.

Take responsibility for group comfort. Be sure the room is comfortable and well lighted. Open or close windows/ doors to shut out noise. Change room temperature if needed. Be sure everyone can hear you and see your visual aids.

If a group is distracted, or if intra-group tension or confrontation arises, redirect their attention with an open-ended question, a shift in pace, or change in topic. Sometimes a riveting statistic or thought-provoking observation can effectively regain attention and interest. Know that you have the right to ask "hecklers" and other disruptive audience members to leave. If an audience member insists on being inconsiderate, you can ask them to leave if they are not interested in the topic. Minor infractions can be ignored, but serious interruptions must be addressed, or else you will lose credibility with the rest of the audience. One individual should not endanger other group members' right to learn.

"Check" audience members for derogatory language: *You must confront language and behaviors that are offensive or disrespectful to members of any cultural group.*

Listen Actively. Pay attention to the verbal and non-verbal cues of audience members: is participation low? are they interested? do people seem bored? are people asking a lot of questions on a certain topic? or are they just confused? Be prepared to speed through some topics and elaborate on others depending on group response, interest, and knowledge. Always plan ahead for these types of situations. Clarify and paraphrase.

Be creative. Use visual aids with colorful graphics, pictures, and big writing. Make up game shows or other interactive activities that require group input and participation, or that require audience members to get up and move around. Add riveting facts and bits of trivia throughout the workshop. Use humor, as long as it is not

offensive and does not undermine or contradict your message. Think up a snazzy, catchy name for your workshop—market yourself! Incorporate theater (role plays, etc.). Use other media (book quotes, videos, cartoons, poetry, music, etc.) to help demonstrate concepts or get a discussion going.

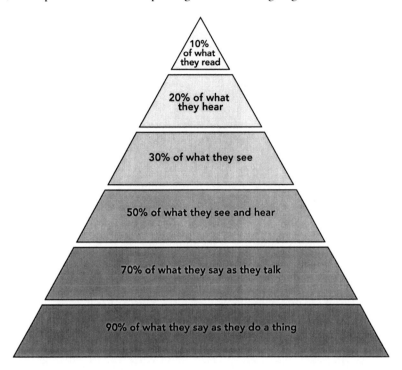

Figure 7: *Retention of information. A graphic representation of a learner's ability to retain information*

Using Culturally Inclusive Language

When leading a workshop, it is important to be aware of your language and word choices. One single word can make the difference in whether you include or exclude members of a certain cultural group. While members of a cultural group may not necessarily agree on which term they prefer others to use in referring to their group, using the following terms will minimize the likelihood of offending someone. In addition, because the comfort and safety of your audience members are in your hands, **it is your responsibility to challenge and respectfully correct members of the audience who use terms that are offensive and disrespectful to others during the workshop.**

There is certainly considerable debate and disagreement about which terms to use when referring to various cultural groups. The following only represents a guide; it is not 100% fail proof. You may use these terms and still offend a particular individual. Some possible ways to minimize offending audience members are to use several terms to refer to the same group during the course of a workshop (when appropriate), or to ask audience members themselves at the beginning of the workshop which terms they would prefer that you use. Finally, using inclusive language is not the same thing as being politically correct. A speaker may use PC language, but if the intent and feeling behind his or her words conveys disrespect or lack of caring, the listener can still be alienated. In general, select the phrase or term that is underlined:

- Person with AIDS (PWA): People who have AIDS are not "patients" or "victims." Referring to them as such implies powerlessness, passiveness, and incompleteness, none of which are necessarily true about people who have AIDS. You can also use "person with HIV infection."
- Multiple partners: "Promiscuous" has a lot of negative connotations. In addition, society has a double-standard for men and women with regard to their sexuality. There are many more terms for women who have multiple sexual partners than there are for men; almost all of them have a degrading connotation (e.g., "slut," "whore"). Furthermore, some individuals are trying to deal with the problem of sexual addiction; labeling them as "promiscuous" merely oppresses them further.
- Sexual orientation: "Sexual preference" wrongly implies that the individual had a choice in their sexual identity. In fact, many studies demonstrate that being gay is genetically determined.
- Gay/Lesbian/Bisexual: "Homosexual" was first established as a medical term; some people believe that it implies that being gay or lesbian is a disease or is abnormal. On the other hand, the term "heterosexual" is preferred over "straight"; the latter term makes a statement about normalcy. However, it is often acceptable to use gay/lesbian/bi and "straight" in the same context.
- Partner, significant other, lover, spouse: These are nonjudgmental terms. "Boyfriend/girlfriend" and "husband/wife" are gender-specific terms that require that you make an assumption about an individual's sexual orientation.
- African American: This is the most commonly used term. "Black" has historically connoted negative stereotypes for many individuals, while "Negro" and "nigger" are insulting, reminiscent of slavery and pre-Civil Rights segregation. Nevertheless, some African Americans refer to themselves as "Black" or "Black American" out of pride. This is an instance when alternating "African American" and "Black" might be appropriate.
- Asian American: "Oriental" carries patronizing overtones originating from American military presence in the Pacific Ocean. Use "Oriental" only to refer to food, furniture, etc. When used to refer to people, it has connotations of being exotic, passive, etc.
- Hispanic American: This is the most widely accepted term to refer to a wide variety of people representing various ethnic backgrounds, including those individuals from Mexico and Latin America. Depending on the region of the country that you are in, particular cultures within the larger Hispanic population may prefer that you use Latino/Latina (from Central and South American), or Mexicano/Mexicana/Mexican and Chicano/Chicana (ONLY if they are from Mexico). It is an insult to Hispanic peoples of non-Mexican origin to be labeled Chicano/Chicana.
- Native American: These people are not "Indians" from the sub-continent of India; they were the first to populate the North American continent. In addition, the term "Indians" has the negative connotation of being savages or uncivilized—which is how Hollywood typically portrayed Native Americans until recently. Other acceptable terms might include American Indian or Native Indians.
- Person with a physical/psychological/learning disability: This term emphasizes the person, while terms such as "handicapped," "disabled," or "retarded" focus on the disability. Another term that is acceptable is "physically/mentally challenged." Furthermore, individuals who are visually or hearing-impaired prefer to be referred to as blind and deaf, respectively.
- International students: "Foreigners" conveys an ethnocentric tone, and implies that the US is the center of the world. It is typically used to put down or patronize those who come from other countries. When traveling to other parts of the world, citizens of the US would be considered internationals.

- Older adults: We forget that age is used to discriminate against individuals in this country. "Old people" conveys the notion that older adults are useless and not valued. In contrast, "older adults" emphasizes the fact the as we age, we accumulate wisdom, knowledge, and experiences that are of benefit to younger adults.

The following phrases are important to keep in mind particularly when you are conducting a program addressing sexual health issues. Again, using these phrases does not guarantee that you will never offend, but they will minimize the likelihood.

- High-risk behaviors: "High-risk group" conveys the false and misleading notion that some people are inherently immune or prone to HIV infection. In reality, it's what you do and not who you are that determines your level of risk.
- Safer sex: "Safe sex" can create a false sense of security. We want to convey that certain practices and precautions can minimize the risk of contracting HIV and STIs but do not completely eliminate the risk.
- Sexual activity/behavior: "Dangers of sex" or any other judgmental term for sexual intercourse or sexual behavior places a negative connotation on sexuality. Similarly, phrases such as "normal sex" imply that some forms of sexual expression are abnormal or wrong.
- Vaginal or anal intercourse: Terms like "heterosexual sex," "gay sex," or "normal sex" are ambiguous, misleading, and judgmental. Anal intercourse is practiced by both heterosexual and gay couples.
- Contract/transmit HIV: People do not "catch," "get," or "spread" AIDS. Such terms are inaccurate and propagate the myth that a person can become infected with AIDS through casual contact. Emphasize that the virus is what is contagious. AIDS takes years to develop.
- HIV Antibody Test: No test for AIDS exists. When we screen, we are looking for the presence of antibodies to HIV—the virus that causes AIDS—in the blood. AIDS must be diagnosed by a physician.
- Sexually Transmitted Infection (STI): "VD" or "venereal disease" is an outdated term that traditionally refers only to syphilis and gonorrhea. Likewise STI is often preferred over STD (Sexual Transmitted Disease), as the word "infection" implies a person can be infected and can infect another person without the knowledge of having a disease. "VD" also has a more negative connotation than STI. Technically, AIDS is not an STI because it can be transmitted by other than sexual means. However, by saying "AIDS and other STIs" we instill the notion that AIDS is not the only disease people should be worrying about.
- Needle use: Not all drug use involves needles. We want to emphasize the dangers of any kind of needle sharing—for street drugs, steroids, estrogen, tattooing, or ear piercing.
- Intravenous/injecting drug user (IVDU): "Drug addict" or "drug abuser" often implies a moral judgment. In addition, not all people who use drugs are addicts. You don't have to be an addict to be at risk.
- Rape survivor: "Rape victim" only serves to emphasize the social stigma associated with rape.
- Reduce the risks of rape: "Prevent rape" implies that rape is caused by the victim and that s/he therefore can do something to stop it. In fact, rape is the responsibility of the perpetrator. Therefore, potential victims can only reduce their risks.

Become comfortable talking about sexual behavior. It is important to use the current and appropriate jargon and correct terms for different sexual behaviors so your audience knows exactly what you are referring to.

If there is a doubt, explain what you mean. If you appear comfortable talking about sex, your audience will be more comfortable listening to you.

Protecting Confidentiality

Interacting with audience members. After peer educators conduct a program, members of the audience frequently have questions they would like to ask. Many students also wish to share personal anecdotes relative to the program topic. As soon as you realize that a student is approaching you with information of a sensitive nature, be proactive and initiate a discussion in which you reassure the student that you will maintain his or her confidentiality. Do not wait until the student expresses concern about confidentiality. If a student begins a discussion when others are present:

- Create a safe, private space for discussion, e.g., a corner of the room, another room if available, and draw the person away.
- Create a safe space for the student whether or not s/he appears to be concerned about privacy.
- If the student is especially upset or emotional, block visual access to him or her by positioning your body between the student and others in the room.

In any situation where a student's confidentiality could potentially be compromised, avoid the appearance of closely watching an interaction between that student and a health center staff member. Avoid eye contact if necessary to ensure the above. Maintain a calm, nonverbal body response if a student discloses highly disturbing information.

Oftentimes, a student will preface his or her interaction with you by asking you not to tell anyone else what they are about to say. **Never promise that you will keep your interaction a secret.** Instead, say that you will do your best to maintain their confidentiality. This is important, because **there are three exceptions when a peer educator must violate confidentiality:**

1. If a student indicates a desire or intention to hurt him- or herself, e.g., suicide threat;
2. If a student indicates a desire or intention to hurt another individual; or
3. If a student reveals that s/he has committed an act that violates state statutes or federal laws (i.e., child abuse).

You must tell the advisor as soon as possible when a student shares this information with you. Should a student begin revealing information of such a nature, stop them tactfully; let him or her know you are willing to listen, but say that, given your paraprofessional role as a peer educator, you are required to convey such information to the advisor. Encourage him or her to continue sharing, but let the student decide if s/he wishes to continue the conversation. In either case, inform your advisor immediately of the interaction.

Common dilemmas peer educators face in protecting confidentiality include encountering students around campus outside a program, or a relationship with a student prior to the program. A good "rule of thumb" is to avoid eye contact and maintain a calm, nonverbal body response when encountering a student from a program. Even if you had a prior relationship with a student, treat any information they share with you in your capacity as a peer educator as private and confidential.

Discussion with other peer educators. Peer education work can sometimes produce stress and anxiety. It can be overwhelming to have students share emotions and experiences with you. It is important that you have someone with whom you can "process" the feelings that you have as a result of doing peer education work. Individuals who are included in the "bubble of confidentiality" include fellow peer educators and your advisor; you can go to these individuals for support, reassurance or guidance.

- It is still important to protect student confidentiality in these instances. For example, when discussing a previous interaction with a student **during a closed meeting of peer educators,** eliminate or change identifying details, e.g., alter age, race, sex, dates, and location. When discussing an interaction with a student with another peer educator **in an unsafe setting,** arrange for a safe place to discuss the situation
- use first name only, a different name, or no name
- eliminate unnecessary details
- minimize necessary details
- use clinical shorthand terminology
- lower your voice

Remember, if you need to process your feelings about an interaction with a student: (1) Identify safe people to discuss this with in advance, e.g., other peer educators, the advisor; and (2) If you can't talk to one of these individuals, talk about your feelings, not about the event, until you can reach another peer educator or the advisor.

Handling the curiosity of friends, family, and partners. "Significant others" frequently feel they have the "right to know" what is going on with a friend, relative, or partner. This could include your own network of friends and family, who are curious about your work, or those of a student you have interacted with. The concern of significant others may be genuine and pressing; however, you are never at liberty to discuss a student's situation with significant others—not even a parent. Respectfully inform the inquiring person that as a peer educator, you are bound by confidentiality. Encourage them to speak to the student directly. If they continue to pressure you, refer them to the advisor.

Never assume a friend or partner has the same motivation to maintain confidentiality as a peer educator does. Don't give anyone that burden of responsibility for protecting someone else's confidentiality when s/he may not be able to nor motivated to keep it over time.

Instead, be proactive; tell people that your peer educator role calls for special limits on revealing information, even when it appears to be safe. In others words, you cannot violate confidentiality.

Be aware of your own vulnerabilities to peer pressure. Be very clear about when the boundaries of your paraprofessional role as a peer educator may impinge on those of your social life. Finally, realize that alcohol or other drugs, or emotional peaks and valleys, can influence your judgment regarding protecting confidentiality.

When confidentiality is breached. The consequences of breaking confidentiality can be detrimental to a peer education organization and to its affiliated departments. Students lose trust in peer educators. Real and imagined "grapevine" rumors are created. The individual peer educator, the entire peer education organization, and the affiliated department lose credibility. Personal conflicts may erupt if the peer educator had a prior relationship with the student involved. Additionally, breach of confidentiality constitutes a potential liability to the organization, the department, and the institution.

It is important to confront other peer educators who may be jeopardizing confidentiality. Always inform the advisor if you believe that confidentiality has been breached. If confidentiality is seriously compromised, it is better to forewarn the advisor in case of possible complaints. Each case will be handled individually, as circumstances will vary. Know that it is natural to make a mistake; as a peer educator, you will not be without support from your advisor or the affiliated department.

All peer educators should be required to read and sign a confidentiality statement. This form is kept in your file. You should receive a copy of this statement; keep it in an accessible location, and refer to it if you have questions about your responsibility to maintain confidentiality. See Figure 8 for a sample confidentiality form.

Each student participating in a peer education organization affiliated with the Student Health Center of University X is hereby advised that all information pertaining to patient visits, individual contacts, and educational programming is to be kept in strictest confidence. There shall be no disclosure, whether in writing or verbally, of any such information to anyone outside the Student Health Center except as otherwise specifically and explicitly authorized by Student Health Center policy or by the Director.

Disclosure of information to professional staff of the Student Health Center or to fellow peer educators is permissible if: (1) the person is currently employed by the Student Health Center, or is currently an active member in a peer education organization; and (2) such disclosure is for the sole purpose of providing the peer educator with information necessary for the performance of his/her duties as a paraprofessional representing the Student Health Center.

Access to Student Health Center medical or mental health records of patients will not be allowed for peer educators. Access to files related to the business and activities of the peer education organization to which a peer educator belongs shall be limited to those circumstances in which the peer educator requires such access in the performance of their assigned duties.

All peer education organization contact records are the sole property of the Student Health Center and shall not be removed from the facility, nor shall the record be copied except as specifically authorized by the Advisor or the Director. Peer educators shall not be given the opportunity to review the contents of their records unless under the direct supervision of the Advisor or the Director. Violation of the above guidelines pertaining to confidentiality shall be grounds for immediate dismissal of the peer educator serving in an official capacity with the Student Health Center.

I have read and understand the above guidelines and agree to comply.

_____   _____
Signature of Peer Educator   Date

_____   _____
Print Name of Peer Educator   Organization

_____   _____
Signature of Advisor   Date

Figure 8: Confidentiality Statement

Questions to Consider

1. As a peer educator, you will be asked to facilitate on many different topics. Which do you feel most ready to facilitate and which do you feel least comfortable with and why?
2. Thinking back to a time when you were involved in a conversation with a peer, give an example of poor and/or good listening skills. Give specific examples.
3. Why is it important to generate discussion in the programs we facilitate? Why do many people stay away from this?
4. Based on the section on culturally inclusive language, which will be most difficult to change and why?

References

Covey, S. R. (1989). *The seven habits of highly effective people.* New York: Simon & Schuster.

Egan, G. (1990). *The skilled helper* (4th ed.). Belmont, CA : Brooks Cole.

Chapter 5

Overview of Campus Health

By Luoluo Hong and Jason Robertson

The Student Wellness Model

Adapted from Hettler's (1980) seven-part wellness model, the following are the eight interrelated and interdependent components of healthy living for the peer educator. A holistic approach to health and well-being must address all eight components. Imbalance in one area will affect other areas.

Emotional	The emotionally well student is able to appropriately express and manage the entire range of feelings, including anger, fear, happiness, and sadness. S/he possesses high self-esteem, a sense of humor, and positive body image. This person also seeks support from a mental health professional when needed.
Physical	The physically well student eats when hungry and selects a varied and nutritionally balanced diet. S/he also gets an adequate amount of sleep, engages in moderate to vigorous exercise 3–5 times a week, gets routine medical check-ups appropriate to his or her sex, age, and risk factors, and takes safety precautions.
Spiritual	The spiritually well student displays a sense of purpose in life and makes life choices with integrity. S/he acknowledges a higher power of some kind, and engages in prayer, meditation, or other means of connecting to humanity. Maslow's "self-actualization" is comparable to spiritual wellness.
Sexual	The sexually well student accepts his or her sexual orientation, engages in sexual relationships that are consistent with his or her values and development, and refrains from using sex to manipulate or influence others. Also, s/he minimizes unwanted consequences through communication and contraceptives.
Social	The socially well student has a network of friends and family to whom s/he can turn for support, validation, and sharing of life experiences. These relationships are based on interdependence (rather than codependence), mutual trust and respect, equity of power, and cultural competence.
Intellectual	The intellectually well student values education and engages in lifelong learning, and pursues activities that increase knowledge, develop moral reasoning, foster critical thinking, and expand world views. Also, s/he appreciates the fine arts, and values intuition, empathy, and understanding as forms of knowing.
Occupational	The occupationally well student fulfills a socially defined role that is both stimulating and inherently rewarding. S/he chooses a role (or several roles) that are consistent with beliefs, goals, lifestyle, personality, and values.
Environmental	The environmentally well student recognizes the Earth's preciousness, and strives to minimize wasteful consumption or unnecessary destruction of animals, plants, elements, or energy. S/he engages in recycling and conservation, protects natural resources, and strives for living spaces free of health hazards.

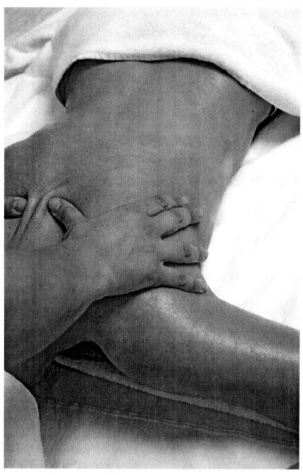

Quick Reference Guide to College Health Statistics

Alcohol consumption. These data are based on a study Presley, Meilman, and Cashin (1996) of N = 45,632 students from two- and four-year institutions in the US. Of the total sample, 83.6% reported consuming alcohol at least once in the past year. Annual prevalence was highest among white students (86.9%) and lowest among students of Asian/Pacific Islander descent (69.0%). Alcohol use by African American students was almost as low as that of Asians (70.1%). Use by Native American/Alaskan Native and Hispanic students was 83.0% and 82.2% respectively. With respect to gender, 27.6% of the males and 14.0% of the females reported drinking three or more times per week.

Students across the nation reported consuming an average of 4.5 drinks per week, with males consuming an average of 6.8 drinks and females consuming an average of 2.8 drinks. The Northeast region consumption levels (5.9 drinks per week per student) were almost 70% greater than that of the South (3.5 drinks per week per student). The North Central region had the second-highest consumption level (4.6 drinks per week per student, and the West ranked third (4.1 drinks per week per student).

Students living on campus consumed more alcohol and engaged in binge drinking more often than students living off campus. Students under the legal drinking age consumed greater quantities of alcohol than those for whom the drug is legal, and they engaged in binge drinking more often.

The heaviest drinkers obtained the lowest grades; this finding is especially pronounced for males. Average number of drinks per week correlated with G.P.A.: A = 3.4 drinks, B = 4.5 drinks, C= 6.1 drinks, and D or F = 9.8 drinks.

Overall, 44% of the students reported having binged (five or more drinks in one sitting for men, four or more for women) in the last two weeks (Perkins 2002). Almost 16% reported binge episodes three or more times in the past two weeks (23.6% of the males, 9.9% of the females).

Other drug use. Presley, Meilman, and Cashin's study (1996) found the following rates of drug use in their sample of college students:

- Tobacco Use: 41.6% have ever used tobacco; 15.1% use tobacco daily (17.3% of men, 13.5% of women);
- Marijuana: 27.7% have ever used marijuana; 16% use marijuana once a month or more often;
- Cocaine: 4.1 % have ever used (5.7% of men, 2.8% of women);
- Amphetamines: 6.8% have ever used (6.0% of men, 7.4% of women);
- Sedatives: 2.6% have ever used (3.1% of men, 2.2% of women);
- Hallucinogens: 6.8% have ever used (9.4% of men, 4.9% of women);
- Opiates: 0.8% have ever used (1.4% of men, 0.4% of women);
- Inhalants: 2.3% have ever used (3.3% of men, 1.5% of women);
- Designer Drugs: 2.3% have ever used (2.9% of men, 1.9% of women); and
- Steroids: 0.7% have ever used (1.2% of men, 0.2% of women).

Consequences of alcohol or drug use. In Presley, Meilman, and Cashin's study (1996), the following were reported consequences of alcohol or other drug use:

- Had a hangover: 59.6% (64.7% of men, 56% of women);
- Performed poorly on a test or project: 25% (Perkins 2002);
- Trouble with police/other campus authorities: 11.7% (17.6% of men, 7.5% of women);
- Damaged property, pulled fire alarm, etc.: 7.7% (14% of men, 3.3% of women);
- Got into an argument or fight: 29.6% (33% of men, 27.1% of women);
- Nauseated or vomited: 47.1% (50.1% of men, 45.0% of women);
- Driven a car while under the influence: 32.6% (40.2% of men, 27.1% of women);
- Missed a class: 27.9% (13.4% did so three or more times; 34.0% of men, 23.6% of women);
- Been criticized by someone I know: 27.1% (32.2% of men, 23.4% of women);

- Thought I might have a drinking/other drug problem: 12.0% (15.6% of men, 8.0% of women);
- Had a memory loss: 25.9% (28.9% of men, 23.8% of women);
- Done something I later regretted: 35.8% (39.1% of men, 33.4% of women);
- Arrested for DWI, DUI: 1.7% (3.0% of men, 0.7% of women);
- Tried unsuccessfully to stop using: 5.7% (7.9% of men, 4.2% of women);
- Been hurt or injured: 12.9% (15.9% of men, 10.8% of women);
- Have been taken advantage sexually: 11.4% (10.6% of men, 12.0% of women);
- Have taken advantage of someone sexually: 6.0% (10.3% of men, 3.1% of women);
- Tried to commit suicide: 1.6% (1.7% of men, 1.5% of women); and
- Thought about committing suicide: 5.1% (5.8% of men, 4.6% of women).

Binge drinking. Almost half (44%) of college students surveyed (N = 17,592) were binge drinkers (consumed five or more drinks in one sitting in the past two weeks, four or more for women), including almost one fifth (19%) of students who were frequent binge drinkers (engaged in binge drinking three or more times in one week). Frequent binge drinkers were seven to ten times more likely than non-binge drinkers not to use protection when having sex, to engage in unplanned sexual activity, to get into trouble with campus police, to damage property, or to get hurt or injured (Wechsler et al. 1994).

Sexual assault. According to the National College Health Risk Behavior Survey (NCHRBS), one in five undergraduate women has been raped (Douglas et al. 1997). The most frequently cited data regarding campus rape were collected by Mary P. Koss, Ph.D. for the 1985 *Ms. Magazine Campus Project on Sexual Assault.* Funded by the National Institute of Mental Health, the study surveyed 3,187 women and 2,972 men at undergraduate institutions across the US (Warshaw 1988), and yielded these results:

- one in four women surveyed had an experience that met the legal definition of rape or attempted rape;
- eighty-four percent of those raped knew their attacker;
- fifty-seven percent of the rapes occurred on dates;
- one in twelve of the male students surveyed had committed acts that met the legal definitions of rape or attempted rape;
- for both men and women, the average age when a rape incident occurred (either as perpetrator or victim) was 18.5 years old;
- only 27% of the women whose sexual assault met the legal definition of rape thought of themselves as rape victims;
- about 75% of the men and at least 55% of the women involved in acquaintance rape had been drinking or taking drugs just before the attack;
- forty-two percent of the rape victims told no one about their assaults, only 5% reported their rapes to the police, and only 5% sought help at rape crisis centers;
- forty-two percent of the women who were raped said they had sex again with the men who assaulted them, while 55% of the men who raped said they had sex again with their victims;
- whether they acknowledge their experience as rape or not, 30% of the women identified in the study as rape victims contemplated suicide after the incident;
- eighty-four percent of the men who committed rape said that what they did was <u>definitely not rape;</u>
- sixteen percent of the male students who committed rape and 10% of those who attempted a rape took part in episodes involving more than one attacker, i.e., gang rape; and
- eight percent of the women who had been raped were 14, 15, 16, or 17 years old at the time of the assaults.

Fighting. Over 90% of physical assaults involve men as both the perpetrators and the victims (Miedzian 1991). Results from the NCHRBS conducted by the Centers for Disease Control and Prevention (CDC) indicate that about 15% of male students have participated in physical fights—twice the number among females (Douglas et al. 1997). Among American men of all ages, nearly half report having ever been punched or beaten by another person (US Department of Justice 1994). Based on the NCHRBS, 14% of male college students carried a weapon on campus, and 5% carried a gun (Douglas et al. 1997).

Stress, depression, and suicide. According to the NCHRBS, 10.3% of all students (10.8% of the women, 9.7% of the men) have thought seriously about attempting suicide. Nearly 7.0% had made a suicide plan (6.3% of the women, 7.2% of the men), and 1.5% had attempted suicide (1.3% of the women, 1.7% of the men)—one third of them requiring medical attention as a result (Douglas et al. 1997). In general, while men and women are equally likely to become depressed in college, males account for six out of every seven college-age suicides.

Women attempt suicide three times as often as men do, but men successfully commit suicide three times more often than women do. In general, men use methods with high lethality and little chance for intervention, such as hanging or gunshot, while women use methods with low to medium lethality, e.g., sleeping pills, slitting wrists, etc. While the suicide rate has remained constant since 1946 in other age groups, it has increased 250% for those aged 16–25 years. For college-age white males, suicide is the second leading cause of death.

Body Image and Eating Disorders. Anywhere from 0.5–2.0% of the female population is anorexic, while as many as 30% of college females are bulimic. Also, 86% of bulimics are between the ages of 15 and 30 years. The 1995 NCHRBS asked female students how they had lost weight or had kept from gaining weight in the thirty days prior to the survey. Of respondents, 42% of female students were dieting, 67% of them exercised, 4% vomited or took laxatives, and 7% took diet pills. Women were significantly more likely to engage in all of these behaviors than their male counterparts (Douglas et al. 1997).

Preliminary research data also indicate that female athletes, because of their tendency to engage in crash dieting and other quick weight-loss techniques, are at increased risk for developing eating disorders (Eating Disorder Awareness and Prevention, Inc. 1994). Sorority women are similarly prone to disordered eating.

While women constitute the majority (90%–95%) of eating disorder cases, there has been an increase in the number of eating disorders that mental health professionals diagnose in men.

Reproductive and sexual health. According to the NCHRBS, 86.1% of the students had sexual intercourse (87.8% of the women, 84.0% of the men). About a third (34.5%) of students had six or more partners in their lifetime (31.8% of the women, 37.8% of the men). At last sexual intercourse, only 29.6% reported using condom (25.8% of the women, 35.2% of the men). Consistent condom use was reported by 27.9% of those surveyed (25.1% of the women, 32.4% of the men). At last sexual intercourse, 79.8% reported using a contraceptive method (80.1% of the women, 79.3% of the men) (Douglas et al. 1997).

One in 250 college students is currently HIV-positive. Nearly half of all HIV infections now occur in individuals under the age of 30.

One in four college students will contract at least one sexually transmitted disease before graduating (American College Health Association 1989). The most common STIs are chlamydia, human papilloma virus or HPV (which causes genital warts and many cancers, including of the tongue), and herpes. One in fifteen college women become pregnant each year (Healthy People 2000 1990).

Questions to Consider

1. How do you perceive your overall wellness? Why is this important to understand as a peer educator?
2. How does an understanding of the wellness model help you as a peer educator assist peers with their concerns?

References

American School Health Association, Association for the Advancement of Health Education and Society for Public Health Education, Inc. (1989). *National adolescent student health survey: A report on the health of America's youth.* Oakland, CA: Third Party Publishing Company.

Douglas, Kathy A., et al. (1997). *Results from the 1995 National College Health Risk Behavior Survey.* Journal of American College Health, 46: p. 55–66.

Miedzian, M. (1991). *Boys will be boys: Breaking the link between masculinity and violence. New York: Doubleday.*

Perkins, H.W. (2002). Surveying the damage: A review of research on consequences of alcohol misuse in college populations. Journal of Studies on Alcohol, 14, p. 91–100.

Presley, C. A., Meilman, P. W., and Cashin, J. R. (1996). *Alcohol and drugs on American college campuses, Volume IV: 1992-1994.* Carbondale: Southern Illinois University, The Core Institute.

Warshaw, R. (1988). *I never called it rape.* New York: Harper and Row Publishers.

Wechsler, H., Davenport, A., Dowdall, G., Moeykens, B., and Castillo, S. (1994). Health and behavioral consequences of binge drinking in college. *Journal of the American Medical Association* 272(21), p. 1672–1677.

Chapter 6

Women's Health—Rethinking the Superwoman Myth

By Luoluo Hong, Lindsay Walker McCall, and Julie Catanzarite

What is the Superwoman Myth?

The "superwoman myth" refers to the false belief that women can be everything and do everything. The belief is fostered by pressure imposed on women by themselves, by their families, by their partners, by their friends, and by society. Women are asked to be perfect in every way—physically, emotionally, intellectually, and interpersonally. Such a state of perfection is inherently impossible, but women will strive unceasingly to achieve this myth. In addition, the myth asks women to be and do contradictory things. As a result, women may engage in a lot of unhealthful behaviors, and experience a lot of oppression.

According to McGrath (1994), author of *When Feeling Bad is Good,* the superwoman syndrome is typified by the following:

- *Victimization Depression* from the emotional, economic, physical, and sexual abuse targeted at women;
- *Relationship Depression* from poor quality or quantity in a woman's relationships;
- *Age-Rage Depression* from cultural devaluation and restriction of activity because of aging;
- *Depletion Depression* from the energy drain from women's typical role overload and role conflict;
- *Body-Image Depression* from impossible standards of physical perfection imposed on women; and
- *Mind-Body Depression* from the physical illness caused by depression, and the depression caused by physical illness.

This chapter strives to debunk the superwoman myth, and provide a framework by which women can heal themselves and begin to build a more balanced life, based on the following concepts:

1. realistic expectations of self and others;
2. self-love;
3. healthy relationships; and
4. wellness choices.

Epidemiology of Women's Health

Alcohol, tobacco, and other drug abuse. Women are more susceptible to alcohol's intoxicating effects and to the physiological effects of heavy drinking. They possess less *alcohol dehydrogenase,* the enzyme that breaks down alcohol, and they have less total body water (45%–55%) as compared to men (55%–65%) with which to dilute the alcohol. Today, 34.4% of women ages 18–20 binge drink (consume four or more drinks in one sitting) (Center for Science in the Public Interest 2008), whereas only 6% of female college students binge drank in 1950 (Young, Morales, McCabe, Boyd, and D'Arcy 2005).

Women are more likely than men to be cross-addicted with alcohol and prescription drugs. Sixty percent of tranquilizers, 71% of all antidepressants, and 80% of all amphetamines are prescribed for women. More and more, female college students are more likely to experience negative consequences, such as breast cancer, liver damage, academic difficulties, and unwanted sexual encounters as a result of drinking (Smith and Berger 2010).

Disordered eating and eating disorders. Women represent over 90% of diagnosed eating disorder cases. Forty percent of newly identified cases of anorexia are in girls and young women 15–19 years old. Ninety-one percent of women recently surveyed on a college campus had attempted to control their weight through dieting; and 22% dieted "often" or "always" (National Eating Disorders Foundation (NEDF) 2010).

On any given day, 25% of women are on diets, with 50% finishing, breaking or starting one. Nine out of ten women think about food excessively. Eighty-one percent of 10-year-olds are afraid of being fat (NEDF 2010)

Since 1960, each year's Miss America winner got thinner, but the average young adult woman got heavier. The average model is 23% slimmer than the average American woman; she is probably 5'9" tall, and weighs 110 pounds. In contrast, today's average woman is 5'4" tall and weighs an average of 142 pounds. If Barbie were a real woman, her measurements would be 36-18-33, and she would be too thin to have a menstrual period. Each year, the diet industry grosses $60 billion, the cosmetic industry $40 billion, and the cosmetic surgery industry $13 billion.

Overweight females are 40% less likely to go to college, are 20% less likely to marry, make on average $6,700 less per year than other women, and are more likely to be found guilty by a jury (NOW Foundation 2008).

Violence against women. **Pornography** is defined as writing or imagery that objectifies, degrades, and brutalizes a person in the name of sexual stimulation or entertainment The pornography industry grosses over $10 billion a year, which is more than what is spent in other forms of entertainment (movies and sporting events). There are four times as many pornographic bookstores in the US as there are McDonald's, and *Playboy* and *Penthouse* outsell *Time* and *Newsweek* ten to one on the newsstand.

One in four girls is sexually abused by the age of 18. Sexual assaults occus in the US every two and a half minutes (RAINN n.d.). One out of every six American women has been the victim of an attempted or completed rape in her lifetime (RAINN n.d.). The National College Women Sexual Victimization Study estimated that between one in four and one in five college women experience completed or attempted rape during their college years (Fisher 2000). One in six college women have experienced sexual harassment (Hill and Silva 2006). Females aged 12 to 24 years are at the greatest risk for experiencing a rape or sexual assault (DOJ 2001).

Sixty-four percent of women who reported being raped, physically assaulted, and/or stalked since age 18 were victimized by a current or former husband, cohabiting partner, boyfriend, or date (Tjaden and Thoennes 2000). In 2000, 1,247 women were killed by an intimate partner. In recent years, an intimate partner killed approximately 33% of female murder victims (Rennison 2003). A woman is physically assaulted within her home every fifteen seconds. Nearly 6 million women will be battered in any single year, and more than 25% of adult women in this country are likely to be victimized during an intimate relationship (Strengthenoursisters.com n.d.). More than one million abused women seek medical help for injuries caused by battering each year. Twenty percent of visits by women to emergency services are due to domestic violence. Half of all battered women will be beaten in their stomachs when they are pregnant (Strengthenoursisters.com n.d.).

In a survey of children aged 11–14 years, 31% of boys and 32% of girls say it is okay for a man to rape a woman who had past sexual experiences, while 65% of boys and 47% of girls believe it is okay for a man to rape a woman if they have been dating for more than six months.

Sexual and reproductive health. About 50% of women become sexually active before they graduate from high school (Kaiser Family Foundation 2005). One in four sexually active women aged 16–25 will contract a sexually transmitted infection. "Women account for a growing share of new AIDS diagnoses, rising from 8% in 1985 to 27% in 2005 Based on the CDC's HIV/AIDS prevalence estimate, approximately 300,000 women are living with HIV and AIDS in the US. Women of color are particularly affected. Black women account for two thirds (66%) of new AIDS cases among women in 2005; Latinas and white women each account for 16%" (Kaiser Family Foundation 2007). According to the CDC (2008) the largest number of HIV/AIDS diagnoses during recent years was for women aged 15–39. A woman is more likely to contract HIV from her male partner during vaginal intercourse than he is from her (CDC 2008). The presence of another STI greatly affects the likelihood of transmitting and contracting the infection.

As reported by the Guttmacher Institute, 750,000 women become pregnant each year (2010). According to the New Mexico Teen Pregnancy Coalition (2004), the US has the highest rate of teen pregnancy in the industrialized world. Additionally, four out of ten girls become pregnant at least once before they reach 20 years of age.

Economic hardship. Women are paid approximately $.77 for every dollar a man earns for equivalent work. Despite the fact that women now make up over half of the US work force, they still perform the majority of household and childcare tasks. A woman with a master's degree makes on average as much as a man with a high school diploma. The jobs that are most accessible to women are also the lowest-paying jobs. The poorest households in the US are those headed by a single female.

Mental health. While nearly half of men score high on self-esteem tests, only one third of women do. About one third of women want an overhaul of their entire appearance, and 99% of women want to change something about their appearance.

Body image is defined as the beliefs about one's own attractiveness, sexuality, and physical characteristics, as well as the perceptions of how others view one's own body, coupled with the inseparable emotions and thoughts that result from such beliefs and perceptions. Women's body image satisfaction is more highly correlated with self-esteem than that of men. Men, for the most part, view their bodies as functional and active; a man tends to feel satisfied as long as his body is healthy and working well. Women are prone to feel good about their bodies only if they are aesthetically pleasing to themselves and others.

Women are more likely than men to become clinically depressed or to be diagnosed with anxiety disorders. Women attempt suicide three times as often as men do.

Quotable Quotes from Women

One is not born a woman, one becomes one.
—Simone de Beauvoir, French writer

One of the things about equality is not just that you be treated equally to a man, but that you treat yourself equally to the way you treat a man.
—Marlo Thomas, actress

A woman without a man is like a fish without a bicycle.
—Unknown

Don't compromise yourself. You are all you've got.
—Janis Joplin, singer

I don't need a man to rectify my existence. The most profound relationship we'll ever have is the one with ourselves.
—Shirley MacLaine, actress and dancer

Rape is not sex. If someone hit you over the head with a rolling pin, would you call that cooking?
—Unknown

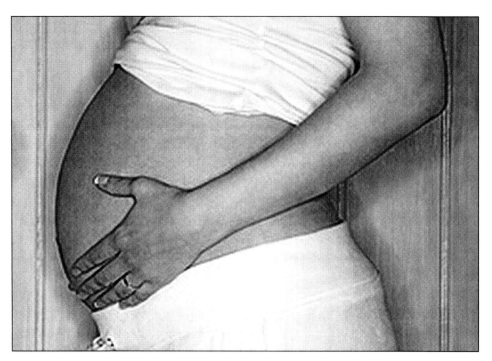

The Wellness Way for Women to Achieve Balance

Physical

- Exercise regularly a minimum of three or four times a week, 45–50 minutes at a time. Choose a moderate to intense activity that you enjoy. Pick an exercise buddy and you can motivate each other. Refrain from using exercise as a punishment for eating.
- Eat at least two regular meals each day. Eat because you are hungry. Choose from a variety of foods from all parts of the food guide pyramid. Be sure to include at least five fruits and vegetables, and eat plenty of fiber. Fat is a necessary part of everyone's diet, but limit intake to no more than 25–30% of total calories. Limit sodium, sugar, and caffeine. Do not use food as a reward system for yourself.
- Get 7–8 hours of sleep each night. Go to bed and wake up each day at approximately the same time. Develop a nurturing bedtime ritual to help you relax and transition into a restful state.
- Limit alcohol consumption to no more than two drinks in one sitting, two or three times a week. Avoid cigarette and cigar smoking completely. Use prescription medication only as directed by a physician and do not mix with alcohol. Avoid all other drug use.
- **Take a self-defense course.**

Emotional

- Give yourself permission to feel and express anger in constructive ways.
- Cry, yell, scream, laugh heartily, and never apologize for it—be most "unladylike."
- Use the creative arts both to document and express feelings (drawing, painting, music, dance, singing, writing, journaling, etc.). Refrain from emotional eating.
- Seek professional help and support when negative feelings become overwhelming or begin to take over your life.
- You aren't perfect, never have been, never will be. Get over it. Perfectionism can literally kill your spirit and your soul.
- Nurture your "inner child." Play.

- If you are a survivor of incest, a child of an alcoholic, etc., get help for working through these issues now.
- Reward yourself for small and big achievements: see a movie, visit a close friend, take a vacation alone, read a good book, go for a drive, etc.
- **Make peace with your body.** Buy clothes that feel good on you and look good on you. Don't look at the size. Don't buy what your friends wear.

Social

- Choose and remain only in healthy relationships—those in which there is mutual and equitable respect, trust, and caring. **If it feels wrong, it probably isn't right.**
- Friendship shouldn't be about popularity. All you really need is two really close, supportive friends.
- Don't buy into the competition model of female relationships when it comes to romance, academics, or career. Successes can be mutually shared, and failures can be faced together. Mentor younger women.
- You can't take care of anyone else in your life if you don't take care of yourself first.
- Develop assertiveness skills. Don't hesitate when saying "no."
- Don't confuse recreation with relaxation. You need relaxation for balance; recreation may or may not get you there.
- If your lifestyle and finances allow it, get a pet. Animals are wonderful for giving unconditional love.
- Support (rather than judge and label) other women for the sexual boundaries they choose.
- **Select friends and experiences to enrich your multicultural understanding and sensitivity.**

Sexual

- In sexual relationships, set boundaries that are consistent with your values and desires, then stick to them. Know that you never have to compromise those boundaries, no matter what.
- **Insist on consistent condom use, or abstain from sexual activity.**
- If you are sexually active, use a reliable method of birth control.
- Acknowledge and learn about all five aspects of your sexuality: *sensuality, sexual intimacy, sexual identity, reproduction/sexual health,* and *sexualization.* (See Chapter 5 for definitions).

Environmental

- A sloppy, uncontrolled, crowded, or unsafe living space can foster anxiety, tension, and stress. Create a space for yourself that is comfortable and reflects your personality.
- Conserve energy and resources. Recycle or reuse whenever possible.
- Every woman's "must-have" list: scented candles, bubble bath, dried flowers, stuffed animal, and silk pajamas.
- Keep your relaxation space separate and distinct from your working space, e.g., don't study in bed.
- **Challenge cultural norms and media messages that ask real women to achieve and become unrealistic ideals.** Engage in consumer activism, e.g., don't buy products from companies that foster unhealthy expectations for and of women.

Intellectual

- Commit yourself to lifelong learning. A mind is like a parachute: it only works when open.
- **Distinguish between needs and wants.** Needs are essential to survival and subsistence—air, water, food, sleep, shelter, clothing, intimacy, and (to a certain extent in modern society) money.

All other desires are wants; that is, they are choices you can make, with both positive and negative consequences or outcomes.

- **Establish clear goals and priorities.** Keep this list with you always. Reevaluate and revise them on a regular basis. Stagnation can lead to low productivity, lack of motivation, and unclear direction. If life is becoming cluttered, chuck those activities that do not contribute to achieving one of your goals.
- Turn off that "inner critical voice." Learn to compliment yourself and to accept compliments from others gracefully.
- Stop griping and start changing.
- Stop worrying and start planning.
- Learn to forgive, but never forget. Pain, anger, failure, and rejection will be your best teachers—and your best motivators.

Occupational

- They key to long-term success and satisfaction is finding a career that you would do for free, but are (luckily) able to get paid for doing. Don't select a professional field on the prestige basis.
- Remember that your job is only part (albeit an important part) of who you are; maintain balance at all times.
- Just because you have a job doesn't mean you still can't volunteer to serve your community. Service is an important way to remain connected with and grounded in your community.
- Hobbies help to maintain balance.

Spiritual

- A sense of purpose and connectedness with others is essential to balance.
- Seek out and surround yourself with humor. Laughing is one crucial way of connecting and of living.
- Don't forget to connect with nature.
- Set aside time for prayer, meditation, introspection and/or contemplation on a regular basis.
- Guilt can be immobilizing. Forgive yourself.
- Unfortunately, bad things do happen to good people. A flexible attitude helps you cope with the challenges of life. Sometimes asking why is not as important as accepting it is.

Questions to Consider

1. In what ways has women's health improved? In what ways has it not?
2. How can peer educators work to improve the health of women on college campuses nationwide?
3. Sexual assault remains a big problem on college campuses and in the world in general. How can you as peer educators work to address this concern?

References

Boston Women's Health Collective. (2005). Our bodies, Ourselves: A new edition for a new era. New York: Simon & Schuster, Inc.

Center for Disease Control and Prevention (2008). HIV/AIDS among women. Retrieved from http://www.cdc.gov/hiv/topics/women/resources/factsheets/pdf/women.pdf

Center for Science in the Public Interest. (2008). Binge drinking of college campuses. Retrieved from http://www.cspinet.org/booze/collfact1.htm

Eberhardt, L.Y. (1995). *Bridging the gender gap.* Duluth, MN: Whole Person Associates.

Fisher, B. S., Cullen, F. T. & Turner, M. G. (2000). *The sexual victimization of college women (NCJRS Publication No. 182369).* Washington, DC: US Department of Justice.

Guttmacher Institute (2010). Facts on American teens' sexual reproductive health. Retrieved from http://www.guttmacher.org/pubs/FB-ATSRH.html

Hill, C & Silva, E (2006). Drawing the line: Sexual harassment on campus. American Association of University Women Education Foundation. Retrieved August 30, 2010 from http://www.aauw.org/learn/research/upload/DTLFinal.pdf

Kaiser Family Foundation. (2005). U.S. teen sexual activity. Retrieved from http://www.kff.org/youthhivstds/upload/U-S-Teen-Sexual-Activity-Fact-Sheet.pdf

Kaiser Family Foundation. (2007). HIV/AIDS policy fact sheet. Retrieved from http://www.kff.org/hivaids/upload/6092-04.pdf

McGrath, E. (1992). *When feeling bad is good.* New York: Bantam Books.

National Eating Disorders Foundation. (2010). *Statistics: Eating disorders and their precursors.* Retrieved from http://www.nationaleatingdisorders.org/uploads/statistics_tmp.pdf

New Mexico Teen Pregnancy Coalition (2004). 10 teen pregnancy facts. Retrieved August 30, 2010 from http://www.health.state.nm.us/phd/fp/Forms/NMTPC%2010TeenPregFacts.pdf

Now Foundation. (2008). Fact sheet: Size discrimination. Retrieved from http://loveyourbody.nowfoundation.org/factsheet4.html

Rape, Abuse, and Incest National Network (n.d.). Statistics. Retrieved August 30, 2010 from http://www.rainn.org/statistics

Rennison, C.M.. (2003). Bureau of Justice statistics crime data brief: Intimate partner violence, 1993–2001. (US Department of Justice Report). *Retrieved from* http://www.ojp.usdoj.gov/bjs/pub/pdf/ipv01.pdf

Smith, M. A, & Berger, J. B. (2010). Women's ways of drinking: College women, high-risk alcohol use, and negative consequences. *Journal of College Student Development, 51(*1). doi: 10.1353/csd.0.0107

Strengthenoursisters.com (n.d.). Domestic violence statistics. Retrieved August 30, 2010 from http://www.strengthenoursisters.org/domestic_violence_statistics.html

Tjaden, Patricia & Thoennes, Nancy. National Institute of Justice and the Centers for Disease Control and Prevention, "Extent, Nature and Consequences of Intimate Partner Violence: Findings from the National Violence Against Women Survey." July 2000.

US Department of Justice. Criminal Victimization 2000: Changes 1999–2000 with trends 1993–2000. Washington (DC): US Government Printing Office; 2001. Publication No. NCJ 187007 Retrieved August 30, 2010 from http://www.ojp.usdoj.gov/bjs/abstract/cv00.htm

Young, A. M., Morales, M., McCabe, S.E., Boyd, C.J., & D'Arcy, H. (2005). Drinking like a guy: Frequent binge drinking among undergraduate women. *Substance Use and Misuse, 40,* 241–267. doi: 10.1081/JA-200048464

Chapter 7

Men's Health

By Luoluo Hong and Jason Robertson

Introduction: The Five-Year Gap

On average, men in the US live five fewer years than women. In addition, for twelve of the fifteen leading causes of death in this country, men have higher death rates (Mahalik, Burns, and Syzdek 2007). While this is true at every age, the gap is greatest among college-age males. Considerable research has been conducted to examine why this disparity exists. As a result, a subfield of medicine has emerged, known as *men's health*. Additional information can be obtained by visiting the **Men's Health Consulting Website** at http://www. menshealth.org or the Male Health Center of Dallas, TX at http://www.malehealthcenter.com.

The Effects of Masculinity and Male Sex-Role Socialization

Many health experts believe that the higher rates of morbidity and mortality among men are attributable to the ways in which boys are raised (Mahalik, Burns, and Syzdek 2007). While there are many exceptions to this rule, in general, intimate relationships and interpersonal communication are more challenging for men than they are for women. Men are more likely to take risks with their health, and men are less likely to seek emotional support or professional help when they need it for health-related concerns. Finally, even if they do receive education or treatment for a medical condition, men often fail to adopt health promoting behaviors.

Brannon (1976) identified four metaphors for describing the traditional role expectations of US men: (1) "No Sissy Stuff" (avoid behaving in a manner that can be perceived or labeled as feminine); (2) "Be a Big Wheel" (strive for dominance, power, wealth, and success); (3) "Be a Sturdy Oak" (be independent, controlled, unemotional; show no vulnerabilities); and (4) "Give 'em Hell" (take risks, be daring). Allen (1993) argues that men are confined by this "Man Box"—a sort of masculine code of conduct that prescribes appropriate and acceptable roles for men: providing and protecting. While the advantage for men of living in the "Man Box" is male privilege, the negative consequences are poorer health status and less intimate relationships with other men. Similarly, Courtenay (1998) believes that men who adhere to more traditional views of manhood have greater health risks because they are more likely to conceal their vulnerability to pain and illness, as well as perceive themselves as invulnerable to injury or death.

These aspects of masculinity are reflected in mainstream culture. *Sports Illustrated,* the magazine read most by young men, has more alcohol advertisements than any other magazine. Like television beer commercials, these advertisements overtly link drinking with being a man, taking risks, and facing danger without fear. The sports culture, which is inextricably woven into the growing-up years of many American boys, promotes aggression, competition, and risk-taking. Even when men are injured, they are expected to grin through the pain and keep on playing the game. Winning is frequently demanded at any cost (Messner 1992). Finally, Hollywood churns out a mind-numbing string of buffed-up male action-heroes who appear nearly indestructible, keep their women at

arm's length, and cling with ease to the grate of an 18-wheeler going 75 miles per hour despite numerous gunshot wounds to the torso, arm, and shoulder. How is the average guy next door to compete with such an image?

The Top Six Leading Causes of Death for College Men

#1: Accidents and Injuries. Males account for 75% of college-age accidental deaths. Almost half of all male deaths between the ages of fifteen and twenty-four are due to accidents, most often in a motor vehicle. Nearly three times more males than females die in motor-vehicle accidents. Drowning, the second leading cause of accidental death, is responsible for twelve times more male than female deaths in college. Males sustain most of the estimated 3–5 million sports injuries that occur each year. Traumatic spinal cord injury among college-age males is five times that of females. Male adolescents have 174% more injuries (Rivara, Bergman, LoGerfo, and Weiss 1982) and more likely to be hospitalized as a result of these injuries.

#2: Homicide. Five times more college-age males than females die by homicide. Every day, fourteen young men are victims. Most young males are killed by someone they know. For African American males in this age group, homicide is the leading killer. According to the National Center for Health Statistics (NCHS), male homicide victims are most likely to be killed by a firearm. Five times as many college men as college women (5% versus 1%) reported carrying a gun on campus over the past year in the NCHRBS (Douglas et al. 1997).

#3: Suicide. While men and women are equally likely to become depressed in college, males account for six out of every seven college-age suicides. Women attempt suicide three times as often as men do, but men successfully commit suicide three times as often as women do. In general, men use methods with high lethality and little chance for intervention, such as hanging or gunshot. Every day, eleven young men take their own lives. For college-age white males, suicide is the second-leading cause of death.

#4: Cancer. Twice as many college-age males as females die from cancer. Leukemia, the leading cause of cancer death in college aged individuals, kills over one and a half more males than females.

Testicular cancer is the most common of solid tumors in college-age males, and they are among those at highest risk for this cancer. Poor nutrition, steroid abuse, and tobacco (including smokeless) use are all accountable for these deaths (DHHS 1990).

#5: Cardiovascular Disease. Nearly twice as many college men as women die from cardiovascular disease (e.g., stroke and heart attack). Contributing factors include high blood pressure, high cholesterol, and smoking—for which men are at increased risk during the college-age years (DHHS 1990).

#6: HIV Infection. About 85% of college males are sexually active by the time they arrive on campus. Of sexually active college men, one in four will contract at least one sexually transmitted infection before graduating. Males account for nine out of ten college-age deaths due to HIV infection. One in 250 Americans is HIV-positive; nearly half of men (and women) with HIV are under the age of 30.

1	Accidents and injuries
2	Homicide
3	Suicide
4	Cancer
5	Cardiovascular disease
6	HIV infection

Figure 9: *Leading causes of death among men. A chart summarizing the six leading causes of death for college men.*

Options for Change

Men can begin incorporating the following lifestyle changes to close the five-year gap and increase both their well-being and life-expectancy:

Foster true friendships with other men. A true male friend is more than just a drinking buddy or somebody you shoot hoops with. Learn to share your feelings, hopes, and fears with a close male friend. Don't let friends get away with doing things that harm themselves.

Seek close relationships with women. Research shows that men whose primary social affiliations are all male tend to adhere most rigidly to traditional male role norms. This rigidity translates into poorer health. Many women have a higher comfort level with emotional and physical intimacy, and possess the skill of communicating honestly about health. Men can learn from them.

Visit a health care provider regularly. You should do so at least once a year. Be sure to report any signs and symptoms—even those you think are minor. Withholding information can mean the difference between early detection and long-term complications. Also, don't be afraid to ask questions.

Manage alcohol, tobacco, and other drug consumption. Limit your intake of alcohol to no more than three or four drinks at a time, no more than two or three times a week. If you are a tobacco user, seek assistance immediately for help in quitting. Avoid all other drugs. When taking prescription medications, carefully follow your physician's directions.

Eat regular, balanced meals. Be sure to drink plenty of fluids (at least six to eight glasses a day). Reduce your intake of sugar, salt, fats, saturated fats, and caffeine. Limit your daily meat intake to no more than three four-ounce servings. Be sure to eat at least five fruits and vegetables every day. Fast food is acceptable to eat, as long you limit your visits to a drive-through to once a week.

Exercise regularly. You should do so three or four times a week, 30–45 minutes each time. Be sure to include exercises that improve flexibility and cardiovascular health, in addition to strength-building activities.

Manage anger and fear effectively. Hidden away, these emotions can literally cause a slow death. Anger and fear are normal, healthy emotions for men and women to experience. However, societal constraints limit the ways in which men can express these feelings. Learn how to get in touch with anger and fear, and develop a repertoire for constructively and appropriately expressing them.

Seek assistance from a counselor when you start to feel out of control. Getting help is a sign of courage. Mental health professionals are trained to help you cope with stressful situations. Nobody can solve major life challenges alone, so don't hesitate to use crisis hotlines, support groups, and counseling centers.

In addition to becoming informed about their risks, men must work individually and collectively to understand how the ways in which men are socialized contribute to their increased morbidity and mortality and poorer health status. For support or additional information, please contact your campus health service or health education department, your family physician, or a local public health office.

Questions to Consider

1. Why is men's health an important issue to discuss in college?
2. Why do men typically not seek help?
3. Name three health issues related to men and how at least one theory from previous readings would apply to each.

References

Allen, M. (1993). *Angry men, passive men: Understanding the roots of men's anger and how to move beyond it.* New York: Fawcett Columbine.

Brannon, D. (1976). *The forty-nine percent majority: The male sex role. Reading,* MA: Addison-Wesley Publishing Company, Inc.

Courtenay, W. H. (1998). College men's health: An overview and a call to action. *Journal of the American College Health Association,* 46, p. 279–290.

Douglas, Kathy A., et al. (1997). Results from the 1995 National College Health Risk Behavior Survey. Journal of American College Health, 46: p. 55–66.

Mahalik, J.R., Burns, S.M., & Syzdek, M. (2007). Masculinity and perceived normative health behaviors as predictors of men's health behaviors. Social Science and Medicine, 64, p. 2201–2209.

Messner, M. A. (1992). *Power at play: Sports and the problem of masculinity.* Boston: Beacon Press.

Rivara, F., Bergman, A., LoGerfo, J., & Weiss, N. (1982). Epidemiology of childhood injuries. *American Journal of Disabled Children. 136.* p. 502–506.

Chapter 8

Campus Party Survival Guide

By Luoluo Hong and Julie Catanzarite

Partied Out?

It's 2:15 AM after a Thursday evening of partying. You're stranded in the parking lot of your favorite local bar. Your date Steven is passed out on the hood of your car, and your best friend Gina has very graciously recolored the upholstery in your car with puke, the texture of which looks suspiciously like dinner. Your hand is still killing you after that freak on the dance floor bumped into it with the burning end of her cigarette. This is the last thing you needed: your biochem exam is at 9:00 AM and you've got to ace it this time. Just how, exactly, did you get yourself into this situation once again? And how can you ensure that you don't always end up cleaning up the mess created by your friends?

This chapter is here to help you do just that. Whether it's tips on socializing or making new friends and keeping your old ones, or suggestions for how to improve your dating life and just plain getting along better with people, this chapter is your rulebook for making it through the next four, or five, or six … years of college. Alcohol is a part of many social situations during college; their use and abuse are related to many aspects about student life: academic performance, fights and campus rapes, verbal harassment and vandalism incidents, automobile and pedestrian accidents, poor sexual decision-making, and so forth. In this chapter, all of these issues will be talked about frankly and straightforwardly, because we want your memories of college to be fun-filled, positive ones, and for you and your friends to be alive and healthy to enjoy many years of alumni reunions to come.

This chapter doesn't intend to judge. The decision to drink is yours and yours alone. Sometimes, however, we make decisions based on misconceptions or what friends believe. Here's where this chapter can help. Let's lay out the bare facts so you can be the one in control. As an adult, you have the capability to make decisions on your own. This chapter has been provided to help you make informed choices. Whatever your decision, decide on healthy, low-risk consumption or no consumption during your time in college and beyond.

The "Beer" Facts

According to the Office for Substance Abuse Prevention, 75% of all beer bought in the US is consumed by 18–25-year-olds. This isn't so surprising given that college students on your campus spend more money on alcohol than they do on textbooks, or than your college spends on library purchases and scholarships together. In fact, all of the students on your campus combined consume enough beer, wine, and hard liquor to fill an Olympic-sized swimming pool.

Drinking has been part of the collegiate tradition since colonial times. In fact, college students engage in heavy drinking at twice the rate of their noncollege counterparts. Rituals related to alcohol and alcohol drinking have been immortalized in such films as *Animal House*, *Old School*, and *The Hangover*. It's almost a rite of passage to go to college and take part in a keg party or funnel at a tailgate. However, what these films fail to do is show

you the very real fact that alcohol can hurt, even kill, students. As many of today's college students will eventually die from alcohol-related causes as will go on to get advanced degrees, masters and doctorates combined (Eigen 1991).

In a national survey of 17,592 college students at one hundred forty US colleges and universities, Henry Wechsler (1994) and his fellow researchers at the Harvard School of Public Health found that almost half (44%) of college students were binge drinkers, and almost one fifth (19%) were frequent binge drinkers (those who binged three or more times in the past two weeks). *Binge drinking* is defined as consuming five or more drinks at one sitting for men, four or more drinks at one sitting for women, at least once in the past two weeks.

Alcohol can result in several negative consequences for students. At least 90% of campus rapes, 80% of campus vandalism acts and 75% of campus violence incidents are committed under the influence of alcohol (Eigen 1991). And as many as one in five college students experiences a drinking problem while in college, says the American College Health Association. Wechsler's (1994) study also found that frequent binge drinkers were seven to ten times more likely than non-binge-drinkers to not practice safer sex, to engage in unplanned sexual activity, to get into trouble with law enforcement, to damage property, or to become hurt or injured.

Alcohol abuse incurs many personal, financial, and societal costs, particularly when you consider that up to 10% of all drivers on a weekend night are legally intoxicated. In addition, 35% of highway deaths are attributable to alcohol, and 16–21-year-olds account for a disproportionately high number of those deaths.

Selling alcohol is also a lucrative business. Over $1 billion a year is spent on TV commercials by the top five beer distributors, including Budweiser, Miller, and Coors. These alcohol distributors are out to recruit lifelong, name-brand loyalty among consumers, and they aren't afraid to target those as young as eleven.

The Rules and Regs

It's important to recognize that alcohol, unlike other drugs such as marijuana, heroin, or cocaine, is legally available to those who are of age. Every state in the US allows drinking at the age of twenty-one. That is, it's illegal for anyone under the age of twenty-one to purchase or consume alcohol. In fact, a citation for underage drinking can remain on your legal record forever—possibly ruining your chance for graduate school or a job; it is not the same as a parking ticket. Similarly, if you are over twenty-one, you are criminally liable if you purchase alcohol for anyone who is underage. Legislators recognize that alcohol can play a positive role in people's lives—when used in moderation—and have designated the ability to choose to drink or not to drink to a certain sector of citizens.

The law is cracking down on the retailers, too. They are required to sell alcohol *only to buyers who submit a legitimate form of identification saying that they are twenty-one or older.* Retailers must not accept identification that is "expired, defaced, mutilated, or altered." With duplicate I.D. cards, the buyer must submit additional identification. Your student I.D., bank card, or employee identification card are not considered legitimate forms of I.D. To ensure that retailers ask for I.D., the law says that lack of knowledge of the person's age **cannot be used as a defense for selling to underage students.**

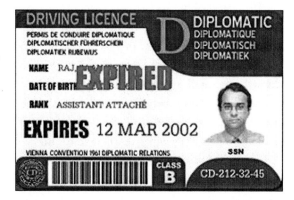

The law may have certain variations from state to state, so be sure to become familiar with the alcohol-related laws in the city and state in which your campus is located. Additionally, many colleges and universities have some type of institutional alcohol policy that may exceed the requirements and limitations imposed by local laws. Call the Dean of Students Office on your campus for a copy of that policy and familiarize yourself with it.

So What's In a Drink?

One Drink Is …
12 oz. beer x 5% ethanol = .6 oz.
5 oz. wine x 12% ethanol = .6 oz.
1.5 oz. liquor x 40% ethanol = .6 oz.

The active ingredient in alcoholic beverages is *ethanol*—the stuff that makes you feel drunk. The "proof" indicates the amount of alcohol in the drink; it is equal to twice the percentage of ethanol. For example, Everclear (or grain alcohol) is 200 proof, or 100% ethanol. Regular beer has 5% ethanol content, so it is 10 proof.

Alcohol is frequently referred to as "empty calories." While high in calories (which predisposes heavy drinkers to the proverbial "beer belly"), alcohol contains little or no nutritional value. In fact, frequent and heavy drinking interferes with your body's natural abilities to effectively absorb vitamins and minerals. A bottle of regular beer contains anywhere from 140 to 200 calories (the so-called light beers only have 100 calories); wine has about 110 to 120 calories per glass, while shots of hard liquor vary widely in their caloric content (usually between 85 and 100 calories). So those of you who save up your money by skimping on meals to go out for that Thursday night binge are doing yourselves a double whammy—poor nutrition and a major dent in your dieting!

Because ethanol contents vary across types of alcoholic beverages, what constitutes "one drink" varies. A twelve-ounce can of beer, a five-ounce glass of wine, or a one-and-a-half-ounce shot of hard liquor all constitute one drink. This is because all three contain approximately 0.60, or two thirds, ounces of ethanol in them. The math calculations in the chart above indicate why.

This is Your Brain. This is Your Brain on Beer.

To most of us with any experience with drinking or with drinkers, it seems pretty obvious what alcohol does to the body's functioning. But what exactly is going on physiologically when alcohol enters the system? The liver is the organ responsible for metabolizing, or "breaking down," 95% of the ethanol we ingest into the waste products of water and carbon dioxide. Only 5% is eliminated from the body unchanged via perspiration, breath, or urine (despite the fact that frequent trips to the urinal yields a liquid that looks suspiciously similar to beer in color). That alcohol strips your body of fluids accounts for most of the physical feelings of being "hung over," e.g., puffy eyes, cotton mouth, stiff joints, massive headache. Because of alcohol's dehydrating effects, drinking alcohol to quench your thirst during strenuous exercise, a day at the beach, an outdoor summer barbecue, or an afternoon football game can be a sure invitation to heat exhaustion and heat stroke (fainting, nausea, and other fun stuff).

The liver metabolizes alcohol at roughly the rate of one drink per hour (or ½–⅔ oz. of ethanol) per hour. This rate can't be messed with. Urinating, taking a cold shower, drinking coffee, or such vigorous exercises as ten laps around the house can't alter this rate. Time is the only method of sobering up.

Only 20% of alcohol is absorbed into the bloodstream through the stomach. Most absorption takes place through the small intestine. Note that carbonated drinks speed up the rate of absorption, hence we "feel" the alcohol faster. This is because carbonation "tickles" the pylorus valve—a membrane that allows the contents of the stomach to enter the small intestine—causing it to open faster. So, your rum and Coke, seven-n-lemon, and sparkling wines or champagne will tend to "hit" you faster than straight vodka or plain old beer.

Alcohol dehydrogenase (ADH) is the enzyme responsible for breaking down ethanol. In general, women have less ADH than men; this means that, drink for drink, women are much more susceptible to alcohol's intoxicating effects than men are (Blume 1986). Similarly, Asians and Native Americans have less ADH as compared to members of other ethnic groups. Repeated, continued drinking increases your body's production of this enzyme, thus resulting in increased tolerance for alcohol. This increased tolerance, however, also can mean increased risk for alcohol addiction. Alcoholics who have "bottomed out" have lost the ability to produce ADH and therefore have no tolerance for alcohol. Hence the term "dry drunk."

Blood alcohol content (BAC) is a measure of the amount of ethanol present in your bloodstream. BAC is affected by several factors:

- **Body size.** The heavier you are, the slower your BAC rises.
- **Amount of alcohol consumed and rate of consumption.** Obviously, drinking alcohol more quickly, or drinking greater amounts of alcohol elevate your BAC more rapidly.
- **Drinker's mood.** Some drinkers report that being depressed or being extremely upbeat can impact how soon they being to feel intoxicated.
- **Amount of food in the stomach.** Eating before drinking, particularly foods higher in starch or fat, slows down the rate of alcohol's absorption, and thus keeps your BAC lower. A shot of vodka on an empty stomach can reach blood cells in your brain within ninety seconds! Remember, eating while you drink can increase your staying power.
- **Type of "mixers" used.** As we discussed before, certain mixers such as carbonated soda can impact the rate of absorption.
- **Stage of menstrual cycle.** Some women report feeling drunk more quickly when they drink during certain times of their menstrual cycle (especially during or right after their period and around ovulation). This is attributable to changes in hormonal levels.

Alcohol is a central nervous system (CNS) depressant. It impairs brain functions in an order opposite to how they developed. Figure 10 summarizes the connection between BAC and behavior. The areas of your brain are affected in the following progression.

Higher Cortical Functions. These are the types of skills and abilities that biologists say differentiate us from other animal species. They include our reason, logic, and intellect—the things that enable us to make sound judgments and effective decisions. Because alcohol affects this area of the brain first, there are significant implications for your physical safety. The ability to determine whether or not you are a good driver goes out the window with the first drink, which is why designating a driver is so important. Second, sex under the influence can lead to such unpleasant afflictions as "beer goggle syndrome." Any of us who've gone down that merry way know that things happen when we're drunk that may not have happened if we were sober. Lastly, students

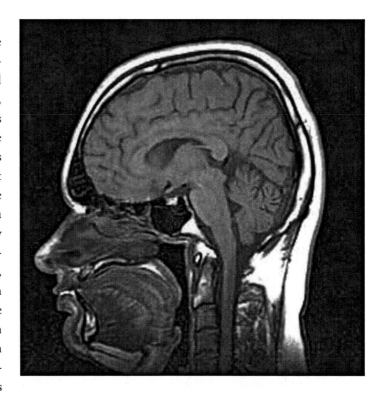

are much more likely to get into fights after drinking. "Liquid courage" may enable even the smallest person to think that he can take on six football players, or the cop, or the stop sign, or the Herculean bouncer at the bar.

Fine Motor Skills. These include such important skills as fitting your key into the lock of your car door without first keying your car, or lighting a cigarette without setting your bangs on fire. Minute muscle manipulations and precise tasks require fine motor skills, and those talents are lost soon after judgment leaves.

Figure 10: *Blood Alcohol Level and Effects On Behavior*

BAC Level	Average # of Drinks	Behavior
.05	1–2	• Usually a feeling of well-being • Some release of inhibitions • Judgment impaired • Coordination and level of alertness lowered • Increased risk of collision while driving
.10	3–5	• Reaction times significantly lowered • Muscle control and speech impaired • Limited night vision and peripheral vision • Loss of self-control • Crash risk greatly increased
.15	6–7	• Consistent and major decreases in reaction time
.20	8–10	• Loss of equilibrium and technical skills • Sensory and motor capability depressed • Double vision and legal blindness (20/200) • Unfit to drive for up to ten hours
.25	10–14	• Staggering and severe motor disturbances
.30	10–14	• Not aware of surroundings
.40	14–20	• Surgical anesthesia • Lethal dosage for a small percentage of individuals
.40+	14–20+	• Lethal dosage for about 50% of individuals • Severe circulatory and respiratory depression

*It is highly recommended that you establish your **drinking limit** as the point at which your fine motor skills have been affected.* Drinking more than that can have serious consequences on your health, safety, and well-being.

Gross Motor Skills. Walking, balancing, and talking are basic physical skills that you learn when growing up. People who are intoxicated to the point that they can't walk properly, bump into walls and excuse themselves, or drool when speaking have consumed an excessive amount of alcohol. At this point, the risk of acquaintance rape becomes a serious reality. Potential perpetrators or victims are not cognizant of their strength or their vulnerability.

Semi-Voluntary Reflexes. These are things your body may do on its own but you still have some control over. Blinking is one example. Extremely intoxicated individuals have either the droopy-eyed or wide-eyed look as they struggle to control eyelids. Urinary continence is also a semi-voluntary reflex. This explains why drunken people may unknowingly go to the bathroom all over themselves. *This is a danger stage. Hopefully, most drinkers don't get to this stage of inebriation, but as a date, friend, or bartender, you should not allow a person in this condition to continue drinking.*

Vital Functions. Breathing, heart rate, and circulation are all essential to living. When a person has consumed so much alcohol that vital functions are impaired, he or she is at risk for cardiac arrest, stroke, or death. This is called *alcohol poisoning*. Drinkers in this state have cold, clammy skin, carry a glazed look in their eyes, and are unresponsive to questions. This is a medical emergency and should be treated as such. "Passing out" is the body's natural defense mechanism against a person consuming enough alcohol to affect vital functions. However, rapid ingestion of alcohol during "funneling" or drinking games can sidetrack this defense mechanism, allowing the person to overdose on alcohol. This should not be confused with blacking out, which is temporary amnesia from excessive drinking.

What is Healthy Drinking?

Drinking in moderation isn't in and of itself bad or unhealthy. Rather, most college students are hurt by the negative consequences that follow from high-risk, excessive drinking (Canterbury et al. 1992; Smith and Smith 1988). These consequences can affect a wide array of student life, including:

- Academic success;
- Athletic performance;
- Financial stability;
- Long-term health promotion;
- Mental health and life-skills development;
- Nutritional status;
- Safety and physical well-being; and
- Sexual and reproductive health.

You can abstain from alcohol altogether, or you can opt to be a low-risk drinker. A low-risk drinker is defined by the National Institute on Alcohol Abuse and Alcoholism to be a person who:

1. recognizes that alcohol is a potent drug and adopts behaviors that minimize the risk associated with drinking;
2. knows his or her family alcohol history and adjusts behaviors accordingly;
3. consumes no more than two or three drinks daily, two or three days weekly, which constitutes moderate (or "social") drinking;
4. periodically abstains from alcohol in order to allow the body to detoxify;
5. avoids drunkenness; and
6. drinks for positive reasons, whereby alcohol is part of, but not essential to, a good time.

The following are some good strategies for putting healthy, low-risk drinking into play. These tips will minimize the potential negative consequences of drinking and maximize your partying power:

- *Decide beforehand how much you'll drink.* Stick to your predetermined limits. Never drink until you're drunk.
- *Consume* no more than two or three drinks daily, two or three days a week. Moderation is the key to low-risk drinking.
- *Never gulp drinks.* Drinking too rapidly will lead to passing out and alcohol poisoning. It's safest to sip your drink.
- *Eat before you drink.* Eat while you drink. Eat after you drink. The foods that slow down alcohol absorption most effectively are *heavy meals* and *dairy products.*
- *Avoid salty foods* such as popcorn, pretzels, and spicy tortilla chips; they will only make you thirstier.
- *Alternate* alcohol with juice, water, or soft drinks. This will give your body time to absorb the alcohol you've already consumed.
- *Drink only when and where it is appropriate.*
- If you don't know how much alcohol is in a beverage—such as a "spiked" punch at a party—*don't drink it.* You want to keep control over what and how much you're drinking.
- *Drink diluted alcoholic beverages,* such as beer, wine, and mixed drinks, rather than straight shots.
- *Periodically allow the body to detoxify* by abstaining from alcohol. Remember, ethanol is a toxin to your body.
- *Never drive after drinking.*
- *Avoid sexual activity during and after drinking.*
- *Respect* the choices of nondrinkers.
- *Know and obey laws and campus policies* related to alcohol consumption.
- If you find yourself drinking too much despite your limits, *recognize that you may need help.* Refer to the end of this chapter for how and where to seek help.

Consistent adherence to these strategies will ensure that alcohol can be a pleasurable part of your social and partying life during college, and not the source of unnecessary heartache and expense.

Making the Grade?

The balancing act between studying and partying is a tough one to master. The key is to restrict your drinking to times and levels that won't interfere with school—which, after all, is supposed to be the reason you're in college.

According to the Carnegie Institute, nationally, alcohol is a contributing factor in 25% of all college dropout cases. In fact, the Core Survey conducted at schools across the US found that alcohol was a factor in bombing a test or important project for 21% of students, missing class for 30%, and experiencing memory loss for 27% of students (Presley, Meilman, and Cashin 1996). Because passing exams, class attendance, and remembering what you read or study are essential to academic performance, excessive drinking

certainly does not help your cause. In fact, the same data from the Core Survey indicated that students' GPAs are inversely correlated with the number of drinks consumed per week. In other words, the more you drink, the lower your GPA. (Of course, what Einstein had to figure that one out?)

Ever had a "blackout" before? A *blackout* is like experiencing temporary amnesia because of excessive drinking. It is not the same thing as "passing out," which is when you lose consciousness. You may be walking, talking, dancing, climbing trees, or perhaps even engaging in sexual activity while under the influence. However, when you inhale a lot of alcohol, the ethanol interferes with the biochemical process called *synapses*. In other words, stimuli fail to get encoded in short-term memory. This is why the next morning everyone else is looking at you with a smirk and you can't remember a single thing about what you did, who you saw, or where you went between 11:45 PM and 1:15 AM last night. If you're blacking out frequently during drinking bouts, you're probably drinking too much, and probably not helping your brain power too much.

The Bumbling Klutz—Alcohol and Athletics

Just as alcohol can interfere with intellectual processes, your physical coordination and skills are similarly impacted. Due to the many media images that focus on athletes and drinking, as well as the tremendous number of beer ads that associate drinking with athletic prowess, student-athletes carry the reputation of being some of the hardest drinkers on campus. Whether that rep is deserved or not, drinking clearly has some deleterious effects on your ability to throw or catch a ball, run quickly, or conduct any of the other physical maneuvers essential to athletic excellence.

Scientific research demonstrates that drinking on a Friday night can affect a student-athlete's hand-eye coordination, muscle reflexes, quick judgment, and physical coordination during Saturday evening's game.

Athletics, exercise, and physical fitness are important aspects of college extracurricular life. Including them in your daily activities not only helps in reducing stress, but aids in promoting lifelong wellness as well. Because you're already committed to improving your health, why not consider foregoing those drinks this Tuesday night?

Bankrolling a Bad Habit

Being a college student is synonymous with being poor, or at least not rich. While some of the drink specials advertised by bars may appear to be a great deal, any college student can easily get "nickled and dimed" to death. Relatively speaking, going out can become an extremely expensive endeavor, particularly when you've got rent to pay, car insurance to keep up with, food to buy, books to get, cell phone bills to meet, and the occasional must-have fashion accessory to acquire.

In addition, frequent and excessive alcohol use usually requires the drinker to start getting harder and harder stuff in order to achieve the same "high." What starts out freshman year as a couple of beers can escalate within a couple of years into a fifth of Crown or Jack Daniels—which don't come cheap.

In certain pockets of the country, the gambling industry has become well established. Many gambling establishments are located near campuses. Alcohol use is often paired with gambling, and in most gambling venues (such as casinos, the riverboats, and video poker games) alcohol is easily accessible—in fact, many casinos provide drinks to the customers free of charge. What with the thousands of football game betting pools and other sports-related betting, it is unclear just how many college students engage

in gambling or are addicted. If you enjoy gambling, be aware that gambling addiction is the most expensive addiction there is. Because gambling *can* be so much fun, it has already caused academic and financial problems for a number of college students.

Even if you don't classify as a compulsive gambler, it is always a good idea to lay out certain guidelines for yourself before you head to the casinos or the slot machines. Most importantly, keep alcohol consumption to a minimum or don't drink at all if you choose to gamble. As in all situations, liquor can cloud your judgment and cause you to think you have a bigger bank account than you actually do. Read Chapter 13 for suggested guidelines to adopt when gambling.

"Getting Smashed Every Now and Then Never Hurt Anyone." (Not!)

Between 240,000 and 360,000 of students who currently attend college will eventually die of alcohol-related causes. That's equivalent to the student populations of all the "Big Ten" campuses. Every year in the US more than 150,000 college students develop health problems that are alcohol-related. Excessive alcohol use is a contributing factor to many of the terminal illnesses and diseases that most Americans end up succumbing to. It affects immune, endocrine, and reproductive functions. Heavy alcohol consumption is a well-documented cause of neurological problems, and such conditions as cirrhosis, chronic gastritis, hepatitis, hypertension, and coronary disease.

Many cancers are correlated with long-term, over-use of alcohol. The tongue, larynx, esophagus, lung, stomach, colon, rectum, pancreas, and liver are especially prone to disease and cancer resulting from excessive alcohol consumption. Reproductive health of both men and women is affected by chronic alcohol use, while women who drink heavily experience more gynecological problems than women who are moderate or light drinkers.

While these conditions may not seem real or relevant to the person who's still young and healthy, medical research has clearly demonstrated that lifestyle choices made today can have a significant impact on longevity and the quality of life tomorrow.

Stressed Out!

Is it sometimes easier to guzzle away your sorrows following a bad break up or an embarrassing class presentation with cheap wine instead of hashing the feelings out with your roommate? Do you find it easier to let out certain types of feelings—anger, fear, horniness—when you're slightly toasted? Do you end up in a lot of arguments after you've been drinking? Do you find yourself funnier and more attractive after tossing back a few? The world is getting to be a tougher and tougher place to live in, and young adults bear the brunt of the stress. As our society becomes increasingly dehumanized, computerized, and technologized, people also have a tendency to feel more isolated, alienated, and oppressed. It appears that winning is the only thing that matters, and feelings are relatively inconsequential. Just because you're on a campus surrounded by hundreds or thousands of other people doesn't make that go away.

Alcohol, weed, or other substances might help you cope, but these things only work for the short term at best. Try to find other ways of managing and coping with your stress. Exercise and massage therapy are examples of how you can reduce physical tension. Relaxation techniques, guided imagery, and other psychological methods can also increase your coping power. Seeing a counselor or therapist is a way to get an entire hour to talk specifically about just you. Take advantage of advice from your church leader, a trusted professor or supervisor, or a close relative or good friend when making decisions.

Children who grow up with at least one alcoholic parent are four times likelier to develop some sort of addiction themselves as adults. In addition, studies show that 75%–90% of women in treatment for drug addictions, alcoholism, or eating disorders report a history of childhood sexual abuse. In fact, substance abuse and eating disorders frequently occur together. Similarly, we know that there is a connection between domestic violence and substance abuse. Alcohol and other drugs may ease the pain at times; in the long run, however, it's more important to seek help and start working out stuff so that the cycle of abuse doesn't have to continue.

Studies tell us that heavy alcohol use is a sign of *major depressive disorder* for both men and women, but for women in particular (Deykin et al. 1997). One might assume that people who are depressed are turning to alcohol as a result of their mental state; however, studies also show that alcohol abuse actually precedes major depressive disorders in many cases. If you or a family member is already prone to depression, be aware that drinking may only increase your chances of becoming chemically depressed.

And You Thought Beer Was a Food Group ...

Trying to shape up for the upcoming 5K Run/Walk sponsored by the campus recreational center? Hoping to lose that beer belly before summer arrives? Just started a diet in preparation for that Spring Break getaway? Well, if alcohol and pizza presently compose the two major "food groups" in your daily eating habits, you might want to consider skimping on the mixed drinks and wine coolers as an immediate way to decrease your caloric intake.

As we talked about before, the "empty calories" in beer (remember, beer has little to no nutritional value) can add up pretty quickly. In addition, ethanol can affect your metabolism in the following ways:

- Fatty acid synthesis **increases**;
- Mineral loss **increases**;
- Protein synthesis **decreases**; and
- Your brain's use of *glucose, its primary energy source,* **decreases**

Below are some additional facts about alcohol's effect on health and nutrition:

- Alcohol can interfere with your body's use and absorption of *calcium*. Also, its diuretic properties may promote loss of calcium through the urine.
- Alcohol displaces necessary nutrients from your diet while increasing your body's demand for them.
- Beer does have some nutritional value, but the vitamins and minerals are in such low amounts that you would have to drink an inordinate number of beers to reap its nutritional benefits. For example, to meet his body's niacin needs, an adult male would need to drink a *six-pack of 12-ounce cans of beer*. That equals many trips to the bathroom. To meet his protein needs, that same male would have to drink *eight additional six-packs*.
- Your *liver* prefers to use fatty acids as fuel. When alcohol is present, however, it uses the alcohol as fuel, leaving fatty acids to accumulate in vast stockpiles. The liver is also forced to lay aside the functions of protein synthesis. Additionally, necessary nutrients and oxygen have trouble getting to the liver cells in the presence of alcohol.
- Your brain needs *glucose* to operate at top speed and efficiency. Alcohol basically puts glucose activity at a standstill, thus causing the brain to slow down for lack of glucose energy. Alcohol anesthetizes and kills brain cells.

So, why aren't all alcoholics fat, you ask? It doesn't seem to make sense: alcohol is full of empty calories, so why are many heavy drinkers thin, even gaunt? Well, alcohol also depresses the appetite (among other things), causing heavy drinkers to eat poorly—if they eat at all. However, because alcohol is composed of empty calories, alcoholics fail to obtain essential nutrients. In addition, alcohol reduces muscle mass, further reducing weight. Long-time drinkers also suffer from B-vitamin depletion, iron deficiency, and folic acid deficiency.

The Date that Lasts a Lifetime ...

Rarely does someone expect it will happen to him or her. The sad reality on college campuses is that one in four college women will be sexually assaulted before graduating. Many men and women report being the target of sexual coercion or pressure. A vast majority of these incidents are the result of gross miscommunication between partners. More recently, Rohypnol and Gamma-hydroxy-butyrate, or GHB, (more commonly known as the "date rape drugs") have been implicated in several campus assaults. These substances when combined with alcohol can produce severe intoxication and even memory loss in the drinker.

Talking about sex is hard enough when you're sober; eight beers or five shots later, it's basically impossible. When potential sexual partners can hardly remember their names by the time the clothes get peeled off, the risks for unplanned and unwanted sex become imminent. Crime reports show that in almost all campus rapes, the victim knows the perpetrator. Anywhere from 75% to 90% of these incidents involve alcohol use by either the perpetrator, the victim, or both prior to the assault. This makes sense given alcohol's effects on the brain. The chances of miscommunication are high; potential victims don't tune in to "red flags" their dates are giving off, and potential perpetrators don't realize that crying or stone silence might be someone's way of communicating "no."

Alcohol is never an acceptable excuse for rape. Nevertheless, students need to know that their risks for sexual assault—either as victim or as perpetrator—are increased if they do drink to the point that their judgment or physical control is distorted. Unfortunately, until we as a society stop rape, this is a reality that women—who compose the majority of victims on campus—and some men will have to confront. If you do drink and are raped, it wasn't your fault—nobody ever asks to be raped.

Men (who make up the majority of perpetrators), on the other hand, should realize that having sex with an intoxicated partner is "playing with fire." *You are always responsible for your own actions, no matter how wasted you are.* Unless you clearly have consent from your partner, don't have sex with someone. Anything except a "yes," should be taken as a "no." So, just to clarify, someone who is passed out, dead to the world, on a bathroom floor, is by definition unable to give consent.

If you're going out on a date or to a party, men and women should set sexual boundaries with their partners early in the evening, especially if drinking will be taking place. Nothing fancy, something basic will do, like,

> "Hey, I just wanted to kind of, you know, clear the air and all, and just let you know that I'm really looking forward to spending some time with you tonight, but I don't want the pressure of wondering if we're going to do 'it' or not, so let's just agree right now to stop with just _____ [insert your activity of choice]."

If your partner is too immature to appreciate your forthrightness and honesty, or gets offended, they can get lost. Clear, assertive communication from the beginning will alleviate heartache and pain the next morning.

Remember, there has been an increase in the number of men who report being sexually assaulted. Alcohol is oftentimes a contributing factor in those instances. The bottom line is that rape affects all individuals—not just the immediate victims.

"Liquid Courage" and "Beer Balls"

Approximately 285,000 serious crimes are committed on America's college and university campuses *in a single year.* And these are the *reported* crimes; most crime reports don't include the tens of thousands of unreported brawls, fights, rapes, acts of vandalism, and other violent incidents. **A large proportion of these crimes are committed by college students under the influence of alcohol or other drugs against other college students who may or may not be under the influence.** Newsweek (Adler 1994) reported that 95% of violent crime on campus is alcohol- or drug-related. In that same year, the New York Times reported that nearly all campus rapes occur when either the assailant or the victim (or both) is intoxicated.

According to the NCHRBS, about 15% of college men have been in a fight (Douglas et al. 1997). Clearly, drinking and other drug use increase the likelihood that a student will be a victim or perpetrator of crime (Brain 1986); this is especially true in the case of assault. With the "liquid courage" provided by alcohol, a student is much more likely to initiate fights, arguments, and acquaintance rapes, or get into a car and drive recklessly. In fact, the Core Survey profiles students' experiences in a typical academic year:
- six percent reported taking advantage of another person sexually while under the influence;
- twelve percent got in trouble with police, residence hall staff, or other campus authorities while drinking;
- eight percent had committed minor infractions such as damaging property and pulling fire alarms while drunk;
- thirteen percent were hurt or injured while drinking;
- thirty percent got into an argument or fight after drinking; and
- thirty-two percent drove a car while intoxicated (Presley, Meilman, and Cashin 1996).

An aggressive temperament isn't necessary for a person to become violent under the influence. Men and women are just as likely to become testy, and size makes no difference to the wasted mind. Drunken people have been known to threaten three cops at a time, pick a fight with a stop sign, or accuse walls of deliberately shoving them. Unfortunately, when a drinker gets violent, he or she potentially isn't the only one who can get hurt. We all have a vested interest in making sure that fights get diffused or conflicts get resolved in a peaceable manner, especially when alcohol is present.

Designate a peace-maker when you go out drinking. Take yourself less seriously; know that the better person is the one who has the strength to walk away from an insult.

So You Got Picked to Be the Designated Driver ...

First of all—celebrate! This means you now have the unique privilege of going out to a bar or party, acting like a total nut (maybe you can tell off that jerk who sits behind you in Psych 101 class to get over himself), and

having everyone else assume you were bombed! Plus, you now have the added advantage of watching all the drunken people around you do stupid stuff, only you'll remember the next morning, and they won't. In fact, being the designated driver could become a really habit-forming thing.

Designating a driver is an important thing that friends do for their friends. While the term may seem obvious, let's clarify just how exactly you designate the driver. *Most importantly, you select the DD before anyone has started drinking.* This avoids the typical "designated least drunk person" scenario that sometimes happens:

> It's 2:10 AM. As you and your drinking buds exit the bar, one shouts out, "How much did you have?"
> "I had six beers!" "Hey—I did four shots!" "Well, I had five drinks!" "Okay, four wins—you drive!"

This is not acceptable or proper designation of a sober driver, because sober implies not drunk, which implies not drinking. The DD does not drink any alcohol that evening. He or she collects the others' keys before heading out—this alleviates the need to engage in bribery and other forms of manipulation to obtain keys from drunken individuals who would be drivers. Finally, the DD then ensures that each friend gets home (that would be the friend's own home) safely after the partying's done. For safety reasons, make them get into your car. No after-party visits to the apartments of people whose names no one knows. This reduces the likelihood for date rape and other unwanted situations. Car keys get returned to their respective owners the next morning so that no four o'clock morning joyrides can take place.

Some sororities and fraternities on campuses have created an organization-wide designated driver system that is easy to adopt and implement in your student organization. Simply

- Print and distribute stickers to all members with the phone number;

- Place the stickers on the back of everyone's driver's license;
- Have members of the group sign up for certain dates on which they will take the night off from drinking and be the designated driver for the night; (Note: Fraternities and sororities—try not to overly abuse your pledges and throw this responsibly wholly on them) and
- When those who are out drinking need a ride home, simply call the driver for a safe and convenient ride home.

If for some reason, a driver didn't get designated, and you are confronted with a drunken date or friend insisting that he or she is the world's best driver, despite the vast puddle of drool surrounding his or her feet, you can try several things. First, if the drinker is not too intoxicated, reasoning with him or her may work. Be firm and persistent; the main goal is to get the car keys away from the drinker; you don't have to always be polite about it. Then, either get him or her a cab, or take the drinker home yourself (if you're brave enough to risk having your car baptized with hurl).

Individuals who are severely intoxicated can probably have their keys wrestled away from them. However, make the decision to engage in a physical confrontation cautiously. The risk of getting hit shouldn't outweigh the danger of having a drinker out on the road. A better option would be to call the police or get the bouncer; he or she can handle the altercation for you. Although babysitting your grownup friends may seem like a hassle, you owe it to them not to let them drink and drive.

A car is a big hunk of metal; it can result in homicide or serious injury even when operated by a perfectly sober individual. You don't have to be drunk to be unable to drive. Drinking even moderately before driving—just one beer, for instance—can markedly impair judgment, reaction time, vision, and decision-making just enough to make you a horror on the road.

Note that the legal level of intoxication in all states is at least .10 BAC, or 10% (it is less in some states; other states have a lower BAC or "zero tolerance" for underage drinkers). On any given weekend evening, up to one in ten drivers on the road is legally intoxicated. If you are pulled over by a cop and found to be intoxicated, you can be ticketed for a DUI (driving under the influence); BAC levels lower than .10 are still at the discretion of the cop to ticket.

The penalties for a conviction of driving while under the influence vary from state to state. These costs alone are substantial; but when you add in legal fees, time off from work or class to attend court hearings, and potential future lost wages, and higher insurance premiums because of a DWI conviction, you've got a real whammy. The best bet is always to choose no alcohol if you have to drive, and to choose no driving if you want to drink.

On a similar note: *walking under the influence (let's call that "WUI") can be just as hazardous.* According to the National Highway Traffic Safety Administration, nearly half of all adult pedestrians killed in traffic accidents in 1990 had recently been drinking. More than a third of them were legally intoxicated.

Drinking Games Can Kill

When 20-year-old Benjamin Wynne, a transfer student at Louisiana State University passed out early in the morning of August 26, 1997, his fraternity brothers never suspected he would never wake up. As part of bid night, Wynne, like the other new pledges in Sigma Alpha Epsilon Fraternity went out to celebrate first at an alum's house, and then at a popular campus bar. In addition to beers, the pledges consumed pitchers of "Three Wise Men"—a lethal combination of whiskey, rum, and bourbon. Fraternity members operated under the very wrong assumption that the pledges would be able to "sleep it off" or vomit out the excessive alcohol. Unfortunately, Wynne died of acute alcohol intoxication; his BAC was .588. The fraternity was fined; some of that money will

go to alcohol awareness programs on the campus. Benjamin could easily have been Any College Student, the fraternity could easily have been Any Student Organization, and LSU could easily have been Any College Campus.

Whenever someone passes out from drinking an excessive amount of alcohol, he or she is in a potentially dangerous situation. "Passing out" (losing consciousness) is the body's self-defense mechanism, in essence saying, "Whoa, stop drowning us brain cells in this toxic dump!" Sometimes, however, the body is unable to shut down before the drinker has consumed enough alcohol to cause *acute intoxication* (also known as alcohol poisoning). During drinking games such as "quarters," a student can easily bypass the "passing out" self-defense mechanism, consume enough alcohol to kill him- or herself, pass out, then die. A BAC level of 0.30 to 0.40 is sufficient to kill someone, or at least render them a lifetime vegetable. At 30%–40% BAC, an individual can suffer cardiac arrest, stroke, and brain and other central nervous system damage. The student may or may not be successfully resuscitated.

Once a student has passed out, DO NOT ATTEMPT TO POUR ANY MORE ALCOHOL INTO THEM. If you suspect that someone is at risk for alcohol poisoning, you must act quickly and call for emergency medical assistance. Signs of acute alcohol intoxication include:

- total unresponsiveness;
- severe disorientation;
- cold, clammy skin;
- weak or no pulse;
- shallow or no breathing;
- dilated pupils; or
- blue or gray pallor.

If any of these symptoms appear following excessive or rapid ingestion of alcohol, call 911 immediately (at many universities, students can also call the campus police department). Don't even stop to consider such trivial things as, "What will my mother think of me?" or "Will the police get us for underage drinking?" The life of your friend is the most important thing. Always err on the side of being over-cautious!

If you feel sure that someone who has passed out is not in any danger and simply needs to "sleep it off," it's still important to take the following precautions:

- Prop the person up on his or her side against a wall or with the help of several pillows. Check that no items are in the drinker's mouth (cigarette butt, gum, etc.)—these can cause choking or suffocation. Face the mouth downward; this way, in case the person vomits, it won't go back down the trachea (breathing tube). Individuals can drown in their own vomit!

Figure 11: *Alcohol Emergency Response Guide*

If the person is drunk but not unconscious ...

DO	DON'T
• **Do** be aware of the potential dangers. • **Do** remain with the person if he or she is vomiting. • **Do** be a "babysitter." It's no fun, but you may prevent the death of both the drunken person and countless others on the road.	• **Don't** let the person leave a party alone. Even if just walking to a residence hall, he or she is at risk for pedestrian injury and other dangers of walking alone at night. • **Don't** administer anything orally (food, liquid, or drug) to sober up the person. • **Don't** attempt to constrain anyone who has become violent unless you have (sober) assistance. • **Don't** give the person a cold shower. The shock may cause unconsciousness and result in injury.

If the person is unconscious . . .

DO	DON'T
• **Do** keep the person still. • **Do** lie the person down with his or her head to the side to keep it from falling back. • **Do** monitor the person's breathing.	• **Don't** leave the person lying face-up. The person potentially could choke on their own vomit. • **Don't** leave the person alone.

If you suspect alcohol poisoning . . .

DO	DON'T
• **Do** check the person's breathing regularly. A good way to remember what to do is "**ABC**": Check the **A**irway; see that the person's air passage is clear of debris. Check to see that the person is **B**reathing regularly. Check **C**irculation: feel regularly for a discernible pulse. • **Do** call 911 immediately if the person's breathing or pulse is weak.	• **Don't** refrain from seeking medical attention for a drinker under twenty-one. A person's life is more important than legal repercussions for underage drinking. Rarely will the police arrest a student when the student's life is in immediate danger. • **Don't** leave the person alone. The alcohol ingested could be absorbed to toxic levels while the person is passed out.

- Continue to check on the person throughout the night. Follow the ABC guide of

Airway

Breathing

Circulation

If anything is wrong, handle it as you would an alcohol emergency and call 911.

If a drinker has smoked marijuana or used it in any other form, you will want to keep an especially close eye on them throughout the night. Marijuana suppresses the gag reflex, causing the person to choke on his or her own vomit.

In general, using alcohol in conjunction with other drugs is extremely dangerous. Using vodka to chase down sleeping pills, tranquilizers, and other "downers" can result in cardiac arrest, because you're ingesting a "double whammy" of depressants. Women, especially, who receive over 70% of all prescriptions for tranquilizers such as Valium, are at risk of this kind of overdose.

Alcohol taken with GHB, diet pills, stimulants, and other "uppers" is equally risky—they don't "cancel" each other out just because alcohol is a depressant. Finally, alcohol taken with hallucinogens such as LSD and "mushrooms" can take a "bad trip" and turn it into your worst nightmare, resulting in self-mutilation or other injury.

As a friend, it is your responsibility to take care of those you care about. If an alcohol emergency occurs, act immediately. It could be the difference between life and death. The steps for responding to an alcohol emergency are summarized in Figure 11.

Worshipping the Porcelain Deity?

One of the strongest arguments against drinking excessively is the probability that you'll have to deal with the tortuous morning after: the headache, the queasiness, and yes, your hard, cold, but ever-so-comforting and faithful porcelain landmark, the toilet.

Just as there's no quick or easy way to "sober up" once you're intoxicated, there's no sure-fire remedy for the common hangover that follows. You can, however, make decisions before and while you drink to decrease the unpleasant morning-after effects of your favorite alcohol.

- *Eat while or before you drink.* Fatty foods are best when it comes to slowing the rate of alcohol absorption into your bloodstream. If you eat while drinking, you might also decrease the total amount you drink, which, in turn, should result in milder hangover symptoms.
- *Drink one cup of water for each drink consumed.* Alcohol's dehydrating effects are part of what make hangovers what they are. Drinking plenty of water helps reduce such morning-after symptoms as "cotton mouth" and dry eyes.
- *Watch what you drink.* Some alcoholic beverages produce a more severe hangover than others. Certain drinks, such as red wine and brandy, contain methanol (wood alcohol) in addition to ethanol. Methanol is broken down much more slowly by the body, and its prolonged presence in the bloodstream can increase a hangover's severity.
- *Don't ingest caffeine or other stimulants to cure your hangover.* While these drugs may perk you up, they won't sober you up.

- *Don't take aspirin to fend off a hangover.* Studies suggest that aspirin may interfere with the enzyme that breaks down alcohol, increasing the amount of alcohol in your body. This can actually worsen your hangover. Aspirin, however, may relieve your "morning after" headache later on. Avoid Tylenol, however: recent studies indicate that Tylenol (acetaminophen) combined with alcohol can inflame the liver and cause liver disease.
- *Don't count on other tried but NOT true sobering-up activities,* which include exercising and cold showers. These activities won't hurt you, but they won't cure your hangover either.
- *Sleeping* may keep you off the road, but it's not always a successful sobering activity. Although your blood alcohol level will have returned to zero, studies show that your judgment and performance might remain impaired even after forty winks. If you're planning to drive a car in the morning, you may want to consider staying sober the night before.
- *Don't switch alcoholic drinks.* "Beer before liquor, never sicker; liquor before beer, in the clear"

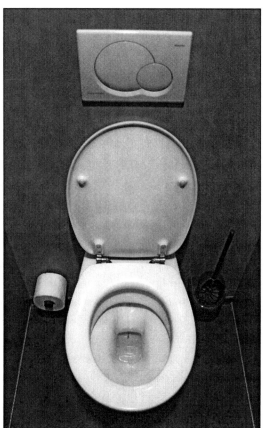

sometimes rings true and sometimes doesn't. Switching drinks can make you violently ill—the night before and the morning after.

Not everyone gets hangovers. In fact, what happens "the morning after" does depend to a great degree on what and how much you drink, but it also depends on your genetic factors and drinking history. Genetically, some people can process alcohol more effectively than others. Some individuals rarely or never get hangovers after drinking.

Most students aren't so fortunate, however, and must simply acknowledge hangovers as part of a lifestyle that allows them a few hours of unabashed partying every now and then. There is no "hangover cure" once the alcohol is in your system. The only real "cure" is, and always has been, not drinking at all. If, however, you're repeatedly desperate for a hangover remedy, think twice—this may mean you're drinking more than you should.

The Beer Goggle Syndrome

Case 1. He steps just inside the doorway of the favorite campus bar. The huge beer stain down the front of his shirt has clearly left him undaunted. Reeking of Taco Bell and Milwaukee's Best, he thinks he's God's gift to women, that his jokes are actually funny, and that he's a good dancer. As he pays his cover charge, he's thinking to himself, "Every woman in this bar wants me!" He intends to "get lucky" tonight.

Case 2. The boyfriend has just told her "adios." She wouldn't put out, so he's moving on. Angered, she's decided that tonight's the night to let it all hang out. She's going to get plastered, and the first guy she meets, she's planning on "shacking with."

What do these two students have in common? A bad case of "beer goggle syndrome" about to hit, the strong potential for engaging in regrettable sex, and a lot of embarrassment and self-anger the next morning.

While most drinkers are fairly well-versed in the "don't drink and drive" motto, many have yet to learn that the best sex—assuming you choose to have it at this point in your life—is sober, planned, and responsible sex. While it may alleviate insecurities about our bodies, physical attractiveness, and sexual prowess, as well as assuage church-generated, self-generated, or parentally imposed guilt about sex and sexuality, rarely does engaging in "sex under the influence" result in mutually pleasurable, satisfying, just plain good sex. Rather, you wake up mortified the next morning wondering who this person is in bed with you; vague flashbacks of the previous night's clumsy gropings come back to you, and you begin to feel two inches high. Repeated mornings of this stuff can start to make you think you don't deserve any better than hasty, forgotten one-night stands.

If you choose to wait to have sex—more power to you! If you think you're ready to have sex and take on the emotional and physical responsibilities it entails, then know that sex is never 100% safe. Engaging in sex while sober ensures that sex will be a positive experience for both you and your partner. Sober sex enables you to (1) communicate honestly and clearly with your partner; (2) consistently and correctly use safer-sex methods; and (3) effectively weigh and prepare for the costs and benefits of engaging in sexual activity. However, students who engage in sexual activity during or after drinking place themselves and their partners at tremendous risk for sexually transmitted infections, HIV infection, unplanned pregnancy, and nonconsensual sex.

Key aspects of sexual decision-making, such as listening, communication, and boundary-setting require that both (or all) participants are sober and cognizant of the choices they are making. Unfortunately, given the depravity of sex education that many students receive, you may or may not adhere to the following two myths about alcohol and sex.

Myth #1. **Alcohol improves sexual performance**. Well, alcohol may make you hornier, or give you permission to get in touch with your horniness, but it greatly decreases sexual pleasure and performance. Males have a difficult time achieving or maintaining an erection (remember—alcohol is a depressant!), and if you do manage to "get it up," orgasms may be hard to reach. Women experience vaginal dryness, inability to achieve orgasm, and lowered sexual response when under the influence of alcohol. As Shakespeare so aptly wrote, "Alcohol provokes the desire but takes away the performance." So avoid a case of penis disobedience and save sex for when you're both sober—it's definitely a lot better that way, and you'll be sure to rock your partner's world!

Myth #2. **Alcohol acts as a social lubricant**. Only if you consider slurred speech, drooling like a baby, and inability to maintain a complete thought as strong indicators of good communication. Because judgment and sense of propriety are the first to deteriorate after just a few drinks, the things that intoxicated people say and do tend to offend, hurt, or objectify those around them. If you're shy or uncomfortable meeting new people, alcohol may create the perception that socializing at a party or in a bar is easier, but you aren't making a good impression on anybody but yourself.

If you're nervous about meeting new people, plan a few non-corny opening lines that you can rely on, practice them in front of the bathroom mirror, and next time you go out, take a deep breath, walk up to that special someone, and go for it! Or, try the "networking system"—have mutual friends do the introductions, relieving some of the first-time-meeting-someone-so-what-do-I-say-to-not-look-stupid pressure.

Sex is a very important step in anyone's life. It should not be a decision taken lightly. Drinking before sex robs you of the ability to make safe, healthy choices for yourself and your partner. Consider the following statistics:

- One in 250 college students are HIV-positive.
- Half of all HIV-infections occur in individuals under the age of 30.
- One in four college students will contract at least one sexually transmitted infection before graduating.
- One in fifteen college women become pregnant each year.

Alcohol is highly correlated as a contributing factor in the incidence of each of these health concerns. It decreases the likelihood of effective communication, of practicing safer sex, and of having consensual sex. Furthermore, alcohol depresses the body's immune system, rendering you more vulnerable than usual to diseases and infections.

Sex is important enough to plan for, and that planning has to take place before you touch a single drink. **Alcohol should never be used as the excuse for having sex.** Consider the following questions:

- *What role does sex play in my life now? What role do I want it to play?* If you're content with the role sex plays or doesn't play in your life, awesome! Do you feel strongly enough about it to practice low-risk drinking or even abstain from alcohol and other drugs if you think that role may be threatened? What if sex doesn't function in your life the way you want it to? Realize that low-risk drinking or abstinence from alcohol or other drugs is necessary for making wise judgments and building honest sexual relationships.

- *How does alcohol affect the way I make decisions about sex?* Alcohol alters everyone's ability to make wise decisions. If alcohol has led to sexual encounters that were unremarkable, awkward, or embarrassing, are you willing to consider low-risk drinking or abstinence from alcohol and other drugs to ensure that similar encounters are not repeated?

- *How do I learn another person's desires and limits?* Because judgment is clouded by alcohol and other drugs, it's difficult to tell how far another person would be willing to go if he or she were sober. It's best not to take chances if the other person is drunk. Respect the other person's right to a true, sober consent. Protect the other person from later embarrassment and protect yourself from possible accusations of acquaintance rape later on. Your ability to use wise judgment and exercise respect for both yourself and the other person depends on your own clear mental state. This is not possible when you're under the influence of alcohol or other drugs.

- *How do I express my own desires and limits?* Again, this is difficult to do when under the influence, so don't wait until the clothes are on the floor and you've each had five beers to discuss your sexual standards. It's best, of course, to talk about sex with a potential partner when sober. If you do find yourself in a situation where the "heat of the moment" causes things to get out of hand a little too quickly, remember that **you never lose the right say "no" to any unwanted sexual contact.**

Ensure that each and every time you have sex, it's the result of your active choice—not anyone else's. Following are some suggestions and communication to keep in mind as you navigate the complex campus social scene:

- *Decide what your limits are.* Remember them. Communicate with your partner, making it clear what your limits are before you get into a sexual situation.

- *The best communication is sober communication.* Never mix alcohol or other drugs with sexual activity.

- *Attend large parties with friends whom you trust.* Agree to look out for each other as the party progresses. Also, agree to leave with the same friends. Give them the right to stop you from leaving with someone else if you are drunk.

- *Trust your instincts.* If you begin to feel uncomfortable in a sexual situation, you have the right to leave, and do so immediately.

- *Be aware of how much you **and** your date are drinking.*

- *If you do end up in bed with somebody, protect yourself—it's your responsibility.* Even if your partner seems safe, he or she may not realize, or reveal, that you are about to put yourself at risk for contracting an STI.

- *If you are going to have vaginal or anal intercourse, use latex condoms and spermicide containing Nonoxynol-9.* Women, don't assume that men are going to provide them. Both men and women should be comfortable purchasing and using condoms; if you're not, you frankly don't have any business having sex. And if neither of you has a condom, don't have sex until you get one. Once is enough to regret. For protection during oral sex on a man, use an unlubricated latex condom; latex dental dams or a double-layer of microwavable plastic wrap is an effective barrier to use during oral sex on a woman.

- *Remember, while prophylactics nearly eliminate your chance of pregnancy if used correctly, they do NOT protect you 100% against all STIs.* Condoms help prevent STI contraction, but abstinence is your only 100% effective protection.
- *Assume nothing.* Are you getting mixed messages about sex from your partner? If you're not sure, it's best to abstain from sexual activity until you're certain about their signals. Your partner may not yet know what his or her boundaries are regarding sex; respect this. When someone is expressing ambivalence, that is not the time to take advantage of them.
- Don't try to force that person into anything he or she (or *you*) will regret later. If someone continues to send mixed messages, he or she is probably unwilling to accept the adult responsibilities that becoming sexually active entails. Get scarce and find yourself a partner who's willing to take responsibility for sex.
- *You won't eliminate every risk by following these tips, but you **can** make sex safer by taking the necessary precautions.* Remember, you *cannot* make sex safer by drinking alcohol or taking other drugs. For this reason, it's safest *never* to mix alcohol and other drugs with sex.

By the way, if you're gay, lesbian, or bisexual or are struggling with your sexual identity, you'll want to know about alcohol- and other drug-related issues particular to you. Although being gay is not a disease or a sign of dysfunction, many gay men and women are often victims of both physical and emotional abuse. This may be part of the reason that *there is a high prevalence of depression, substance abuse and dependence, and suicide among gays, lesbians, and bisexuals.* If you are experiencing problems related to your sexual orientation, either from society or from within yourself, don't turn to alcohol or other drugs as a coping mechanism. Most likely, there are support services available, both on campus and in the surrounding community.

For counseling, support, or just additional information on these issues, contact your campus counseling center, the health education department, or the gay and lesbian student organization.

The Art of Refusal

Well, being able to cope with issues like drinking and driving, violence, and academic stress is sometimes easier said than done. Obviously, to succeed at keeping a handle on things, you'll have to get an "attitude adjustment."

Refraining from alcohol use is becoming an increasingly common and "cool" decision among college students who are fed up with the stupid, senseless behavior that is linked with getting wasted. People abstain—that is, engage in "creative social outlets"—for various reasons; many individuals choose not to drink because they fear the negative consequences of drinking and prefer to *remain in control at all times.* Others who choose to engage in creative social outlets do so for *health* or *religious reasons,* or simply because they perceive *no need for alcohol.* Finally, a good proportion of creative social outletters have simply decided that finishing school and getting that degree are the most important reasons for coming to college. They choose to have fun in unusual, innovative ways.

It's been said that the sign of a truly great individual is the ability to say "no" without feeling guilty. Therefore, the only thing you need to say when you are offered alcohol and don't choose to drink are these three simple words:

"No, thank you."

Get your best Clint Eastwood glaze in the eyes, look the person in the face and say these three words. In that order. Then walk away, strut a little. Variations might include,

"NO, thank you anyway."

or

"No, **GET LOST**."

or

"No, I can cut up and get wild without a brew!"

If you have made the decision not to drink, stand by that decision; nobody has the right to persuade you to act against your convictions. Your true friends won't ridicule you or pressure you.

Does drinking seem to be the only thing your friends are interested in? If alcohol isn't your cup of tea, seek out friends who enjoy the same things *you* enjoy. If you want to make creative social outlets a part of your lifestyle at college, get involved in non-drinking activities. Play a sport, go to dance clubs or good concerts, head out to a good movie, hit an amusement park, learn a musical instrument (or at least pretend to), join a student club or organization, or find a hobby that suits your interests. Avoid parties where drinking is the primary focus. Instead, spend the money you would have spent on alcohol on a great meal out instead. You'll enjoy it much more, and there

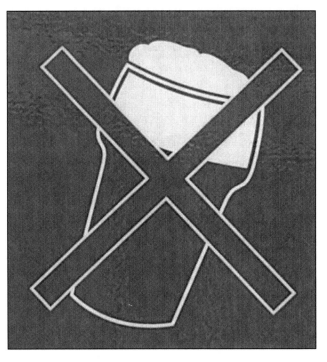

aren't any hangovers! Finally, throw your own party! Make some finger sandwiches, bake some cookies, and get lots of bubble gum. Have a funky theme like a disco retro, Hawaiian luau, 1920s rip-roaring ball complete with swing and big-band music—make everybody dress up in appropriate costume. Then, crank up the tunes. Best of all—you don't have to serve any alcohol!

If you're offered alcohol at a party and you're just not interested, decline politely but firmly. Don't apologize or make excuses for abstaining. If challenged, insist on your right not to drink. Don't be afraid to ask for soda, water, juice, or iced tea. If you want your drink to look like it contains alcohol, you can always ask for a twist of lemon or lime in it.

Remember, certain individuals may choose to periodically abstain from alcohol. That is, you elect not to drink for certain time periods for any of the following reasons:

- you're the designated driver;
- you're diabetic;
- you're on a diet to lose weight;
- you're currently on a medication that cannot be mixed with alcohol (tranquilizers, antibiotics, etc.);
- you're pregnant.

In these situations, creative social outlets are a must. So, go hog-wild!

The Lowdown on N.A.B.s

One way to select creative social outlets and still enjoy the taste of beer is to try out some of the non-alcoholic beers (N.A.B.s) available at many bars, clubs, and package stores. Non-alcoholic beers are smart alternatives if you like the taste of beer (yeah, right) but want to eliminate or at least cut down on your intake.

Are non-alcoholic beers really alcohol-free? No. The term "non-alcoholic" implies that these "brews" or "malt beverages," as they are called, are absolutely alcohol-free. Actually, this is not the case. These beverages do contain substantially less alcohol than regular beer (0.02%–0.05% per 12-ounce bottle, as opposed to regular beer's 5%). For most people, 0.05% is an undetectable trace and will not interfere with driving.

I am a recovering alcoholic. Are non-alcoholic beers an option for me? No. Because these beverages do contain a small amount of alcohol, they are not recommended for recovering alcoholics or children.

Are non-alcoholic beers more nutritious than regular beers? Although non-alcoholic beers are preferable for dieters, neither beverage offers much in the way of nutrition. Like regular beer, non-alcoholic beer is composed primarily of carbohydrates from barley malt and hops. Both regular and non-alcoholic beers do, however, have minuscule amounts of minerals and B vitamins. Also, because they have less alcohol, these brews don't promote dehydration like regular beers do.

Concerned about your weight? Non-alcoholic beers offer about one third to one half the calories of regular beer: regular beers have 140–200 calories as compared to the 100 in light beers and a mere 50–95 in N.A.B.s.

Are You In Control?

The American College Health Association estimates that 20%, or one in five, of undergraduate students experience a drinking problem. While most will "grow out" of the problem, some will go on to develop alcoholism, a serious and debilitating disease, in later adult life.

Becoming a problem drinker is not so much a marker of individual weakness as it is a reflection of how potent a drug alcohol is. While studies show that children of alcoholics are four times as likely to develop an addiction to alcohol or other drug themselves, any student who elects to drink is at potential risk for psychological or physical dependence on alcohol.

Signs of alcohol or other drug dependency are not always dramatic or obvious. The warning signs to watch out for in your friends and in yourself are actually more attitude- and relationship-related. The following list cites some common behaviors and symptoms associated with problem drinking. If you or your drinking buddies are exhibiting several of these behaviors, you might want to consider seeking help.

Increase in Tolerance. Most adult drinkers reach a plateau of tolerance after regular, repeated drinking. This is what most drinkers refer to as their "limit." However, about 30% of adult drinkers will demonstrate increased tolerance, meaning that they require more and more alcohol to achieve the same level of intoxication.

Frequent Blackouts. A drinker who experiences many bouts of alcohol-induced "amnesia" is getting a lot of alcohol into his or her system. This is a sign of increased alcohol tolerance.

Preoccupation with Alcohol. Problem drinkers think about (and frequently talk about) alcohol all the time—about the next time they'll be able to get a drink, when the next party is, how much alcohol will be provided ... you get the picture. This is the person who will take a leisure class on wine tasting very seriously.

Inability to "Cut Down" Despite Intentions to. Problem drinkers will very often swear off alcohol after a particular intimate morning with the porcelain deity or an exceptionally horrific case of beer goggle syndrome. Two days later, they (and your nerves) are down the same road. This happens over and over.

Continued Drinking Despite Negative Consequences of Drunkenness or Intoxication (Academic, Financial, Health, Legal, Professional, Sexual, Social, Etc.). For most individuals, a particularly hairy encounter with the cops, failing a core requirement for his or her major, or a diagnosis of chlamydia will dampen and put a reign on excessive boozing. For the problem drinker, the need for the alcohol supersedes all others.

Personality Changes; Altered Lifestyle; Loss of Interest in Hobbies. The never-ending cycle of nights of excessive drinking followed by excruciating pain-filled mornings would make anyone cranky. Problem drinkers may become hostile. Hobbies get thrown by the wayside because alcohol has become the primary obsession. Problem drinkers have been known to forfeit athletic or music scholarships because of alcohol dependency.

Repeatedly Cutting Classes or Missing Work Due to Hangovers. This is particularly problematic because most would agree that class attendance is necessary to getting good grades, and keeping a job is essential for paying those rent bills.

Distancing from Friends, Family, or Partners, Especially After a Conversation about Drinking Habits. Most problem drinkers know that they are in trouble. Hearing about it from those closest to them simply aggravates the self-disappointment and self-anger. It's easier to shut those people out rather than confront an issue they aren't ready to deal with yet.

Poor Grooming and Hygiene; Frequent Illness. People who frequently drink to excess rarely look good, smell good, shave, or iron. They don't care about themselves any more. And because constant drinking suppresses the immune system, interferes with good nutrition, and decreases appetite, most problem drinkers are easily prone to whatever "bug" is going around at the time.

Excessive Debt, Frequent Borrowing of Money, or Engaging in Theft. Any drug habit eventually gets expensive, because the user will need more and more of the same substance to get the same "high." When the goodwill of generous friends and family runs out, the problem drinker may try his or her hand at gambling (which doesn't work), theft, or credit card fraud. In extreme cases, some abusers will trade sex for drugs (as is very commonly the case with cocaine and heroin addicts).

Drinking Alone or at Socially Inappropriate Times. Being able to keep up with the alcohol cravings will eventually require around-the-clock consumption. The problem drinker can hide his or her addiction in activities where drinking is socially acceptable, but then drink alone and at times that are inconsistent with social norms.

Hiding Alcohol. Fearing that he or she won't have enough to stave off alcohol craving and keep off the withdrawal symptoms, problem drinkers will stash away great quantities of liquor in clever hiding places.

Withdrawal Symptoms When Alcohol is Unavailable. Similar to withdrawing from nicotine, cocaine, or heroin, the abuser will experience symptoms associated with not having the drug available, including night sweats, the "shakes," hallucinations, and nightmares. At this point, alcohol has become essential to basic functioning, rather than a mere enhancement.

Apparent Depression; Suicide Attempts. The stress of maintaining a substance addiction can result in poor mental health status. Other life stressors may result in depression, and drinking serves to mitigate the fear of being sucked into the "black hole." However, the attempts to self-medicate with alcohol only work for a while. Eventually, the drinker will have to confront whatever is the source of his or her depression.

Violence, Aggression, and Other "Acting Out" Behaviors. The sadness and anger, rather than being turned inward, can also be exhibited toward others. Oftentimes, these are cries for help.

Memory Loss. Repeated "black outs" over time result in loss of brain matter.

Denial; Blaming Others for Problems. This is the classic sign of a substance abuse problem. According to the drinker, his or her excesses are the result of everyone else's incompetence, stupidity, etc. It's easier to blame others than to confront oneself. Your job as a partner, friend, or relative is to keep yourself from falling into the problem drinker's trap; his or her reality shouldn't be yours. Avoid enabling his behavior by taking notes for him because he missed class due to a hangover, calling her boss to say she's sick when she's actually stone drunk, cleaning up the mess he made of the living room after an alcohol-induced violent episode, or apologizing for her to the neighbor next door because she called him a fat, ugly toad while in a drunken stupor.

Living with a problem drinker is a trying experience. Always remember that as the person who cares about him or her, your job is to assist the problem drinker in getting help; it's not your job to "fix" the person.

Confronting the Problem Drinker

It's unpleasant at best; it could cost the friendship at worst. As a friend who cares, however, it's your responsibility to intervene when your friend's in trouble. Most problem drinkers need the support of their significant others in order to get into help. The student services staff on your campus can help students who are experiencing problems with alcohol, but students have to reach out first.

The first thing you can do is to familiarize yourself with the signs and "red flags" of a drinking problem—which if you've read this far, you already have. These can act as a roadmap for the conversation you have with your friend. Be sure to confront the problem drinker in a confidential environment. Honesty and forthrightness will be best fostered if no strangers are around to eavesdrop, and confronting in a public place will only embarrass him or her. Time the confrontation for when the individual is sober—no need to get into an unconstructive yelling match that can result in your nose being broken.

Begin the conversation by saying you are concerned about his or her welfare. Exhibit a nonjudgmental manner and a supportive tone at all times. You can do this by confronting specific alcohol-related behaviors that concern you, rather than attacking the drinker's personality or integrity. Keep the focus on what the drinker has done, not on innate values he or she does or doesn't possess. Cite specific and clear examples of drinking incidents and the negative consequences they generated on both the drinker and on you.

Be prepared for defensiveness, anger, or denial. Don't resort to patronizing or pitying the drinker, or to coming across as the "expert." However, do remain firm, and keep the confrontation focused on the drinker; problem drinkers are intelligent and manipulative, and will try to turn the tables on you by bringing up irrelevant, distracting points (e.g., "Who are you to judge? You go out drinking, too!").

Tell the problem drinker that you would like him or her to go talk to someone. Provide the list of campus and community resources listed in the next section. Stress that help-seeking is a sign of courage, not a sign of weakness.

Most importantly, avoid enabling the drinker's abusive behavior, and recognize your limits in changing another. Change only occurs if the person wants it and is willing to take the responsibility to initiate it. You can't "fix" someone else's problem, no matter how tempting it is. If coping with a significant other's drinking problem is causing undue stress in your life, seek professional support for yourself. And you might want to consider whether or not this relationship or friendship is worth keeping in its unhealthy state.

Our society has taught us to value independence. The reality of today's world is that social problems such as substance abuse and violence won't be solved until each and every one of us recognizes our mutual interdependence—we owe it to each other to not let those close to us get away with self-destructive behavior. Failing to speak up is as hurtful as commiserating in a loved one's self-destruction.

Resources for Information and Support

Your campus most likely has a wide variety of staff resources and literature available to answer your questions or to provide the help and support that you need for an alcohol-related concern. Try visiting the student health center, making an appointment at the counseling center, talking to your RA, or approaching a trusted professor.

Community resources that might be available to student include twelve-step organizations such as Alcoholics Anonymous and Al-Anon. You can easily find the phone numbers for a local contact by doing a Google search. Similarly, nearby hospitals will have treatment and detoxification centers, as well as support groups for problem drinkers.

Below are some websites containing substance abuse information that might be of interest to students. They cost nothing to use. All you need is an Internet browser.

- **Higher Education Center for Alcohol and Other Drug Prevention:** *www.edc.org/hec*
- **BACCHUS and GAMMA Peer Education Network:** *www.bacchusgamma.org*
- *Go Ask Alice!* **(Columbia University):** *www.columbia.edu/cu/healthwise/alice.html*
- **The Core Institute:** *www.siu.edu/~coreinst*
- **Facts on Tap:** *www.factsontap.org*

Questions to Consider

1. Your friend decides to go out and drink. Name four harm-reduction strategies.
2. What myths or misconceptions about alcohol are most prevalent on the campus? What could be done to change this?

3. You notice one of the other peer educators out at a party and they have obviously been drinking. How would you address this? What are steps or techniques to address/confront a problem drinker?

References

Adler, J. (1994, December 19). The endless binge. *Newsweek. Retrieved from* http://www.newsweek.com/id/112602

Brain, P. F. (Ed.). (1986). *Alcohol and aggression.* London: Croom Helm.

Canterbury, R. J., Gressard, C. F., & Vieweg, W. V. R. (1992). Risk-taking behavior of college students and social forces. *American Journal of Drug and Alcohol Abuse,* 18, p. 213–222.

Deykin, E., Levy, J., & Wells, V. (1987). Adolescent depression, alcohol and drug abuse. *American Journal of Public Health,* 77, p. 178–182.

Douglas, Kathy A., et al. (1997). *Results from the 1995 National College Health Risk Behavior Survey.* Journal of American College Health, 46: p. 55–66.

Eigen, L. (1991, September). *Alcohol practices, policies, and potential of American colleges and universities: A white paper* (DHHS Publication No. ADM 91-1842). Rockville, MD: Office for Substance Abuse Prevention.

Presley, C. A., Meilman, P. W., & Cashin, J. R. (1996). *Alcohol and drugs on American college campuses, Volume IV: 1992–1994.* Carbondale: Southern Illinois University, The Core Institute.

Smith, S., & Smith, C. (1988). The college student's health guide. Lost Altos, CA: Westchester Publishing Company.

Wechsler, H., Davenport, A., Dowdall, G., Moeykens, B., & Castillo, S. (1994). Health and behavioral consequences of binge drinking in college. *Journal of the American Medical Association 272(21),* p. 1672–1677.

Chapter 9

Tobacco Cessation

By Luoluo Hong and Jason Robertson

Cigarette smoking is correlated with more of the top ten leading causes of American death than any other single risk factor. Cigarette smokers, who represent less than one-third of the adult population, account for about 83% of all cases of lung cancer. In fact, the risk of developing lung cancer is ten times greater for smokers than for non-smokers. Cigarette smokers have 70% more heart attacks than non-smokers, and they have an abnormally high number of strokes. Incidence of emphysema (deep, persistent coughing), heart attacks, and strokes are also higher among smokers. Cigar smoking, pipe smoking, cigarette smoking, and use of smokeless tobacco have also been implicated as causes of cancers in the mouth, pharynx, larynx, esophagus, bladder, and pancreas (Hamilton 1997).

Men who smoke less than half a pack a day have a death rate 60% higher than nonsmokers; for 1–2 packs a day, the death rate is 90% higher; for two or more packs a day, it is about 120% above average. Leukemia, the leading cause of cancer death in college-aged individuals, kills over one and a half more males than females.

The number of female smokers has almost caught up with men. The death rate for women who smoke and use oral contraceptives is much higher than for non-smoking pill users.

However, unless irreversible damage has already occurred, the health benefits of quitting begin immediately. After one year, there is a drop in the risk of heart attacks among quitters. Your risk of lung cancer is cut in half after five years of quitting, even sooner if you were not a heavy smoker (i.e., more than twenty cigarettes a day, twenty years). After ten years, death rates from all causes of ex-cigarette smokers are approximately as low as those who never smoked.

On Quitting Successfully

About 46 million Americans smoke (CDC 2009). More than 70% of them say they would like to quit. While 18 million try each year, only 3% have long-term success, according to the American Cancer Society. Each day 1,000 persons younger than 18 years become regular smokers. Most smokers who have successfully "kicked the habit" tried to stop three or four times before succeeding. The beginning is most difficult, mainly due to the physiological withdrawal symptoms from nicotine addictions. Consequently, half of relapses occur within the first week of quitting. Still, failed attempts need not mean permanent failure. More than 40% of people who have ever smoked have now quit.

Many smokers try to quit "cold turkey" and can, without first reducing their smoking, planning a special program, or seeking professional help. However, other successful quitters have given up cigarettes after several weeks of practice replacing them with new habits. Included below are a variety of tips and helpful hints on kicking the smoking habit. These methods can make your own efforts a little easier.

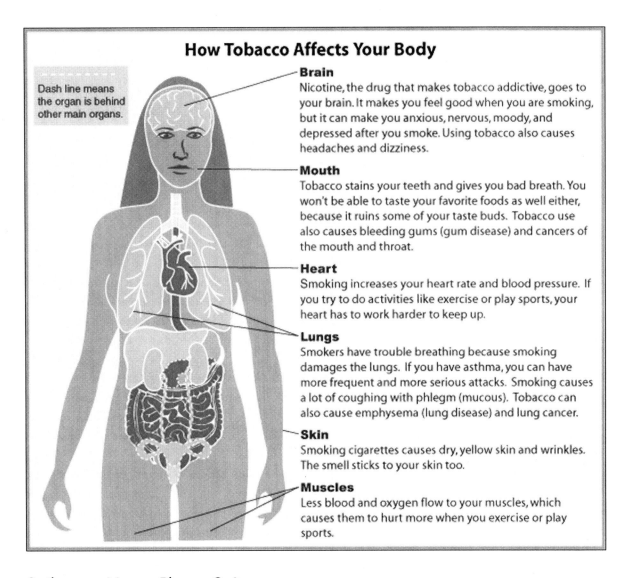

How Tobacco Affects Your Body

Dash line means the organ is behind other main organs.

Brain
Nicotine, the drug that makes tobacco addictive, goes to your brain. It makes you feel good when you are smoking, but it can make you anxious, nervous, moody, and depressed after you smoke. Using tobacco also causes headaches and dizziness.

Mouth
Tobacco stains your teeth and gives you bad breath. You won't be able to taste your favorite foods as well either, because it ruins some of your taste buds. Tobacco use also causes bleeding gums (gum disease) and cancers of the mouth and throat.

Heart
Smoking increases your heart rate and blood pressure. If you try to do activities like exercise or play sports, your heart has to work harder to keep up.

Lungs
Smokers have trouble breathing because smoking damages the lungs. If you have asthma, you can have more frequent and more serious attacks. Smoking causes a lot of coughing with phlegm (mucous). Tobacco can also cause emphysema (lung disease) and lung cancer.

Skin
Smoking cigarettes causes dry, yellow skin and wrinkles. The smell sticks to your skin too.

Muscles
Less blood and oxygen flow to your muscles, which causes them to hurt more when you exercise or play sports.

Strike up a Master Plan to Quit

1. Develop a list of strong personal reasons and incentives to quit (significant other will kiss you, win a bet, better health, save money, better sex life, nicer smile, smell better, etc.). Be sure to include reasons other than your health and your obligation to others. For example, think of all the time you waste (taking cigarette breaks, rushing out to buy a pack, hunting a light, standing outdoors in the cold to smoke, etc.). Every night before you go to bed, read these reasons.
2. Decide positively that you want to quit. Try to avoid negative thoughts.
3. Set a realistic target date for quitting—perhaps a special day at work, or quit during your vacation. Make the date sacred, and don't let anything change it.
4. Begin to condition yourself physically. Start a modest exercise regimen. Drink a lot of water (to cleanse your body of nicotine) and eat at least three well-balanced meals every day to maintain a constant blood-sugar level (to prevent urges to smoke). Get plenty of rest and avoid fatigue.
5. Bet a friend you can quit on your target date. Put your cigarette money aside every day, and forfeit it if you smoke.
6. Ask your friend or spouse to quit with you, or find someone who will be a committed and supportive "cheerleader" throughout the entire time you are quitting.
7. Switch to a brand you find distasteful.

8. Change to a brand that's low in tar and nicotine a couple of weeks before your target date. This will change your smoking habit. Try not to smoke two packs of the same brand in a row.

Cut Down on the Number of Cigarettes You Smoke

1. Smoke only half of each cigarette.
2. Each day, postpone lighting your first cigarette one hour.
3. Decide you'll smoke only during odd or even hours of the day.
4. Decide beforehand how many cigarettes you'll smoke during the day. For each additional smoke, give one dollar to your favorite charity.
5. Don't smoke when you first experience a craving. Wait several minutes; during this time, change your activity, talk to someone, or take a deep breath and hold it for a few seconds.
6. Stop buying cigarettes by the carton. Wait until one pack is empty before buying another.
7. Stop carrying cigarettes with you at home and work. Make them difficult to find.

Preparations Before Quitting

1. Speak to your doctor about your decision to quit. Inform him or her of your quit date and report on your progress.
2. Collect all your cigarette butts in one large glass container as a visual reminder of the filth smoking represents.
3. Practice going without cigarettes. Don't think of never smoking again. Think of quitting in terms of one day at a time. Tell yourself you won't smoke and then don't.
4. Keep a log of the types of emotions and situations that typically precede a desire to smoke. Be aware of and temporarily avoid activities that strongly "trigger" your desire to smoke (parties, coffee, alcohol, sweets, watching television, etc.). Avoid friends who smoke.
5. Develop a plan to manage your stress and anxiety more effectively without relying on nicotine (e.g., improving time management skills, adopting relaxation techniques, and positive visualization).

The Day You Pack It In

1. Throw away all cigarettes and matches by breaking them in half and wetting them down. Hide lighters and ashtrays.
2. Visit the dentist and have your teeth cleaned and polished to get rid of tobacco stains. Notice how nice they look and how fresh your breath smells; resolve to keep it that way.
3. Make a list of things you'd like to buy for yourself or someone else. Estimate the cost in terms of packs of cigarettes, and put the money aside to buy these presents.
4. Keep very busy on the big day. Go to the movies, exercise to relive tensions, take long walks, go bike riding, etc.
5. Buy yourself a treat or do something special to celebrate.

After Quitting

1. The first few days after you quit, spend as much free time as possible in places where smoking is prohibited, like libraries, museums, theaters, department stores, and churches.
2. Drink large quantities of water and fruit juice to cleanse your body of nicotine. Try to avoid alcohol, coffee, and other beverages with which you associate smoking.
3. Strike up a conversation with someone instead of striking a match for a cigarette.
4. Find something else to keep your hands occupied (e.g., pencil, paper clip, marble, ben-wa balls). If you miss having something in your mouth, try toothpicks or gum.

Avoid Temptation

1. Find new habits to replace smoking. For example, get up from the table and brush your teeth or take a walk after meals. If you always smoke while driving, take public transportation for a while, or sing to the radio or a favorite CD while driving.
2. Develop a clean, fresh non-smoking environment around yourself, both at work and at home.
3. Until you are confident of your ability to stay off cigarettes, limit your socializing to healthful outdoor activities or situations where smoking is prohibited.
4. If you must be in a situation where you'll be tempted to smoke (such as a party), try to associate with the non-smokers there.
5. Look at cigarettes ads more critically to better understand the attempts to make individual brands appealing.

Find New Habits

1. Change your habits to make smoking more difficult, impossible, or unnecessary. Try activities such as swimming, jogging, tennis, or riding a bike. Wash your hands or the dishes when the desire for a cigarette is intense.
2. Eat three or more small meals. This maintains constant blood sugar levels, thus helping to prevent urges to smoke. Avoid sugar-laden foods and spicy items that can trigger a desire for cigarettes.
3. Do things to maintain a clean taste in your mouth, such as brushing and flossing your teeth frequently or using mouthwash.
4. Do things that require you to use your hands. Try crossword puzzles, needlework, gardening, playing an instrument, or house chores.

5. Stretch a lot. Get plenty of rest. Pay attention to your appearance. Look and feel sharp.

When You Get the "Crazies"

1. Keep low-fat and low-calorie oral substitutes handy (vegetable sticks, dill pickles, sunflower seeds, fruit, sugarless gum, etc.).
2. Take a shower or bath if possible.
3. Learn to relax quickly and deeply. Make yourself limp, visualize a soothing and pleasing situation, and practice deep breathing.
4. Never allow yourself to think, "One won't hurt." It will.
5. Don't forget that your doctor can help. S/he is proud that you've made it this far and can get you over these last hurdles.

On Becoming an "Ex"

1. Each month, on the anniversary of your quit date, plan a celebration.
2. Periodically write down reasons why you're glad you quit. Keep these reasons with you at all times in your date book or journal, and post these reasons where you'll be sure to see them.
3. Make a calendar for the first ninety days. Cross of each day and indicate the money you saved by not smoking.

About Weight Gain

Many people who are considering quitting are concerned about gaining weight. If you are one of them, keep these points in mind:

1. Giving up cigarettes is far healthier for you than gaining a few extra pounds. It would take the addition of more than 75 pounds to offset the health benefits that a normal smoker gets by quitting.
2. Just because you quit doesn't mean you'll automatically gain weight. Because nicotine can suppress a person's appetite, people usually gain weight because they have begun to eat more once they quit.
3. Eating a well-planned and balanced diet that is low in fat will help minimize the weight gained. Start yourself on a healthy eating program while preparing to quit.
4. Don't set a target quitting date right after a holiday when the temptation of high calorie and high fat foods or drink may be hard to resist.
5. Incorporate a regular exercise routine of moderate to vigorous activity.

Nicotine Replacement Therapy: Using Nicotine in Smoking Cessation

Since 1991, first by prescription only, and now over the counter, products are available that allow those seeking to stop smoking address the often-painful symptoms of nicotine withdrawal that accompany smoking cessation. The use of these products is referred to as "nicotine replacement therapy (NRT)." NRT means administering nicotine by means of (1) wearing an adhesive patch, (2) chewing gum, or (3) using a nasal spray. By providing nicotine in amounts that are mild but consistent, one may tackle the psychological challenges of smoking cessation while minimizing the physical symptoms of withdrawal.

Taking nicotine to end nicotine addiction may seem paradoxical; however, the harmful effects of tobacco use are only partly due to nicotine. Numerous clinical tests comparing the patch with placebos demonstrate the relative effectiveness of the patch. At the end of six months, 20% of patch users had successfully quit. Similar figures have been recorded for the use of nicotine gum. Nicotine spray, the most recently approved method of NRT has slightly better success rates. However, when NRT is combined with behavioral modification programs, the success rate approaches 45%.

It is strongly advised that people not use tobacco while wearing the patch or using any NRT. Smoking while using NRT can be dangerous, especially for those who are pregnant, or who have high blood pressure or other cardiovascular disease.

The Nicotine Transdermal Patch. Available over the counter, the nicotine patch is a bandage-like adhesive that is applied to the body somewhere above the waist but below the neck—usually on the upper arm or back—where it then gradually administers nicotine directly to the blood. Upon initiating a smoking cessation program, the patch is worn for a full 24-hour period. A new patch is applied daily upon waking in the morning. Studies show that both the 16- and 24-hour patches are equally effective.

Nicotine patches come in varying strengths. Step One patches administer 21 mg. of nicotine over a 24-hour period, which is nearly one mg. of nicotine per hour—roughly the amount of nicotine from one cigarette. The manufacturer recommends wearing the 21 mg. patch for up to six weeks, following it with two weeks of the Step Two 14 mg. patch, and two final weeks with the Step Three 7 mg. patch. This method permits the smoker to learn to cope with both the psychological and physiological changes of quitting. The patch may be removed at bedtime.

For those who smoke less than half a pack a day, weigh less than 100 pounds, or have heart disease, it is recommended skipping step one and beginning treatment with the 14 mg. patch.

The gradual administration of nicotine is intended to reduce addiction to the patch itself. While the patch is a source of nicotine, it is preferable to cigarettes and smokeless tobacco, which contain tar, carbon monoxide, and potential carcinogens. Those who are pregnant or have heart conditions are encouraged to stop smoking by means of planned behavioral modification, but if such a program alone is not successful, the nicotine patch is clearly preferable to continued cigarette or cigar use.

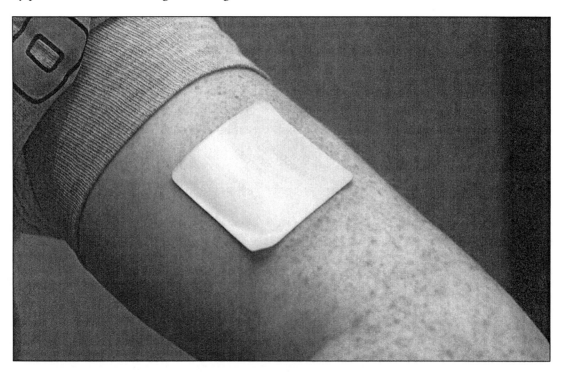

The success of the patch is greatly enhanced by completely abstaining from cigarettes and by combining the patch with a behavioral modification system. Conversely, if one smokes while beginning use of the patch, the likelihood of successfully quitting is reduced. In fact, 83% of those using the patch who were still smoking after six months had smoked during the first two weeks of using the patch.

Both patches are distributed with behavioral aids, consisting of a CD, booklets, and tip cards. The cost, on average, is around $30 for a week's supply (seven) of patches. Skin irritation is almost universally reported by users of the nicotine patch, and for some that irritation prohibits wearing the patch at all. Sites for the patch should be rotated and the same site shouldn't be used more than once in a seven-day period. A severe allergic reaction to the patch is one reason to consider using nicotine gum or nasal spray.

Nicotine Polacrilex Chewing Gum. Nicotine polacrilex chewing gum is a gum with nicotine in it. There are several versions available on the market in two different strengths: 2 mg. or 4 mg. of nicotine per piece.

The gum is chewed slowly until a peppery taste or tingling sensation is perceived in the mouth. The gum is then held between the cheek and gums. When the taste or tingling has diminished, the gum is chewed and held again, this time in a different spot. This process is continued for up to one-half hour. The manufacturer recommends not eating or drinking during the fifteen minutes before or during gum chewing.

With one hundred pieces costing about $45, nicotine gum is potentially more expensive than patches. Using one piece per hour, one hundred pieces will last almost a week.

Some people experience side effects with gum use, including soreness of the mouth, aching jaw, hiccups, and upset stomach. Because nicotine dosage is self-administered when using gum, some individuals chew the gum long past the two or three months recommended. Evidence indicates that use of the gum for more than eleven months may elevate the risk for cardiovascular disease. However, many physicians believe the benefits of using the gum in smoking cessation far outweigh the possible harm of abusing the gum through prolonged use.

Nicotine Nasal Spray. Nicotrol NS is available by prescription only. It is manufactured by the same company that makes the Nicotrol patch, and is distributed with the "Pathways to Change" program, as well. Because nicotine is absorbed more rapidly through the nasal membranes, the spray is more likely to provide pleasurable sensations associated with tobacco use. For this reason, the spray is recommended only for those who are heavy tobacco users, and is not intended for use longer than six months.

One dose (two sprays) provides the same amount of nicotine as one cigarette. Patients use one or two doses per hour, up to forty per day. The spray costs about $40–$55 for two hundred sprays, or one hundred doses. The manufacturer claims that in clinical trials, between 31%–35% of nasal spray users were tobacco free at the end of six months. Because the spray has been on the market a relatively short amount of time, independent tests have yet to be run.

Almost all users experience some initial irritation with the spray. The most commonly reported side effects include a runny nose, throat irritation, watering eyes, sneezing, and coughing. Side effects should diminish with continued use. There are inadequate data about the effects of the nasal spray on allergies, sinusitis, nasal polyps, or asthma. Again, because nicotine dosage is self-administered, combined with the "rush" similar to that provided by a cigarette, users of the spray are much more likely to abuse it.

Pharmacological Means of Quitting

Zyban

Bupropion Hydrochloride (Zyban) is a non-nicotine medication recognized as a smoking cessation aid. It is available only with a doctor's prescription. It acts on the parts of the brain that are affected by nicotine.

It seems to reduce craving and withdrawal symptoms such as frustration and anxiety, difficulty concentrating, restlessness, and negative mood. Some people should not take it, including people who:

- have ever had seizures
- have had head injuries
- take some anti-depressants (MAO inhibitors)
- take another medication containing bupropion
- have, or have had, eating disorders.

Caution: It is very important to discuss thoroughly and completely with your provider your suitability to use Zyban.

Chantix

Chantix (also known as Varenicline) is a non-nicotine drug to aid with smoking cessation. It comes in tablet form and works by stimulating receptors for nicotine in the brain. This produces an effect that relieves the craving and withdrawal symptoms you can get when you stop smoking. At the same time, Chantix prevents any nicotine inhaled in tobacco smoke from having a rewarding and enjoyable effect.

Some people should not take Chantix if:
- they are allergic to any of the ingredients that Chantix contains;
- are under 18 years of age; or
- are pregnant, planning a pregnancy, or breastfeeding.

Before being prescribed Chantix by a doctor, it is important to disclose:
- allergies to any other medicines, foods, etc.;
- a history of kidney problems, hemodialysis treatment, or repeated fits or convulsions;
- a history of mental illness.

Smokeless Tobacco

Smokeless tobacco use defined as any tobacco use that excludes the inhaling of smoke. Users either dip snuff or chew tobacco supplied in tins, pouches, or individual pouches called "bandits." Both require frequent swallowing or spitting out of saliva.

Smokeless tobacco manufacturers have targeted their products to young males 18–25 years of age, particularly athletes, by promoting a "macho" image of smokeless tobacco use. In fact, 20% of males 18–25 used smokeless tobacco in the past year (National Institute of Drug Abuse [NIDA] 2010). About 12% of college males (compared to less than 1% of college females) are current users of smokeless tobacco (NIDA 2010).

Health hazards associated with smokeless tobacco include:

Leukoplakia. Leathery white patches appear inside the mouth as a result of direct contact with and continued irritation by tobacco juice. One in twenty cases develops into oral cancer.

Decreased sense of taste and ability to smell. The user may need more salt and sugar to enhance the taste of food.

Dental problems. Tobacco is a chemical irritant. As a result, users are more prone to such problems as receding gums, periodontal (gum) disease, erosion of tooth enamel, and tooth loss. In addition, increased saliva production, bad breath (halitosis), discolored teeth, and "black hairy tongue" all result from smokeless tobacco use. Because sugar and molasses are added to smokeless tobacco to enhance taste, users have a three to four times' greater chance of losing their teeth than non-users.

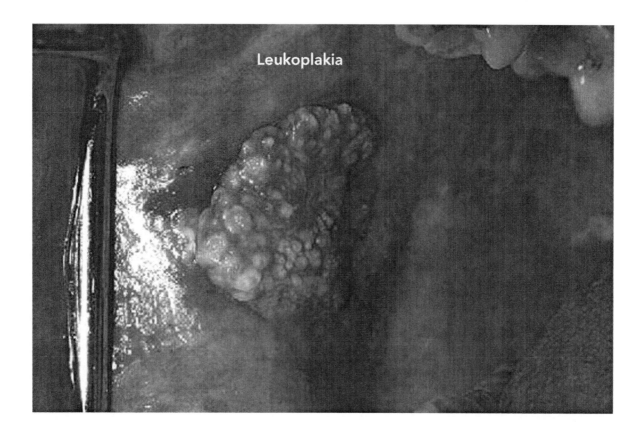

Leukoplakia

Nicotine addiction. While smokeless tobacco has been marketed as the safer alternative to cigarettes, it is much more addictive because of its greater nicotine concentration. In smokeless tobacco users, 90% of the nicotine is absorbed directly into the bloodstream within fifteen seconds.

Cardiovascular problems. In addition to being addictive, nicotine causes the blood vessels to constrict. The heart then has to pump harder to circulate blood, resulting in higher blood pressure. Smokeless tobacco is a risk factor for heart disease, strokes, and arteriosclerosis.

Cancer. Continued smokeless tobacco use is associated with a variety of cancers in young adults, including cancers of the mouth, larynx, esophagus, and stomach—all parts of the body that come into direct contact with the carcinogens contained in tobacco juice.

As with cigarette smokers, users of smokeless tobacco can quickly become addicted. There is a variety of methods for quitting. Users can either quit "cold turkey," adopt a behavioral modification plan as described above, or take advantage of over-the-counter and prescription nicotine replacement therapies (i.e., nicotine patches, gums, and nasal sprays). Alternative therapies might include hypnosis. In addition, the user can seek the support and expertise of a mental health provider for assistance in quitting.

Questions to Consider

1. What is the impact of tobacco on American society? What about college students?
2. What are five methods to getting a person ready to quit?
3. Why is it important for peer educators to be knowledgeable about cessation aids? Should they recommend one over another? Why or why not?

References

Hamilton, K. (1997, July 21). Blowing Smoke. *Newsweek Magazine*, 130(3) p. 54–61.

National Institute on Drug Abuse (2010). NIDA InfoFacts: Cigarettes and other tobacco products. Retrieved from http://www.drugabuse.gov/infofacts/tobacco.html.

Chapter 10

Abuse of Drugs Other Than Alcohol

By Luoluo Hong and Julie Catanzarite

Psychoactive drugs are most frequently used for social or recreational purposes. Many psychoactive drugs produce tolerance or dependence (psychological, physical, or both). The more frequently a person uses a drug and/or the larger the dose, the greater is his or her tolerance to the drug. This means that over time larger quantities may be needed to produce the desired effect.

Although dependence is associated with tolerance, it is not the same thing. A person who is physically dependent on a drug needs it to function "normally." Discontinued use of the drug results in withdrawal symptoms that can be painful and even life-threatening. Taking the drug again relieves these symptoms, but only temporarily. A person who is psychologically dependent feels s/he cannot function normally without the drug. While there may be no physical illness associated with quitting, there can be severe emotional and mental distress that prompting the person to resume using the drug.

There are three basic categories of psychoactive drugs:

1. **Stimulants**, including amphetamines, meth-amphetamines, cocaine/crack, nicotine, and caffeine, which increase alertness, energy, physical activity, and feelings of well-being;
2. **Depressants**, including alcohol, barbiturates, inhalants, opiates/narcotics, and tranquilizers, which decrease body processes such as breathing, heartbeat, and brain activity; and
3. **Psychedelics/Hallucinogens**, including marijuana and LSD, which cause auditory, visual, and other sensory hallucinations.

PCP has characteristics of all three categories.

Amphetamines/Methamphetamines

Amphetamines are synthetic central nervous system (CNS) stimulants with actions similar to the naturally occurring substance in our bodies known as adrenaline. The best known members of this drug group are dextro-amphetamine (Dexedrine), benzamphetamine (Benzedrine, Didrex), methamphetamine (Methedrine, or "ice"), and methylphenidate (Ritalin). These drugs have been used by physicians to treat narcolepsy, attention deficit disorder in children, obesity, and certain other disorders. Although medical use of amphetamines has declined greatly in the last twenty years, people continue to use them illegally.

Amphetamines can be taken orally, dissolved in water and taken intravenously, or by sniffing it through the nose (also known as "snorting"), although the latter is less common. Injection is preferred by chronic, high-dose abusers. As pure crystals, amphetamines appear as an odorless, bitter-tasting, white or off-white power that is water-soluble. Illicit preparations of amphetamines are often mixed with other materials and may appear as off-white powders, crystals, or chunks. They may also be packages as capsules or tablets to resemble commercial preparations. Illicit amphetamines may have a strong odor from solvents used in their manufacture.

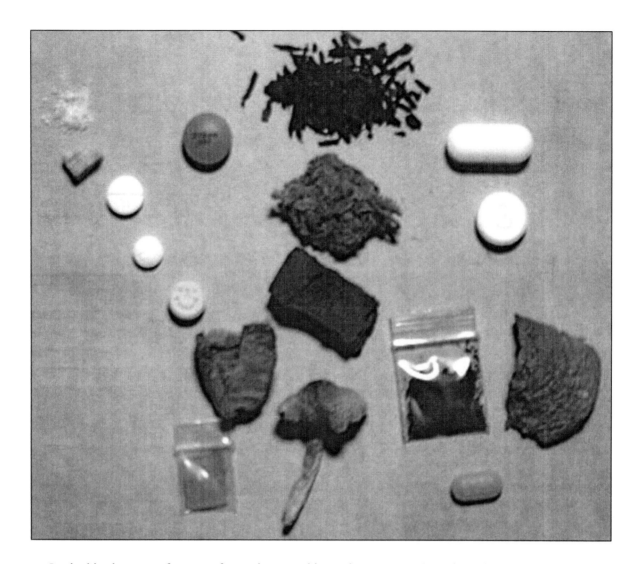

Look-alike drugs are often manufactured to resemble amphetamines, or "speed," and marketed as such. They rarely contain amphetamines, however; rather, they contain a blend of three common drugs: caffeine, ephedrine, and phenylpropanolamine (PPA, used in over-the-counter appetite suppressants and decongestants). Also, amphetamines are sometimes combined with other drugs and illegally sold on the street. Such combinations include "goofballs" (amphetamines and barbiturates), "speedballs" (methamphetamine or cocaine and heroin), and less commonly, combinations of amphetamines with LSD or PCP (phencyclidine).

A relatively new kind of synthetic methamphetamine, called "ice," is smoked in a pipe. (A single-chambered glass pipe, called a "bong" is used for smoking ice.) Ice is an extremely pure, highly addictive form of methamphetamine. It first appeared in the US in Hawaii in 1985, smuggled from Asia. One gram of ice costs $350–400 in Hawaii, and yields ten to fifteen hits. Ice has become the illicit drug of choice for many stimulant user because:

1. It produces a high that lasts up to thirty hours, compared to the thirty-minute high one gets from smoking crack;
2. The vapors are odorless, making use of the drug difficult for law enforcement officers to detect; and
3. It is less expensive to manufacture than crack, but sells for more on the street.

Street Names: Speed, bennies, Black Beauties, diet pills, white cross, co-pilots, crystal, dexies, eye openers, meth, pep pills, uppers, or wake-ups. Methamphetamine is known as speed, crank, go fast, go, zip, ice, chris, cristy, cream, chalk, glass, shabu, and batu. "Snot" refers to methamphetamine-oil (methamphetamine powder dissolved in water with baking soda added to raise the pH) that is smoked in a pipe.

Short-Term Effects: Wakefulness, alertness, talkativeness, increased breathing and heart rate, elevated body temperature and blood pressure, dilation of pupils, increased energy, suppressed appetite, and heightened sense of well-being. A user may take high doses every few hours for extended periods of time (called a binge or "run")—staying awake 72 hours or more, and experiencing disinhibition, confusion and anxiety, dizziness, head-aches, palpitations and tremors, impaired judgment, grandiosity, impulsiveness, hypervigilance, compulsively repeated acts, hypersexuality, and atypical sexual behavior. An overdose of ice can cause delirium, circulatory collapse, nausea and vomiting, seizures, coma, and death.

Long-Term Effects: Severe anxiety, agitation, malnutrition, chronic sleeplessness, irritability, high blood pressure, poor coordination, tremors, blurred vision, high blood pressure, rapid and irregular heartbeat, skin rash, body sores and hives, increased susceptibility to disease, chronic fever and excessive perspiration, dry mouth and skin, damage to internal organs (especially brain, heart, lungs, liver, and kidneys), visual and auditory hallucinations, memory loss and mental confusion, and paranoid psychosis. Chronic use of methamphetamine depletes reserves of both dopamine and norepinephrine.

Drug Interactions: **(See Figure 12.)** *Synergistic:* Amphetamines taken with the class of antidepressants known as MAO (monoamine oxidase) inhibitors can result in death by hypertensive crisis. Antagonistic: Chronic amphetamine users often take marijuana and depressant drugs to combat adverse side effects and come down from a "crash."

Special Hazards: Amphetamine use interferes with concentration, impairs vision, and increases risk-taking; therefore, driving or operating machinery while under the influence can be dangerous. Abuse of amphetamines can lead to poor nutrition and insufficient sleep, thus lowering the body's immune system; combined with impaired judgment, chronic users are therefore at increased risk for HIV. Methamphetamines should not be used by people with glaucoma or who are diabetic.

Dependency Risk: Physical—high. Psychological—high.

Figure 12: *Drug Interactions*

Additive effects between drugs occur when one drug combined with another produces an effect that is like simple addition, expressed by the equation $1 + 1 = 2$.

Synergistic effects occur when one drug combined with another produces an effect that is greater than the sum of the effects of the two drugs alone, as in $1 + 1 = 3$.

Antagonistic effects occur when one drug combined with another produces an effect that is less than the sum of the effects of the drugs acting alone, as in $1 + 1 = 1$, or even $1 + 1 = 0$.

Barbiturates

Barbiturates are CNS depressants that are prescribed for a variety of therapeutic purposes, including sleep disorders, anxiety, and seizure disorders. People misuse barbiturates to help them relax, to induce a sense of euphoria, or to counteract the adverse effects of other drugs.

Barbiturates are generally white, bitter, water-soluble powders that are marketed in capsules and tablets of various colors and sizes. They are also available in suppositories and in liquid form that can be taken orally or by injection.

Once thought to be safe, barbiturates were popular medical drugs in the first half of the 1900s. However, widespread reports of abuse led physicians and consumers to question the usefulness of the drugs. The federal government has increased its control over their prescription and administration, and made nonmedical use illegal. Since the 1960s their medical use has been largely superseded by the benzodiazepine tranquilizers (such as Valium) and other sedatives/hypnotics. These drugs were developed as safer alternatives for treating anxiety and sleep disorders.

Though more than 2,500 barbiturate compounds exist, only a dozen of these are currently prescribed. Some well-known barbiturate compounds include *amobarbital* (Amytal), *butabarbital* (Butisol), *pentobarbital* (Nembutal), *phenobarbital* (Luminal), *secobarbital* (Seconal), *thiopental* (Pentothal), and *secobarbital-amobarbital combinations* (Tuinal). Barbiturates vary in composition and effects. Methaqualone is a CNS depressant that, like the tranquilizers, was promoted in the 1960s as a safer alternative to barbiturates. It was found to have a high liability for abuse, however, and was banned by Congress in 1984. It is still used illicitly by some people.

Barbiturates have been classified into three groups, based on the duration of their "half-life" (the time it takes for 50% of the drug to be eliminated from the body:

- Ultrashort-acting barbiturates are administered intravenously for induction of anesthesia both before and during surgery. Example: thiopental has a half-life of 11–15 hours.
- Short- and intermediate-acting barbiturates are prescribed for daytime sedation and sleep induction. Examples: secobarbital has a half-life of 19–34 hours, and amobarbital has a half-life of 8–42 hours.
- Long-acting barbiturates are also used for daytime sedation and induction of sleep, as well as to control epileptic seizures. Example: phenobarbital has a half-life of 24–140 hours.

Street Names: Blues, blue heavens, blue birds, blue angels, blue devils, amies (amobarbital, or Amytal). Yellow jackets, yellow dolls, yellow bullets, nembies (pentobarbital, or Nembutal). Purple hearts or phennies (phenobarbital). Reds, red dolls, red birds, red bullets, red devils, Mexican reds, seccies (secobarbital, or Seconal). Rainbows, reds and blues, tuies, tootsies, double trouble (secobarbital-amobarbital combinations, or Tuinal).

Short-Term Effects: Low doses produce muscular relaxation, a sense of tranquility, mild euphoria, dizziness, lethargy, drowsiness, mild incoordination, mild impairment of thinking and short-term memory; mild release of emotional inhibition, exacerbation of preexisting pain, and nausea, vomiting, or stomach pain. Moderate doses produce oversedation, confusion, slurred speech, confused sensory impressions (e.g., disturbed vision), slight drop in blood pressure and heart rate, slight respiratory depression, and induced sleep. High doses produce slow, shallow, and irregular breathing; constriction of pupils, followed by unchanging dilation; impaired reflexes; low body temperature; very low blood pressure; weak pulse; and coma.

Long-Term Effects: Chronic fatigue, slurred speech, incoordination, visual disturbances, vertigo (extreme dizziness), slower reflexes, reduced sex drive and impotence, menstrual irregularities, and certain respiratory disorders. Chronic use of high doses can produce a state of chronic inebriation, coupled with some or all of the following: impaired memory, judgment, and thinking; hostility, depression, and mood swings; reduced attention span; and exacerbation of preexisting emotional disorders, which may lead to paranoia or suicidal thinking.

Drug Interactions: *Additive:* Barbiturates can intensify the high from weak street heroin or supplement a heroin dose to which the abuser has become tolerant. Combining barbiturates with other CNS depressants, especially alcohol, can be deadly. MAO inhibitors can prolong the effects of barbiturates. *Synergistic:* Antihistamines can potentiate the effects of barbiturates, causing respiratory weakness. *Antagonistic:* Abusers of stimulants often take barbiturates to reduce severe agitation and sleeplessness. Because barbiturates increase metabolic breakdown, they decrease the effectiveness of tricyclic antidepressants, oral contraceptives, and metronidazole (or Flagyl, used in the treatment of many sexually transmitted infections), as well as increase their side effects.

Special Hazards: Barbiturates can pass through the placenta and harm the developing fetus, resulting in birth defects. Barbiturates impair judgment, vision, and reflexes, thus interfering with a person's ability to operate any vehicle.

Dependency Risk: Psychological—high. Physical—high.

Caffeine

Caffeine is the most widely consumed drug in western society. It is a CNS stimulant commonly found in coffee, tea, cola and some other soft drinks, cocoa, chocolate, and the South American beverage known as yerba mate. It is also found in several prescription and nonprescription medications, including analgesics, cold and allergy remedies, diet pills, and over-the-counter stimulants. Another source of caffeine is street drugs misrepresented as another drug (e.g., amphetamines).

Pure caffeine is a white, crystalline substance that is extracted from the seeds, leaves, and fruits or more than sixty plant species found throughout the world. The amount of caffeine in a cup of coffee or tea depends on the brewing method, the amount of beans or leaves used, the brewing time, and the plant species the beans or leaves come from. Caffeine content in coffee ranges from 70–150 mg. per six-ounce cup, and from 25–75 mg. per six-ounce serving of tea. A 12-oz. can of Coca-Cola contains 45 mg. of caffeine, while one ounce of baking or sweet chocolate has 20–35 mg. An OTC stimulant such as No-Doz (used by many high school and college students to stay awake during late-night studying) contains 100–200 mg. of caffeine in each tablet.

Caffeine produces effects that vary considerably from one individual to another. While many people use caffeine because it makes them feel particularly alert or energetic, others find that the drug makes them jittery. Children and older adults are more sensitive to the effects of caffeine than younger adults.

When a person drinks coffee, 99% of the caffeine ingested is absorbed and distributed to all the body's tissues and organs. Peak blood levels of the drug are attained in 15–45 minutes; the drug effects begin 15–30 minutes after ingestion. Caffeine is metabolized primarily in the liver. Only 3%–6% of ingested caffeine is excreted unchanged. The rates of metabolism and clearance vary by individual. Clearance is slower in individuals who are pregnant, take oral contraceptives, or who have liver disease. The clearance rate is affected by other drugs the individual may be taking; for example, smoking increases clearance.

Many coffee or soda drinkers become tolerant to some of caffeine's stimulant effects after a few days of regular use. Regular use of coffee also leads to dependence—a craving for the drugs' effects. A habitual coffee drinker may need a cup or two in the morning to "get going." People who are dependent on caffeine experience withdrawal when deprived of the drug; these symptoms include headache, drowsiness and lethargy, yawning, irritability and nervousness, depression, and nausea.

Street Names: N/A.

Short-Term Effects: A regular coffee drinker might feel pleasantly energetic after a cup or two of the beverage (about 125 mg. caffeine per cup), while an infrequent coffee drinker might feel nervous and restless. Use of caffeine often causes alterations in mood and sleep patterns, particularly for infrequent users. If consumed

before bedtime, caffeine can delay the onset of sleep, shorten sleep time, reduce the depth of sleep, and increase the amount of dream (REM) sleep early in the night. Other short-term effects may include increases in general metabolism, body temperature, peripheral blood flow (except in the brain, where it constricts blood flow), production of urine (a diuretic effect), blood pressure, blood sugar levels, and stomach acid secretion. Caffeine may also impair the action of the sphincter muscle in the esophagus, resulting in heartburn. Some studies indicate that use of caffeine aggravates symptoms of premenstrual syndrome (PMS).

As little as 32 mg. of caffeine can shorten reaction time to visual and auditory stimuli. Caffeine has also been found to enhance the performance of athletes in endurance activities by increasing fatty acid metabolism, masking fatigue, and increasing the force of skeletomuscular contraction. Claims that caffeine can improve intellectual capacity, short-term memory, numerical reasoning, or verbal fluency have not been substantiated.

High doses of caffeine (600 mg. or more for an experienced user) can cause an intensification of lower-dose effects, as well as irritability, restlessness, tremor, insomnia, rapid and irregular heartbeat, nausea, and a mild form of delirium. Overdose rarely occurs, but may result in seizures and death from respiratory failure. These toxic effects can be blocked by barbiturates or narcotics, which are CNS depressants.

Long-Term Effects: Daily use of low to moderate doses of caffeine (up to 300 mg., or about two cups of coffee) does not generally produce adverse effects in healthy adults. However, heavy use (600 mg. or more daily) can result in chronic sleep problems, anxiety, restlessness, depression, gastrointestinal irritation, and abnormally rapid and irregular heartbeat.

Regular use of extremely high doses of caffeine (1,000 mg. or more) may lead to a syndrome called "caffeinism," marked by an intensification of the symptoms of heavy use. Other symptoms may include headache, abnormally heavy breathing, tremors and muscle twitches, ringing in the ears, and excessive sensitivity to pain, touch, or other stimuli.

There have been reports of increased incidence of heart attacks and certain cancers, particularly pancreatic cancer, among heavy coffee drinkers. These studies have not been confirmed, however; because many heavy coffee drinkers also smoke cigarettes, the results may be confounded. Caffeine consumption has also been associated with the incidence of breast cysts in some women. While caffeine may not cause such disorders as ulcers and diabetes, it does appear to aggravate existing problems.

Drug Interactions: *Additive:* It may be risky to mix caffeine with another stimulant, such as pseudoephedrine or phenylpropanolamine (PPA), which are ingredients in some oral decongestant preparations and weight loss products. Caffeine is combined with aspirin or ergot alkaloid in many OTC products. Because caffeine constricts blood vessels in the brain, it aids in the relief of migraines. *Antagonistic:* Contrary to popular belief, caffeine will not counteract the effects of alcohol. Some nonprescription cough and cold remedies contain caffeine to counteract the drowsiness caused by antihistamines.

Special Hazards: Low to moderate doses of caffeine may help a driver stay alert. Caffeine's effect on a fetus, or on the body's immune response is unclear.

Dependency Risk: Psychological—high. Physical—moderate.

Cannabis (Marijuana)

Cannabis is the name for a group of drugs prepared from the Asian Indian hemp plant, *Cannabis sativa L.* The most common of these drugs in the US is marijuana. Marijuana consists of the leaves and flowering tops of both male and female plants. Users most commonly smoke it, either as a cigarette or in a pipe or other paraphernalia. Users sometimes ingest marijuana by adding it to certain foods, including brownies. Hashish (often known simply as "hash") is the unadulterated resin that is scraped from the flowering tops of cultivated female hemp plants. The resin is often pressed into cakes or slabs. Users most often smoke hash.

Cannabis contains more than four hundred chemicals, including sixty that are called cannabinoids. Cannabinoids are found only in the cannabis plant. The chemical in cannabis with the greatest mind-altering effect is THC (delta-9-tetrahydrocannabinol). A synthetic cannabinoid, dronabinol (brand name Marinol) is sometimes prescribed by physicians to treat vomiting and nausea caused by chemotherapy. Substances sold as THC on the street usually turn out to be hallucinogens, PCP (phencyclidine), or chemical relatives. Tests of confiscated street marijuana

around the country have shown little adulteration by other drugs. Occasionally, however, marijuana leaves are soaked in formaldehyde, which is toxic.

The average potency of marijuana confiscated in the US has increased since the 1970s. Confiscated samples now average 3.5% THC. One common form of marijuana, called sinsemilla, comes from a female plant that has been kept unfertilized. The plant produces more flowers, more resin, and more THC. Confiscated samples of sinsemilla usually contain 6.5%–12% THC. The user cannot determine the potency of marijuana by its appearance or aroma. Hashish is usually more potent than marijuana, containing 3%–15% THC. Hash oil, a highly refined distillate of cannabis, may contain up to 70% THC.

Cannabis's effects depend on the potency, dosage, and method of administration. The dosage, in turn, depends on how deeply the user inhales and the length of intervals between puffs. Its effects also depend on characteristics of the user and setting; a person's mood and expectations can influence their response to the drug, as can when and where it is used. Age is an important factor; youth are more susceptible to some effects because they are still developing physically, mentally, and emotionally. Tolerance—the loss of sensitivity to the drug's psychoactive effects—is also important.

People can become tolerant to the effects of cannabis after long-term heavy use; they will need a stronger dose to achieve the same effects. This tolerance decreases after several days of abstinence. Reverse-tolerance (also known as sensitization)—in which a smaller dose can produce the same effects—may occur among some regular users. This effect may result from psychological acclimation to the drug or more efficient smoking. The use of marijuana does not necessarily lead to the use of stronger drugs. However, it is highly correlated with the use of other drugs, especially alcohol and tobacco.

The high from one joint usually lasts 2–3 hours. If the drug is ingested, the effects can last up to 24 hours. Inexperienced users may feel the effects more intensely. Some first-time users, however, report almost no effects at all. Cannabinoids remain in the body, stored in fatty tissues, for several weeks after use. Cannabinoids can be detected in the urine up to 77 days after a user stops.

On the street, the combination of cannabis and PCP is called "supergrass" or "killer weed." Cannabis and opium together are called "O.J." Cannabis and heroin are referred to as an "atom bomb."

Street Names: Grass, pot, weed, MJ, Mary Jane, doobie, dope, ace, bhang, jive, sativa, ganja, reefer, tea, and Thai sticks. Many names are associated with the supposed place of origin, such as Acapulco or Columbian Gold, Jamaican, and Panama Red. A "joint" is a marijuana cigarette. A "roach" is the butt of a joint.

Short-Term Effects: Effects are so unpredictable; users should be aware of possible adverse reactions. Low to moderate doses can produce feelings of well-being, relaxation, and drowsiness; panic and anxiety; or exhilaration, arousal, and enhanced sexuality. Perceptions of time and distance may be distorted. Visual, auditory, and tactile sensations may be enhanced. Users tend to laugh and talk more than usual. Cannabis can impair speech, thinking, short-term memory, physical coordination, and balance; interfere with judgment, concentration, attention span, and overall intellectual performance; or cause delusions, hallucination, or acute psychosis in some cases. Cannabis can also cause increased heart rate, reddening of the eyes and reduction of ocular pressure, dampened sexual response, dryness of the mouth and throat, increased body temperature, a slight drop in blood pressure when moving from sitting to standing position, increase hunger, bursts of spontaneous laughter, and drowsiness. At higher doses, adverse reactions are more likely, and they are more likely in those who are anxious, depressed, under stress, or borderline schizophrenic before using the drug. It can also precipitate seizures in people with epilepsy.

Long-Term Effects: Heavy, extended use can cause physical and psychological damage. Smoking the drug can lead to upper respiratory problems, sore throats, and bronchitis; a marijuana cigarette contains twice as much tar as a tobacco cigarette. In addition, marijuana smoke is usually unfiltered, inhaled deeply, and held in the lungs for longer periods, so the user gets almost four times as much tar from smoking marijuana as from tobacco. Marijuana tar also contains higher concentrations of some carcinogens (cancer-causing chemicals), increasing the risk of lung damage and cancer. Memory and concentration impairments are often seen in chronic heavy users, although these effects generally disappear after several weeks of discontinued use. Some animal studies suggest that chronic heavy cannabis use may cause brain damage.

Some researchers believe that regular use of cannabis, particularly among young people, leads to *amotivational syndrome,* marked by a loss of drive, energy, and motivation; moodiness and inability to handle frustration, as well as an increase in passivity, sluggishness, and withdrawal. Consistent features of this syndrome include apathy, loss of ambition and effectiveness, diminished ability to carry out long-term plans, difficulty in concentration, decline in school/work performance, and problem behavior in relationships with parents/teachers/employers. Youthful users who fit this syndrome develop a lifestyle revolving around procurement and use of marijuana at the expense of other activities.

Drug Interactions: Additive: THC increases the effects of depressants. *Synergistic:* Cannabis combined with alcohol creates greater impairment of coordination and reaction time. Cannabis combined with sedatives and opiates can also cause anxiety and hallucinations. Increased heart rate and blood pressure have been noted when amphetamines are combined with cannabis. *Antagonistic:* Cannabis has unpredictable effects when combined with stimulants.

Special Hazards: Because it leads to impaired judgment, dizziness and/or drowsiness, slower reaction time, poor control of speed and inaccurate reading of signs, cannabis interferes with the ability to operate a vehicle or other machinery safely. Preliminary research shows that THC can accumulate in reproductive tissues before and during pregnancy and pass through the placenta—resulting in chromosomal damage, miscarriage, premature birth, lower birth weight, and birth defects. Animal studies have shown THC lowers the immune response, thus increasing the susceptibility to certain viruses. Human studies indicate that cannabis interferes with the T-lymphocyte function, which plays a major role in resistance to viruses. Because it impairs reasoning and judgment, cannabis use reduces the likelihood of practicing safer sex.

Dependency Risk: Psychological—moderate.

Cocaine/Crack Cocaine

Cocaine is a powerful CNS stimulant derived from the Erythroxylon coca bush (not to be confused with the cacao plant, which produces cacao), grown in mountainous regions of South America. Cocaine hydrochloride is chemically a salt produced from coca paste (cocaine sulfate). Coca paste is the first product extracted from the coca bush leaf. Very soluble in water, cocaine is an odorless, white crystalline substance in powder or lump form. When sold on the streets, cocaine is often diluted with other white powders, such as cornstarch, baby laxatives (mannitol), sugars (lactose, inositol), local anesthetics (lidocaine, benzocaine), or other CNS stimulants (ephedrine, caffeine, phenylpropanolamine).

Users commonly sniff the powder through the nose (known as "snorting") or dissolve and inject it intravenously ("shooting"). Users also frequently smoke cocaine ("freebase"). Making freebase involves converting the powdered cocaine hydrochloride into a more volatile form. This is done by heating the drug with flammable solvents such as ether or lighter fluid. Users then smoke the cocaine in a pipe or mix it with tobacco or marijuana.

Cocaine powder may also be converted into a freebase form known as "crack" or "rock." The process involves heating cocaine hydrochloride powder with ammonia or baking soda (sodium bicarbonate) and water to remove the hydrochloride and some impurities. The resulting powder is pressed into chunks or "rocks" and smoked in a two-chambered glass pipe. The drug is burned in the top section; as the user inhales, the smoke is cooled and filtered through water in the lower chamber. Sodium bicarbonate remaining in the final product may cause the crackling sound the drug makes when heated. Crack is absorbed immediately and enters the brain within a few seconds, producing an intense "rush" or sense of euphoria that wears off in 10–15 minutes, followed by a "crash." Because of its potency and short-lived "high," crack is extremely addictive.

Effects of cocaine depend on several factors, including the dose, how the drug is taken, or whether the user has developed tolerance or sensitization to the drug. Depending on the route of administration, the drug's effects begin within a few seconds and diminish within 10–40 minutes.

Freebased cocaine produces more intense effects almost instantaneously. Effects last about 30–90 seconds, with an "afterglow" that may last 10 minutes or more. Usually, when the "afterglow" disappears, users crave more of the drug to avoid the acute feelings of anxiety and confusion that rapidly follow. Hence, the potential for addiction to freebased cocaine is higher. Users often binge on the drug, readministering it every 10–15 minutes over a period of several hours. In addition, those who heat highly flammable solvents to make freebase are also at great risk for fire and subsequent burns.

Cocaine injected in combination with heroin is called a "speedball." Crack smoked in combination with heroin is called "parachute," "moonrock," and "50-50." These drug combinations increase the risk of toxicity, overdose, and death.

Street Names: Coke, "C," toot, cola, nose, snow, flake, white, gold dust, leaf, pearl, stardust, blow. Crack is one street name for a form of freebased cocaine; it takes its name from the crackling sound made when the drug is heated. Other street names for crack include rocks, roxanne, ready-rock, gravel, French-fries, or teeth (3" sticks with ridges); purple crack or space base (crack doused with PCP); geek, cav, fry daddy, grimmie or primo (combination of marijuana and crack); and caviar or cocktail (cigarette laced with crack).

Short-Term Effects: At low doses, cocaine produces a short-lived "rush" or sense of euphoria—sometimes compared to the feelings of a sexual orgasm. The rush is usually accompanied by a longer-lived "high" marked by feelings of enhanced energy, mental alertness, increased self-esteem, heightened sensory awareness, greater sociability, motor activity, and arousal. Cocaine reduces the perceived need for food and sleep, and increases heart rate, blood pressure, respiratory function, and body temperature. Cocaine can also alter heart rhythm, dilate pupils, and produce sweating, pallor, restlessness, and excitement.

High doses of cocaine produce more intense euphoria and can cause a variety of adverse reactions, including bizarre and violent behavior; extreme anxiety and restlessness; twitches, tremors, spasms, and loss of coordination; hallucinations and delusions; and chest pain and nausea. High doses of cocaine can also produce seizures, respiratory arrest, cardiac arrest, and high fever, all of which can result in death. Death from cocaine use is not extremely common, however, because illicit cocaine is usually diluted with other less-toxic materials. However, even small doses (one gram or less) can be dangerous or fatal for persons with heart conditions, epilepsy, or high blood pressure. Lung damage, seizures, and overdose are more likely to occur when freebasing cocaine.

Binges are often marked by extreme alertness and watchfulness, disinhibition, impaired judgment, feelings of grandiosity, impulsiveness, compulsively repeated acts, hypersexuality, and atypical sexual behavior. Binges frequently lead to anxiety, irritability, panic, and paranoid psychosis—some users may attempt suicide. After a binge, a user will be extremely exhausted and crave sleep; some users turn to depressant drugs at this point to reduce any lingering agitation and induce sleep. After several hours, the user enters withdrawal, marked by decreased energy, limited interest in surroundings, and limited ability to experience pleasure—feelings that increase over the next 1–4 days, eventually returning to normal. Memories of the euphoria produced by the drug may result in strong cravings for another binge after weeks, months, or years of abstinence.

Long-Term Effects: Impotence in male users, loss of appetite and weight, dehydration, constipation, rapid tooth decay, and difficulty urinating. When snorted, cocaine can damage nose and nostrils, as well as result in stuffiness and runny nose, eczema around the nostrils, tissue deterioration inside the nose, and perforation of the nasal septum (the cartilage dividing the nostril). Users of injected cocaine are at increased risk of overdose and infections and disease from unsterile needles. Those who freebase are at higher risk for significant, long-term damage to their lungs, chronic sore throat, and hoarseness. Extended use of cocaine can lead to high blood pressure, seizures, damage to lungs, difficulty breathing, and heart attacks. Cocaine also produces significant long-term psychological damage; user may develop cocaine psychosis—rather than feeling euphoric, the user experiences extreme excitability, restlessness, anxiety, insomnia, hallucinations, and paranoia, as well as a very uncomfortable sensation that feels like bugs crawling under the skin. The chronic user is likely to withdraw from others, focusing on the internal sensations caused by the drug. Social effects of cocaine include family problems, crime and law-enforcement problems, work-related problems, financial difficulties, violence, and community breakdown.

Drug Interactions: Additive: Cocaine mixed with mild stimulants such as caffeine or OTC products such as diet pills and or antihistamines produces an enhanced CNS-stimulant effect. *Synergistic:* Taking cocaine with certain psychotropic drugs (e.g., MAO inhibitors and other antidepressants) can result in stroke or heart attack from extremely high blood pressure. *Antagonistic:* Some users combine cocaine with alcohol or sedatives to cushion the "crash"—the feelings of depression and agitation as the effects of cocaine wear off. Research indicates that alcohol and cocaine produce both additive and antagonistic effects, depending on the respective doses of each drug.

Special Hazards: Low doses of cocaine have been found to enhance performance on driving tests, but at higher doses, the drug simply masks fatigue. Because it results in impaired coordination and vision, greater risk taking and confusion, bingeing on cocaine can impair the ability to operate a vehicle safely. Use of cocaine impairs the immune system, thus increasing risk for infections and disease; similarly, users who intravenously inject the drug are at risk for HIV infection from contaminated needles. Cocaine that crosses the placenta can cause problems for the developing fetus, including premature birth, low birth weight, CNS dysfunction, retarded growth, underdeveloped organs or systems, an increased risk for Sudden Infant Death Syndrome (SIDS), and withdrawal symptoms for up to six months following birth.

Dependency Risk: Psychological—high. Physical—moderate (especially crack).

Designer Drugs

Designer drugs, also known as analogs, are synthetic substances related to illegal drugs in their chemical formula and psychoactive effects. Underground chemists began to synthesize most of these drugs in the late 1970s in an attempt to circumvent existing drug laws. Although molecular structures of these preparations differ only slightly from those of the drugs they mimic, the new drugs were legal until the mid-1980s. In 1986 federal drug laws were rewritten to classify any analogs of a controlled substance.

Designer drugs can be dangerous because of their direct effects and because of the impurities and unknown byproducts resulting from their preparation. In addition, these drugs can be several hundred times more potent than the drugs they are designed to mimic. This can result in accidental overdose even for sophisticated users.

There are currently two major categories of designer drugs: the *opiate analogs* (specifically those related to fentanyl and meperidine), and the *hallucinogenic amphetamine analogs* (phenylethylamines that are structurally similar to methamphetamine but with the psychoactive properties of mescaline). The *fentanyl* analogs include: (1) alpha-methylfentanyl (AMF)—the first substance to be called a designer drug; (2) 3-methyl fentanyl; (3) parafluoro fentanyl; and (4) several others. These analogs are fast-acting but short-lasting.

Analogs of *meperidine* include: (1) 1-methyl-4-propionoxy-piperidine (MPPP)—a potent chemical cousin of the synthetic narcotic analgesic known as Demerol, and (2) 1-(2-phenylethyl)-4-acetyloxypiperidine (PEPAP).

Analogs of the hallucinogenic amphetamine group include: (1) 3,4-methylenedioxy-methamphetamine (MDMA); (2) 3,4-methylenedioxy-ethamphetamine (MDEA); and (3) 1-[1,3-benzodioxol-5-y1]-2-butanamine (MBDB).

Phencyclidine (PCP) analogs are sometimes considered as a third category, although they are also groups with the hallucinogens as PCP itself once was. Analogs of PCP include cyclohexamine (PCE).

All of the designer drugs may appear as a white powder that looks like pure heroin. The powders may be inhaled through the nose (snorted), smoked, or dissolved and injected. The hallucinogenic amphetamine analogs are usually taken orally, either in the form of a tablet or capsule or dissolved in liquid. New synthetic analogs of known psychoactive drugs are developed every year.

Street Names: Because designer drugs have been difficult to document, little is known about their street names. Some of the most well-known include China White, Persian white, and Mexican brown (for AMF); "new heroin" (for MPPP); Ecstasy, XTC, Adam, Essence, Decadence, and M & M (for MDMA); Eve (for MDEA); and rocket fuel (for PCE).

Short-Term Effects: *Fentanyl analogs*—a typical dose may produce the following effects: euphoria, mental confusion, a feeling of warmth, dry mouth, dizziness, drowsiness, constriction of the pupils, constipation and nausea, as well as rigidity of the muscles (especially those involved in breathing), which can lead to respiratory failure. Overdose can cause coma and death by respiratory depression. AMF has caused a number of deaths by overdose.

Meperidine analogs—a low dose can cause the following effects, lasting up to three hours: euphoria, disorientation, mild mental confusion, dizziness, drowsiness, visual disturbances, and slight respiratory depression. The most common adverse side effects of using MPPP are caused by the presence of MPTP of MPTP (1-methyl-4-phenyl-1,2,3,6-tetrahydropyridine)—a toxic byproduct in the synthesis of MPPP that destroys nerve cells in the brain. Exposure to MPTP can result in symptoms clinically similar to Parkinson's disease, including slowed voluntary muscle functioning, difficulty speaking or swallowing, progressive muscle rigidity, flexed posture, tremor, drooling, and flattened facial expression.

PEPAP has been found to be contaminated with a byproduct identified as PEPTP, creating symptoms of another neurodegenerative disease called Huntington's chorea, which is associated with spasmodic movements of the limbs and facial muscles and progressive deterioration of brain tissue, resulting in loss of mental function.

Higher doses of MDMA and other similar analogs may cause confusion, anxiety, depression, nausea, dilated pupils and blurred vision, chills and sweating, fainting, increased blood pressure, pulse and body temperature, and extreme physical fatigue lasting up to two days.

PCP analogs—have stimulant, depressant, and hallucinogenic effects. Low dose effects include mental confusion, slurred speech, drowsiness, general numbness of the extremities, muscle stiffness and incoordination, sweating and flushing, increased heart rate, and euphoria. High doses of PCE reduce sensitivity to pain and cause perceptual distortions, mood swings, and bizarre and violent behavior. Toxic effects may include seizures, respiratory depression, fever, and brain hemorrhage resulting from a sudden rise in blood pressure. A few deaths have been attributed directly to PCE overdose.

Long-Term Effects: There is little known about the direct health effects of long-term use of opiates, hallucinogenic amphetamines, or PCP analogs.

Drug Interactions: Additive: Opiate users exposed to fentanyl analogs may experience a more potent effect. Synergistic: Opiate analogs may increase the depressant effects of alcohol. MPPP should never be taken with MAO inhibitors, as a rapid increase in blood pressure can cause heart attack or stroke.

Special Hazards: It is dangerous to drive a vehicle or operate other machinery while under the influence of designer drugs, as they interfere with thought and concentration, produce visual distortions, and perceptual distortions of time and distance. Distractions and drowsiness caused by the drugs can also exacerbate the danger. Little is known about the effects of designer drugs on the developing fetus. Use of designer drugs can increase an individual's chances of being exposed to HIV (impaired judgment, unsterile needles, etc.).

Dependency Risk: Psychological—moderate to high. Physical—high.

GHB

GHB, or gamma-hydroxybutyrate, is a normal, low-toxicity component of mammalian metabolism, and is believed to be a neurotransmitter. During the 1980s GHB was widely available over the counter in health-food stores, purchased largely by body-builders for its ability to stimulate growth hormone release that aids in fat reduction and muscle building. In recent years, GHB has gained in popularity among high school and college students as a recreational drug offering a pleasant, alcohol-like, hangover-free "high" with potent prosexual effects (Morgenthaler and Joy 1994).

GHB temporarily inhibits the release of dopamine in the brain, possibly causing increased dopamine storage and later increased dopamine release when the GHB influence wears off. This effect could account for the middle-of-the-night wakings common with use of higher GHB doses, and the general feelings of increased well-being, alertness, and arousal the next day (Chin and Kreutzer 1992).

GHB also stimulates pituitary growth hormone release by a mechanism that is unknown. Because it induces remarkable hypotonia (muscle relaxation), it has gained popularity in France and Italy as an aid to childbirth; it causes more rapid dilation of the cervix, as well as greater intensity and frequency of uterine contractions.

The amount of GHB required for a given level of effect will vary from person to person; however, because small increases in the amount ingested lead to significant intensification of the effect, overdosing can frequently occur. Tolerance to GHB does not develop.

Street Names. "Grievous bodily harm."

Short-Term Effects: Most users find that GHB induces a pleasant state of relaxation and tranquility. Frequent effects are placidity, sensuality, mild euphoria, and a tendency to verbalize. Anxieties and inhibitions tend to dissolve into a feeling of emotional warmth, well-being, and pleasant drowsiness. The "morning after" effects of GHB lack the unpleasant or debilitating characteristics associated with alcohol and other relaxation-oriented drugs. In fact, many users report feeling particularly refreshed, even energized, the next day. The effects can generally be felt within 5–20 minutes after ingestion and usually last no more than one and a half to three hours.

The effects of GHB are very dose-dependent. Higher levels feature greater giddiness, silliness, and interference with, mobility, and verbal coherence, and maybe even dizziness, nausea, and vomiting. Even higher doses usually induce sleep or loss of consciousness. At very high doses, cardiac and respiratory depression can occur.

Anesthetic (large) doses of GHB are accompanied by a small increase in blood sugar levels and a significant decrease in cholesterol. Respiration becomes slower and deeper. Blood pressure may rise or fall slightly, or remain stable, but a moderate bradycardia (slowing of the heart) is consistent. A slight drop in body temperature also occurs.

Four main prosexual properties of GHB have been identified: (1) disinhibition; (2) heightening of the sense of touch (tactility); (3) enhancement of male erectile capacity; and (4) increased intensity of orgasm. Most users find that 0.75–1.5 grams is suitable for prosexual purposes, while 2.5 grams is sufficient to induce sleep.

Drug Interactions: GHB should not be combined with benzodiazepines ("minor tranquilizers" such as Valium or Xanax), phenothiazines ("major tranquilizers" such as Thorazine), various painkillers (barbiturates and opiates), alcohol, anticonvulsants (phenobarbital), and many over-the-counter allergy and sleep remedies without direct medical supervision. GHB-related poisonings usually involve the simultaneous ingestion of one of these substances with the drug.

Special Hazards: Any dose can be deadly for individuals with epilepsy, severe cardiovascular disease, severe hypertension, or Cushing's syndrome.

Dependency Risk: Physical—none. Psychological—low to medium.

Hallucinogens

Hallucinogens are a chemically diverse group of drugs that alter mood, thought, perception, and brain function. Some of these drugs are synthetic; others are compounds extracted from plants and fungi. The best-known hallucinogen and the most potent psychoactive drug known is *LSD* (d-lysergic acid diethylamide), but the use of others dates back thousands of years. The three main classes of hallucinogens are

- **the LSD family**, including LSD, *LSA* (d-lysergic acid amide), psilocybin, and *DMT* (dimethyltryptamine)—all of which are natural alkaloids that can be produced in the laboratory;
- **the phenylethylamines**, including *mescaline,* elemicin, *MDA* (3,4-methylenedioxyamphetamine), *PMA* (paramethoxyamphetamine), *DOM,* or STP (4-methyl-2,5-dimethoxyamphetamine, *TMA* (trimethoxyamphetamine) and MDMA—of which only mescaline and elemicin are natural alkaloids; and
- **the atropinic drugs, or belladonna alkaloids**, including atropine, scopolamine, and hyoscyamine.

PCP and cannabis also have hallucinogenic properties.

Pure LSD is a white, odorless, crystalline powder. It is derived from ergot, a fungus that grows on rye and other grains. The standard dose is so small that the chemical must be mixed with or added to something else for handling. Street doses range from 40–700 micrograms. On the street LSD appears as tablets, capsules, and other solids, or liquids of different colors. Sometimes it is added to a sugar cube; a small, thin square of gelatin (called a "windowpane"); or a piece of blotting paper, which can be chewed to release the drug. LSD can be chewed to release the drug. LSD is usually taken orally, but it is also "snorted" through the nose or dissolved in water and injected.

Morning glory seeds contain LSA, which is chemically related to LSD but is only one-tenth as potent. Morning glory seeds, which are small and dark in color, can be purchased legally at garden supply stores. They are often treated with fungicide for planting or a chemical designed to induce nausea to prevent abuse. If eaten whole, untreated seeds of this plant usually pass through the digestive tract with little effect on the user. However, if the seed are ground or chewed, a dose of roughly 300 seeds produces effects equivalent to 200–300 micrograms of LSD.

Psilocybin is the active ingredient in certain species of mushrooms. In pure form, psilocybin is a white crystalline powder, it can be taken orally as a capsule containing a powder of any color; it can also be taken orally as a crude mushroom extract or as dried mushrooms. It can also be injected. Average doses range from 4–10 mg. of pure compound, although amounts of up to 60 mg. are not unusual.

DMT is a synthetic chemical that resembles psilocybin. It is usually used with marijuana. The marijuana leaves are soaked in a solution of DMT, then dried and smoked in a pipe or cigarette. DMT can also be made into tea.

Mescaline is found in the "buttons" or disk-like tops of the peyote or mescal cactus. The buttons are dried, then chopped or ground—sometimes placed in capsules. The drug is usually taken orally, but ground buttons can be smoked. Typical doses of mescaline range from 300–500 mg., equal to the amount found in 3–6 peyote buttons. A dose in this range will produce effects equivalent to those caused by 50–100 micrograms of LSD. Most street preparations sold as mescaline are impure—if they contain any of the drug at all; more often, they contain PCP or LSD.

The nutmeg plant contains elemicin, a chemical relative of mescaline. Nutmeg kernels can be eaten or powdered and sniffed. Because of the long, unpleasant hangover that follows elemicin intoxication, this drug is not frequently used.

MDA, which is chemically related to mescaline and the amphetamines, is synthesized as a white to light brown powder or as an amber liquid. MDA is usually taken orally, though it can be sniffed as a powder or dissolved and injected. A typical dose is 120 mg. MDMA, closely related chemically to MDA, is a rarely encountered drug.

Pure PMA is a white powder that is rarely found on the street. It has both hallucinogenic and CNS stimulant effects and is highly toxic. A typical dose of PMA is 50–75 mg. DOM (STP), a synthetic drug, occurs as a tasteless, odorless, white crystalline powder. It is also rarely encountered as a street drug any longer. TMA is a yellow or beige powder sometimes sold on the street as MDA or other hallucinogens. Like PMA, it is a synthetic hallucinogen in the amphetamine group.

The atropinic drugs also are not common street drugs; they are used medically. Hallucinogenic alkaloids are present in certain parts of many species of the potato family and in deadly nightshade. It is found in all plant parts of the jimson weed, which grows wild across the US. Usually the leaves or seeds ("berries") are eaten. As few as ten seeds can produce vivid hallucinations.

Hallucinogens produce changes in thought, perception, and emotions without serious side effects on the CNS. However, the short-term effects vary greatly from use to use and from one user to another. Factors affecting the drug experience include the dose, the setting, the user's personality and emotional state, as well as the user's attitudes, expectations, and previous experiences with hallucinogens.

People can rapidly become tolerant to the psychoactive effects of most hallucinogens; they will need higher doses to achieve the same effects. In the case of LSD, repeated doses over as little as three or four days can result in complete tolerance, in which the psychoactive effects no longer occur even at high doses. Sensitivity is restored after several days of abstinence. A pattern of episodic use that is called "weekend tripping" often develops.

Street Names: The street names for LSD are numerous to list; a few are acid, green or red dragon, white lightning, blue heaven, sugar cubes, microdots, barrels, windowpanes, blotters, California sunshine, mellow yellow, purple haze, Lucy in the Sky with Diamonds, contact lens, domes, flats, lids, tabs, wedges, and frogs. Street names for other hallucinogens include heavenly blues, flying saucers, pearly gates (LSA); magic or sacred mushrooms, shroom, noble princess of the waters, hombrecitos, las mujercitas (psilocybin); business man's lunch (DMT); button, cactus, electric adobe, moon, plants (mescaline); love drug (MDA); ecstasy, XTC, Adam, decadence, hug-drug (MDMA); death drug (PMA); and devil's weed, and locoweed (jimson weed).

Short-Term Effects: LSD is the most potent psychoactive drug known. A dose as small as 40 mcg. (microgram) can produce significant changes in perception, emotions, and thought. The drug is rapidly absorbed through the gastrointestinal tract and diffuses to all tissues, including the brain. LSD interferes with the normal action of 5-HT (5-hydroxytryptamine), a natural chemical messenger that acts on main sites in the body, especially neurons. The behavioral effects of LSD can be felt within 30 to 90 minutes of ingestion, peaking at two to four hours and gradually tapering off. Most effects subside within 6 to 12 hours. Physical effects of a typical dose of LSD include numbness, muscle weakness and twitching; rapid reflexes and impaired coordination; increased heart rate, blood pressure, and body temperature; tremors; dilation of pupils; reduced appetite; and nausea, vomiting, and abdominal discomfort. Other effects include distortions in vision, time, space, and body image. Users often report seeing visual patterns and shapes that they know are not real. True hallucinations, those that the user thinks are real, may occur at higher doses. The user may experience *synesthesia,* in which sensations seems to "cross over," giving the user the impression of hearing colors or seeing sounds. LSD impairs the ability to distinguish boundaries between objects and between self and surrounding objects, causing some users to panic. The user often has little control over thought and concentration.

A person can have a "bad trip," or adverse psychological reaction to LSD regardless of dose or past experiences with the drug. A bad trip, which may last a few minutes to several hours, may involve severe emotional depression, panic, or psychotic episodes. Previously existing fears may be exaggerated. A person experiencing a bad trip may feel helpless and out of control, and believe the experience will never end or that they will go crazy. Bad trips are often accompanied by dilated pupils, rapid heart rate, and fever. Bad trips are more likely if the user is in a hostile environment, rather than in a calm, familiar one. While frightening, a bad trip is rarely a medical emergency. Emotional support, reassurance, and a quiet environment in the company of one of two trusted adults is the best treatment. Those "talking down" a bad trip should remain calm and steady as the user may react negatively to fear. Avoid physical restraint, and reassure the user that the experience is a temporary drug reaction. Despite the potency of LSD, overdose is virtually unknown. However, there have been many deaths attributed to LSD-induced accidents and suicides.

Effects of other hallucinogens such as psilocybin, DMT, mescaline, elemicin, MDA, MDMA PMA, DOM (STP), and TMA vary according to dose, and can include:

- mental and physical relaxation
- fatigue
- sleeplessness
- detachment from surroundings
- visual, auditory, and tactile hallucinations and delirium
- panic, anxiety, and paranoia
- mild euphoria
- memory loss
- feelings of physical heaviness or, conversely, lightness
- dizziness and lightheadedness
- numbness of the tongue and lips

- shivering
- yawning
- facial flushing
- fever and excessive perspiration
- dilated pupils
- agitation
- muscle spasms
- nausea and vomiting
- increased heart rate, body temperature, and blood pressure
- seizures
- coma

Effects of DMT, DOM (STP), and mescaline resemble those of LSD, except that DMT has an immediate onset and mescaline has a delayed effect. Elemicin, MDA, and MDMA possess mild stimulant properties along with hallucinogenic ones. PMA is a strong CNS stimulant.

Low doses of atropinic drugs are used medically to reduce gastric secretions and secretions of the nose, mouth, and pharynx, to dilate pupils, slow heart rate, relax muscle spasms, suppress tremors, and induce sedation. At higher doses, all of these drugs have hallucinogenic and CNS stimulant effects that may last for twenty-four to forty-eight hours. Effects are similar to those listed above.

Long-Term Effects: Little information is available regarding the long-term effects of prolonged, chronic use of hallucinogens. Studies to determine the incidence of brain and chromosomal damage are inconclusive. An "amotivational syndrome" involving symptoms of apathy and listlessness has been correlated with long-term use of LSD. LSD can also precipitate severe psychotic episodes in a small number of users who do not have a history of mental illness. "Flashbacks," lasting only a few seconds or minutes or as long as several hours, happen when certain sensations of a drug experience (particularly visual distortions) recur spontaneously when the person is not under the influence of the drug. Flashbacks can be pleasant or frightening.

Drug Interactions: *Synergistic:* Amphetamines mixed with hallucinogens add a stimulant "rush," while sedatives/hypnotics are used for a quieter psychedelic experience. *Antagonistic:* Some toxic effects of MDA can be blocked by cocaine.

Special Hazards: Because these drugs interfere with thought and concentration, as well as produce visual, auditory, and tactile distortions and distortions of time and space, it is dangerous to drive a vehicle or operate machinery while under the influence of hallucinogens. Studies also indicate a higher incidence of spontaneous abortions and birth defects in offspring of women who regularly used LSD while pregnant.

Dependency Risk: Psychological—low to moderate. Physical—none.

Inhalants

Inhalants are a diverse group of chemicals that easily evaporate and can cause intoxication when their vapors are inhaled. Because many of them are household products that were never intended to be used as drugs, people often do not think of inhalants as drugs. Exceptions to this are local anesthetics, such as nitrous oxide and amyl nitrite (used in treatment of severe chest pain, or angina pectoris). Most inhalants are CNS depressants. Use of these drugs slows down many body functions and results in intoxication similar to that produced by alcohol. High doses can cause severe breathing failure and sudden death. Chronic abuse of some of these chemicals can lead to irreversible liver damage and other health problems. Inhalants fall into four main categories:

- ***Solvents*** are contained in model airplane glue, typewriter correction fluid, lacquer thinners, nail polish remover, lighter fluid, plastic cement, cleaning fluids, shoe polish, and gasoline. Users inhale their fumes. Primary psychoactive components include acetone, toluene, trichloromethane, ketone, and naphtha.
- ***Aerosols*** are propellant gases discharged from such products as hair sprays and spray deodorants, insecticides, medications, and paints. Psychoactive ingredients include hydrocarbons and methylene chloride, and fluorocarbons (including freon gas to a lesser extent). Most of these solvents and aerosols contain additives that are at least as toxic as the psychoactive solvents or gases themselves.
- ***Gases*** used for intoxication include nitrous oxide, ether, and chloroform. Nitrous oxide is frequently used in dentistry for its anesthetic and sedative effects. It is also used as an aerosol propellant in whipped cream. Ether is a volatile liquid; its fumes are inhaled. Chloroform can be very hazardous and is not commonly used as a drug of abuse.
- ***Other chemicals*** used as inhalants include the volatile liquids amyl nitrite and butyl nitrite. Amyl nitrite is a prescriptive drug used medically to dilate blood vessels. It was a popular drug of abuse until 1979, when it was made a prescription drug. Butyl nitrite, originally marketed as a locker room deodorizer, has taken its place as a recreational drug.

The vapors of liquid solvents can be sniffed directly from the container. Alternatively, liquid solvents may also be poured onto a rag and held over the mouth for inhalation. A popular method for using solvents involves emptying the product into a bag and holding its opening firmly over the mouth and nose for inhalation. The rebreathing of exhaled air causes an oxygen deficiency, which can intensify the intoxicating effect of the solvent. Use of a plastic bag is hazardous, though, because a user who vomits or passes out could suffocate. The practice of heating a flammable solvent to concentrate the vapors is also hazardous. Less common routes of administration involve use of perfume atomizers, mixing the solvent with an alcoholic beverage, or intravenous injection.

Some abusers of aerosols spray the commercial products directly into their mouths for inhalation. Most prefer to separate the propellant gas from other ingredients. There are a number of ways to do this. The pressurized container can be held and the valve pressed in such a way as to permit only to propellant to be released. This method is often used to get

nitrous oxide from pressurized cans of whipped cream. Some users filter the contents of the container through a cloth held firmly over the mouth and nose. Another method is to spray the contents into a bag or balloon for inhalation.

Amyl and butyl nitrite are translucent, yellow liquids that are dispensed in cloth-covered glass ampules. The ampule is broken or "popped" in the hand and the vapors inhaled immediately. Oral ingestion of amyl nitrite is rare.

Inhaled vapors generally enter the bloodstream rapidly. They are then distributed to many organs, especially those with a large blood circulation, such as the liver and brain. Most volatile hydrocarbons are absorbed quickly into the CNS, depressing many body functions, including breathing. Some volatile hydrocarbons are eliminated unchanged, primarily through the lungs. The odor of a solvent may remain on the user's breath for several hours after inhalation. This is a tell-tale sign for many sniffers.

People can become tolerant to the intoxicating effects of inhalants. They will need a stronger dose to achieve the same effects. Users of certain solvents can also develop sensitization (reverse tolerance) after chronic use. Some users binge on inhalants, taking in small amounts repeatedly in the course of a day.

Street Names: Glue, gas, and sniff. "Laughing gas" refers to nitrous oxide. "Poppers" refers to amyl or butyl nitrite. Amyl nitrite is also known as snapper, pearls, or amys. Butyl nitrite is often sold at drug paraphernalia shops, record shops, and bars under a variety of trade names used to advertise it as a "liquid aroma" or "liquid incense": Locker room, Rush, Bolt, Hardware, Quick Silver, Discorama, and Highball.

Short-Term Effects: Within seconds of ingestion, the user may experience a feeling of euphoria, which may be marked by lightheadedness, numbness, exhilaration, excitation, and sexual arousal. Inhalants cause intoxication similar to that of large doses of alcohol, involving giddiness, emotional disinhibition, muscle weakness, incoordination, slowed reflexes, and slurred speech. Inhalants may cause temporary sensory and perceptual distortion, or "pseudohallucinations." Some solvents and aerosols can cause true hallucinations. These distortions are often accompanied by delusions of grandeur and may lead to bizarre and reckless behavior, as well as fear and anxiety. Some people experience severe emotional depression when intoxicated by inhalants, occasionally to the point of attempting suicide. After sobering up, the user may not be able to remember any of the events that took place during the period of intoxication. Short-term physical effects of inhalant intoxication may include:

- rapid and/or irregular heartbeat
- decrease in blood pressure
- relaxation of sphincter muscles
- depressed respiratory rate
- sneezing and coughing
- increased salvation and thirst
- irritated eyes, nose, and mouth
- nausea and vomiting
- drowsiness
- visual disturbances
- headache

In addition to these effects, amyl and butyl nitrite cause flushing of the face and upper torso. Some abusers of nitrite report that the drugs enhance sexual performance and orgasm. However, this effect is unpredictable and often offset by unpleasant side effects, such as severe headache.

Long-Term Effects: There is building evidence that chronic exposure to aerosol paints and certain solvents (for both abusers and industrial workers) can cause brain damage, characterized by tremors, poor coordination, and difficulty walking. Long-term sniffing can also damage the lungs, liver, and kidneys. Chronic exposure to industrial solvents containing benzene, a suspected carcinogen, can lead to a reduction in the formation of blood cells in the bone marrow. Chromosomal abnormalities have also been found in youths who sniff glue and in industrial workers exposed to benzene and other solvents. Other physical effects that appear following chronic use of inhalants include fatigue, pallor, weight loss, and excessive thirst. Most of these long-term effects are reversible after drug use has stopped. However, cleaning fluid (trichloromethane) and aerosol sprays (especially those containing fluorocarbons) can cause permanent damage. People who abuse solvents and aerosols risk adverse health effects caused by other ingredients in commercial products. For example, toxic metals in spray paints may accumulate in the body; leaded gasoline is particularly hazardous because of the high toxicity of lead.

Drug Interactions: Synergistic: Combining inhalants with other CNS depressants such as heroin or alcohol can be deadly; the depression of the respiratory centers of the brain is greatly increased when these drugs are combined.

Special Hazards: Inhalants can impair the ability to drive a vehicle or operate machinery safely. It can be dangerous to use inhalants during pregnancy; animal studies indicate that solvents cross the placental barrier and cause birth defects—possibly resulting in microcephaly (small head size), CNS dysfunction, attention deficit and hyperactivity, growth retardation, facial abnormalities, and urinary tract disorders. These drugs are also believed to contaminate breast milk.

Studies have linked use of nitrite inhalants with the development of Kaposi's sarcoma in people infected with HIV. Use of inhalants can also impair the cognitive ability to practice safer sex.

Dependency Risk: Psychological—high.

Opiates/Narcotics

Opiates, or narcotic analgesics, are drugs that cause sedation and euphoria. Opiates stimulate the higher centers of the brain and slow down the activity of the CNS. The term "opiate" refers to natural drugs produced from Oriental poppy, such as opium, morphine, and codeine. There are also many semisynthetic opiates, including heroin (a chemically treated derivative of morphine), as well as wholly synthetic substitutes, called opioids, such as meperidine and methadone. Opiates are derived from the thick, white secretion found in the unripe seed pods of the opium poppy, *Papaver somniferum.* Opium contains many naturally occurring alkaloids, of which only morphine and codeine have psychoactive properties. Crude opium is a brown substance with a tar-like texture. It has an unpleasant odor and a bitter taste. Pure opium is smoked or eaten.

Morphine, which is isolated from crude opium, appears as white crystals, tablets or solutions to be smoked, sniffed, swallowed, or dissolved and injected.

Heroin, which is derived from morphine, is a fine crystalline powder, white in its pure form and dark brown when impurities are present. "Black tar" heroin (or "gumball") is a form of the drug that may resemble a tootsie roll or may also appear in powdered form. It originated in Mexico and is a relatively inexpensive form of heroin with a high level of purity. Although heroin can be swallowed, this is not preferred because it is rapidly destroyed in the liver. Heroin is often smoked with cigarettes and marijuana, and its effects are more potent than those of smoked opium. Inexperienced users inhale heroin through the nose ("snorting") or inject it under the skin ("skin popping"). Dependent users prefer intravenous injection ("mainlining") as the quickest means of attaining euphoria.

Codeine is available in capsules, tablets, cough remedies, and other solutions for oral or intravenous administration. Other opiates are also available in liquid, powder, tablet, or capsule form. **Methadone** appears as a solution that is taken orally in treatment programs or injected by dependent users who obtain it illegally.

Some forty opiate preparations are used by physicians for a variety of reasons. They are used as pain relievers for people with cancer, and as surgical anesthetics. They are known for their ability to reduce people's sensitivity and emotional response to pain. Those who take prescribed opiates report therapeutic effects ranging from less discomfort to complete analgesia. Opiates are also used in the treatment of diarrhea and dysentery to reduce stomach acidity, delay food digestion, and decrease the peristaltic waves of the large intestine (the motion that allows food to pass through the gastrointestinal tract). In addition, low doses of opiates (primarily codeine) are also used to help suppress certain types of cough. The active ingredients of these medications include morphine and codeine; semisynthetics such as oxycodone (Percodan) and hydromorphone (Dilaudid); and opioids such as meperidine (Demerol), propoxyphene (Darvon), pentazocine (Talwin), and methadone (Dolophine). Although therapeutic doses of these drugs are carefully measured to minimize side effects, opiates are often abused and are highly addictive.

Another class of opiates, called antagonists, counteracts the effects of these drugs; they are used to reverse respiratory depression and other effects of narcotic overdose. Levallorphan (Lorfan) and Naloxone (Narcan) are two of the most widely used antagonists. In a drug-dependent person, however, administration of an antagonist will stimulate withdrawal symptoms.

Opiate users rapidly become tolerant to many of the drug effects, including the euphoric, analgesic, sedative, and respiratory depressant effects. A regular user may increase the daily dose by a factor of 10 or more to experience the euphoria s/he seeks. Eventually, the user cannot achieve the pleasurable effects at any dose level but must continue taking the drug to avoid withdrawal.

Street Names: Street names for heroin include smack, horse, junk, dust, H, Harry, scat, scag, brown sugar, and black tar. Morphine is called M, morph, sweet Morpheus, god's drug, and Miss Emma. Codeine is known as schoolboy, and cough syrups containing narcotics are often called "juice." Heroin and cocaine or methamphetamine injected together is called a speedball, while an injection of heroin and a barbiturate is a goofball. Heroin smoked with crack is known as parachute, moonrock, and 50-50. Cannabis and opium smoked together is called O.J., while a "cigarette" of cannabis and heroin is called an atom bomb. Other street names include Demerol (doctors), Dilaudid (lords, dillies), Talwin (butterballs, bananas), Darvon (yellow football), and methadone (dollies, methadose, biscuits).

Short-Term Effects: The onset of effects depends on the drug taken and the route of administration. Intravenous injection produces the most rapid onset and is the preferred route of abusers because it produces an intense "rush." Although many opiates lose some potency when taken orally, those manufactured as legal pharmaceuticals have very strong effects. In the body, opiates bind to receptor sites on the neurons (nerve cells), interacting with chemically related, naturally occurring, or "endogenous," opiates produced by brain chemicals. These endogenous opiates were first called "enkephalins" and then "endorphins," a contraction of endogenous morphine.

Endorphins are produced in the pituitary gland and elsewhere in the body. They are constantly released into the bloodstream. They attach to the millions of opiate receptor sites and stimulate the electrochemical or hormonal messages that flow across the nerve cells and affect the perception of and emotional response to pain and stress. Endorphins regulate the intake of food and water and many other physiological functions. Endorphins also appear to influence mood and serve as the reward pathway of the brain. Disruption of their function has been associated with certain psychiatric disorders. By acting on the same receptors as endorphins, opiate drugs enhance pleasurable effects and negate painful ones, thereby reinforcing the psychoactive properties of the drugs.

Patients who take therapeutic doses of medically prescribed opiates sometimes report that they feel warm and their extremities feel "heavy." Higher doses can produce additional effects, including:

- euphoria
- mental confusion
- drowsiness, and sometimes sedation
- dizziness
- constriction of the pupils ("pinpoint pupil")
- nausea and vomiting in inexperienced users

Some opiate drugs, such as codeine, Demerol, and Darvon, also have stimulating effects, including CNS excitation, increased blood flow, elevated blood pressure, increased heart rate, tremors, and seizures. Very high doses can result in low blood pressure, decreased heart rate, low body temperature, muscle constriction, cyanosis (lack of oxygen in the bloodstream), and respiratory depression. These symptoms are pronounced in overdose; respiratory depression usually occurs before depression of heart rate, so death from an overdose is almost always from respiratory arrest. A person who is suffering adverse side effects of opiates should receive immediate medical attention.

Long-Term Effects: Opiates have relatively few direct, serious adverse health effects besides addiction. However, chronic abusers generally have higher rates of illness and early death than the general population. Some direct health effects of long-term use include:

- chronic constipation
- impaired vision, especially at night
- reduced sex drive
- menstrual irregularity
- higher risk of pulmonary complications
- nightmares and hallucinations in some users

- mood swings and instability due to short action of the drug

Chronic needle use may lead to local irritation and infection at the site of administration, abscesses and collapsed veins.

Social effects of opiate abuse include family problems, crime and law-enforcement problems, work-related problems, financial problems, violence, and community breakdown. These problems appear most visible among "street" addicts. Addiction to morphine and Demerol is high among medical personnel who have ready access to these drugs.

Drug Interactions: *Additive:* Barbiturates can intensify the high from weak heroin or supplement a dose to which the user has become tolerant. THC in cannabis increases the depressant effects of opiates and can also cause anxiety and hallucinations. *Synergistic:* Alcohol greatly increases the depressant effects of opiates and can lead to respiratory arrest. Meperidine should never be taken with MAO inhibitors; a rapid increase in blood pressure can cause heart attack or stroke. Highly potent analogs to fentanyl when combined with heroin have caused a number of deaths. *Antagonistic:* Some users inject heroin mixed with cocaine or methamphetamine ("speedball") for a stimulant effect.

Special Hazards: Even at low to moderate doses, opiates produce drowsiness, mental confusion, and visual impairment, so operating a vehicle or machinery under the influence is prohibited. Intravenous injection of opiates is linked with increased risk for HIV infection. In addition, because opiates suppress the immune system, they render the user more susceptible to disease. Opiate use during pregnancy reduces the amount of oxygen to the fetus, resulting in higher incidence of prematurity, miscarriage, stillbirth, and infant mortality. In addition, infants exposed to opiates before birth are likely to be born addicted and to suffer withdrawal symptoms that may be more severe than those experienced by adult users.

Dependency Risk: Psychological—high. Physical—high.

PCP

PCP (phencyclidine or 1-(1-phencyclohexylpiperidine)) is a synthetic anesthetic that has stimulant, depressant, and hallucinogenic effects. Special effects vary by user and by drug episode. Factors that affect how a person responds to PCP include dose, route of administration, past drug experiences, and individual personality differences. The term "dissociative anesthetic" is used to describe this drug. The person is aware of physical sensations (touch, pressure) but pain is not perceived by the brain. Because analgesia is provided without sleep, there is no significant cardiovascular or respiratory depression. PCP binds to receptor molecules in the brain and blocks action of certain chemical messengers that affect the neurons. When PCP is smoked, the drug effects can be felt within five minutes, reaching a peak about thirty minutes later. The high maintains a plateau that lasts four to six hours, with a gradual abatement of effects that may take up to twenty-four hours. The onset of effects after oral administration is about one hour. It may take up to four weeks for the user to feel normal after taking PCP.

PCP is one of the most widely available psychoactive drugs in the US. First developed in the 1950s as a general anesthetic and analgesic for animals, PCP was also used for humans for a short time. However, because of severe adverse side effects, such as delirium and its liability for abuse, the drug is now illegal. Commonly known as "angel dust" on the street, PCP is easy and inexpensive to manufacture. It is often misrepresented on the street as another more expensive and desirable hallucinogen, such as LSD, mescaline, or THC. The effects of

PCP are highly unpredictable; the drug experience can be different each time an individual takes PCP. Adverse psychological reactions ("bad trips") are common events for PCP users.

Pure phencyclidine is a white crystalline powder that is highly soluble in water and alcohol. On the street it is available as a powder, liquid, tablet, or capsule of any color. The powder can be sniffed (snorted); the liquid form can be taken orally or used for dipping cigarettes in. Users often soak marijuana, tobacco, parsley, or mint leaves in a solution of PCP, dry the leaves, and smoke them. Less frequently, the drug is injected. Because virtually all PCP on the streets is illicitly manufactured, the purity and dosage levels are unknown. Sometimes a drug sold as PCP is actually a dangerous byproduct of the drug. Thus, drug users cannot be sure of the identity or quantity of the drug they are buying. In addition, analogs have been developed in recent years to sidestep the law. These analogs have effects that may or may not resemble those of PCP and cannot always be detected by routine urine drug screenings.

Chronic users often engage in "runs" or "binges." They take repeated doses of the drug from a period of two to three days without sleeping and with little or no nourishment. The run is followed by prolonged sleep, which leaves the user feeling disoriented and depressed.

Tolerance to the effects of PCP has not yet been clearly demonstrated. However, there is some evidence that chronic users can become tolerant to the euphoric and stimulant effects of the drug.

Street Names: Angel dust, PeaCe Pill, dust, hog, elephant, DOA (dead on arrival), horse tranquilizer, rocket fuel, cadillac, cyclone, goon, mist, ozone, scuffle, surfer, embalming fluid, and Mr. Lovely. When combined with marijuana leaves, PCP is called crystal joints, super grass, peace weed, whack or whacky weed, and killer weed.

Short-Term Effects: Physical effects of a low intake (5 mg. or less) can include increased blood pressure and heart rate; sweating, nausea, and vomiting; increased water intake and urinary output; rapid, shallow breathing; speech disturbances; constricted pupils and blurred vision; dizziness and drowsiness; and impaired muscle coordination (often resulting in disjointed gait or "zombie walk").

Psychological effects of a low dose can include euphoria, which may be mild or intense; a pleasant stimulation, or conversely, relaxation and sedation; sensory distortions of sight, sound, space, time, and body image (users may feel they are floating or weightless); impaired concentration and thinking; memory loss; and feelings of apathy or indifference. Users often become incommunicative or feel lost in fantasy; they may have slurred speech or be incapable of speaking or moving. Hallucinations are rare at low doses.

Adverse psychological effects at low doses are unpredictable, and may include feelings of anxiety, agitation, confusion, isolation, paranoia, panic, and terror. Feelings of depression and alienation can be severe enough to provoke a suicide attempt. Sometimes the psychological effects of PCP can lead to irrational, hostile, violent, or bizarre behavior. Occasionally, use of PCP triggers a psychosis even in people with no previous history of mental illness. Amnesia for events occurring while using PCP may occur.

Higher doses (10 mg. or more) intensify both physical and psychological effects. There is a greater likelihood of an adverse psychological reaction, bizarre or aggressive behavior, and psychosis. Users may experience hallucinations and have delusions of grandeur. They may be preoccupied with trivial matters. These effects may last several days.

Physical effects of higher doses of PCP may include irregular heartbeat; abnormally high blood pressure alternating with periods of abnormally low blood pressure; slow, shallow, and irregular breathing; muscle rigidity, tremors and bizarre posturing; nausea and vomiting; heavy salivation and sweating; high fever (up to 108°F); and decreased urinary output.

Very high doses (150–200 mg.) of PCP can cause coma, seizures, and death due to respiratory or cardiac arrest or ruptured blood vessels in the brain.

Because PCP is stored in body fat and muscle tissue, it can take weeks to be excreted. Thus the drug accumulates in the body and increases the risk of overdose with repeated low doses. Taking PCP combined with other CNS depressants such as alcohol increases the risk of overdose. However, many PCP-related deaths are not the result of overdose. Numerous accidental drownings, leaps from high places, vehicular accidents, suicides, homicides, and self-mutilations have occurred because of the unpredictable psychological effects of this drug. Emergency treatment of persons with adverse PCP reactions is difficult because of the unknown dose and identity of the drug taken. However, cases of overdose or potential overdose call for immediate medical attention. Persons experiencing adverse reactions should be protected from physically harming themselves.

In the case of adverse psychological reaction, a quiet, dimly lit, comfortable setting and the company of a skilled, supportive person may be helpful. "Talking down" a bad trip, a technique often used for adverse psychological reactions to LSD, may not work with PCP. More likely, it will increase the user's agitation and paranoia. Certain tranquilizers and other drugs are used under medical supervision in emergency rooms to sedate persons intoxicated with PCP.

Long-Term Effects: Long-term use of PCP often results in symptoms that may last several weeks after stopping use of the drug. These symptoms include:
- memory loss (especially for events that occur during use)
- disorganized thought processes
- speech difficulties (stuttering, slurred speech, or an inability to articulate or to speak at all)
- visual and auditory hallucinations
- anxiety and depression.

Some users report unpleasant flashbacks similar to those experienced by LSD users. However, PCP flashbacks differ in that they are induced by the release of PCP stored in the body rather than by psychological association.

Toxic psychosis, similar to that caused by chronic amphetamine use or acute schizophrenia, has been observed in some chronic users of PCP who had no history of mental illness before using the drug. The psychosis is marked by aggressive or assaultive behavior, paranoia, delusional thinking, and auditory hallucinations.

Although most PCP users initially take the drug in the company of others, they often withdraw socially as they continue to use the drug. Long-term use (and even short-term use of regular or high doses) interferes with family, social, work, and academic lives of many PCP users. However, the degree to which PCP use is responsible for these problems is unknown as most regular PCP users also smoke marijuana and use other drugs that may contribute to this syndrome. PCP use is particularly dangerous for adolescents because of its prolonged effects on emotions and memory. It impairs judgment and affects the user's affective response, often resulting in bad relationships with family members, teachers, and adults in general.

Drug Interactions: *Synergistic:* High doses of PCP and other CNS depressants such as alcohol, opiates, or sedatives/hypnotics, can cause respiratory arrest. *Antagonistic:* Because there is no known antagonist to PCP, emergency medical treatment for a person who has overdosed or is suffering extremely adverse reactions is limited.

Special Hazards: It is dangerous to operate a vehicle or machinery while under the influence of PCP. Use of PCP also suppresses the immune system, rendering the user more vulnerable to infection and diseases such as

HIV. The extent of fetal damage by PCP is unknown; however, it is safest for the baby if pregnant and nursing mothers, or women contemplating pregnancy, do not use PCP.

Dependency Risk: Psychological—high. Physical—low to none.

Tranquilizers

Tranquilizers are depressant drugs that act primarily on the nervous, skeletomuscular, and cardiovascular/respiratory systems. These drugs fall into two categories: (1) **anxiolytics** (anti-anxiety); and (2) **sedatives/hypnotics** (sleep-inducing). Tranquilizers are legally obtainable only by prescription. They produce a calming effect without excessive sedation in most people. Physicians prescribe them to treat anxiety, insomnia, and skeletomuscular spasms. There is little evidence that use of these drugs for more than three to six months is effective medically, yet they are often prescribed for long-term use with increased dosages.

Tranquilizers appear as white, off-white, or light yellow crystalline powders, usually in pills or capsules of a variety of colors. Powders can also be dissolved in water or alcohol for intravenous or intramuscular injection.

Low doses of tranquilizers have a calming effect. They may also cause drowsiness and a sense of well-being. High doses can result in a lack of coordination and stupor. People can become dependent on tranquilizers. Tranquilizers vary in dosage, rate of absorption, action in the body, duration of effects (half-life), and addiction potential. High-potency, quick-acting drugs with a short half-life (the amount of time for 50% of the drug to be excreted) have a higher addiction potential. While these drugs have a relative margin of safety, there has been some concern that tranquilizers are prescribed too frequently and abused, especially by women. Benzodiazepines are prescribed too often for women, who are therefore at greater risk for addiction.

Three chemical groups comprise tranquilizers: (1) *meprobamate* (Equanil, Miltown); (2) *benzodiazepines* (Librium, Valium, Serax, Xanax, Ativan, Clonopin, Dalmane, Restoril, and Halcion), which act as either anti-anxiety agents or sedatives/hypnotics; and (3) *buspirone* (BuSpar), a new anti-anxiety tranquilizer that is not sedating and presumed to be less addicting.

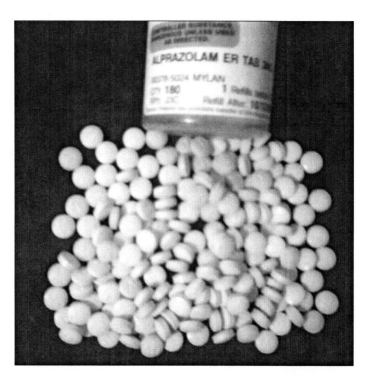

Users can become tolerant to the psychoactive or sedative effects of tranquilizers. Cross-tolerance occurs among different kinds of tranquilizers and other sedatives/hypnotics, such as barbiturates. That is, an individual who has become tolerant to the effects of one of these drugs will also be tolerant to an equivalent dose of another drug that produces the same effect.

Street Names: Tranks, downers, sleepers. Valium tablets are known as "Vs."

Short-Term Effects: Therapeutic doses can cause relief of mild anxiety or tension, sense of relaxation, sense of well-being, temporary memory impairment, drowsiness, confusion (especially in the elderly), and stupor. The intensity and duration of these effects varies according to the particular drug, the dose, and the individual user. Medical supervision is recommended for the use of these drugs.

Taking tranquilizers at higher than the recommended dose can produce impaired thinking and memory, emotional instability, altered perceptions, slurred speech, and staggering gait and motor incoordination. Because tranquilizers can affect the way the mind and muscles work together, use of these drugs can cause blurred or double vision and impaired muscular coordination. Some users may experience overstimulation, hallucinations, insomnia, nightmares, and rage.

Severe cardiovascular and respiratory depression may occur at extremely high doses of benzodiazepines or at low doses when combined with other CNS depressants, such as alcohol or barbiturates. Though tranquilizers are often used in suicide attempts, deaths from overdoses of these drugs alone are very rare.

Long-Term Effects: Long-term users of daily therapeutic doses of benzodiazepines may experience a number of side effects, including lethargy and oversedation, decreased motivation, irritability, vivid or disturbing dreams, nausea, headache, skin rash, impaired sexual functioning, menstrual irregularities, and increased appetite leading to weight gain, or loss of appetite and weight.

Chronic, heavy use of tranquilizers can cause the symptoms above and the following: impaired thinking, memory, and judgment; disorientation and confusion; slurred speech; muscle incoordination and weakness; dizziness; anxiety and depression; sleep disorders; loss of appetite; tremors; apathy or lack of interest in surroundings; and emotional disinhibition and rage.

Drug Interactions: *Additive:* Some persons in methadone treatment programs use benzodiazepines to enhance the effects of methadone. *Synergistic:* Even low doses of tranquilizers combined with alcohol or other CNS depressants produce effects than can produce severe cardiovascular and respiratory depression than can be fatal. Alcohol increases the absorption of benzodiazepines and slows their breakdown by the liver. *Antagonistic:* Users of stimulants sometimes take tranquilizers to offset the agitation and sleeplessness.

Special Hazards: Any use of tranquilizers can make it dangerous to operate a vehicle or other machinery. Pregnant or nursing women can damage a developing fetus and pass the drug on to the unborn child or infant. Use of tranquilizers during the first trimester of pregnancy increases the risk of congenital malformations.

Dependency Risk: Psychological—moderate. Physical—moderate.

Questions to Consider

1. Describe the importance of understanding drug interactions.
2. What are the three most prevalent drugs on the campus? Develop an outline on how you would facilitate a group discussion on these three drugs.

Chapter 11

Steroid Abuse

By Luoluo Hong, Elizabeth Livingston, and Jason Robertson

What are Steroids?

Steroids are an entire class of chemicals whose structures are very much alike. Two of the three types of steroids are familiar to most college students are hydrocortisones (which help control rashes and itching) and female sex hormones (estrogens and progestogens). However, it is the class of steroids known as anabolics (or androgenics) that are most frequently abused by college men and some women, primarily student-athletes. Anabolic steroids are substances that promote the building of muscle tissue or the accumulation of nitrogen in muscle protein. These steroids are taken by injection or orally, often in cycles instead of continual use. The male sex hormone testosterone is the body's natural anabolic steroid.

Who Abuses Steroids?

More than half a million US adolescents use steroids. Approximately 2%–3% of college men report ever having used steroids. Steroid abuse occurs most frequently among young men aged 18–25, especially those participating in organized sports.

Anabolic steroids enable athletes in certain sports to build up muscle tissue during training more quickly than training without drugs. Use of steroids decreases the amount of time necessary (ordinarily 48 hours) for recovery from muscle injury, so trainings can occur at a much more rapid pace. In addition, many athletes experience a psychological boost from using steroids that they report increases their competitive edge and performance. However, steroid abuse is no longer limited to the world of sports. A growing number of steroid abusers are high school and college students not involved with any organized sport. When surveyed, students who were not athletes became steroid abusers in an attempt to improve their appearance or their fitness.

What are the Physiological Effects of Steroid Use?

Anabolic steroids are known to increase muscle size, increase muscle water content, and increase body weight. Steroid use also increases some of the building blocks of muscle, such as potassium and nitrogen, while it causes relative decreases in the energy-carrying component of muscle, mainly phosphate. In addition, steroid use has been associated with increased aggression, which may have a positive effect on athletic performance. While steroids can cause a possible increase strength performance, there is no scientific proof that they directly increase physical strength. Excess anabolic steroids are metabolized into female sex hormones, such as estrogen.

What are the Health Consequences of Steroid Use?

There is substantial evidence that taking excessive amounts of steroids leads to negative consequences on virtually every system of the body. These effects include:

- premature stunting of bone and body growth
- decreased elastin and increased collagen, resulting in hardening of the arteries
- enlargement of the heart and killing of heart tissue
- high blood pressure
- increased likelihood of blood clot formation
- increased risk of heart attacks and strokes
- liver disease and cancer of the liver
- atrophy of the male sexual organs
- decreased sperm production and temporary sterility
- development of female sex characteristics (in men), including breasts (known as "gynecomastia")

- decreased libido and impotence
- increased serum cholesterol level and decreased HDL cholesterol, which lead to coronary heart disease
- mild to severe acne
- male pattern baldness
- mood swings, euphoria, feelings of guilt, and temporary personality changes
- decreased levels of immune globulin A, G, and M, resulting in increased risk of illness and infection
- Women can grow facial hair, experience a change in menstrual cycle, and have a deepening of the voice

Living Steroid-Free

When steroid use becomes compulsive, and the user loses control—continuing to use steroids despite its adverse consequences—an addiction has developed. The pressure for men and women to perform and excel in athletics is tremendous. Similarly, non-athletes experience pressure to conform to the unrealistic, oftentimes unattainable, body size and shape that typically is expected of men. In either case, those who are abusing steroids for performance or body image reasons should consult a mental health care provider on campus. The lifelong health consequences of steroid abuse are costly, and certainly are not worth the time-limited benefits that some college students derive from it. For more information about steroids, visit the Website for the **Center for Substance Abuse Research**, at http://www.cesar.umd.edu/cesar/drugs/steroids.pdf

Question to Consider

1. Based on your understanding of steroids, create a program outline for the campus.

Chapter 12

Gambling—The Drugless Addiction

By Luoluo Hong and Julie Catanzarite

Few recreational activities have seen more growth in the past few years than gambling. For many communities it seems that new opportunities for gambling arrive daily; newspaper headlines and radio commercials are a clear indication of its dominance in public attention. Forty-eight states have legalized gambling, offering a wide range of gambling opportunities (e.g., casinos and slots, off-track betting, Indian gambling venues, riverboat gambling, lotteries, bingo, and video poker). While the intent is to generate state revenues, a painful side effect of the gambling industry parallels that of the alcohol and tobacco industries; industry patrons are inevitably at risk for addiction, and addiction can destroy careers, marriages, even lives.

Many people find a great deal of fun and excitement in gambling; taking a chance is exciting, gambling with friends is fun, and the thrill of winning is … well, thrilling! An occasional weekend at the casinos makes for an entertaining and even profitable diversion from everyday life—although most occasional and social gamblers know that the odds of winning are against them.

For some individuals, however, gambling is not just a "diversion." **Pathological gambling**, diagnosed as a compulsion disorder by the American Psychological Association in 1980, is, like the industry that feeds it, a growing phenomenon in the United States. Pathological gambling's essential feature, as defined by the fourth edition of the *Diagnostic and Statistical Manual of Mental Disorders (DSM-IV)* (1994) is "persistent and recurrent maladaptive gambling behavior [...] that disrupts personal, family, or vocational pursuits." If help is not sought by the gambling addict, an activity that began as an entertaining "diversion" can spiral into a destructive addiction.

The "Drugless Addiction"

Gambling has been referred to as the "drugless addiction" for many, possibly up to 3% of the population. Arnold Wexler, former Executive Director of the Council on Compulsive Gambling in New Jersey, reported that "compulsive gamblers experience that same euphoria of 'high' related to endorphin release that is also associated with chemical addiction." This endorphin release produces a soothing, morphine-like effect for the addict of gambling or drugs. A compulsive gambler's overwhelming need to gamble, then, is similar to an alcohol's compelling need to drink. Pathological gamblers, in fact, do not gamble so much "for the money" as for that "high" related to feelings of relief or freedom from life's stresses. Although many pathological gamblers believe that money is both the cause of and the solution to all their problems, the power ultimately driving their "money-chasing" addiction is not monetary. It is, instead, the same sort of "high" craved by addicts of alcohol, nicotine, and other drugs and activities.

Pathological gambling is related to other problems, including marital, emotional, occupational, financial, and legal difficulties. The problems that drive compulsive gambling are often, ironically, the very ones aggravated by it: separation and divorce, depression and even suicide (by either the gambler or the gambler's spouse), lost or decreased productivity at school or work, exorbitant debts, and medical problems. These, along with illegal

gambling or borrowing, can and do result in civil and even criminal court appearances. In addition, gambling may be "drugless," but in many ways it can prove just as harmful as an addiction to alcohol or other drugs.

Signs of Pathological Gambling

- You take time from work, school, or family to gamble.
- You gamble in secret.
- You feel remorse after gambling and repeatedly vow to quit (you may even quit for a while and then start up again).
- You do not plan to gamble—you just "end up" gambling, and you gamble until your last dollar is gone.
- You gamble with money to pay bills or solve financial problems.
- You lie, steal, borrow, or sell things to get gambling money.
- You gamble in an attempt to win back your gambling losses.
- You gamble in an attempt to increase your gambling winnings, dreaming of the "big win" and what it will buy.
- You gamble when you feel down or when you feel like celebrating.
- Your friends or family have criticized your gambling in the past.
- You need to gamble with increasing amounts of cash to achieve your desired "high."
- You are restless or irritable when trying to cut down on or quit gambling.
- Your gambling habits have jeopardized or even ruined a personal relationship, job, or educational or career opportunity.

Setting Gambling Guidelines

Even if you don't classify as a compulsive gambler, it is always a good idea to lay out certain guidelines for yourself *before* you head to the casinos or the slot machines. *Most importantly, keep alcohol consumption to a minimum or don't drink at all if you choose to gamble.* As in all situations, liquor can cloud your judgment and cause you to think you have a bigger bank account than you actually do.

Consider adopting the following suggestions as your gambling guidelines:

- **Establish acceptable losses before you gamble.** No matter how much money is won by casino patrons, the "house" is always the big winner. Set aside a certain amount of money for "entertainment funds" and consider any cash you lose as money spent on entertainment.
- **Be careful when mixing alcohol and other drugs with gambling activities.** These substances can distort your judgment, interfering with your ability to stick to your predetermined gambling limits.
- **Never borrow money to gamble.** You'd be surprised at how often this seemingly obvious precaution is ignored. When you run out of your own money, it's time to stop. Leave your ATM and credit cards at home!
- **Don't gamble to relieve unpleasant emotional conditions** such as stress, anger, depression, or loneliness. If these conditions are plaguing you, seek help from a friend, a family member, or a therapist. Gambling away your (or your partner's, or your parents') money will only aggravate your personal problems.
- **If you have a current problem with alcohol or other drugs**, or are in stages of recovery, you may be wise not to gamble at all, as there is an apparent connection between compulsive gambling and alcoholism and drug addiction.

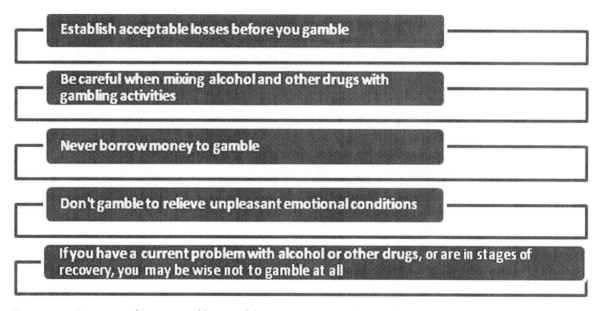

Figure 13: *Summary of setting gambling guidelines. Strategies to reduce problem gambling.*

If You Need Help

Don't wait until all bets are off! While gambling is known as the most expensive addiction, it is among the least expensive to remedy. There are a number of resources for help available. The national office for **Gamblers Anonymous** can be reached by dialing 888-GA-HELPS. The toll-free hotline sponsored by the National Council on Problem Gambling is 1-800-522-4700.

Question to Consider:

1. What other drugless addictions are there than gambling?

Reference

American Psychiatric Association. (1994). *The diagnostic and statistical manual of mental disorders (DSM-IV)* (Rev. 4th ed.). Washington, DC: American Psychiatric Association.

Chapter 13

Toward Campus Communities Free of Sexual Violence—Rewriting the Cultural Norms about Sex, Power, and Relationships

By Luoluo Hong

Introduction: The Reality of Campus Rape

The presence of sexual violence on the college campus is perhaps one of the greatest inhibitors to effective student learning and full student engagement in all that campus life has to offer. As such, students, faculty, staff, and administrators alike have a vested interest to closely examine the phenomenon of sexual violence and take affirmative, proactive, and courageous steps to reduce the incidence of rape and sexual assault, as well as address the "root causes" of sexual violence.

The movement to end rape and sexual assault began in the late 1960s as part of the Women's Liberation Movement. While many of the individuals working in the field of sexual violence prevention might observe that our country has come a long way during the intervening decades in terms of acknowledging the problem of rape and directing more resources and attention to this topic, the reality of rape and sexual assault on college campuses has in many ways also remained the same. Research conducted and data collected on sexual assault years ago unfortunately are still applicable and relevant today.

The most frequently cited data regarding campus rape were collected by Dr. Mary P. Koss for the 1985 *Ms. Magazine Campus Project on Sexual Assault.* Funded by the National Institute of Mental Health, the study surveyed 3,187 women and 2,972 men at undergraduate institutions across the US. Highlights of Dr. Koss's findings are summarized below:

- One in four women surveyed had an experience that met the legal definition of rape or attempted rape.
- Eighty-four percent of those raped knew their attacker.
- Fifty-seven percent of the rapes occurred on dates.
- One in twelve of the male students surveyed had committed acts that met the legal definitions of rape or attempted rape.
- For both men and women, the average age when a rape incident occurred (either as perpetrator or victim) was 18.5 years.
- Only 27% of the women whose sexual assault met the legal definition of rape thought of themselves as rape victims.
- About 75% of the men and at least 55% of the women involved in acquaintance rape had been drinking or taking drugs just before the attack.
- Forty-two percent of the rape victims told no one about their assaults; only 5% reported their rapes to the police; and only 5% sought help at rape crisis centers.
- Forty-two percent of the women who were raped said they had sex again with the men who assaulted them; 55% of the men who raped said they had sex again with their victims.
- Whether they acknowledged their experience as rape or not, 30% of the women identified in the study as rape victims contemplated suicide after the incident.

- Eighty-four percent of the men who committed acts that met the legal definition of rape said that what they did was definitely not rape.
- Sixteen percent of the male students who committed rape and 10% of those who attempted a rape took part in episodes involving more than one attacker, i.e., gang rape.
- Eight percent of the women who had been raped were 14, 15, 16, or 17 years old at the time of their assaults (Warshaw 1994).

Over a decade later, the *National College Women Sexual Victimization* (NCWSV) telephone survey was conducted of 4,446 women to examine the prevalence of rape, sexual assault, and stalking on campus (Fisher, Cullen, and Turner 2000). Sponsored by the US Department of Justice, this study found that:

- 1.7% of college women had experienced a completed rape and 1.1% an attempted rape in the seven months prior to the study; using this finding, the survey authors projected that nearly 5% of college women were victimized annually and up to 25% were assaulted during their college years.
- In nine out of ten cases reported in the survey, the victims knew the perpetrators.
- Rapes also occur during dates: 12.8% of completed rapes, 35.0% of attempted rapes, and 22.9% of threatened rapes.
- Nearly 60% of on-campus rapes occurred in the victim's residence, 31.0% happened in other housing areas, and 10.3% took placed in a fraternity house.
- Approximately thirteen percent (13.1%) of respondents had been stalked since the beginning of the academic year.
- In 10.3% of the stalking incidents identified through the survey, the stalker "forced or attempted sexual contact."
- Four in five victims knew their stalkers, and known perpetrators were most likely to be a boyfriend, ex-boyfriend, classmate, acquaintance, friend, or coworker.

These data coincide with findings from the Fall 2009 administration of the *American College Health Association's National College Health Assessment* (ACHA-NCHA) survey, in which data from 32,208 students and 57 institutions of higher education were analyzed (ACHA 2009). The ACHA-NCHA indicated that in the last 12 months college students reported experiencing:

Type of Intepersonal Violence
Source: ACHA-NCHA, Fall 2009

	Percent (%)		
	Male	Female	Total
Sexual touching without their consent	3.6	7.2	6.0
Sexual penetration attempt without their consent	0.9	3.1	2.4
Sexual penetration without their consent	0.8	2.0	1.6
Stalking	4.2	8.2	6.9
An emotionally abusive intimate relationship	7.1	11.2	9.8
A physically abusive intimate relationship	2.3	2.3	2.4
A sexually abusive intimate relationship	0.9	2.0	1.7

In addition, college students who reported consuming alcohol during the last twelve months on the survey reported the following consequences occurring as a result of their own drinking:

Consequences of Alcohol Consumption
Source: ACHA-NCHA, Fall 2009

	Percent (%)		
	Male	Female	Total
Had sex with someone without giving your consent	1.7	2.1	2.0
Had sex with someone without getting their consent	0.7	1.6	2.6
Physically injured another person	4.2	1.6	2.6

Definitions of Sexual Assault and Consensual Intimacy

In general, sexual assault is any kind of sexual activity in which consent is not freely given or obtained. The US Department of Justice's Office on Violence Against Women defines sexual assault as "… any type of sexual contact or behavior that occurs without the explicit consent of the recipient of the unwanted sexual activity. Falling under the definition of sexual assault is sexual activity such as forced sexual intercourse, sodomy, child molestation, incest, fondling, and attempted rape," (US Department of Justice 2010). Note that "freely given" implies that the individual giving consent is not feeling psychologically or socially pressured, verbally or emotionally coerced, or physically intimidated into giving their consent.

Sexual assault prevention education consultant Dr. Alan Berkowitz has provided one of the most useful set of guidelines for college students to use to ensure they have achieved mutual, uncoerced consent in their intimate relationships. He believes that consent is composed of four characteristics, or conditions, all of which must be present before one can consider that consent has been given or received:

1. **Both sexual partners are fully conscious**, meaning both individuals are awake and their judgment not overly impaired due to alcohol or other drugs.

2. **Both sexual partners are equally free to act**, meaning that neither partner feels physically threatened or disadvantaged, emotionally coerced, or psychologically pressured, nor is there an imbalance in power and authority, e.g., faculty member with a current student or supervisor with a current employee.

3. **Both sexual partners have clearly communicated their willingness/permission**, meaning that direct and unambiguous dialogue about sexual intent and specific sexual activities has been taken place without any assumptions or guesswork taking place, while remembering that silence or passivity are not the same as consent and that consent for certain sexual activities does not automatically confer consent to all sexual activities; and

4. **Both sexual partners are positive and sincere in their desires**, meaning that both individuals have been truthful about their wishes and desires and refrained from saying things, e.g., "I really love you," they do not mean in order to "get sex" (Berkowitz 2002a).

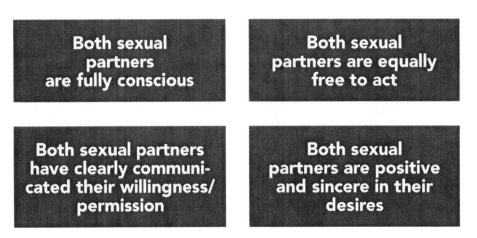

Figure 14: *Summary of consent. Four characteristics or conditions that must be present before consent can be considered to have been given or received.*

Note that the person who initiates sexual activity—male or female—bears the greater responsibility for ensuring that all conditions of consent have been met. Berkowitz (2002a) believes that consent is not impossible when one or both sexual partners are under the influence of alcohol; however, it is considerably more difficult to meet all four of the above conditions when one or both partners are intoxicated.

Laws about Rape and Sexual Assault

The legal statutes defining rape, sexual assault, sexual abuse, sexual battery, and other similar types of behavior vary greatly from state to state, but rape is considered illegal in all fifty states. Almost all states have stipulations that minors under a certain age are not able to give consent. Some states do not recognize spousal rape, e.g., an individual cannot be tried or convicted for sexually assaulting a legally married partner. Still other states impose higher penalties if a person is convicted of drug-facilitated rape, e.g., uses GHB, Rohypnol, or other substances to render the victim more vulnerable. The current statutes for sexual assault for any particular state can be found by searching the Website for that state's Office of the Attorney General or state legislature.

It is important to note that while every state has laws that prohibit sexual assault and rape, these laws have historically not been effective as deterrents to sexual violence. In fact, the likelihood of accused perpetrators

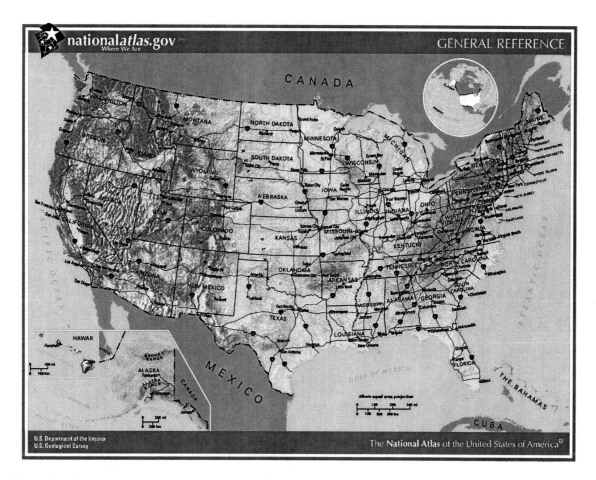

of sexual violence ever receiving consequences for their actions is minimal. Consider the following analysis conducted by the National Center for Policy Analysis in 1999:

In addition, there are a variety of pieces of federal legislation that provide guidelines for how colleges and universities, law enforcement agencies, health care entities, and community-based organizations must either enact measures to reduce the likelihood of sexual assault incidents, or for how these organizations must respond when they receive a report of a sexual assault. College students should in particular be familiar with The Campus Security Act of 1990, Title II of Public Law (later amended in 1999 and renamed *The Jeanne Clery Disclosure of Campus Security Policy and Campus Crime Statistics Act* in recognition of Jeanne Ann Clery, a 19-year-old Lehigh University student who was raped and murdered in her residence hall room in 1986). This law governs how and when public and private colleges and universities should disclose information about crime on and around their campuses to students, staff, and faculty.

Title IV of the *Violent Crime Control and Law Enforcement Act of 1994, P.L. 103-322*, which is more commonly referred to as the *Violence Against Women Act* (or VAWA 1994), authorized significant amounts of federal funding for activities to help prevent, investigate, and respond to violence against women. Congress later added provisions to VAWA in order to provide greater statutory protections for trafficking victims when it passed the *Victims of Trafficking and Violence Protection Act of 2000, P.L. 106–386.* Most recently, VAWA was reauthorized in 2005 as the *Violence Against Women and Department of Justice Reauthorization Act of 2005, P.L. 109–271,* revising and extending many of the activities that are authorized under the original VAWA legislation.

If a rape is reported there is 50.8% change of an arrest.

If an arrest made, there is an 80% chance of prosecution.

If there is a prosecution, there is a 58% chance of a conviction.

If there is a felony conviction, there is a 69% chance the convict will spend time in jail.

Of the 39% of attacks that are reported to the police, there is only a 6.3% chance that the rapist will end up in prison.

Individual and Interpersonal Factors that Contribute to Sexual Assault

Rape and sexual violence are the result of a complex interrelationship between individual, interpersonal, group, societal, political, and cultural factors, and a wide range of researchers have examined each of these areas. *Regardless of the wide range of contributing factors, it is important to recognize and acknowledge that ultimately, each perpetrator is the person who is most responsible for committing sexual assault and therefore has the greatest ability and choice to ensure that a sexual assault does not happen.*

Alan Berkowitz proposed a behavioral model that posits sexual assault is the result of a combination of perpetration and victim socialization experiences, beliefs, and attitudes toward sexuality; the situational characteristics or context of the situation; and the perpetrator's misperceptions of the victim's sexual intent (Berkowitz, Burkhart, and Bourg 1994). For example, attitudinal factors on the part of a perpetrator that might contribute to a greater likelihood of sexual assault include holding more traditional attitudes about male and female gender roles, demonstrating a higher level of hostility toward women, regarding use of force in relationships as normal, believing that relationships are based on power and control, and subscribing to "rape myths" and other false ideas about sex and violence (Abbey and McAuslan 2004).

"Rape myths" are false ideas and assertions about sexual assault perpetrators and their victims. In general, they serve to place the blame for rape on its victims to ameliorate the perpetrator's responsibility (Burt 1991). When invoked in the courts of law, in the system of medical care, or in schools and in churches, rape myths reduce the seriousness of sexual violence, and thereby invalidate the experiences of individuals who are raped. The most common examples of rape myths include the following:

Myth	Information
Myth 1 "If she really didn't want it, she would have fought back harder." *The "You Can't Thread a Moving Needle" Myth*	This myth is rooted in the cultural norm that women are the traditional "gatekeepers" of sexual activity; men are expected to be the sexual aggressors and to always be interested in sexual activity, while morally upstanding women are expected to set the boundaries on sex.
Myth 2 "When she says 'no,' she really means 'yes.'" *The "Token No" Hypothesis*	From an early age, many boys and men are taught the false notion that many girls and women enjoy playing "games" and prefer to be taken be overcome and/or overwhelmed by their sexual partner in order to be sexually aroused.
Myth 3 "Most women secretly want to be raped." *The "Rape Fantasy" Theory*	This is a more extreme variation of Myth 2, and has been largely propagated by the pornography industry. While it is true that some women do fantasize at times about being swept away into the arms of a sexually aggressive partner, that is not the same thing as being raped or sexually assaulted against one's wishes or desires.
Myth 4 "Women just make false accusations of rape to get back at a man." *The "Women Just Cry Rape" Theory*	This myth is rooted in men's fear that women merely use a rape accusation as retaliation for not calling back or for being rejected. The myth asserts that accusations of rape are easily made but difficult to defend against. While the fear is understandable, in reality, the false reporting rate for rape is lower than that of most criminal acts and rape is one of the most *underreported* crimes; furthermore, many victims who report rape find it very hard to have their reports taken seriously by law enforcement and the vast majority of reported sexual assaults are never investigated or prosecuted. This myth invalidates women's experience of rape as a real violation and makes it harder for women to be believed when they report sexual assault. A corollary to this myth is that physically attractive men or men who have available sexual partners would never rape, when in fact neither of these factors reduce the likelihood of sexual assault perpetration.
Myth 5 "A woman can't be raped if she has had sex with lots of men." *The Virgin-Whore Dilemma*	In this "good girl/bad girl" double-standard, the false assumption is that women who are sexually active are automatically interested in sex with any partner at any time. In truth, sexually active women should no more lose their right to control their own bodies than women who are virgins. Even a professional sex worker has the right to refuse service or to say "no" to sex at any time.
Myth 6 "If a woman leads a man on, then she deserves to be raped." *The "Point of No Return" Premise*	This myth asserts that there is an essentially an "invisible line" (e.g., going up to a man's room after 2:00 AM, letting him pay for her steak and lobster dinner, drinking alcohol or smoking pot, performing oral sex for him, dating him for one whole year, etc.) over which once a woman "steps" she is no longer allowed to say "no" to sex. In other words, "consenting" to those other activities was a form of giving consent to sexual intercourse, as well. This myth is rooted in an unhealthy notion that sex is about an exchange of goods or services.
Myth 7 "Men have no choice but to rape because they can't control themselves sexually." *The "Blue-Balls" Myth*	This myth implies that it is unhealthy and even painful for boys and men if they become highly sexually aroused and then do not engage in sexual intercourse or ejaculate. To date, there are absolutely no research data to confirm this assertion. Rather, this myth demeans men and male sexuality and reduces men to mere animals unable to control their sexual urges, which is of course not true.

What is especially disturbing about rape myths is how early we acquire them. Both boys and girls are socialized to believe rape myths beginning early in life. In one survey of 1,700 11–14-year-olds conducted by the Rhode Island Rape Crisis Center, 31% of the boys and 32% of girls said it was okay for a man to rape a woman who had past sexual experiences, while 65% of the boys and 47% of the girls believed it was okay for a man to rape a woman if they had been dating for more than six months (White and Humphrey 1991). In another study of adolescent youth, 56% of girls and 76% of boys believed forced sex is acceptable under certain circumstances. For instance, if "he spends a lot of money on her" during a date, 39% of the males and 12% of the females said forced sex would be justified. Similarly, if "she's led him on" sexually, 54% of boys and 27% of girls believed forced sex was acceptable (Goodchilds et al. 1988, as cited by White and Humphrey 1991).

Beyond rape myth adherence, interpersonal and situational dynamics that might contribute to sexual assault include differences in how men and women interpret verbal and nonverbal cues and attribute sexual intent differently. Research has shown that men tend to overestimate women's interest in them as sexual partners based on behavioral "signs" such as friendliness, touching, social attentiveness, and style of dress (Abbey 2002). Based on socialization they receive from peers or from messages they receive from mainstream media, men may also believe that women initially will offer "token" resistance to maintain their reputation as virtuous women, but actually want their partners to be sexually aggressive with them.

Alcohol constitutes one of the most significant situational factors in sexual assaults. Its consumption increases the risk of sexual assault in several ways. First, drinkers may use alcohol as an excuse to engage in sexually aggressive behavior, or use it as a tactic to make their sexual partner more vulnerable and less able to resist sexual advances. Further, because alcohol interferes with judgment and cognition, the drinker may be more likely to overestimate their female partner's sexual interest, show decreased concern about her experience, and be less able to accurately evaluate whether or not consent has been given (Marchell and Cummings 2001; Abbey, Zawacki, Buck, Clinton, and McAuslan 2001). Conversely, women's alcohol consumption may render them more likely targets of sexual aggression as they are less able to resist an assault and more likely to be perceived as sexually available (Abbey 2002). In fact, alcohol is associated with a "double standard" in incidents of sexual assault, whereby female victims are regarded as more culpable for the assault but male perpetrators are absolved of their responsibility.

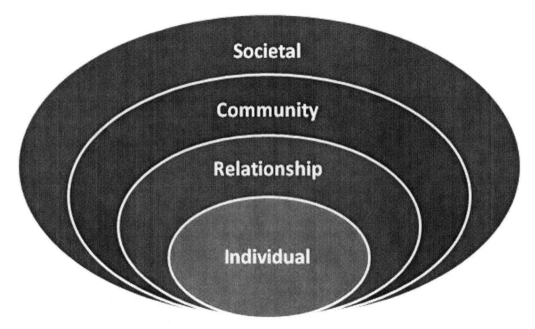

Figure 15: *The Socioecological Model (Source: World Health Organization 2002)*

Understanding the Link Between Traditional Masculinity and Sexual Violence

Increasingly, colleges and universities are recognizing that rape, sexual assault, and gender violence are not only the product of individual, interpersonal, or situational factors. Broader societal and cultural forces play a major role in sustaining an environment that allows rape to continue happening in our communities.

The Centers for Disease Control has adopted a four-level socioecological model (see Figure 15) to help "map" the factors that contribute to violence and to help guide the planning of potential prevention interventions. To be most effective prevention strategies should include a continuum of interventions that address all levels of the model; these interventions must be developmentally appropriate and culturally relevant, as well as conducted across the lifespan (Dahlberg and Krug 2002).

In applying this model to analyze the risk factors associated with sexual assault, we can see the risk and protective factors associated with perpetration of sexual violence (see Figure 16), which include (Jewkes, Sen, and Garcia-Moreno 2002):

Figure 16: *Analysis of Risk and Protective Factors For Sexual Violence Perpetration.* (World Health Organization 2002)

Risk Factors

Individual Risk Factors	• Heavy alcohol and drug use • Attitudes and beliefs supportive of sexual violence, including coercive sexual fantasies • Impulsive and antisocial tendencies • Preference for impersonal sex • Hostility toward women • Hypermasculinity • Prior history of childhood sexual and/or physical abuse • Witnessed family violence as a child
Relationship Risk Factors	• Association with sexually aggressive and delinquent peers • Family environment characterized by physical violence and few resources • Strong patriarchal relationship or familial environment • Emotionally unsupportive family environment • Family honor considered more important than health and safety of the victim
Community Risk Factors	• Poverty and associated factors (e.g., neighborhood disadvantaged) • Lack of employment opportunities • Lack of institutional support from police and judicial system • General tolerance of sexual violence within the community • Weak community sanctions against sexual violence perpetrators • High levels of crime and other forms of violence
Societal Risk Factors	• Societal norms that support sexual violence • Societal norms that support male superiority and sexual entitlement • Societal norms that maintain women's inferiority and sexual submissiveness • Weak laws and policies related to sexual violence and gender equity • Economic inequality

Protective Factors

Protective factors may lessen the likelihood of sexual violence victimization or perpetration by buffering against risk. These factors can exist at individual, relational, community, and societal levels. Because there is so little research on protective factors, this list does not show any specific items.

The women's and men's movements have also adopted a systemic approach to understanding the perpetration and prevention of sexual violence. A growing number of researchers are analyzing how dominant male culture and the associated prevailing values might socialize boys and men to see violence as a normalized and accepted way for interacting with their sexual partners (Kimmel 2005; Marshall 1993; Messner and Sabo, 1994; Katz 2006; Flood 2003). Most of us do not think of men as having a "culture." While we must be cautious about overgeneralizing with regard to men's values and masculine norms, women's and men's studies scholars have largely recognized that there is value in acknowledging the common socialization that most men in the US experience—a socialization that can and does transcend generations, race/ethnicity, socioeconomic status, and educational background (Connell 2005). Many men have actively strived to resist some of the expectations and norms of masculinity, finding them limiting, counterintuitive, and harmful; yet, just as many boys and men subscribe to and live unconsciously and uncritically by the "rules of manhood."

One of the earliest definitions of "dominant" masculinity describes the prevailing male sex role through four metaphors: (1) *"Don't Be a Sissy"*—avoid acting in ways that can be perceived as feminine; (2) *"Be a Big Wheel"*—strive for power, status, and control; (3) *"Be a Sturdy Oak"*—act tough and unemotional; and (4) *"Give 'em Hell"*—be aggressive and take risks (David and Brannon 1976). It is important to note that these metaphors do not describe the actual lives of the vast majority of boys and men in the US. Rather, they offer a social construct referred to as "real men" and suggest how boys and men ought to behave. Although men may subscribe to a wide range of masculinities, one ideal or concept of masculinity becomes dominant and subsumes other definitions. This hegemony is reinforced by societal institutions such as political power, mass media, education, church, and corporate culture (Connell 2005).

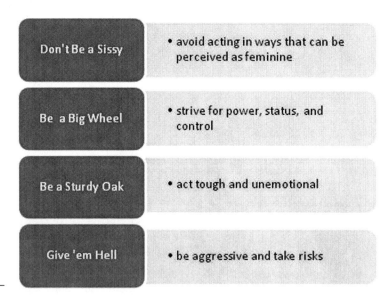

Figure 17: *Male sex-role metaphors.*

Surprisingly, David and Brannon's (1976) metaphors remain largely relevant as ways to describe the pressures that men today face. Consider ways in which each metaphor might manifest itself in sexual encounters. As a result of feeling pressure to prove their manhood, some men may choose to use sexual activity and violence as a means of confirming their masculinity, especially to other men. For example, almost two-thirds of men surveyed in one study had engaged in unwanted intercourse, primarily because of male peer pressure or wanting to be popular (Berkowitz 2004). This is an example both of "Don't be a Sissy" and "Give 'em Hell."

Because normative gender roles assign men the role of "aggressor" and women the role of "gatekeeper" with respect to issues of sexual intimacy, the typical heterosexual encounter becomes a battle of wills in which the man maneuvers to obtain sexual favors from the woman while she "holds the line." For the male, sex becomes the goal of the date or interaction; the woman is regarded as a potential "conquest" or "prize." This adversarial view of dating and sex is captured in many of the slang terms used for sex by boys and men: "scoring," "homerun," "hitting that," etc.—many of which carry a violent subtext. This approach to sex and sexual relationships is reflective of both "Be a Big Wheel" and "Be a Sturdy Oak" mentalities.

The research also suggests that the dynamics of all-male groups can reinforce rape-supportive beliefs, attitudes, and norms by generating a "group think" environment that encourages conformity. For example, some male students indicate that they feel pressure from their friends, teammates, or fraternity brothers to perform sexually or to be sexually aggressive; some even fear "losing face" if they do not participate in individual or group sexual assaults (Sandler and Ehrhart 1985; Sanday 2007; Schwartz and DeKeseredy 1997; Benedict 1999). It is therefore not surprising that most campus gang rapes are perpetrated by members of fraternities or intercollegiate athletic teams. Membership in these groups serves to protect the perpetrator from doubts about the wrongness of such behavior, especially when such groups are associated with high status and special privileges on campus. Participation in or observation of gang rape fosters group cohesiveness and resolves doubts about heterosexuality caused by close, intimate relationships among men (Sanday 2007).

When considered against the context of male sex role socialization, sexual violence can no longer be regarded as deviant, abnormal acts of a few individuals. Rather, the sexual coercion and violation of women is normalized in the ways boys and men are raised to view women, sex, and sexual relationships. However, because peer pressure and male socialization may increase adherence to attitudes, beliefs, and behaviors that support sexual violence, this also means that male friendships and communities of men can also serve to develop new norms and expectations that do not support gender violence (Schwartz and DeKeseredy 1997; Hong 2000; Flood 2003; Katz 2006).

Because of the recognition that men's culture plays a major contributing role in preventing sexual assault and rape, scholars have argued that all-male programs about sexual assault are a better starting place for involving boys and men in sexual-assault-prevention efforts. Alan Berkowitz cites the following reasons:

- Men are more comfortable, less defensive, and more honest in all-male groups;
- Men are less likely to talk openly and participate in the presence of women;
- Mixed-gender discussion can become polarized and thus less constructive;
- Single-gender groups reveal a diversity of opinions and views among men that may not express when women are present;
- Men feel safer disagreeing or putting pressure on each other in all-male groups; and
- Focusing on risk reduction strategies in mixed-gender groups can result in men assigning responsibility for the assault to women (Berkowitz 2002b).

As a result, numerous programs have been developed and designed for all-male college student audiences (Jackson 1995; Kilmartin 1996; Foubert and McEwen 1998; Hong 2000; Men Can Stop Rape 2007).

"Mickeys" and "Roofies": Drug-Facilitated Rape

(Santa Monica-UCLA Rape Treatment Center 2010; Fitzgerald and Riley 2000)

What Are Date Rape Drugs? While alcohol has long been used by potential perpetrators to facilitate sexual assault, there also exists an entire class of sedating drugs known informally as "date rape drugs"—the most common of which include gamma hydroxybutyrate (GHB, "Liquid Ecstasy," "Liquid X," "Grievous Bodily Harm," or "Easy Lay"), flunitrazepam (Rohypnol), scopolamine, burundanga, and ketamine (Special K). As with alcohol, these drugs are used to render the victim involuntarily helpless and vulnerable. Laboratory tests conducted on the urine of survivors of drug-facilitated sexual assault have revealed the use of other substances as well, including amphetamines, barbiturates, benzodiazepines, cocaine, marijuana, and opiates. All of these drugs can come in any form such as powders, pills, tablets, or liquids, and they are typically slipped into the victim's drink when the victim or her friends are not looking.

Effects of Sedating Substances. The effects of sedating drugs differ from person to person, and depend on such other factors as dosage, sensitivity to the substance, and the presence of alcohol or other drugs. The universal "telltale" signs that an individual may be under the influence of a sedative substance include impaired judgment, loss of inhibition, dizziness, and confusion. In addition, sedating substances can temporarily inhibit a person's ability to remain conscious, cause sudden and unexplained drowsiness, and impair motor coordination.

Brief periods of impaired memory also may result from sedative use, making GHB, Rohypnol, and similar substances the "drug of choice" for potential rapists, as their use means the victim cannot remember what happened while under the drug's influence. Depending on the substance and the presence of alcohol or other drugs in the person's system, more dangerous and life-threatening side effects may occur.

Rohypnol, the Prototypical Date Rape Drug. Rohypnol is banned in the United States and Canada, but it is used legally in sixty-four countries prior to surgery, and prescribed as sleeping pills in eighty countries. Odorless and colorless, this substance dissolves in ten minutes in a can of Diet Coke, and costs as little as $1.50 for a small white pill. A potent hypnotic sedative, Rohypnol creates an intoxicating effect that can last over eight hours when ingested. Ten times more powerful than Valium, it enhances the effects of alcohol and causes loss of inhibition, extreme drowsiness, relaxation, and amnesia. Rohypnol acquired the nickname "date rape drug" after police in Broward County, Florida, arrested several men in connection with administering "roofies" to their victims prior to sexually assaulting them.

Reducing the Risk of Being Drugged. Never leave your beverage unattended. Don't take any beverages, including alcohol, from someone you do not know well and trust. At a bar or club, accept drinks only from the bartender or server; watch carefully while he or she pours or mixes the drink. At parties, do not accept open-container beverages from anyone; if possible, bring your own beverage. Finally, be alert to the behavior of friends and ask them to watch out for you. If an individual appears extremely intoxicated after consuming a non-alcoholic beverage or only a small amount of alcohol, they have probably unknowingly ingested a sedative. Get them to medical assistance immediately.

If You Think You've Been Drugged and Sexually Assaulted. If you feel any of the symptoms of sedative use described above after consuming any kind of beverage, immediately contact a trusted family member, friend, law enforcement authority, physician, or 911 for help in getting to the hospital. Follow the procedures outlined in the section later in this chapter entitled *What to Do If You Are Sexually Assaulted.*

Proving Involuntary Drug Use. If you suspect that you have been drugged against your will, do not go home with or accept a ride from someone you do not know well. Instead, have a trusted friend or family member drive you to a rape crisis center, the hospital emergency room, or the police station. Ask to have a urine (usually 100 ml is needed) or blood (30 ml is typically drawn) sample taken as soon as possible. Most substances can be detected through appropriate drug testing up to 96 hours (four days) after ingestion. The findings of such tests can become valuable evidence in a court of law if you wish to press charges.

What to Do If You Are Sexually Assaulted

If you are sexually assaulted, there are several things you should know about taking care of your mental and physical health. It is important to seek emotional support as soon as possible after the assault. If available, call your local rape crisis center's 24-hour hotline for emotional support. Its staff is trained specifically to address issues of sexual assault. In addition, your campus's student health services or counseling center may also offer individual counseling and support groups for sexual assault survivors.

Be sure to seek medical attention at a nearby emergency room or go to your campus medical clinic, even if you have no visible injuries from the assault or do not intend to press charges. Internal injuries may have been sustained that will require attention; you may also want to be tested for HIV and other sexually transmitted infections as well as receive preventative treatment. The examining health care provider may also administer the sexual assault (or forensic) evidence collection kit in the event that you wish to press charges at a later date. Finally, prophylaxis in the form of antibiotics is available for syphilis, gonorrhea, and chlamydia; women who are concerned about pregnancy may want to request emergency contraceptives (or "morning-after pill") to prevent conception.

If you do wish to press charges, it is important to seek medical attention as soon as possible. Do not change clothes, shower, or douche before going to the emergency room, as doing so may destroy crucial evidence.

The FBI estimates that only one in ten stranger sexual assaults and one in one hundred acquaintance sexual assaults are reported to police. Reporting is essential to reducing the likelihood of future rapes occurring, so whenever possible, report the incident. However, **know that the decision to report a sexual assault to the police or to press charges is yours alone**, for only you know what is best for you. While the law recognizes sexual assault as a crime punishable by imprisonment, the courts do not always work that way. Legal proceedings can add additional and sometimes unnecessary trauma to a victim who is already under a lot of duress. Many victims do not report a sexual assault for fear of repercussion by the assailant, or because they do not want to embarrass their family and friends.

If you wish to hold a perpetrator accountable for sexual assault, several options are available to you. First, you can choose to file a criminal charge according to your state's statutes on rape. Note that legal definitions of rape and penalties for a conviction of rape vary from state to state. Call the local district attorney's office, or the sex crimes division of your local law enforcement agency, for more information about your legal options or to press charges.

Second, you can elect to pursue a civil case in order to gain monetary and other compensation for pain and suffering resulting from the attack. Many sexual assault survivors choose this route because the standard of proof is not as stringent; criminal courts require guilt "beyond a reasonable doubt" (a 99% standard of proof), while civil courts only require a "preponderance of evidence" (a 51% standard of proof). In a crime that typically involves "his word against hers," civil cases can be a more viable option for sexual assault victims for ensuring that the perpetrator face consequences for the sexual assault. Consult a private civil litigation attorney who specializes in sexual assault cases for more information.

Additionally, students victimized by a peer, professor, or university staff member can frequently seek recourse through internal disciplinary proceedings. These campus hearings occur independently of criminal or civil court charges. Students accused of sexual assault who are found to have violated campus codes of conduct may receive probation, suspension, or expulsion for their acts. Contact the office of the Dean of Students on your campus for more information or to file a charge. Faculty/staff perpetrators may face consequences under human resource policies and other institutional procedures, including sexual harassment policies. Contact the director of the office of human resources for more information about filing a complaint if the perpetrator is employed by your college or university.

As days and weeks lapse after the assault, you may find yourself experiencing unusual feelings or behaving in an atypical manner. Similar to post-traumatic stress disorder experienced by war veterans, *rape trauma syndrome* (RTS) refers to the cluster of feelings, behaviors, and psychological reactions commonly exhibited by both male and female sexual assault victims in response to such a life-threatening situation, and are summarized in Figure 18. RTS was first identified by two Boston City Hospital health care professionals, Ann Burgess (a nurse) and Lynda Holmstrom (a sociologist), in 1974 (Burgess and Holmstrom 1974). One of the most common reactions is denial—refusing to acknowledge that the rape happened. If you will recall, only 27% of women whose experiences meet the legal definition of sexual assault recognize themselves as sexual assault victims (Warshaw 1988).

Many sexual assault survivors wrongly blame themselves for the sexual assault. They may feel ashamed about what happened to them, or

feel like "used" or "dirty goods." Some become disgusted at the thought of sexual contact; others feel extremely angry and guilty. You may believe that the assault could have been averted if you had only done things differently; men, especially, are taught that they should always be able to defend themselves or be in control of a situation. However, you need to know that nothing you said or did caused the sexual assault to happen; nobody ever "asks" or deserves to be sexually assaulted.

Sexual assault victims frequently feel out of control during the first few weeks following the attack, exhibit an unusually high level of fear for their safety, and are unable to concentrate. You may become depressed, experience sleep and eating disturbances, have nightmares or flashbacks, or withdraw from friends and family out of mistrust. About one third of college rape survivors attempt suicide (Warshaw 1988).

Some survivors make major life changes such as moving away, quitting a job, or transferring to another school in order to cope with the pain of sexual assault. Still others may turn to substance abuse; on average, 75% of women in treatment for alcohol, drug, or food addictions report a history of childhood or adult sexual assault (Root 1989).

Feelings	Behaviors
• Guilt, Self-blame	• Disturbances in sleep or eating patterns
• Ashamed	• Drop out of school or quit job
• Fear	• Loss of interest in sex
• Anger	• End or withdraw from relationships
• Anxiety	• Change jobs or quite school
• Out of control	• Takes extreme safety precautions
• Violated	• Move to a new home or community
• Like "dirty" or "used goods"	• Flashbacks or nightmares
• Numbness	• Difficulty concentrating
• Humiliated	• Unwilling or unable to make decisions
• Mistrust of others	• Substance abuse and/or eating disorders
• Depression	• Suicide attempts
• Denial	• Self-mutilation
• Self-efficacy for having survived	• Enter helping professions

Figure 18: *Rape Trauma Syndrome (Adapted from: Burgess and Holmstrom 1974)*

All of these responses are normal, but can be difficult for you to understand. The best way to cope and begin your recovery process is to talk about these feelings with a supportive friend or a trained mental health professional. Some survivors find that journaling, painting, dancing, or music can be powerful and helpful ways for expressing the feelings associated with being a rape victim. While sexual assault certainly has a serious and lifelong impact on its victims, men and women who have experienced sexual assault can and do go on to lead happy, healthy, and productive lives—transforming a trauma into a source of strength and personal courage.

If your partner, friend, family member, classmate, or coworker is the victim/survivor of sexual violence, see Figure 19 for what you can do to help them begin the journey to recovery.

Women Fighting Back: How to Reduce Your Risk

Due to the pervasive rape culture in US society embedded in the media, the medical system, and legal institutions, victims of sexual violence are often blamed for their own victimization. In reality, **sexual assault is never the victim's fault.** However, until such time that men stop rape, there are things that a potential victim can do to fight back and, if faced with a sexual assault, effectively survive the experience. Both men and women are the victims of sexual assault, but on college campuses, women do still compose the vast majority of victims, so this section will be written with women in mind.

First, **know that you never lose the right to refuse or choose sex.** Women have just as much autonomy over their sexual desires as do men. It doesn't matter how long you have known your partner, or how much money your date has spent on you. Your body is not an item for sale. Similarly, we must validate both women who have made the choice to wait before becoming sexually active, as well women who have chosen to become sexually active (regardless of the number of sexual partners they choose to have).

Second, **be aware of the risks that young women and college women in particular face.** Adolescent and young adult women are at the highest risk of being victims of sexual assault. Therefore, a heightened sense of awareness on the part of women in their teens and twenties can help to avert a potential attack. Furthermore, realize that in most cases the greatest threat to your safety are people that you know, not strangers; in fact, over 75% of women are sexually or physically assaulted by their intimate male partners.

When in public or walking on the street, be sure to **carry yourself in an assertive posture, remain**

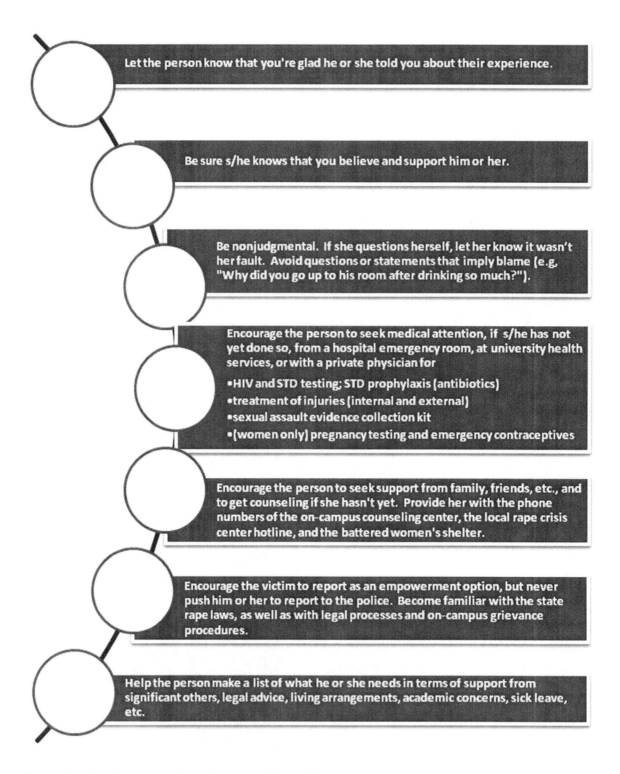

Figure 19: *How To Support Victims/Survivors of Sexual Violence*

alert and demonstrate that you are in full control of your mental faculties. This demeanor communicates to potential attackers that you care enough about yourself to fight back. However, don't forget that sexual assault is also a crime of opportunity—even if you do everything within your power, you may be chosen as a target.

Resist and speak out against rape-supportive myths and stereotypes. When women judge and label each other as "sluts" or "whores," they imply that some women are less deserving of respect than others—especially when they use this kind of language in the presence of men. Be sure that your language and actions do not inadvertently support the existing rape culture. Speak up against sexist comments or jokes about sexual harassment/assault.

Use common sense and trust your "gut." Take precautions to guard your own safety and that of your friends. Don't let friends walk home alone from a party or bar. When meeting someone for the first time, refrain from giving out your home phone number; get his number instead. If you are going on a date with someone for the first time, insist that you drive; let your roommate know where you will be for the date and about what time to expect you home. Similarly, refrain from going back for an intimate rendezvous to an empty apartment where you and he will be alone. Public places are the safest option for the first date.

Similarly, recognize **"red flags" and act on them.** If a man you are with is sending out vibes that make you uncomfortable or frightened, don't be too embarrassed to get out of the situation immediately. While there is no surefire way to pick out potential rapists, keep in mind that men who consume a substantial amount of pornography (magazines or films), use degrading terms to refer to women, or attempt to control your actions (who you talk to, the way you dress, what you eat, etc.) are probably not the type of men who truly respect and value women.

Manage alcohol consumption. Alcohol and other drugs (such as Rohypnol) are a major contributor in acquaintance rapes. Perpetrators frequently ply the victims with alcohol in order to render them vulnerable. That a woman has been drinking or is drunk is never a justification to rape her; however, it is important to realize that even small amounts of alcohol can interfere with your sense of judgment, your ability to fight back, and your memory of the attack should you be assaulted.

Say "no" unambiguously. Talking about sex honestly and openly has frequently caused women to be regarded as "aggressive" or "loose." Challenge these limiting and patronizing attitudes about women's sexuality by communicating directly and clearly about your sexual wants and your sexual limits before the date gets too "hot

and heavy." Verbal and body language that convey unequivocally your sexual boundaries will leave less room for doubt (or hope) in your partner's mind. And be sure that your verbal and non-verbal cues are in alignment. A male partner who has difficulty accepting that you can be frank and forthright about sexual activity is most likely not the kind of sexual partner who will respect you as an equal.

Learn, practice, and decide on a self-defense strategy now. There is no formula for making the decision to fight back. Some women who find themselves the target of an attack may physically fight back, while others choose not to. Both choices are right and only the victim can make this choice for herself at the time of an assault. Know that saying "no" is enough; you don't have to be injured or beaten up to "prove" you were raped. However, some women have elected to fight back and successfully averted a rape. Your voice is probably the best weapon you have to fight back. Yelling in a manner that demonstrates that you are fully cognizant of what is going on will frequently scare off attackers who assumed you were easy prey. However, if you do choose to defend yourself physically, be sure to evaluate your comfort level with regard to use of physical force or carrying a weapon. Be prepared to use any weapon you carry (mace, gun, etc.) correctly and quickly. Realize that any weapon you carry can also be used against you, and that use of force can sometimes escalate the violence. In all cases, the goal of fighting back is to momentarily incapacitate the attacker to give you time to get away and seek help.

The Power to Change: What Boys and Men Can Do to Prevent Rape

Ultimately, men, as its primary perpetrators, are responsible for preventing and ending campus rape. Unfortunately, many educational programs label all men as "potential rapists" or simply exclude men as partners in prevention. **While the disproportionate majority of campus sexual violence is perpetrated by college men, most college men are not perpetrators!** Nevertheless, all men are ethically and morally responsible for changing the behavior of the minority of men who do commit violence against women. Men oftentimes have the greatest ability to influence the behavior of other men, and as such, men have the greatest potential to impact other men and deter sexual assault (Katz 1995).

It isn't enough to be "against rape." You would have a very difficult time finding a man who says, "Oh, I think rape is just great. I think all women should be raped." Just about all men believe passionately that they would never rape a woman and that rape is wrong. Yet, most college men who commit acts that met the legal definition of rape fail to recognize their acts as such, even when the victim presses charges or when confronted by campus or law enforcement authorities. These men simply cannot see themselves as rapists—the stereotypical vicious, sex-deprived men wearing ski masks and touting a gun or some other weapon. Yet their behaviors are those of sexual violation.

Take a close look at your own behaviors; instead of reassuring yourself that you're not a rapist, examine the way you treat and feel about women: might you ever be placing yourself in potentially compromising situation? Ask yourself honestly: do you believe in any of the rape myths or some variation of them? Have you ever participated in propagating a rape myth? If so, work on changing them.

Refrain from making sexist jokes or laughing when others tell them. Whether you actively participate in the degradation of women or simply passively listen, you are sending off the message that you implicitly believe women are not as deserving of respect or equal treatment as men are. Jokes, comments, pornography, and other forms of media or communication that objectify or sexualize women foster a rape culture that justifies and normalizes rape. Refuse to tolerate this in your friends or in your own behavior.

Remember that every woman is somebody's sister, daughter, mother, girlfriend, etc. Oftentimes, men demand that the women who are important to them be treated with dignity and respect, but fail to afford the same treatment to other women. Treat all women as you would want the women you care about to be treated.

Never assume; always ask. Dating on the college campus has become virtually extinct; accordingly, the rules of about what is sexually appropriate are not as clear these days. Men are frequently left trying to guess what their companions want from them. As a result, they usually resort to reading "body language" or to interpreting women's actions—both of which can lead to erroneous conclusions. For example, research has shown that men and women interpret non-verbal actions differently; for instance, touching and hugging is often assumed to be a "come on" by many men, whereas women see such physical contact as a way of tuning in and connecting.

Similarly, many men (and women) believe that if a woman goes up to a man's bedroom, then she is interested in sexual intercourse. Rather, there may be numerous possibilities. It is true that a woman may not be acting in the best interest of her safety by going up to a man's room, but her doing so does not alleviate a man's accountability for his own behavior.

While both partners need to assume responsibility for honest, forthright communication regarding sexual desires and boundaries, there is no reason that men cannot initiate a mature conversation. Remember, our social norms unfairly inhibit women from being more comfortable expressing their sexuality for fear of being judged; be sure that as a man, you don't exacerbate that norm. When a woman is comfortable enough to be responsible for her own sexuality and for expressing her sexual desires, she needs to be reinforced and appreciated for that, not judged. If a woman is still trying to play "head games" or is using sex to manipulate you, find another partner who is mature enough to handle the responsibility of sex.

Always establish clear consent with your sexual partner. Remember, take everything except a verbal, audible, and sober "yes" from your partner as a "no."

Abandon the virgin/whore double standard. When men (and women) haphazardly designate some women as "whores" or "sluts" on the basis of the number of sexual partners she's had, they are reducing women's worth as an intimate partner to their sexual behavior. The number of partners that any individual has should not be used to judge or categorize him or her. Labeling some women as "whores" implies that some women are less deserving of respect and perhaps more deserving of mistreatment—or to be raped.

Manage alcohol consumption. The vast majority of campus rapes involve alcohol or other drug use on the part of perpetrator and/or victim. Research studies demonstrate that alcohol increases male sexual aggression by exacerbating the effects of testosterone. At the same time, drinking on the part of the victim is perceived as increasing her culpability but mitigating the blame placed on the perpetrator—one of the more prevalent rape myths. In reality, men and women are both responsible for their actions and words even under the influence. Men should especially be aware that when they are intoxicated, they may not listen as well, be able to hear "no," or be aware of their own physical strength.

Intervene with a male friend when he is getting too sexually aggressive. Rape is typically referred to as a crime with no witnesses. In actuality, however, there are many signs preceding a sexual assault incident to indicate that trouble might be brewing. All too often, however, men and women are reluctant to intervene with friends. The attitude is one of "live and let live." If you care about your male friends, don't let them bring intoxicated sexual partners up to their rooms, sexually harass women at a party or in a bar, or otherwise place themselves in a potentially risky situation. When sexual assault happens, the entire community is negatively impacted. You have a vested interest to avoid risky situations for yourself and your male friends.

Take a public stand against sexual assault. Join a men's organization on your campus that supports the equal treatment of men and women. Organize a Men Against Violence or Men of Strength chapter on your campus. Write letters to the editor of the college newspaper. Participate in anti-violence marches and rallies. Not enough men's voices are heard in the public arena in support of a non-violence community. Remember, men have the greatest power to affect other men as friends, brothers, fathers, and sons.

Be an ally to women. Women face a reality that is virtually unknown to men. They spend a considerable amount of energy worrying about their physical and emotional safety, and taking precautions to reduce their risk—sometimes inconveniencing themselves in order to feel more safe. Then, once women have become victims or survivors of sexual violence, they spend the rest of their lives coping with the aftermath of that experience—an experience that subsequently ripples and "touches" the lives of those closest to the victim/survivor.

While men are also targets of violence, they do not devote nearly the same amount of time or energy in thinking about violence or about how to reduce their risks of becoming a victim. When women have to take time and energy that could instead be devoted to improving their own quality of life or that of their families and communities, we all lose in some way. Men can also help reduce sexual violence by taking time to listen and understand women's realities and perspectives, and then supporting the issues that are important to women. Being sensitive to the intersections of identity among women is also important, as women of different backgrounds will experience different versions of women's reality.

Resources for Further Learning

Websites

- **California Coalition Against Sexual Assault:** http://calcasa.org/
- **Centers for Disease Control and Prevention:** http://www.cdc.gov/ViolencePrevention/sexualviolence/
- **Higher Education Center for Alcohol, Drug Abuse, and Violence Prevention:** http://www.higheredcenter.org/
- **Men Can Stop Rape:** http://www.mencanstoprape.org/
- **Mentors in Violence Prevention:** http://www.sportinsociety.org/mvp/
- **National Sexual Violence Resource Center:** http://www.nsvrc.org/
- **Rape, Abuse, and Incest National Network:** http://www.rainn.org/
- **Santa Monica-UCLA Rape Treatment Center:** http://www.911rape.org/
- **Sexual Violence Prevention and Education Program:** http://azrapeprevention.org/

Books

- Brownmiller, S. (1993). *Against our will: Men, women and rape.* New York: Ballantine Publishing Group.
- Buchwald, E., Fletcher, P. R., and Roth, M. (Eds.). (2005). *Transforming a rape culture (2nd Edition).* Minneapolis: Milkweed Editions.
- Dines, G., Jensen, R., and Russo, A. (1998). *Pornography: The production and consumption of inequality.* New York: Routledge.
- Katz, J. (2006). *The macho paradox: Why some men hurt women and how all men can help.* Naperville, IL: Sourcebooks, Inc.
- Kilmartin, C. T., and Berkowitz, A. D. (2005). *Sexual assault in context: Teaching college men about gender (Updated Edition).* Mahwah, NJ: Lawrence Earlbaum Associates Inc., Publishers.
- Kivel, P. (1998). *Men's work: How to stop the violence that tears our lives apart* (2nd Edition). Center City, MN: Hazelden Publishing.
- Warshaw, R. (1994). *I never called it rape: The Ms. Report on recognizing, fighting and surviving date and acquaintance rape.* New York: HarperCollins, Publishers.

Questions to Consider

1. What are some ways you as peer educators can help address violence on campus?
2. Why should men be engaged in sexual assault programming?
3. What is the socioecological model and what is its usefulness in violence-prevention programming?

References

Abbey, A. (2002). Alcohol-related sexual assault: A common problem among college students. *Journal of Studies on Alcohol, Supplement No. 14,* p. 118–128.

Abbey, A. & McAuslan, P. (2004). *A longitudinal examination of male college students' perpetration of sexual assault. Journal of Consulting and Clinical Psychology, 72 (5),* p. 747–756.

Abbey, A., Zawacki, T., Buck, P.O., Clinton, A. M., & McAuslan, P. (2001). *Alcohol and sexual assault. Alcohol Research and Health, 25(1),* p. 43–51.

American College Health Association. (2009). *American College Health Association-National College Health Assessment II: Reference group executive summary, Fall 2009.* Linthicum, MD: author.

Benedict, J. (1999). *Public heroes, private felons: Athletes and crimes against women.* Boston, MA: Northeastern University Press.

Berkowitz, A., Burkhart, B. R., & Bourg, S. B. (1994). *Research on college men and rape. In A. Berkowitz (Ed.), Men and rape: Theory, research, and prevention programs in higher education: New directions for student services #65.* San Francisco: Jossey-Bass

Berkowitz, A. D. (2002a). *Guidelines for consent in intimate relationship. Campus Safety and Student Development, 3 (4),* p. 49–50.

Berkowitz, A. D. (2002b). *Fostering men's responsibility for preventing sexual assault. In P.A. Schewe (Ed.), Preventing violence in relationships.* Washington, DC: American Psychological Association.

Berkowitz, A. D. (Ed.). (2004). *Men and rape: Theory, research, and prevention programs in higher education: New Directions for Student Services #65.* San Francisco: Jossey-Bass, citing Muehlenhard & Cook, 1988.

Burgess, A.W. & Holmstrom, L.L. (1974). *Rape trauma syndrome. American Journal of Psychiatry, 131,* p. *981–986.*

Burt, M. R. (1991). Rape myths and acquaintance rape. In Andrea Parrot & Laurie Bechhofer Eds.), *Acquaintance rape: The hidden crime.* New York: John Wiley & Sons.

Connell, R.W. (2005). *Masculinities (2nd Edition).* Berkeley: University of California Press.

Dahlberg, L.L. & Krug, E.G. (2002). Violence—a global public health problem. *In E.G. Krug, L. L. Dahlberg, J.A. Mercy, A. B. Zwi & R. Lozano (Eds.), World report on violence and health.* Geneva: World Health Organization.

David, D. S. & Brannon, R. (1976). *The forty-nine percent majority: The male sex role.* Reading, MA: Addison-Wesley Publishing Company, Inc.

Fisher, B.S., Cullen, F. T. & Turner, M. G. (2000). *The sexual victimization of college women (NCJRS Publication No. 182369).* Washington, DC: U. Department of Justice.

Fitzgerald, N. & Riley, K.J. (2000, April). *Drug-facilitated rape: Looking for the missing pieces. National Institute of Justice Journal,* 8–15.

Flood, M. (2003). *Engaging men: Strategies and dilemmas in violence prevention education among men. Women Against Violence: Issue Thirteen,* 2002–2003, p. 25–32.

Foubert, J. D. & McEwen, M.K. (1998). *An all-male rape prevention peer education program: Decreasing fraternity men's behavior intent to rape. Journal of College Student Development, 39(6),* p. 548–556.

Hong, L. (2000). *Toward a transformed approach to prevention: Breaking the link between masculinity and violence. Journal of American College Health, 48 (6),* p. 269–279.

Jewkes, R., Sen, P. & Garcia-Moreno, C. (2002). *Sexual violence.* In Krug, E.G., Dahlberg, L.L., Mercy, J.A, Zwi , A.B., & Rafael Lozano (Eds.), *World report on violence and health.* Geneva: World Health Organization.

Katz, J. (1995). Reconstructing masculinity in the locker room: The mentors in violence prevention project. *Harvard Educational Review*, 65(2): p. 163–174.

Katz, J. (2006). *The macho paradox: Why some men hurt women and how all men can help.* Naperville, IL: Sourcebooks, Inc.

Kilmartin, C. T. (1996). The white ribbon campaign: Men working together to end men's violence against women. *Journal of College Student Development, 37,* p. 347–348.

Kimmel, M. (2005). Clarence W, Iron Mike, Tailhook, Senator Packwood, Spur Posse, Magic—and us. In E. Buchwald, Fletcher, P. R., & Roth, M. (Eds.). *Transforming a rape culture* (2nd Edition). Minneapolis: Milkweed Editions.

Marchell, T. & Cummings, N. (2001). Alcohol and sexual violence among college students. In A. J. Ottens & K. Hotelling (Eds.). *Sexual violence on campus: Policies, programs and perspectives.* New York: Springer Publishing Company, Inc.

Marshall, D. L. (1993). Violence and the male gender role. *Journal of College Student Psychotherapy, 8:* p. 203–218.

Men Can Stop Rape. (2007). Trainings and workshops: Men Creating Change. Retrieved from http://www. mencanstoprape.org/info-url2697/info url_list.htm?section=MEN%20CREATING%20CHANGE

Messner, M. A. & Sabo, D.F. (1994). *Sex, violence and power in sports: Rethinking masculinity.* Freedom, CA: Crossing Press.

Rape, Abuse & Incest National Network (RAINN). (2010). *Reporting rates.* Retrieved from http://www.rainn.org/ get-information/statistics/reporting-rates

Root, M.P. (1989). Treatment failures: The role of sexual victimization in women's addictive behavior. *American Journal of Orthopsychiatry, 59* (4), p. 542–549.

Sanday, P. (2007). *Fraternity gang rape: Sex, brotherhood, and privilege on campus* (2nd Edition). New York: New York University Press.

Sandler, B. & Ehrhart, J. K. (1985). *Campus gang rape: Party games?* Washington, DC: Project on the Status and Education of Women, Association of American Colleges and Universities.

Santa Monica-UCLA Rape Treatment Center. (2010). Drug-facilitated sexual assault—An overview. Retrieved from http://www.911rape.org/drug-facilitated-sexual-assault-dfsa/overview

Schwartz, M.D. & DeKeseredy, W.S. (1997). *Sexual assault on the college Campus: The role of male peer support.* Thousand Oaks, CA: Sage Publications.

US Department of Justice. (2010). The facts about the office on violence against women focus areas. Retrieved from http://www.ovw.usdoj.gov/ovw-fs.htm

Warshaw, R. (1994). *I never called it rape: The Ms. Report on recognizing, fighting and surviving date and acquaintance rape.* New York: HarperCollins, Publishers.

White, J. W., & Humphrey, J. A. (1991). Young people's attitudes toward acquaintance rape. In Andrea Parrot and Laurie Bechhofer (Eds.), *Acquaintance Rape: The Hidden Crime.* New York: John Wiley & Sons, Inc.

Chapter 14

HIV and Other Sexually Transmitted Infections

By Luoluo Hong and Lindsay Walker McCall

While HIV/AIDS have received the most aggressive media attention over the past two decades, HIV infection is just one of many sexually transmitted infections (STIs). While not always as fatal as HIV infection, STIs are far more prevalent in the population. If left untreated, their consequences are very damaging.

Anyone who is sexually active is at risk for STIs. STIs can affect individuals of any gender, age, race, class, or sexual orientation. Many individuals infected with an STI are asymptomatic but still contagious. Because you cannot "tell" if someone has an STI, always practice safer sex and reduce the risks of both HIV and STIs.

Epidemiology

Sexually transmitted infections are bacterial and viral infections that are acquired and transmitted primarily through sexual contact, including vaginal and anal intercourse, as well as oral–genital and oral–anal contact, with an infected partner who may or may not have symptoms. Contrary to myth, STIs cannot be contracted from toilet seats or swimming pools. A few STIs are also transmissible by means other than sexual. The hepatitis B virus (HBV), like HIV, can be contracted through needle-sharing. A mother can pass herpes (herpes simplex virus, or HSV) and genital warts (human papilloma virus, or HPV) to her infant during birth. Crabs can be transmitted by using infected sheets and towels.

Because it is transmitted through blood and needles, as well as through sexual contact, by definition, HIV is not a sexually transmitted infection. Nevertheless, it is always important to discuss "HIV and other STIs" together. This emphasizes the importance of safer sex as a method of HIV and STI prevention.

Each year, approximately 19 million Americans are diagnosed with an STI. Of those, almost 50% are aged fifteen to twenty-four (National Prevention Information Network 2010). In 2007, chlamydia was the most commonly reported STI, with over 1 million cases reported to health departments across the United States. Chlamydia represents the largest number of cases ever to be reported to the Center for Disease Control and Prevention (CDC) for any disease in 2007 and 2008 (National Institute of Allergy and Infectious Diseases 2010). Currently, HPV is the most common STI, with over 40 different types and 20 million Americans currently infected (CDC 2010e).

With the advent of the "sexual revolution" in the 1960s, sex with multiple partners became much more acceptable and openly practiced. Furthermore, women increasingly relied on oral contraceptives and the intrauterine device (IUD) for pregnancy prevention. To compound the problem, many of the STI-causing organisms have undergone mutations and developed new strains, making them resistant to many of the traditional, inexpensive treatments.

STIs now constitute perhaps the greatest health threat to young adults aged fifteen to twenty-five. With an infection rate on the rise, an estimated 50% of sexually active men and women acquire genital HPV at some point in their lives (CDC 2010c). It is estimated that half of all sexually active youth will contract an STI by age 26 (Kaiser Family Foundation 2006). Similarly, one in four college students will be diagnosed with an STI before graduating (American College Health Association 1987). The most common STIs on college campuses, in order of incidence, are (1) chlamydia; (2) genital warts (caused by HPV); and (3) herpes (Type I = oral, Type II = genital). At least 10%–15% of the student population is infected with chlamydia each year. One in eight college women carries HPV, the virus that causes genital warts.

All STIs can be categorized into one of three groups, each of which is characterized by different treatment options:

Category	Treatment	Examples
Bacterial	Treatable with an antibiotic.	Chlamydia Gonorrhea Syphilis Gardnerella Trichomoniasis
Viral	Remain in body for lifetime. Symptoms can only be managed.	Genital warts (HPV) Herpes (Type I, Type II) Hepatitis B HIV
Parasitic	Topical treatment available.	Pubic lice ("crabs")

Common symptoms of STIs include:
- **Itching** on or around genitals;
- Malodorous, discolored **discharge** from urethra or vagina;
- **Bleeding** from urethra or vagina;
- **Sores, lesions, or growths** on or around genitals;
- **Burning** sensation on urination or ejaculation; and/or
- **Pain** during intercourse.

Complications of Untreated STI

Most bacterial STIs, such as gonorrhea, chlamydia, and syphilis, are relatively easy to cure with antibiotics if diagnosed quickly. Viral STIs such as genital herpes, genital warts, and HIV infection, on the other hand, are difficult to treat and often incurable. In fact, once contracted, these viruses typically remain with the person for a lifetime.

Costs attributable to STIs amount to over $16 billion annually. After AIDS, the most serious complications of STIs include:
- Pelvic inflammatory disease (PID);
- Cervical and testicular cancer associated with HPV;
- Sterility;
- Blindness due to advanced syphilis;
- Ectopic (or tubal) pregnancy;
- Fetal and infant death; birth defects;
- Mental retardation; and
- Death.

The most common side effects of untreated STIs are infertility and cervical cancer. The psychological impact of being diagnosed with an STI can be devastating and embarrassing. Having one STI lowers your resistance to other infections. In fact, **coinfection**—infection with more than one STI—is very common. For example, syphilis is often diagnosed with chlamydia. Presence of an STI also increases your vulnerability to HIV infection. The key to minimizing the negative consequences of STIs is early detection and early treatment.

Chlamydia

Chlamydia is caused by the *Chlamydia trachomatis* organism, a highly contagious bacterium. With over 1 million new cases a year, it is the most prevalent STI, but it is also considered the most curable. It commonly occurs with gonorrhea. Appearing within twenty-one days, symptoms in women include unusual vaginal discharge, burning when urinating, lower abdominal pain, pain during intercourse, bleeding between menstrual periods, and low-grade fever; women are asymptomatic 67% of the time. Symptoms in men include a mucous-like discharge from the urethra and/or burning when urinating, itching around urethra, pain and swelling in the testicles, and low-grade fever; men are asymptomatic 50% of the time.

The most common complication of chlamydia for women is pelvic inflammatory disease (PID). PID is an infection of the fallopian tubes accompanied by fever, abdominal pain, heavy bleeding, and excessive discharge; it can result in infertility. NGU, or nongonococcal urethritis, is another possible complication. Untreated chlamydia in men also leads to sterility. Chlamydia can be diagnosed from a cell culture. Infected persons and their partners are treated with antibiotics.

Gonorrhea

Also known as the "clap," "the drip," or "a dose," gonorrhea is also caused by a bacterium. It occurs less frequently than chlamydia, but it is the most commonly reported infectious disease in the US—700,000 cases each year. Men may have a creamy, pus-like discharge and pain on urination within two to ten days after infection. Women usually have no symptoms, but may have vaginal discharge and pain on urination.

Gonorrhea can be detected with a cell culture. Left untreated, gonorrhea can cause arthritis, dermatitis, and heart problems in men and women, and ectopic (tubal) pregnancy in women. It can also be transmitted to infants at birth. Infected persons and their sexual partners are treated with antibiotics.

Herpes

Herpes is caused by the herpes simplex virus (HSV). Once a person contracts HSV, they carry it for life. Approximately one out of six people are infected. There are two types of herpes. The Type I (HSV-1) virus produces cold sores around the mouth (oral herpes), while the Type II (HSV-2) virus generates small painful blisters on the genitals, cervix, or anus (genital herpes). The lesions may be tender and itchy. A herpes Type I infection is often the result of overexposure to the sun, while Type II infections are sexually transmitted. However, oral herpes can be transferred to the genitals.

A herpes episode includes the sores, fever, headache, muscle aches, problems urinating, and swollen glands. Although the first herpes episode is usually the most severe, they can recur at any time and are usually triggered by stress. The number of recurrences varies from person to person. Many individuals experience itching or tingling—"prodromal symptoms"—at the blister site just before a recurrence, indicating that the virus is present on the skin.

Herpes is contagious from the time any prodromal symptoms appear until the blister have cleared up; a person with herpes should not have any genital–genital or oral–genital contact during this time. Herpes symptoms will usually begin within two to twenty days after infection. Women with herpes are at increased risk for cervical cancer and may pass HSV to an infant during childbirth. There is no cure for herpes, but the blisters may be treated with Acyclovir capsules or ointment.

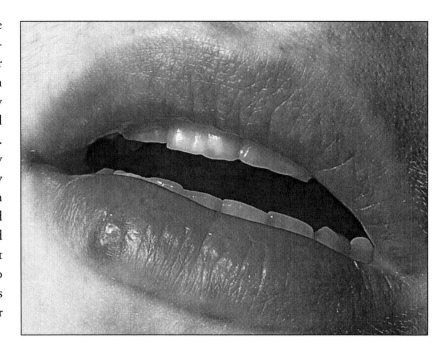

Hepatitis B

The hepatitis B virus (HBV) is found in bodily fluid and excretions; concentrations in blood and semen are most infectious. HBV is transmitted through sexual intercourse or needle-sharing with infected individuals. The virus can also be transmitted during childbirth. Most cases of Hepatitis B are asymptomatic. However, early symptoms include nausea, general malaise, fever, and loss of appetite. Symptoms can last several days to several weeks. In the later stages, dark urine or jaundice may appear.

A diagnosis is confirmed with serologic testing. There is no specific treatment for Hepatitis B. Adequate diet and fluid intake, rest, and decreased alcohol consumption alleviate symptoms.

HIV Infection

Current estimates by the CDC and the American College Health Association put the number of college students infected between one in every 250 to 500 students. In the general population, over 1 million Americans are infected with HIV, equivalent to 22.6 cases per 100,000 (Center for Disease Control and Prevention 2010a). National data state 45 percent of new HIV infections were among blacks or African Americans. Additional findings in 2007 suggest 53% of new infections occur in gay and bisexual men (Center for Disease Control and Prevention 2010a).

HIV, or *human immunodeficiency virus,* is the virus that causes AIDS. HIV has been found in infective concentrations in the following bodily fluids: blood, semen, vaginal secretions, and breast milk. HIV can be transmitted through direct contact with any of these fluids. Minute traces have been discovered in saliva and tears, but there is no evidence that HIV is transmissible through them.

HIV is a "wimpy" virus relatively speaking. Ordinary household bleach and isopropyl alcohol can inactivate HIV. Theoretically, one HIV virus is enough to infect an individual, but in reality HIV infectivity occurs on a concentration gradient. It is not transmitted by casual contact. Casual contact includes hugging, handshaking, use of public facilities such as bathrooms or swimming pools, sneezing or coughing, and sharing dishes/utensils/food.

A person can transmit or contract HIV only when bodily fluids are exchanged or come into contact with mucous membranes in the mouth, anus, and vagina, or on the penis. Receptive anal intercourse incurs the highest risk of contracting HIV. However, any unprotected anal, oral, or vaginal intercourse with an HIV-positive partner is risky. Behaviors associated with high risk for contracting HIV include IV drug use, having sex with an IV drug user, exchanging sex for money or drugs, and having multiple partners. Cofactors that increase the likelihood of HIV transmission during sex include a history of genital ulcers or lesions, e.g., herpes or syphilis, and being uncircumcised.

In general, exposure to contaminated blood, blood products, and donor products also increase the risk of HIV transmission. This includes:

- sharing contaminated needles, syringe-barrels, and other drug paraphernalia for IV drug use (street drugs including heroin and cocaine);
- sharing contaminated needles for injecting hormones (steroids and estrogen), e.g., athletes, persons undergoing sex reassignment surgery (transgender), or women on hormone treatment;
- sharing contaminated needles for tattooing and ear-piercing;
- accidents in health care settings;
- receipt of contaminated blood, blood products, or organs, e.g., for an operation, hemophilia;
- receipt of semen from an infected donor for artificial insemination; and
- sharing personal hygiene items exposed to contaminated blood (toothbrushes, razors).

Since March 1985, the entire United States blood supply has been routinely screened for HIV. As a result, the blood supply is much safer today than in the past; the estimated risk of receiving an infected unit of blood is less than one in 2 million. Due to increased precautionary measures, there is virtually no risk associated with donating blood.

HIV causes AIDS by weakening the immune system. A retrovirus, HIV consists of a tightly packed core of RNA surrounded by a protein coat. When the virus infects a host cell, it uses reverse transcriptase to manufacture *proviral DNA*, from which viral proteins can then be made.

The primary target of HIV is the T-4 helper cell. This is a white blood cell that directs the body's immune response against invading organisms. Once the HIV finds a T-4 helper cell, it attaches itself to the outside. After entering the T-4 nucleus, HIV uses enzymes to facilitate replication. New viral particles then enter the bloodstream and infect other T-4 helper cells. The presence of HIV in a cell can hamper cell function and destroy the cell completely. When the number of T-4 cells in the blood decreases from a normal level of 1,000 to below 200, the immune system is no longer able to fight infections that previously posed no threat.

Macrophages, another type of white blood cell, can also be attacked by HIV. If a macrophage with HIV attached crosses the blood–brain barrier, HIV can then attack the glial brain cells, leading to neurological disorders.

HIV infection undergoes three stages. During the **asymptomatic stage**, individuals do not know they have been infected, but they are capable of transmitting the virus. The virus may or may not be detected by an HIV antibody test. This first stage usually lasts 4 to 5 years, but may last as long as 12 to 17 years (average is 14 years). The amount of time an individual spends in the asymptomatic stage can also be increased with use of AZT/ddI. In the **symptomatic stage**, which can also last several years, the infected person begins experiencing some of the following unexplainable symptoms:

- bruising or bleeding easily and excessively;
- persistent fatigue that interferes with physical and mental activities;
- weight loss in excess of 15 lbs. or 10% of normal body weight in less than two months not related to diet or increased activity;
- fever higher than 100 degrees Fahrenheit lasting longer than several weeks;
- drenching night sweats, shaking, or chills for over a month;

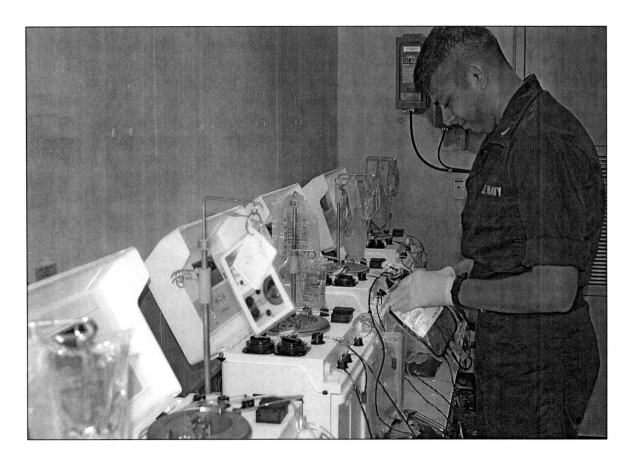

- swollen, enlarged lymph nodes and glands in the neck, armpits, or groin that remain swollen for more than one month;
- white spots or unusual blemishes on the tongue or roof of the mouth;
- persistent watery diarrhea;
- a persistent dry cough, especially if accompanied by shortness of breath;
- pink to purple, flat or raised blotches or bumps under the skin or on mucous membranes that do not disappear; and/or
- blurred vision, severe headaches, or significant memory loss.

In the final stage, the person is diagnosed as having **AIDS**. The onset of one or more opportunistic infections signals the beginning of this stage. Once a person reaches this stage, there is a 90% chance of mortality within two to three years.

Certain **cofactors** can affect the course of HIV transmission to AIDS. Because it taxes your immune system, presence of another STI renders an individual more vulnerable to HIV infection. Similarly, stress, poor health and nutrition, and excessive drinking and drugging lower your resistance to HIV infection. These cofactors can also affect the rate of seroconversion, onset of opportunistic infections, and development of AIDS.

Opportunistic infections (OI) are the primary manifestation of AIDS. Opportunistic infections are those diseases that rarely occur in individuals who have a normal and viable immune system. However, because HIV attacks the body's immune response and lowers resistance, persons with AIDS are extremely susceptible to repeated and numerous bacterial and viral infections. *It is important to remember that people do not die of AIDS, but rather from the OIs that result.* Many OIs result in cancers and acute degenerative diseases. The most common opportunistic infection among intravenous drug users is Pneumocystis carinii pneumonia (PCP); among gay men it is Kaposi's sarcoma (KS); and among women they are chronic yeast infections and vigilant HPV.

Pneumocystis carinii pneumonia (PCP): a fungal infection of the lungs; characterized by a mild cough or chest discomfort lasting two to ten weeks; accompanied by shortness of breath and fever; can be prevented with monthly inhalations of pentamidine; this is the most common opportunistic infection

Kaposi's sarcoma (KS): a type of skin cancer, affecting the blood and lymphatic vessel walls; characterized by pink to purple, flat or raised blotches and bumps; they initially resemble bruises, but they do not disappear

Other infections common to persons with AIDS that do affect people with normally functioning immune systems include chronic cytomegalovirus (CMV) retinitis, AIDS dementia syndrome (ADS), chronic diarrhea, Burkitt's lymphoma, lymphadenopathy syndrome (LAS), unusually severe shingles (Herpes zoster), thrush (Oral candidiasis), primary or recurrent herpes simplex virus, and atypical tuberculosis (TB).

The CDC revised the definition for diagnosing AIDS in 1992, in large part to better account for the growing number of AIDS cases in women. Biological markers (CD4+ T-lymphocyte count below 200/microliter, or CD4+ percentage less than 14) will replace opportunistic infections in heralding the onset of AIDS (CDC 1992).

Human Papilloma Virus (HPV), or Genital Warts

Also known as condyloma, genital warts are one kind of lesion produced by the human papilloma virus (HPV), a family of at least forty strains of viruses. Highly contagious, HPV is transmitted through direct contact with the lesions. An estimated six million cases are diagnosed each year in the US. Once contracted, HPV is never eliminated from the body; rather, the virus remains latent, controlled by the immune system. HPV is often diagnosed upon visual examination or a positive Pap result.

Usually within 6–8 months of infection, a local irritation or itching on, in, and around the genitals occurs, followed by soft, flat, irregularly surfaced growths called warts. Warts can appear on the shaft or head of the penis, in the urethra, or on and around the vagina, vulva, cervix, or anus. Warts often are not visible to the naked eye; other times, they look like small hard spots or have a fleshy cauliflower-like appearance. Warts can be very difficult to get rid of and are highly contagious.

Genital warts have been associated with increased rates of intraepithelial neoplasia (precancerous condition), dysplasia, and cervical cancer among young women. Therefore, women who have HPV must have regular follow-up Pap smears every six months. Treatments for genital warts include topical application with trichloracetic acid, podophyllin, interferon or 5-fluorouracil (5-FU) cream. More extensive warts may require cryotherapy, laser surgery, or liquid nitrogen.

The incidence of HPV on college campuses has recently reached a mini-epidemic. An average of 28 to 46 percent of women under the age of 25 are infected with genital HPV. There is now a vaccine available for both men and women to reduce the risk of HPV of the types that can cause cervical cancer.

Pubic Lice

Also called "crab lice," "cooties," or "crabs," pubic lice are tiny parasites that breed in the pubic hair and cause intense itching. Usually transmitted sexually, they can also be transmitted through contaminated underwear, sheets, or towels. The pubic louse attaches itself to the skin around the genitals and lays eggs ("nits") on the pubic hair shafts. These "nits" can live for almost a week unattached to a human. On rare occasions, lice will migrate to the chest, scalp, or underarms.

If left untreated, pubic lice multiply quickly and cause great discomfort. Treatment in the form of creams and shampoos are available with or without prescription. Everyone with whom the infected person has had close contact should be treated, and all clothes and bedding should be washed in hot water.

Syphilis

Caused by bacteria, this STD is also referred to as "syph," "pox," "bad blood," or "lues." Syphilis occurs in three distinct stages—primary, secondary, and late—associated with three sets of symptoms. The most common symptom of primary syphilis is a painless sore, called a "chancre," which usually appears on the vagina, cervix, vulva, mouth, or penis up to 12 weeks after infection. The chancre disappears after 2–6 weeks with or without treatment. Signs of secondary syphilis occur 6–8 weeks after exposure; they include swollen lymph nodes, skin rash, hair loss, and flu-like symptoms.

If left untreated, syphilis will cause blindness, insanity, permanent disability, or death in the late stage. It can also result in stillbirth or birth defects if contracted during pregnancy. A blood test can detect syphilis. The infected person and their partners are treated with antibiotics.

Treatment of STIs

Treatment for an STI does not provide immunity against future infection. Nor does infection with one STI protect you against other STIs. In fact, infection with more than one STI at a time is very common; once infected, the body's resistance is lowered.

Health care providers will prescribe some sort of topical or oral medication upon diagnosing an STI. It is important to take all of the medication in the prescribed manner, even if the symptoms disappear in a few days before the treatment is finished.

To prevent re-infection and cross-infection, both you and your partner(s) should be treated together. Refrain from sexual contact during treatment. Be sure to take the entire dosage (usually ten days). Avoid alcohol consumption. Women on the pill should use a back-up method. Remember, antibiotics are a treatment, not a vaccine.

STI treatment must include responsible communication. Having an STI can be embarrassing and uncomfortable. However, if you have an STI, refrain from sexual contact until you have completed the entire treatment. Don't delay in notifying all your current and past sexual partners so that they can be treated, as well. This guards against further infection and reduces the likelihood of serious complications.

HIV Antibody Testing

The HIV antibody test is used in screening for HIV. This test actually tests for the presence of antibodies produced in response to HIV infection. Three tests are currently in use for HIV screening. The **ELISA** is the most commonly used and the least expensive, but it is also prone to some error. It detects HIV antibody only and is usually used for screening. The **Western Blot** is a more expensive and specific test, detecting HIV itself; it is used to confirm a positive ELISA test. The most expensive, the **immunofluorescent antibody (IFA) assay** fulfills a similar purpose.

The time period between HIV infection and the presence of detectable antibodies is called **the window period**. Because it takes time for antibodies to build up to a level sufficient for the test to detect, people who are concerned about HIV should wait at least three months after experiencing risky behavior before testing. While many people seroconvert within three months, it can take as long as three years; therefore, follow-up testing every six months is also recommended.

A negative test can be interpreted in two ways. Either it is a *true negative,* that is, the person has not been exposed to HIV, or it is a *false negative*: the person has been exposed to HIV but the amount of antibody produced thus far is insufficient to be detected. A positive test indicates that antibody to HIV is present in the body; it is not a diagnosis of AIDS. Note that *false positives* occur frequently. It is important to remember if a person has had risky behavior, negative results can be misleading. Safer sex practices should continue even when a test is negative. In other words, testing is not a form of safer sex.

Testing can be confidential and/or anonymous. **Confidential testing** means a person's name is attached to the results, but the results of the test remain private; only certain individuals have access to the information. In **anonymous testing**, the person's name is in no way connected to the test result. Given the possibility of discrimination by employers and health insurance companies, people considering testing should carefully weigh the costs and benefits of testing.

Confidential testing: the number of people who have access to the fact that you tested and to the test results is limited

Anonymous testing: your name is not in any way connected to the fact that you tested or to the test result

Regardless of the result, testing is an extremely stressful experience; people who decide to test should receive counseling and seek support from family and friends when possible.

In short, people who want to test for HIV should: (1) Receive pre- **and** post-test counseling; (2) Wait **at least** 3–6 months ("window period") after risk activity to determine if exposed; (3) Know testing is not a substitute for safer sex! Its purpose is for early diagnosis and early intervention; and (4) Know that a high rate of false positives exists. Contact your campus health service or the local office of public health for a list of available testing sites.

As of 1996, **home testing kits** for HIV have been approved by the Food and Drug Administration, and now are available over the counter. A test kit purchaser pricks his/her finger, puts a drop of blood on a piece of blotter paper, sends it off in the mail, and then phones for results and counseling after a specified time. Each test comes with a unique identification number, which patients return to the lab with their blood sample; the lab never knows a name. When calling for results, patients identify themselves by this number alone. Contact your nearest drug store or pharmacy for availability and cost (approximately $60). Note that over-the-counter sales of home access HIV testing may violate laws in some states (e.g., Texas) where face-to-face counseling is mandated (Texas Department of Housing and Community Affairs 2004).

Living with HIV and AIDS

Currently, there is no cure for AIDS. Therefore, the best protection is prevention. There are treatments that can slow down, and in some cases almost stop, the progression of the disease. The Food and Drug Administration has approved seventeen drugs—reverse transcriptase inhibitors (RTIs), protease inhibitors (PIs), non-nucleoside reverse transcriptase inhibitors (NNRTIs), and nucleotide analogues—to combat HIV. Available since 1987,

Zidovudine (ZDV or Retrovir, also called AZT) was the first of the RT inhibitors. *RT inhibitors* slow down the process of viral replication by interrupting the conversion of viral RNA into DNA; they do not destroy HIV. If administered with early detection of HIV, AZT can prolong the lives of persons living with HIV by delaying the onset of symptoms and opportunistic infections. However, potential users should know it has serious side effects, including nausea/vomiting, headaches, and fatigue, which can severely impede quality of life. Dideoxyinosine (DDI), or Videx, is another antiviral therapy approved by the FDA; it improves the body's ability to fight disease. Other RT inhibitors include ddC (HIVID), d4T (Zerit), 3TC (Epivir), and Nevirapine (Viramune).

Protease inhibitors interfere with viral replication by neutralizing the enzyme that allows HIV to splice its DNA into the host cell's chromosomes. Protease inhibitors include Saquinavir (Invirase), Ritonavir (Norvir), and Indinavir (Crixivan); Indinavir is the most common one. Like the RT inhibitors, protease inhibitors have strong, sometimes toxic side effects.

Unfortunately, used alone, these FDA-approved drugs often fail to significantly prolong life because the virus evolves into new strains so quickly. However, certain three-drug combinations of drugs (known as a "cocktail") have proven to be especially effective, in some cases causing a remission in the person with AIDS in which no HIV can be detected in the body. This remission period can last anywhere from six months to several years. Treatments cost over $25,000 a year. Meanwhile, research efforts continue to find a vaccine for AIDS, or to discover a method for destroying HIV and curing AIDS.

Preventive treatments are used to keep an opportunistic infection from starting. For OIs that are common in persons with AIDS, a physician can prescribe medicine before the patient gets sick. For example, pentamidine, trimethoprim/sulfamethoxazole and Dapsone may prevent PCP. Anti-neoplastic agents such as Alpha-interferon are used to treat early KS and other HIV-related cancers. Immune modulators are intended to boost the immune system, but these therapies are still experimental. Finally, numerous alternative therapies have been developed with and without strong scientific study. Examples include acupuncture, visualization, herbal remedies, marijuana, and stress reduction. While these treatments may alleviate pain and symptoms, they have not been shown to stop viral replication.

Women and HIV

The number of new AIDS cases is rising more rapidly among women than in any other group. Today, women account for more than one quarter of all new HIV/AIDS diagnoses. High-risk heterosexual contact was the source of 80% of these newly diagnosed infections. In 2004 HIV infection was the leading cause of death for African American women aged 25–34 years. Luckily these numbers are decreasing. The estimated number of HIV/AIDS in female adults or adolescents decreased from 11,941 in 2001 to 9,708 in 2005 (Centers for Disease Control and Prevention 2010d).

Women at Risk. Women are four times more likely than men to contract HIV from heterosexual intercourse. This is because vaginal tissues are prone to tearing and bleeding, directly exposing a woman to HIV (Padian, Shiboski, and Jewell 1990). The risk is increased if the woman has intercourse during menstruation, uses an IUD (intrauterine device), her male partner is uncircumcised, if she has ectopy (a benign cervical condition), or if she already has another sexually transmitted disease or infection.

The anatomy of the female reproductive system and genitalia put sexually active women at higher risk than men for bacterial and viral infections. Because the vagina is warm and moist, it harbors an abundance of microorganisms. During intercourse, vaginal and cervical tissues are irritated, thus increasing the likelihood of contracting an STI. Furthermore, women tend to experience asymptomatic infections or have "hidden symptoms"; this makes early detection of STIs more difficult in some cases. If a woman contracts an ulcerative STI, her risk of being infected with HIV is at least 3–5 times higher. In addition, use of oral contraceptives from an early age renders the cervix more susceptible to infection and malignancy (Zilbergeld 1988).

Sexual assault, or any kind of sexual intercourse without the woman's consent, by an acquaintance or stranger can put the woman at a slightly higher risk of contracting an STI (Jenny 1990).

Lesbians are not at any lesser risk for contracting HIV or STI. Bacteria and viruses can be transmitted during oral–oral and oral–vaginal contact. Lesbians can also contract HIV or STI from previous or intermittent male partners.

Pregnancy and HIV. HIV can also be vertically transmitted from an infected mother to her child. This can occur during pregnancy, delivery, or breast-feeding. If a woman is HIV-positive and pregnant, there is a 20%–45% chance her baby will be infected during pregnancy, delivery, or breast-feeding (AVERT 2010). Recent research has demonstrated that AZT therapy can greatly reduce rates of mother-to-infant transmission to below 2% (AVERT 2010).

Women who have engaged in risky behavior and who plan to become pregnant may want to consider having an HIV antibody test beforehand. In addition, women who wish to be artificially inseminated have a small chance of receiving sperm from an HIV-infected donor. Finally, HIV-positive women have a higher likelihood of developing HIV-related illnesses during pregnancy due to the additional stress exerted on the immune system.

Epidemiology of HIV. Women tend to experience different kinds of opportunistic infections from those of men. Whereas men will commonly develop KS (Kaposi's sarcoma) or PCP (Pneumocystis carinii pneumonia), women with advanced HIV infection will experience chronic yeast infections, cervical dysplasias or carcinomas, human papilloma virus (HPV) that spreads rapidly, frequent bouts with pelvic inflammatory disease (PID), and recurrent herpes ulcers.

Early diagnosis of HIV is the key to extended survival. Besides having options to begin treatment with various FDA-approved therapies, women with HIV have been able to take control of their health through nutrition, stress reduction, spirituality, education,

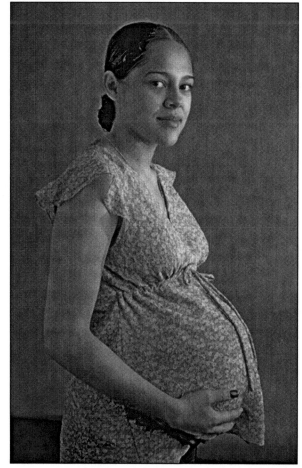

and involvement with other people with HIV. If you think you are at risk, contact your campus health center or the local public health office for the phone number and location of the nearest HIV testing site.

Injecting Drug Use (IDU) and HIV

"Shooting up," or injecting drugs or steroids is a very risky activity. Sharing used or unsterilized needles can expose your to infected blood—which carries the highest (and therefore more infectious) concentration of HIV. HIV, the hepatitis B virus (HBV), and syphilis are all transmissible through using contaminated syringes. Nationally, from one fourth to one third of all new AIDS cases are IDU-associated (CDC 2010b).

To reduce the risks:

1. DON'T SHARE NEEDLES OR SYRINGES. Unless you want to share diseases, too. This means not sharing the cotton or your water, either.
2. USE CLEAN WORKS. Clean needles, syringes, cookers, cotton, and water—all your "works"—with household bleach diluted with water in a 1:10 solution after each use. Rinse twice with water before reusing.
3. KEEP HEALTHY. Eat a balanced diet, sleep and exercise regularly. Drugs weaken the immune system, further increasing risk of infection.
4. GET HELP. If drugs are controlling your life, see a substance abuse counselor.

When a Friend Has AIDS

A person with AIDS is still a person. Having AIDS certainly changes a person's life, but it doesn't change the person. When the person with AIDS is a lover, friend, or relative, we are faced with the possibility of losing somebody we really care about. This feeling may also be accompanied by a fear of "getting AIDS" from the friend. It is difficult to face the reality of AIDS; here are some suggestions on how to help a friend who has AIDS:

1. Don't avoid them. Touch them and hug them.
2. Be there for them. Laugh and cry with them.
3. Encourage and support your friend. Let them know how strong they are.
4. Don't blame them. Nobody deserves to have AIDS; nobody asks to have AIDS.
5. Express sincere concern and caring. If you don't know what to say, be silent: words aren't always necessary.
6. It's okay to talk about AIDS in a sensitive manner if your friend wants to. If they want to go to one, help them find a support group.
7. Ask if you can help out in any way. Offer to buy groceries, write letters, babysit kids, drive them to doctor's appointments, etc.

8. Don't take away their independence. Up until the very late stages, a PWA is capable of doing just about everything for him- or herself.
9. Be prepared to deal with anger and depression—yours and theirs.
10. You can still do all the same things you used to do together: go out for dinner, see a movie, play sports, shop, share hobbies, etc.
11. Practice safer sex. If the person is your lover, intimacy doesn't need to end.
12. Take care of yourself. Dealing with chronic illness can be tiring. Give yourself some breaks

Questions to Consider

1. List three categories of STIs and two examples in each.
2. Why do many people mistake STI symptoms for other infections?
3. List three advances in medical care to help address STIs.

	U.S. 2007
Male	74%
Female	26%
White	29%
Black	51%
Hispanic	18%
Asian	1%
American Indians/Alaska Natives	<1%
Native Hawaiians/Other Pacific Islanders	<1%
Other	n/a
(Men who have sex with men) MSM	53%
IDU	17%
MSM/IDU	3%
Heterosexual	32%
Hemophilia	n/a
Transfusion	n/a
Unknown	<1%
<13	<1%
13–19	4%
20–29	25%
30–39	26%
40–49	27%
50–59	13%
>60	4%

Figure 20: *Prevalence of HIV/AIDS Cases by Gender, Ethnicity, Age, and Exposure Category. (CDC 2009)*

References

ACHA. (1987).

AVERT. (2010). *HIV, pregnancy, mothers and babies.* Retrieved from http://www.avert.org/pregnancy.htm

National Prevention Information Network. (2010). *STIs today.* Retrieved from http://www.cdcnpin.org/scripts/std/std.asp

National Institute of Allergy and Infectious Diseases. (2010). *Sexually transmitted infections: Quick facts.* Retrieved from http://www.niaid.nih.gov/topics/sti/Pages/quickFacts.aspx

Centers for Disease Control and Prevention (CDC). (1992). Projections of the number of persons diagnosed with AIDS and the number of immunosuppressed HIV-infected persons—United States, 1992–1994. *Morbidity and Mortality Weekly Report, 41.*

CDC. (2009). *HIV/AIDS in the United States.* Retrieved from http://www.cdc.gov/hiv/resources/factsheets/us.htm

CDC. (2010). *Basic statistics.* Retrieved from http://www.cdc.gov/hiv/topics/surveillance/basic.htm#hivest

CDC. (2010). *Drug-associated HIV transmission continues in the United States.* Retrieved from http://www.cdc.gov/hiv/resources/factsheets/idu.htm

Centers for Disease Control and Prevention. (2010). Genital HPV infection: CDC fact sheet. Retrieved from http://www.cdc.gov/std/HPV/STDFact-HPV.htm#common

Centers for Disease Control and Prevention. (2010). *HIV/AIDS among women.* Retrieved from http://www.cdc.gov/hiv/topics/women/resources/factsheets/women.htm

Centers for Disease Control and Prevention. (2010). *Human Papillomavirus: What is HPV?* Retrieved from http://www.cdc.gov/hpv/WhatIsHPV.html

Jenny, C. (1990). Sexually transmitted diseases in victims of rape. *The New England Journal of Medicine, 322*(11).

Kaiser Family Foundation. (2006). *Sexual health statistics for teenagers and young adults in the United States.* Retrieved from http://www.kff.org/womenshealth/upload/3040-03.pdf.

Texas Department of Housing and Community Affairs. (2004). *Reporting on program year 2004 [Annual report].* Retrieved from http://www.tdhca.state.tx.us/housing-center/docs/05-CAPER.pdf.

Chapter 15

Safer Sex

By Luoluo Hong and Lindsay Walker McCall

Introduction

Virtually the only two 100% foolproof methods of STI and HIV prevention are complete abstinence, or a mutually monogamous relationship between two non-IV-drug-using virgins. In any college population, such preventive measures are most likely unrealistic for the majority of students. Contrary to myth, talking about sex and protection does not promote sexual activity; rather, it can help delay sexual activity for some students or reduce STI transmission for those who are sexually active (Center for AIDS Prevention Studies [CAPS] 1995).

In this "Age of AIDS" virtually all sexual activity is associated with some risk. Because sexual behavior varies widely, it is difficult to say which sexual behaviors are safe. A good rule to follow—**activities that involve sharing bodily fluids, especially semen and blood, incur high risk of transmitting STIs** (American College Health Association [ACHA] 1987). For example, anal intercourse is associated with very high risk because it commonly causes tears in mucous membranes and skin in and around the anus, allowing blood and microorganisms to be exchanged. Other highly risky activities include internal watersports, fisting, and rimming. On the other hand, fantasy and masturbation on healthy skin are very safe.

We no longer refer to "risk groups." Rather, we talk about "risky behavior" in order to emphasize the fact that anyone can contract HIV or an STI. Remember, it is what you do and not who you are that puts you at risk for contracting STI. Risky practices are risky regardless of your gender, age, class, race, or sexual orientation.

What is Safer Sex?

"Safer sex" means protecting yourself and your partner from STIs, HIV infection, and unplanned pregnancy. Safer sex can mean deciding to abstain from sexual intercourse, or it can mean finding other forms of sexual expression that do not involve exchange of bodily fluids. However, if you do decide to have anal, oral, or vaginal intercourse, always take the following risk-reduction measures.

1. *Use latex condoms with additional spermicide containing Nonoxynol-9 during vaginal and anal intercourse.* Condoms minimize the amount of semen or vaginal fluid that is exchanged. It is important to practice safer sex during any kind of sexual contact. Any skin or mucous membranes on and around the genitals that come into contact with genital warts, herpes sores, and syphilis lesions can become infected. The compound Nonoxynol-9 found in jellies, foams, and creams appears to kill many of the microorganisms that cause STIs. During oral sex on a man, use a condom without spermicide.

    Other barrier methods of contraception such as diaphragms and contraceptive sponges and non-barrier methods such as the birth control pill, provide protection against pregnancy, but they do not provide protection against STIs. Always use condoms with spermicide in conjunction with those methods.

Condoms are prophylactic sheaths usually made of thin latex. Some are made of animal skin. Condoms can be purchased in a variety of shapes (receptacle tip or rounded-end), textures (ribbed, smooth), sizes, flavors, and colors. Some are lubricated and/or contain spermicide. *(See Figure 21 at the end of this section for proper use of a condom.)*

Many students have the mistaken belief that condoms are permeable to HIV and/or to sperm. While lambskin condoms do contain pores large enough to let HIV and other microorganisms to pass through, latex condoms, however are impermeable to HIV and sperm, as well as to many other bacteria and viruses associated with STIs. Condom failure is due rather to the "human factor"—in its manufacturing, improper storage, and improper use.

Like condoms, **spermicide** comes in a variety of textures and flavors. Read the package to make sure the product contains Nonoxynol-9, the chemical that kills sperm and STI microorganisms, including HIV. Spermicide can be purchased as creams, films, foams, gels, jellies, or suppositories. Most are readily inserted into the vagina with the help of a plastic applicator; the applicator usually comes with the spermicide, or it can be purchased separately.

Use spermicides that contain at least 4% Nonoxynol-9. For maximum effectiveness, spermicide should be inserted within five to ten minutes of intercourse. Use one applicator-full of spermicide for each additional act of intercourse. It is not recommended to douche after intercourse; douching may inhibit spermicidal action.

Virtually all spermicidal brands and products are equally effective; a choice about which one to use can be based on individual preference and comfort. For instance, some women experience an allergic reaction to foam because of its high concentration of Nonoxynol-9. Always save and read the directions about how to insert or apply the spermicide.

When used as directed with a condom, spermicide provides substantial STI and pregnancy protection (CAPS February 1995). They are available without prescription at all drugstores and pharmacies.

The newest condom to hit the US. market is the *Avanti* condom, manufactured and distributed by Apex Medical Technologies, Inc. in conjunction with London International Group. Made of polyurethane (a type of plastic), *Avanti* condoms are looser fitting than latex, and supposedly have an advantage over latex condoms because they allow for greater sensitivity with equivalent strength. Research however has demonstrated that latex and plastic condoms have the same breakage and slippage rates. However, for some individuals who are allergic to latex, plastic condoms can be a prophylactic and contraceptive alternative. Plastic condoms are odorless and colorless, do not disintegrate over time, and can be used with any type of lubrication ("Barriers to better" 1994).

2. *Use latex or rubber barriers such as dental dams during any oral-vaginal or oral-anal contact.* This prevents the exchange of fluids between the tongue and vulva or anus.

Dental dams are small latex squares that are used during cunnilingus (oral-vaginal sex) and/ or rimming (oral-anal sex). They come in a variety of colors and flavors. A dental dam should first be rinsed to remove the packaging powder. The square can then be placed over the vagina or anus before oral stimulation. Use each dental dam only once, and use only one side of the dental dam. Partners can be creative in devising methods to hold the dam in place.

If a dental dam is not available, you can also cut off the tip of an unlubricated condom, cut down its length, and unroll into a square. Or use a small section of a double layer of microwavable plastic wrap.

3. *Wash the genital areas with soap and warm water before and after intercourse.* This minimizes the number of infectious microorganisms that cause STIs. Douching is not recommended; the preparations in douches irritate the vagina, upset the normal pH balance, and kill many of the harmless bacteria that are naturally found in the vagina.

4. *Avoid using alcohol, tobacco, or other drugs before and during sexual intercourse.* Use of substances severely depresses the immune system, rendering you susceptible to infections, and decreases the likelihood of practicing safer sex. This includes "shooting up." Sharing needles for drugs incurs a risk of contracting HIV, HBV, and possibly syphilis.

5. *Learn the common STI symptoms and perform a monthly genital self-exam (GSE).* Perform a genital self-exam on a regular basis (at least once a month). (Or you can have your partner do it!) If you notice any suspicious symptoms, see a health care provider as soon as possible and refrain from sexual intercourse until treatment is completed. In addition, don't have sexual contact with any partner who exhibits possible STI symptoms. Remember, however, that a person infected with an STI is still contagious even if s/he has no symptoms. Remember, it's best to treat an STI as soon as possible; this requires early detection.

6. *Have regular medical check-ups.* Regular check-ups facilitate early detection of STIs. A physician or nurse practitioner can observe minute or subtle symptoms that a self-exam would miss.
   a. **Women: Yearly breast/pelvic exam and Pap smear.** All women age 18 and over should have yearly Pap smears, regardless of whether or not they are sexually active. Pap smear can detect HPV on the cervix. Visual exam for warts. Culture needed for chlamydia, gonorrhea, and syphilis. Pubic lice and herpes are diagnosed by their physical symptoms.
   b. **Men: Yearly visit to urologist or dermatologist.** Don't wait for your partner to tell you that they have an STI.

7. *Stay healthy.* You help maintain your body's ability to resist infection if you:
   a. Eat a balanced diet.
   b. Exercise regularly.
   c. Sleep adequately.
   d. Manage stress.

8. *Talk about safer sex with your partners.* This doesn't mean asking about number of partners, or if they have been tested! People will lie about almost anything to have sex.

   Safer sex does not mean just having an HIV antibody test every six months. A negative test doesn't necessarily mean you don't have HIV. Simply asking your partner if they have an STI isn't safer sex either. A 1990 study by Cochran and Mays at California State University showed that 47% of men and 60% of women have been lied to by their partners about sexual history for the purposes of having sex.

9. *Limit the number of sexual partners.* This decreases the possibilities of being exposed to an STI. However, take this with a grain of salt. In terms of HIV, true monogamy requires seven years of mutual faithfulness (that's how long it can take for HIV to seroconvert). What college students typically practice is "serial monogamy," which does not count. Unfortunately, there is a high rate of infidelity even among married couples. Remember, the bottom line is whether or not you protect yourself, not how many partners you've had.

Figure 21: *Steps for Proper Condom Use*

1. Check the expiration date on the package. Do not use old condoms or condoms that have been kept in a wallet, or exposed to heat or cold. Also, use reliable condom brands. Trojans, Lifestyles, Durex are all acceptable. DO NOT use condoms that are scented or flavored; substances placed on

these condoms can erode the latex.

2. Carefully remove the condom from the package. Hold it up against light to check for small punctures. Do not use a condom that shows breakage.

3. If desired, place a drop of water-based lubricant into the tip of the condom before putting it on; this increases sensitivity to the penis.

4. ALWAYS squeeze the tip of the condom to create a pocket, which leaves space for the semen; the pressure of an ejaculation may break the condom if there is no pocket.

5. Unroll the condom over the erect penis. If you make a mistake, start over with a brand new condom.

6. Gently but generously apply a **water-based** lubricant such as K-Y Jelly on the outside of the condom. This decreases the amount of friction (thus reducing likelihood of breakage), and enhances sensation for both partners.

7. After ejaculation, hold the base of the condom while withdrawing the penis to prevent semen from leaking out.

8. Tie the condom in a knot near the rim and throw it out in the garbage. Do not flush it down the toilet: condoms are not biodegradable. Do not use a condom more than once, even if the man does not ejaculate!

Remember:

- Use latex condoms ONLY, not animal, or "natural," skin: lambskin is permeable to HIV. Use water-based lubricants such as K-Y Jelly. Vaseline, Crisco, butter, mayonnaise, or other makeshift lubricants (such as—believe it or not—WD-40) are oil-based and cause microscopic holes to form in the condom. Sputum carries bacteria.

- Always use lubricants with a condom. This decreases the amount of friction and reduces the likelihood of breaking or tearing a condom. Place the lubricant directly in the vagina or anus with an applicator.

- Condoms used with spermicide are an effective method of birth control as well as an essential safer-sex practice.

- Condoms are available at all drugstores, superstores, and even some grocery stores. Even better, your university's Student Health Center will often provide condoms at low or no cost.

Communicating about Safer Sex

Abstinence. The only true "safe sex," abstinence can be primary or secondary. Primary abstainers have not had a sexual experience with another person, while secondary abstainers (also called "secondary virgins") are sexually experienced individuals who have chosen to avoid some or all sexual activity with another person. Whatever your reason to choose to abstain, the following list of suggestions adapted from *Contraceptive Technology* (Hatcher 1998) will help to support and maintain your decisions to abstain from intercourse:

1. Avoid high-pressure sexual situations.
2. Discover the societal pressures that influence your choices.
3. Take ownership of your personal rights in sexual relationships.
4. Decide in advance which sexual activities you will say "yes" to and discuss these with your partner. Learn more about the range of sexual expression.
5. Tell your partner, very clearly and in advance—not in bed—what activities you will not engage in.
6. Learn more about your body and how to keep it healthy.
7. Learn about available birth control methods should you choose to have intercourse. Have a back-up method available to you.

Barriers to Communication. That all-important "safer-sex" conversation looms in front of us before each sexual encounter—a source of awkwardness, embarrassment, and frustration. For most young adults, sex and "doing it" is a touchy subject that is difficult to talk about; AIDS and STIs only further complicate the discussion. More often than not, sexual partners never really get around to talking about safer sex.

The barriers to communicating about safer sex are many. Many young adults don't perceive themselves to be at risk for STI or HIV. Because they believe they are invulnerable, such individuals see no need for a safer-sex conversation. Others who do consider themselves at risk are nevertheless afraid of what their partner or potential partner will think of them if they bring up STIs and safer sex. People often infer different things from a conversation about safer sex:

- infidelity in the relationship
- lack of love or respect for the partner
- lack of trust in the partner
- accusation of being "dirty" or promiscuous

Such issues can deeply affect a sexual relationship.

Still others are afraid to talk about—or talk openly—about safer sex, because they fear losing a sexual opportunity. In other words, it becomes a choice of safer sex or no sex. Research by Cochran and Mays (1990) on 18–25-year-olds in southern California revealed 34% of men and 10% of women admitted telling a lie about sexual history in order to have sex.

For many people talking about safer sex ruins the "spontaneity" or "naturalness" of sex. Condoms and foam don't seem very romantic to most partners, and they are perceived as interrupting sex.

Finally, there are very few role models for talking responsibly about sex. Ours is a society that seemingly values "act first, talk later." In books, movies, and television, people are always having sex without condoms, yet they never get pregnant or contract AIDS. Chances are, our teachers, parents, and friends don't talk about safer sex either; sex is still a taboo subject. Many adults are embarrassed or uncomfortable with issues of sexuality, sending a negative image to their children. It's difficult to talk about safer sex if you don't know where to begin.

Safer is Sexier. In reality, talking about sex is a sign of caring and respect. Partners make themselves vulnerable and share their feelings with each other. It shows that sex is more than a meaningless encounter of two bodies; rather, sex becomes part of an important relationship between two people.

A safer-sex conversation involves more than a discussion about sexual history and diseases; it means talking about contraception and pregnancy, about mutual consent, about feelings for each other. Planning for and talking about sex prevents partners from getting hurt emotionally; safer sex is about being romantic because STIs and pregnancy aren't romantic.

Safer sex doesn't have to be cumbersome; it can be incorporated into lovemaking. Shopping for condoms and spermicide together can be fun. Putting on a condom or inserting spermicide for your partner can be a very sensual activity. Bringing safer-sex issues out into the open and knowing that partners are protecting themselves can relieve a lot of stress, making sexuality less inhibited. The risks are too high not to talk about safer sex.

How to Talk with a Partner. Lynn Bechtel, a mental health educator at the University of Massachusetts at Amherst, offers the following guidelines on how to have a safer-sex conversation:

1. Think before you talk. You need to know why you think it's important to talk about safer sex. You need to know what your expectations are; i.e., do you want monogamy, several partners, an on-going relationship, a casual encounter, etc. You need to think about your own history and about how to share that history with someone else.

   If you have an STI, you might feel worried that the other person will reject you. Don't let this fear keep you from telling them you are infected. Practice telling your potential partner about your situation in a calm, straightforward manner: "I have herpes. I only have occasional outbreaks and I know when they're coming. I was careful with my last girlfriend and she didn't get infected." The other person may react with questions, fear, or uncertainty. Be prepared for this and stay calm. Your openness and honesty can help reassure your friend. If you don't have an STI you should think about how you'll respond if your potential partner is infected. Think about what information you'll need and be prepared to take some time making a decision about sexual activity. Whichever side of the situation you're on, remember that caution is smart.

2. Plan when to have your conversation. If you wait until you're in bed with your partner, aroused and ready to go before saying, "By the way, there's something we should discuss," then chances are you'll have a difficult conversation. Instead plan to talk about sexual history and STI concerns at a time when you both are comfortable, relaxed, sober, and not sexually aroused.

3. Speak for yourself rather than the other person. For example, begin statements with "I feel like …" or "I would like … ." State what you want to talk about and why you think it's important. "I've

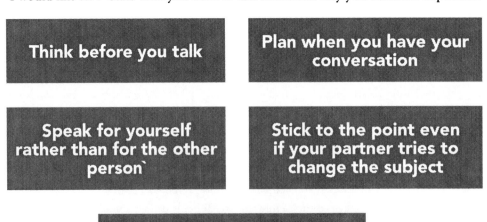

Table 17: *Talking with a partner about safer sex. Summary of how to prepare for this conversation.*

read a lot about STIs and I've got some concerns. I'd like to tell you what I've been thinking and find out more about you. I'll enjoy sex with you more if we talk about this stuff first."

4. Stick to the point even if your partner tries to change the subject. Be a "broken record." Repeat a statement like "I know this is difficult but I think it's important."

5. Be prepared for the person who responds to a discussion of safer sex with denial or rejection. Don't take it personally. Remember, you're the smart one, doing your best to stay healthy.

Negotiating with a Partner. It is important to rehearse or practice beforehand what to say to a partner about safer sex. Safer sex is about negotiation. A partner who is reluctant to use a condom or discuss sexual history will have a lot of convincing reasons why not to. Be prepared for the reasons that they might give so that you'll know how to respond.

If Your Partner Says ...	You Can Respond With ...
I'm on the pill; you don't need a condom.	The pill doesn't protect us from infections.
I'm a virgin.	I'm not. This way we'll both be protected.
It destroys the romantic atmosphere.	It doesn't have to be that way; I'll help you put on the condom.
I know I'm clean; I haven't had sex in six months.	I'd like to use it anyway. We'll both be protected from any infections that we may not realize we have.
I can't feel a thing when I wear a condom. It's like wearing a raincoat in the shower.	You won't feel anything at all if you don't use a condom. Besides, you can't really tell the difference if we use lots of lubricant.
I'll lose my erection by the time I stop and put it on.	I'll help you put it on and help you keep an erection ...
Condoms are unnatural; I want to feel you, not some piece of rubber.	You will feel me ... let's give it a try at least.
This is an insult! Do you think I'm some slut?	I didn't say that. I care for you; a condom protects both of us.
Okay ... just this once.	Once is all it takes.
I love you. I would never hurt you.	Not on purpose, but many people don't even know they have an infection.
Hey, I'm not gay.	You don't have to be gay to get HIV.
I tested negative for HIV.	The test isn't perfect. Besides, there are other diseases besides HIV.
I don't have a condom.	But I do.
None of my other partners used condoms. A real man isn't afraid.	Please don't compare me to them. A real man cares enough about the person he has sex with to play it safe.
I won't have sex then.	Okay, let's not have sex. We can try other things ...

Remember, talking about sex is not only for those who are sexually active, nor is it only about STIs and condoms. It's equally important to talk about desires and consent to avoid unwanted or unplanned intercourse; about how sex will affect the relationship; and about contraception and alternatives in the event of an unplanned pregnancy. Furthermore, it is never the sole responsibility of one partner to bring up the subject. Never assume that the other person will "take care of everything." Play it safe and ask. If a partner is truly resistant to even trying safer sex, then it may be time to reconsider the relationship.

"Creative Sexuality." It is important to remember that all people are naturally sexual beings, regardless of whether or not someone is engaging in sexual activity. "Creative sexuality" may be a better term than "abstinence" when working with young adults, because it emphasizes that choices about sexuality occur on a continuum. Abstinence is regarded not as denying oneself, but rather as only one end of a wide range of behaviors. In other words, an individual can abstain from some types of sexual activities, but still find pleasure and intimacy in others. In addition, abstinence is not an absolute standard; it can represent an individual's choice regarding their body at a particular point in their life.

Eroticizing Safer Sex. Regarding safer-sex practices as a detriment to spontaneity and to intimacy is one of the biggest barriers to their implementation. It is critical that all sexually active young adults see that safer-sex techniques are a natural, exciting, and pleasurable aspect of sexual activity. Safer sex can have benefits that extend beyond just health related ones. For examples, see the *Safer Sex Menu* that begins on page 144.

The Impact of Sex-Role Socialization. We learn about appropriate sex roles, as well as peer and cultural norms/values, from the day we are born from parents, friends, teachers, school, church, television (MTV), Hollywood movies, pornography, ads/commercials, the Internet, magazines, music, books, and romance novels, etc.

The accepted male sexual role is to …
- have sex as often as possible, as long as possible, with as many people as possible;
- always initiate sexual activity;
- be the aggressor;
- always want sex;
- masturbate often;
- hope his partner will take care of contraception and safer sex;
- use alcohol as an excuse for his behavior; and
- publicize his sexual conquests.

The accepted female sexual role is to …
- have sex with only a select few or one individual;
- never initiate sexual activity;
- be the "gatekeeper";
- have sex because her partner wants to (not because she does);
- never masturbate;
- take care of contraception and safer sex;
- be blamed for her behavior when she drinks; and
- be discreet about her sexual encounters.

These expectations are equally damaging to both men and women, and have a significant impact on the ways in which men and women communicate about sex and protection.

Understanding Sexual Response (for Men and Women)

1. **Excitement.** Pelvic engorgement, penile erection. Lubrication and dilation of upper vaginal canal. Increased muscle tension, heart and respiratory rates, and blood pressure. Focus of attention on sexual matters.
2. **Plateau.** Sustained engorgement, muscle tension, elevated heart and respiratory rates, and elevated blood pressure; varies from minutes to hours.

3. **Orgasm.** A beginning of relief from tension. Rhythmic contractions of pelvic involuntary and voluntary muscles. In men, this can result in ejaculation of seminal fluid. May experience a variety of somatic sensations sometimes described as a feeling of warmth arising from the pelvis.

4. **Resolution.** Gradual loss of tension, progressive relaxation, and often a sense of drowsiness and contentment. Blood vessels open to drain pelvic and genital engorgement, and within minutes the individual returns to a nonexcited state.

Either penile or clitoral stimulation is required—"vaginal orgasms" are a fact. In achieving orgasm, men are more mechanical, and women are more psychical. Similarly, women tend to be whole-body oriented in their sexual arousal while men are trained to be more genitally oriented. Women can have multiple orgasms (move between plateau and orgasm several times), while men require a *refractory period*, a "rest period." Increasing with age, this period can last anywhere from a few minutes in adolescent boys to several days for older men.

The Clitoris. There is no such thing as a "vaginal" orgasm—for women, only clitoral orgasms exist. For many women, the clitoris is too sensitive to be directly stimulated. Each woman requires different stimulation (intercourse, oral, manual, masturbation, vibrator, pressure, etc.) for orgasm.

All women have a G spot, but few know it or have any idea of how to guide an intimate partner to it. Not a nebulous or psychic quest, it is the tissue that, had the zygote been awash in the hormones to become male, would have become the prostate gland. It is the source of the vaginal orgasm and of the feminine ejaculate.

The quest is in combining G spot and clitoral stimulation to achieve the Holy Grail of "coming together."

The Penis. The most sensitive spots are the area of frenular attachment on the ventral surface, just behind the glans, and then the coronal ridge of the glans. The flaccid penis may appear to come in all shapes and sizes, but almost all penises when erect are approximately six inches long.

Sexual Problems. Common sexual problems for women include *anorgasmia* (inability to achieve orgasm) and *vaginismus* (tightening of the vagina). For men, *premature ejaculation* (inability to delay ejaculation) and *impotence* (difficulty achieving or maintaining an erection) are the most frequently reported problems.

While some sexual problems are the result of chemical or physiological factors, many are the result of anxiety, ignorance, or lack of communication. Developing realistic expectations for sexual performance, taking the time

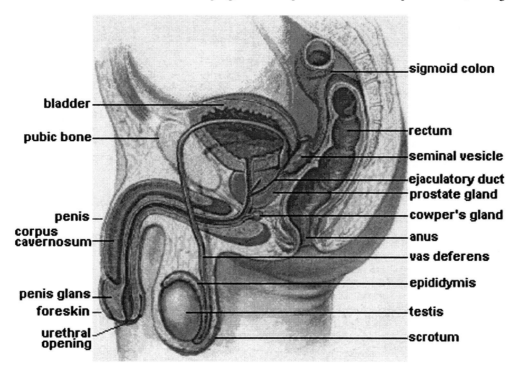

to learn about what is pleasurable both for yourself and your partner, as well as honest, open communication—not to mention patience—will alleviate many sexual problems.

Quiz: Are You and Your Partner Ready for Sex? (Yale Health Services 1994)

	Yes	No
Are you both ready to have sex right now?		
Do you both have a clear understanding of how sex influences your relationship?		
Can I have sex without feeling guilt or regret?		
Do I want to have sex for selfish reasons?		
Have I honestly considered my values?		
Have I discussed birth control with my partner?		
Do I have all the knowledge I need to prevent an unwanted pregnancy and the spread of STIs?		
Are there other ways my partners and I can build loving relationships?		
How do my religious/spiritual beliefs affect this decision?		
Am I afraid I'll lose my partner if I refuse to have sex?		
Have I thought about all of the possible consequences?		
Am I willing to accept all of the consequences?		
Do I want to have sex because of pressure to have friends?		

Safer Sex Menu

In the Age of AIDS practicing abstinence can mean "fasting," which provides the best protection against HIV. Or, you can regard abstinence as "dieting," where you don't have to refrain from *all* sexual contact. On the following pages, our Health Chef suggests some delectable options for exciting sexual encounters between you and your partner that will still reduce the risks of unwanted pregnancy, HIV infection, and other sexually transmitted infections. Bon appetit!

Originally prepared by Luoluo Hong, Peer Education Coordinator

Yale University Health Service, New Haven, CT 1992

Portions of this menu have been adapted from Boston and Phoenix

The Relative Risks of Not Abstaining (Keeling 1989)

High	Sharing IV drug needles
	Unprotected receptive vaginal intercourse
	Unprotected receptive anal intercourse
Medium	Unprotected insertive vaginal/anal intercourse
	Watersports
	Unprotected oral sex on a man with ejaculation
Some	Unprotected oral sex on a man without ejaculation
	Unprotected oral–anal contact
	"Golden showers"
Low	Unprotected oral–vaginal contact
	Unprotected "fisting"
	Blood transfusions
None	Kissing, touching, masturbation, fantasy

Appetizers

Talking to each other about safer sex
Choice of English, Spanish, French,
Chinese, or Swahili

Listening to music and/or dancing together
Chef's suggestion: Ravel's Bolero

Reading erotic literature together
Special: D. H. Lawrence's Lady Chatterley's Lover

Looking at erotic pictures together

Watching erotic movies together
Special: Like Water for Chocolate

Talking sexy or sharing fantasies

Stroking, brushing, washing, or playing with
each other's hair

Playing strip-poker, strip backgammon, or
spin-the-bottle

Burning scented candles or incense

Kissing, hugging, and holding hands

Back and shoulder massages, foot rubs, and
body rubs while still dressed

Caressing, tickling, pinching, and nibbling
each other through clothes

Dry humping

Undressing each other or watching each other
undress

Dressing up in erotic lingerie
Chef's suggestion:
Adam and Eve or Victoria's Secret

Showering or taking a bubble bath together

Kissing, licking, or fondling your partner's
body (except for the genitals and anus).

Rubbing any nonpetroleum-based body
oil or lotion on each other or yourself

Dieter's Delights

Putting a latex condom
Recommended: Trojans on yourself or your partner

Inserting spermicide containing Nonoxynol-9
in your partner's vagina or anus

Petting with no clothes on

Stroking, caressing and fondling
your partner's body
including the genitals and anus

Mutual or simultaneous masturbation
to orgasm with your hands with or
without condoms
With no exchange of semen or vaginal fluids

Mutual or simultaneous
masturbation with a vibrator
No sharing!

Rubbing your penis against healthy, unbroken
skin on your partner's body
Between the breasts, between the lower thighs, or
against the buttocks, making sure not to ejaculate in
or on your partner's body orifices

Rubbing your clitoris against healthy,
unbroken skin on your partner's body
Avoid contact with your partner's body orifices

Entrees

Oral sex
(fellatio, "blow job," "sucking cock")
on your male partner with an
unlubricated condom
with choice of fruit-flavored water-based
lubricant or honey.

Oral sex (cunnilingus, "eating") on your
female partner with a latex dental dam or a
double-layer of plastic wrap
Recommended: Glad Wrap

Oral-anal sex
("rimming," "licking butt")
on your partner with a latex dental dam or
double-layer of plastic wrap

Vaginal or anal intercourse
with a latex condom and spermicide
containing Nonoxynol-9

Vaginal or anal penetration with a sex toy
No sharing!

Desserts

Licking whipped cream, jelly, chocolate syrup, or honey off your partner's body,
Except for unprotected body openings

Masturbating while your partner watches or holds you

Making sexy video or experimenting with a digital camera

Bodypainting with nonpetroleum-based body paints

Soaking in a hot tub or Jacuzzi

Taking a swim together in the ocean or a pool at night

Holding each other

Talking to each other

Sleeping together

Spending the day in bed together
Chef's favorite: a waterbed

Eating breakfast, lunch, or dinner in bed

Starting over

This Month's Special

Order any appetizer and entree from our menu and receive a free dessert!

A Message from the Chef

We do not use lambskin, or "natural skin" condoms, which have been shown to be permeable to HIV and sperm. We use only the freshest, highest-quality water-based lubricants with our latex condoms and dental dams, and we inspect our stockrooms frequently in order to discard latex products that have expired, been exposed to extreme heat or cold, excessive light, or been in somebody's wallet.

Here's what some of our patrons say

"Exquisite! Divine!! Not to be missed!!! Definitely a five-star establishment!"   —Staff reporter, *Campus Newspaper*

"It changed my life—you get the best of both worlds here:
pleasure *and* safety. You've got to try it!"   —Unidentified sorority member

"WOW!!"   —Nurse, Student Health Center

"People used to tell me that getting a Ph.D. meant sacrificing
your sex life. Not so after trying some of these appetizers …"   —Ph.D. candidate, College of Education

"After partaking of your menu, my wife and I have been
enjoying a second honeymoon ever since!"   —Officer, Police Department

"Who needs beer after a taste of this?!"   —Patron, Sports Bar

"If we served this stuff, maybe more students would like us!"   —Server, Food Services

Safer Sex Cafe

WE ACCEPT VISA, MASTERCARD, DISCOVER, AND AMERICAN EXPRESS

Figure 22: *Some Special Considerations for Sexual Health Peer Educators.*

1. Consider your attitudes, beliefs, and religious views about:
   - sexual orientation
   - contraception and abortion
   - menstruation
   - premarital sex and teenage sex
   - infidelity
   - interracial couples
   - sex education
   - virginity and abstinence
   - sex and marriage
   - prostitution
2. Become informed about and practice discussing:
   - sexual intercourse and reproduction
   - sexual development and maturation
   - HIV/AIDS and sexually transmitted infections
   - pregnancy and childbirth
   - contraception and safer sex
   - sexual orientation
   - sexual acts
   - sexual response and sexual fantasies
   - intimacy and relationships
   - sexual assault and incest
   - sexual problems and concerns
   - sexual addiction
3. Be nonjudgmental. Do not impose your values and lifestyle choices on another person. "Normal" behavior should always be defined from the individual's point of reference.
4. Be proactive; set up an atmosphere that is safe for the client to bring up sexual concerns and issues by displaying literature, asking questions, etc.
5. Be direct. For instance, say "anal intercourse," not "sex the other way, you know."
6. Use culturally appropriate and sensitive language that empowers the client. For example, don't refer to prostitutes as "whores," or gay men as "funny" or "fairies"—they are people, too. Also, use "partner" instead of "girlfriend/boyfriend," "rape survivor" instead of "rape victim," and "person with HIV" instead of "AIDS patient/victim."
7. Be familiar with the impact that sex, sexual identity, and sexual health have with mental health issues: alcohol and other drug abuse, eating disorders, relationship problems, stress, self-esteem, violence, etc.
8. An open mind and a willingness to really listen will go far toward establishing trust and rapport with peers. Non-verbal cues are just as important in communicating your genuine desire to discuss sexually related issues.
9. Recognize that sex is not always dangerous but can be a fulfilling aspect of living. Exhibit a positive attitude about human sexuality. Keep a sense of humor.
10. Refrain from reinforcing myths and misconceptions about sex. For example, avoid "Of course it will hurt the first time—it's supposed to," or "Women really should be the ones to take care of birth control because they are the ones who get pregnant."
11. When confused, don't be afraid to ask or to refer to someone who is better equipped to help.

Questions to Consider

1. Safer sex exists on a continuum. Develop a continuum for safer sex listing all forms of sexual activity in terms of risks.

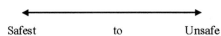

Safest   to   Unsafe

2. How would you advise a peer to talk with a partner prior to having a sexual relationship?
3. How can you use the safer-sex menu in programming?

References

Barriers to better condom 'killing people': regulatory, political hurdles stifle development. (1994 December). *AIDS Alert.*

Center for AIDS Prevention Studies, University of California at San Francisco and Harvard AIDS Institute. (1995, June). *Does sex education work?* San Francisco: University of California.

Cochran, S. D., & Mays, V. M. (1990). Sex, lies, and HIV. *New England Journal of Medicine,* 332(11), p. 774–775.

Hatcher, R. A. (1998). Contraceptive technology (7th Ed.). New York: Ardent Media, Inc.

Keeling, R. P. (Ed.). (1989). *AIDS on the college campus (2nd ed.).* Rockville, MD: American College Health Association.

Peel Public Health. (2009). *Making decisions about sex.* Retrieved from http://www.peelregion.ca/health/sexuality/relations/make-quiz.htm

Chapter 16

Reproductive Health

By Luoluo Hong and Lindsay Walker McCall

Pelvic Exams

All women over 18 or who are sexually active (whichever comes first) should get a pelvic exam at least once a year.

Preparation for the Exam

1. The appointment should be scheduled between menstrual periods. Menstrual bleeding may interfere with the accuracy of some laboratory tests.
2. It may be helpful to make a list of all of your questions and any problems you want to talk about.
3. Douching is not recommended for at least twenty-four hours.

The Exam

1. *External Genital Exam.* The clinician examines the soft folds of the vulva and the opening of the vagina to check for signs of redness, irritation, discharge, or other conditions.
2. *Speculum Exam.* The clinician inserts a sterile metal or plastic speculum into the vagina. The speculum is opened to separate the walls of the vagina, which normally are closed and touch each other. This way, the cervix can be seen. Some clinicians may warm the speculum for your comfort.

   The clinician will then check for any irritation, growth, or abnormal discharge for the cervix. Tests for gonorrhea, HPV, chlamydia, or other STIs may be taken by collecting the cervical mucous on a cotton swab.

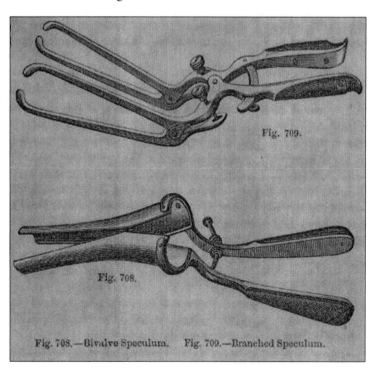

Fig. 708.—Bivalve Speculum.   Fig. 709.—Branched Speculum.

The clinician will take a smear for a Pap test. Usually a small spatula or brush is used to gently collect cells from the cervix. The cells are tested to see if any are precancerous or cancerous cells.

Some clinicians will discuss everything they are doing throughout the process. They may offer you a mirror so that you can observe as well.

3. *The Bimanual Exam.* Wearing a rubber glove, the clinician inserts one or two lubricated fingers into the vagina. The other hand presses down on the lower abdomen.

The clinician will examine the internal organs with both hands to check for pain:

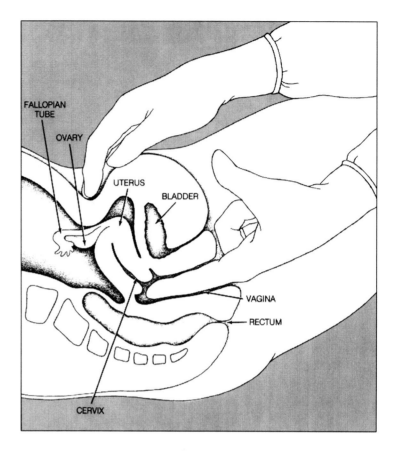

- tenderness or pain—indicator of infection
- size, shape, and position of the uterus
- an enlarged uterus, which could indicate pregnancy
- swelling of the fallopian tubes
- enlarged ovaries, cysts, or tumors

4. *Rectovaginal Exam.* The clinician may insert a gloved finger into the rectum to check the condition of muscles that separate the vagina and rectum. They are also checking for possible tumors located behind the uterus, on the lower wall of the vagina, and in the rectum.

Breast Self-Exam (BSE)

One in eight women in the US will develop breast cancer. Most of these women will be over the age of 50, but it does occur in younger women. Women with a family history of breast cancer are at a higher risk than those who do not have a family history of breast cancer. Two factors that seem to be protective against breast cancer are having your first child before 30 years of age and breastfeeding. Health care providers suggest annual mammograms for women after age 40.

To perform a breast self-exam

1. Choose a day each month to do a BSE. The best time to do it is 2 to 3 days after your period ends because your breasts will not be tender or lumpy from normal swelling.

2. Stand in front of a mirror and check for any changes in size, shape, or appearance (such as puckering of the skin), and for any discharges. Do this with your hands at your sides, then with your hands behind your head, and then with your hands at your waist.

3. To complete the exam stand in the shower with your arm raised or lie on your back with your arm above your head. In a circular motion, press firmly and feel for any lumps or discharge. Move around the breast in a set way. Choose either a circle motion, an up or down line, or a wedge. Make sure you do it the same every time so that you will cover the entire area of the breast.

Testicular Self-Exam (TSE)

Cancer of the testes—the male reproductive glands—is one of the most common cancers in men ages 15–34. It accounts for 3% of all cancer deaths in this age group. Symptoms of testicular cancer include:

- a slight enlargement of one testicle and a change in its consistency;
- dull ache in the lower abdomen and groin area;
- a sensation of heaviness or dragging in the scrotal area; and/or
- lumps or cysts are most commonly found on the front or side of the testicle.

Men who have an undescended or partially descended testicle are at a much higher risk of developing testicular cancer than other men. However, this condition can be corrected with a simple procedure performed by a physician.

The best hope for early detection of testicular cancer is a simple, three-minute, monthly self-examination. The best time to perform a **testicular self-exam**, or **TSE**, is after a hot bath or shower, when the testicles descend and the scrotal skin relaxes. Gently roll each testicle between the thumb and fingers of both hands, placing index and middle fingers underneath and thumbs on top. If you find any hard lumps or nodules, you should see your doctor promptly. They may not be malignant, but only a doctor can make a correct diagnosis. Following a thorough physical examination, your doctor may take x-rays to obtain the most accurate diagnosis possible.

If discovered in its early stages, spread of the disease can be prevented. Surgery is usually the preferred treatment, and in certain cases it may be used in conjunction with radiation therapy or chemotherapy. Studies indicate a 90% cure rate for patients who are treated within three months of feeling a lump, but after three months, the cure rate drops to 30%. The five-year survival rate for all types of testicular cancer is 87%. However, *seminoma*, the most common type of testicular cancer, has a survival rate approaching 100% in cases that are detected and treated early.

For more information about testicular cancer, contact your local chapter of the American Cancer Society, or call their toll-free national hotline, 1-800-ACS-2345.

Genital Self-Exam (GSE)

The GSE supplements the yearly physician's visit. After a satisfactory check-up, perform a "baseline" GSE for future comparison. Thereafter, perform GSE once a month with BSE or TSE. Get a mirror. Find a private place and time. Sit on edge of chair or on a bed.

Men: examine head and shaft of penis for lesions, growths, etc. (if uncircumcised, be sure to pull down foreskin); also, examine color and texture of testicles/scrotum and any discharge from urethra.

Women: spread apart and examine labia ("lips of vagina") and outer vagina for lesions, growths, excessive/malodorous discharge, etc. If anything appears unusual, consult a physician. Alternative: have sexual partner perform it!

Considerations when Selecting a Contraceptive Method

1. User dependence: is the method used in conjunction with the act of sexual intercourse? does the method require the cooperation of the user's partner? does the method rely on the user's memory?
2. Lifestyle, personal habits, culture: what is the user's comfort level with touching his or her own genitalia? what are the user's personal values regarding contraception? what are the user's intentions if an unintended pregnancy occurs? what are the user's beliefs about abortion?
3. Effectiveness: what are the chances of an unintended pregnancy? what risk is the user willing to accept?
4. Side effects: what is the current health status of the user? what unwanted side effects are tolerable? what side effects are undesirable?
5. Type of sexual relationship(s): what is the level of intimacy between partners? is the relationship short- or long-term? is the user monogamous or serially monogamous? what is the level of comfort in communicating with a partner? is the relationship physically, emotionally, or sexually abusive?
6. Long- or short-term family planning: is the method reversible or not? what are the effects on immediate and future fertility?
7. HIV and STI risk-reduction: does the method protect against HIV and other STIs? has the user ever had an STI before, or is she HIV-positive?
8. Family history: did the user's mother have cervical cancer? did the user's mother have other reproductive health problems? is there a history of heart disease, diabetes, stroke, etc.? any other conditions that are contraindications for use?
9. Cost: what is the cost of the method? what is the cost of associated physician visits (if needed)?
10. Convenience: is the method available over the counter or is a physician visit/prescription required?

Depo-Provera

Depo-Provera is an injectable form of contraception (given in a shot) that protects you against pregnancy for three full months at a time. Its active ingredient is a synthetic hormone similar to progesterone. Depo-Provera acts by preventing your egg cells from ripening, therefore suppressing ovulation. Also, it causes changes in the lining of the uterus that make it less likely for contraception to occur. The Depo-Provera injection is administered within the first five days of the menstrual cycle. Depo-Provera is more than 99% effective, making it the most reliable method on the market. Very few contraindications exist.

Advantages: (1) does not contain estrogen; (2) scanty menses to no menses; (3) decreased menstrual cramps; (4) suppression of pain associated with ovulation; (5) decreased risk of developing endometrial cancer, ovarian cancer, and pelvic inflammatory disease; (6) low risk of ectopic pregnancy; (7) no drug interactions; (8) fewer seizures; and (9) can use while breastfeeding.

Disadvantages include menstrual cycle disturbance, weight gain, breast tenderness, bone density loss, and a delay in the return of fertility of an average of six months to one year after ceasing use Depo-Provera (i.e., no immediate discontinuation). Also, must return for injection every three months. High Density Lipoprotein (HDL) cholesterol levels fall significantly in women using DMPA.

Costs $30–$75 per injection. To protect yourself from Sexually Transmitted Infections including HIV, use a latex condom with spermicide each time you have sex.

Birth Control Pill (Combined Oral Contraceptives)

The most commonly used method in the US, oral contraceptives (OC) prevent pregnancy by keeping levels of estrogen and progestin elevated, thus hindering ovulation. In addition, it renders uterine lining and vaginal secretions hostile to sperm and inconducive to conception. Pill packs are available in 21-day cycles (in which all pills contain hormones) and 28-day cycles (21 active pills, seven placebos). Start taking the first pill either on

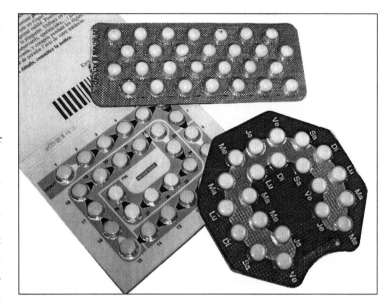

Day Five of the menstrual cycle or on the first Sunday after menstrual flow begins. Take one pill every day at approximately the same time for 21 days; during the fourth week, menstruation should occur. OCs typically are prescribed at 30 or 35 mcg. doses (minipill is less). Need back-up method of contraception during first cycle.

Possible side effects (usually disappear after first month): weight loss/gain, skin and hair changes, change in eyeglass/ contact lens prescription, change in sex drive, break-through bleeding, nausea, mood changes. Contraindications to use: 35+ years, smoker, overweight,
migraines, cardiovascular, or circulatory problems. Non-contraceptive benefits: decreased menstrual bleeding and dysmenorrhea. Certain drugs do decrease the effectiveness of OCs; if you are taking antibiotics, antifungal agents, or anticonvulsants, use a back-up method for the duration of drug use. Oral contraceptives also interact with antidepressants, antidiabetic agents, corticosteroids, and sedatives; always consult a physician before taking any medication. At local pharmacies, prices range from $20–$45 for a month supply.

Emergency Contraceptive Pills (The "Morning-After Pill")

Oral contraceptive pills that contain either ovral or ethinyl estradiol and norgestrel are now given in one dose and should be taken within 72 hours after intercourse. Menstruation should occur within one week. Emergency contraception works by disrupting endometrial development so the uterine lining is unsuitable for implantation. Also, hormone disruption may interfere with fertilization and cause disordered tubal transport. Danazol, a synthetic androgen, and progestin-only pills may be an alternative treatment regimen for those who need or want to avoid estrogen.

The risk of pregnancy with one act of intercourse ranges from approximately 0%–26% depending on the cycle day of exposure in relation to ovulation. Risk of pregnancy is highest during the three days prior to ovulation; rates 15%–26%. Emergency contraceptive pill treatment reduces the risk of pregnancy by approximately 89%. Emergency contraceptive treatment is the only option available to reduce pregnancy risk in circumstances such as rape or mechanical failure of a contraceptive device.

Emergency pills are simple, easy to use, and involve minimal medical risk. Nausea and vomiting are the most common side effects of contraceptive pill treatment. Nausea will occur in 50%–70% of those treated; as many as 22% will experience vomiting as well. Emergency hormone contraception may cause menstrual-cycle disturbance. Less common side effects are breast tenderness, dizziness, and fluid retention. Talk to your clinician before using ECPs if you have ever had a stroke, breast cancer, blood clots in your legs or lungs, diabetes, liver disease, heart disease, kidney disease, or high blood pressure. Emergency contraceptives are available at your Student Health Center. If you have been raped and wish to receive ECPs, go to a hospital immediately. ECP is not licensed as a method of birth control by the FDA.

Diaphragm

Prevents sperm from fertilizing ovum in uterus/fallopian tube. Made of latex rubber. Diameter represents length of the vaginal canal. Fitted by clinician. Place ½ teaspoon of spermicide (cream, gel, jelly) in dimple. Rub a small amount of spermicide on rim. Bearing down, insert high into the vagina with the indentation facing the cervix. If inserted correctly, neither partner should feel it. Insert another applicator-full of spermicide for each additional act of intercourse. Must be left in six hours after last act of intercourse. Do not leave in longer than twenty-four hours (due to risk of Toxic Shock Syndrome). Do not use if menstruating. After removing, clean with warm water and mild soap. Let air dry. Check for holes/wear. Brush lightly with cornstarch. Store in its proper container. Typically needs to be replaced once a year. Requires physician prescription.

Cervical Cap

Prevents sperm from fertilizing ovum in uterus/fallopian tube. Made of latex rubber. Place ¼ teaspoon of spermicide (cream, gel, jelly) in dimple. Bearing down, insert high into the vagina with the indentation facing the cervix. Twist to seal. If inserted correctly, neither partner should feel it. Insert another applicator-full of spermicide for each additional act of intercourse. Must be left in six hours after last act of intercourse. Do not leave in longer than total of twenty-four hours (due to risk of Toxic Shock Syndrome). Do not use if menstruating. After removing, clean with warm water and mild soap. Let air dry. Check for rips/cracks. Brush lightly with cornstarch. Store in its proper container. Typically needs to be replaced once a year. Requires physician prescription. Very few community providers prescribe this method.

Vaginal Condom

The *Reality* female condom is a thin polyurethane sheath 7.8 cm in diameter and 17 cm long. The loose-fitting sheath contains two flexible polyurethane rings. One ring lies inside and serves as an insertion mechanism and internal anchor on the cervix. The other ring forms the external, open edge of the device and remains outside the vagina after insertion. The sheath is pre-lubricated on the inside with a silicone-based lubricant. Additional lubricant is provided with the device. The female condom should not be used in conjunction with latex male condom. The condom can be inserted up to eight hours before intercourse. A new condom should be used with each act of intercourse.

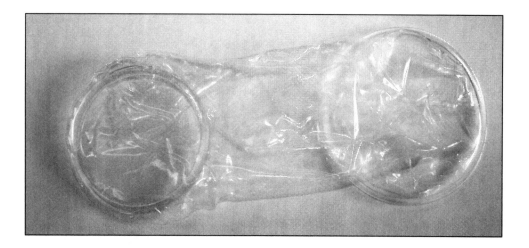

The vaginal condom has a failure rate of 5% for perfect use to 21% for typical use. When completely covering the vagina, the female condom offers protection from sexually transmitted infections including HIV. The vaginal condom is not susceptible to deterioration with exposure to oil-based lubricants and is less susceptible than latex to deterioration during storage. You can insert the vaginal condom yourself. It gives women a way to protect themselves. Does not require a prescription from a physician. Vaginal discomfort and penile irritation are among the most common minor problems associated with the vaginal condom. Also, the outer ring can be pushed inside the vagina during sex, and the penis may slip to the side of the device on entering the vagina. These condoms are usually available at your Student Health Center for a small fee. Can be purchased over the counter at local grocery stores or drug stores at approximately $2.50–$5 each. Store the *Reality* female condom at normal room temperature. Do not use *Reality* after its expiration date because it will not work as well.

Spermicides

Active ingredient Nonoxynol-9 kills sperm and many STI microorganisms, including HIV. Vagina or anus may experience irritation. Never use alone! Come in various consistencies, textures, odors, and flavors (may numb the tongue!). Choice of creams, gels, jellies, film, foam, or suppositories (3%–5% Nonoxynol-9 content, except film and foam contain over 12% Nonoxynol-9). Insert high into the vagina with fingers or with an applicator 3–5 minutes before intercourse (to allow body heat to activate spermicide). Note: some women may be allergic to Nonoxynol-9.

Sterilization

The most commonly used method for women in the US. Includes vasectomy, hysterectomy, removal of ovaries, or tying of fallopian tubes (tubal ligation). Some procedures are reversible. May experience side effects associated with decreased hormone levels. Not recommended for nulliparous college-age women unsure of family plans.

Abortion

Abortion is only one of three options (having and keeping the child, as well as adoption are the other two) available to a woman who experiences an unplanned pregnancy. State laws regarding abortion vary, so check with your state's laws to find out more specifics. Likewise, parental notification laws are different in each state.

In 2005, a total of 820,151 legal abortions were reported to the Center for Disease Control. Approximately 88% were performed during the first twelve weeks of pregnancy.

Suction Curettage (First Trimester)

- A local anesthetic is injected into or near the cervix.
- The opening of the cervix is gradually stretched. One after the other, a series of increasingly thick rods (dilators) are inserted into the opening.
- After the opening is stretched, a blunt tube is inserted into the uterus. This tube is attached to a suction machine.
- The suction machine is turned on. The uterus is emptied by gentle suction.
- After the suction tube has been removed, a curette (narrow metal loop) may be used to gently scrape the walls of the uterus to be sure that it has been completely emptied.

Dilation and Evacuation (D & E) (Second Trimester)

Second trimester abortions are available in some clinics, as well as certain hospitals, up to the twenty-fifth week.
- Absorbent dilators may be put into the cervix where they may remain for several hours or overnight. These dilators absorb fluid from the cervical area and stretch the opening of the cervix as they thicken.
- The woman is usually sent home and given antibiotics to prevent infection. Gradual dilation is more comfortable than having it done all at once. However, pressure and cramping is normal while the dilators in place.
- Intravenous medications may be administered to ease pain and prevent infection.
- A local anesthetic is injected into or near the cervix.
- The dilators are removed from the cervix.
- The fetus and other products of conception are removed from the uterus with instruments and suction curettage. This procedure takes 10–15 minutes.

Abortion after 24 weeks (Third Trimester)

Only one out of every 10,000 women who have abortions have them after 24 weeks. These are only performed when there is a serious threat to a woman's life or health or if the fetus is severely deformed.

Induction Method: The doctor injects salt solution into the uterus to induce contractions that cause a stillbirth. Is usually done in a hospital and may mean staying overnight or longer.

Hysterotomy: In very rare cases, an incision is made through the abdomen. The fetus and placenta are removed and the incision is closed with stitches. Requires general anesthesia and from five to seven days in the hospital.

Complications Due to Abortion

- Allergic reactions to specific anesthetics
- Incomplete abortion
- Blood clots in the uterus
- Infection by germs from the vagina or cervix that get into the uterus.
- Heavy bleeding that requires medical treatment
- A cut or torn cervix
- Perforation of the wall of the uterus

Abortion is about twice as safe as having your tonsils out and eleven times safer than giving birth. Remember, the risks associated with pregnancy are always lower than the risks associated with contraceptive use, especially for young women!

Figure 23: *Summary of Contraceptive Method Failure Rates.* (Trussel 2007)

Method	Rx/OTC	% Women Experiencing an Unintended Pregnancy within the First Year of Use		Mechanism
		Typical use*	Perfect Use	
Depo-Provera (injectable progestogen)	Rx	3	0.3	Synthetic hormones
Female sterilization	N/A	0.5	0.5	Surgical procedure
Male sterilization	N/A	0.15	0.10	Surgical procedure
Oral contraceptives combined and progestogen only	Rx	8	0.3	Synthetic hormones
Evra Patch	Rx	8	0.3	Synthetic hormones
Nuva Ring	Rx	8	0.3	Synthetic hormones
Intrauterine device —ParaGard (copper T) —Mirena	N/A	0.8 0.2	0.6 0.2	Surgically implanted device
Male condom	OTC	15	2	Barrier
Female condom	OTC	21	5	Barrier
Diaphragm	Rx	16	6	Barrier
Vaginal spermicides	OTC	29	18	Chemical
Fertility awareness	N/A	25	—	
Withdrawal	N/A	27	4	
No method	N/A	85	85	

failure rates for men and women whose use is not always consistent or correct

Not For Men Only

The realm of birth control and protection has typically been regarded as the woman's responsibility in a sexual relationship. With increased awareness about HIV and other sexually transmitted infections, many partners are realizing the importance of practicing safer sex. If you choose to be sexually active, then a male condom is the most effective way of reducing risk of disease transmission. This requires the cooperation and participation of the male partner. Therefore, men need to be especially knowledgeable about several issues.

Protecting Yourself and Your Partner. The only 100% method of protecting yourself against unplanned pregnancy, HIV, and other STIs is abstinence. That is, refrain from engaging in any sexual activities that involve the exchange of infectious bodily fluids or tissues. However, this still leaves a wide range of possibilities for sexual intimacy with your partner. Don't be afraid to experiment and be creative. For many men, choosing abstinence is most consistent with their values.

However, if you do choose to be sexually active, you must be ready and willing to accept the emotional and physical consequences of sex. Any boy can have sex; a man does so responsibly and respectfully.

Communicate honestly and openly with your sexual partners about values, desires, and consequences, regardless of whether it's a long-term monogamous relationship or casual one-night stand, or anywhere in between. Doing so prevents misunderstanding, and shows you are a millennium man who takes responsibility for his sex life. It also diminishesthe possibility that you will be accused of rape.

Practice safer sex. That means consistently and correctly use a latex condom each time you have sexual intercourse.

Correct condom use:

1. Purchase a reputable brand of latex condom (such as *Durex* or *Trojans*). Store the condom correctly in a dresser drawer or in a plastic case in your bookbag. DO NOT use a condom that has been in your wallet; the pressure erodes the latex. Also, stay away from lambskin, colored, scented, or flavored condoms; lambskin is permeable to HIV and sperm, and the others contain substances that break down the latex.

2. Check the expiration date, then carefully unwrap the condom package.

3. Always pinch the tip of the condom before unrolling it onto your erect penis. The average male ejaculates at the speed of 35 miles per hour; the pressure is enough to break the condom if there is no space left in the tip. In addition, place a tiny drop of water-based lubricant inside the tip of the condom before putting it on; this will greatly increase sensitivity.

4. Roll the condom all the way down the base of your penis, smoothing out any air bubbles. Generously apply a water-based lubricant such as *K-Y Jelly* or *Astroglide* to the exterior of the condom. This will greatly enhance the sensitivity for both you and your partner.

5. To be even safer, have your partner insert spermicide containing the chemical *Nonoxynol-9* into the vagina or anus 3–5 minutes before initiating intercourse. The spermicide is a back-up in case the condom should break.

6. After ejaculating, be sure to pull out right away, holding firmly to the base of the condom as you do. Discard the condom. If you have both vaginal and anal intercourse, be sure to use a different condom for each act.

Remember, a condom is not foolproof. For example, the parts of your genitalia that are not covered by a condom can be exposed to human papilloma virus (HPV), the virus that causes genital warts, or to herpes if your partner is having an active outbreak. However, a condom is the only method that will reduce the likelihood of HIV or STI transmission if you wish to be sexually active. Therefore, a condom should be worn even if a woman is taking or using birth control, unless she's using a vaginal condom.

Perform a genital self-examination once a month. Look for any unusual lumps, growths, sores, or lesions. Gently squeeze the urethra to see if there is any discharge. If you see anything suspicious, or if you experience pain on ejaculation, a burning sensation when urinating, or blood in urine, see a health care provider immediately to check it out. Early detection leads to more effective treatment.

If you believe you have engaged in high-risk behavior, get an HIV antibody test. Given the wide range of drugs that are now available to physicians, HIV-positive individuals can live many healthy years. The key is to begin early intervention.

However, this test is not a certificate for a "clean bill of health." Due to a "window period"—the time it takes after being infected before a person develops a detectable level of antibodies—the test is not 100% accurate. Remember, testing is never a replacement for safer sex.

Replacing the Myths with Truth. In general, men are not as knowledgeable about reproductive and sexual health. They frequent health providers less often, and generally take more physical risks than women do. However, it is important to debunk the common myths held by men:

TRUTH: "Pulling out," or withdrawal, is not an effective method of birth control. In the fact, over the long run, "pulling out" is as effective a method of contraception as doing nothing; there is a 90% chance of pregnancy after a year. This is because the pre-ejaculatory fluid still contains sperm. In addition, most men cannot withdraw completely before ejaculating. By the way, "pulling out" affords no protection whatsoever against HIV or other STIs.

TRUTH: You can get a girl pregnant if you have sex during her period. While conception is only possible during specific times of a woman's menstrual cycle (mainly during and immediately following ovulation), the typical college woman has an irregular cycle due to stress, poor nutrition, etc. Sperm can live for up to 72 hours in a woman's vaginal canal. Should a woman ovulate soon after her period has ended, it is possible for her to become pregnant.

TRUTH: Men and women are equally sexual. However, traditional sex role socialization has taught women to be more passive and to be less comfortable and open about their sexuality. Men are taught that more, more, and more is better. This is reflected in the sexual double standard; a woman who has slept with several people is labeled a "whore" or a "slut," yet men who have multiple partners are revered and admired by their peers.

TRUTH: Men cannot die of "blue balls." It is true that if a man reaches a high level of sexual arousal and then doesn't achieve an orgasm, he may experience a painful throbbing in his groin and genitals. However, the pain is temporary and not life-threatening. An effective solution to "blue balls" is masturbation. Remember, your partner never has an obligation to alleviate your horniness—no matter what caused it.

TRUTH: AIDS is no longer just a disease that affects gay men. In fact, rates of HIV infection are rising most rapidly among heterosexuals. Heterosexuals now compose approximately 32% of all AIDS cases. In addition, the number of AIDS cases is increasing four times faster among women than among men.

TRUTH: You cannot tell by looking at someone if they have an STI. The vast majority of STIs are not associated with any symptoms. Never assume that just because a person looks "clean" that they do not have a disease. STIs are not so much a reflection of a person's moral character as they are a result of unwise sexual choices. Also, don't bother asking someone if they have a disease; partners may lie, or they may not realize they are infected.

TRUTH: Alcohol and other drugs make for clumsier, less fulfilling sex. While alcohol's intoxicating effects may lead to "beer goggles" and increased sexual desire, they interfere with a man's ability to perform sexually. The intoxicated male may have difficulty achieving or maintaining an erection, and orgasm may evade him. Additionally, substances interfere with good judgment and make practicing safer sex much less likely. In fact, unplanned pregnancy and STI transmission are highly correlated with sex under the influence.

TRUTH: One-size condom fits all. Even though there are several brands of large, max, or plus-size condoms available over the counter, their shape and quality vary greatly. A regular size latex condom can fit easily over a watermelon, so unless your penis is larger than that, stick with the regular size. To alleviate the discomfort or feelings of constriction, use a water-based lubricant such as *Astroglide* on the outside of the condom.

   TRUTH: Even if I'm allergic to latex, I can still wear a condom. The *Avanti* condom is made of polyurethane. The Food and Drug Administration has found it to be comparable to the latex condom as a contraceptive and a prophylactic. It is slightly thicker than latex, so one possible side effect is decreased sensitivity. However, using a generous amount of water-based lubricant on the outside of the condom will help.

Questions to Consider

1. What considerations must be taken while talking to a peer about contraceptive methods? Is it okay to recommend a method? Why or why not?
2. What are ethical considerations you must be considerate of when addressing reproductive health issues?
3. Name two of the most common reproductive health myths on the campus and how as peer educators you would address these.

References

Trussell, J., Hatcher, R.A., Cates, Jr., W., Stewart, F. H., & Kost, K. (1990). A guide to interpreting contraceptive efficacy studies. *Journal of Obstetrics and Gynecology*, 76, p. 558–567.

Trussell, J. (2007). Contraceptive efficacy. In Hater, R.A., Trussel, J., Nelson, A.L., Cates, W. Stewart, F.H., and Kowal, D. *Contraceptive technology: Nineteenth Revised Edition*. New York, NY: Ardent Media.

Chapter 17

Body Image and Eating Disorders

By Luoluo Hong and Julie Catanzarite

What is Body Image?

Body image affects women's health in a way that is unique from that of men. *Body image* is defined as the beliefs about one's own attractiveness, sexuality, and physical characteristics, as well as the perceptions of how others view one's own body, coupled with the inseparable emotions, thoughts, and behaviors that result from such beliefs and perceptions. Body image is context-bound and culturally derived. That is, women with the similar types of bodies who grow up in different cultures may have vastly different body images.

What Are Eating Disorders?

The three most common eating disorders include *anorexia nervosa* (self-starvation), *bulimia nervosa* (bingeing and purging), and *compulsive overeating* (bingeing). Signs and symptoms are fairly similar across all three eating disorders; however the medical complications and nutritionally related sequel, or consequences of each disorder vary (American Dietetic Association 1992).

How Common are Eating Disorders?

Because of the secrecy that tends to surround eating disorders, it is difficult to know the prevalence of the condition. However, numerous research surveys have indicated that anywhere from 0.5%–2.0% of the female population is anorexic, while as many as 30% of college females are bulimic. In addition, 86% of bulimics are between the ages of 15 and 30, and 30% of bulimics report a previous history of anorexia (National Institute of Mental Health [NIMH] 1994).

The 2009 National College Health Risk Behavior Survey asked female students how they had lost weight or had kept from gaining weight in the thirty days prior to the survey. Of respondents, 39% of female students were dieting, 54% of them exercised, 3% vomited or took laxatives, and 4% took diet pills. Women were significantly more likely to engage in all of these behaviors than their male counterparts (Douglas et al. 1997). Preliminary research data also indicate that female athletes, because of their tendency to engage in crash dieting and other quick weight-loss techniques, are at increased risk for developing eating disorders (Powers 1999). Sorority women are similarly prone to disordered eating. While women constitute the majority (90%–95%) of eating-disorder cases, there has been an increase in the number of eating disorders that mental health professionals diagnose in men.

What Causes Eating Disorders?

There is no single cause of eating disorders; rather, the reasons are complex, ranging from emotional and psychological to physiological and sociocultural. In general, people with eating disorders exhibit some level of distorted body image. In other words, what is disordered is the way in which an individual sees him/herself in the mirror and assesses their own appearance; these judgments then result in irrational and irregular eating habits.

Emotional and psychological factors that have contributed to the development of eating disorders include low self-esteem; inability to cope with negative emotions such as fear, anger, or anxiety; depression; experience of childhood sexual abuse; and a family history of alcohol or other drug abuse (The Eating Disorder Foundation 2005).

People with eating disorders tend to have decreased levels of the neurotransmitters *serotonin* and *norepinephrine* (same as in people with depression), and increased levels of the brain hormones *cortisol* (A stress hormone that promotes the retention of new fat and stubbornly clings to existing body fat) and *vasopressin* (similar to individuals with obsessive-compulsive disorder) (NIMH 1994).

Our society places tremendous pressure on young girls and women to be thin, and strong cultural messages say that thin is better (Levine 1987). Fashion magazines, lingerie catalogs, television and Internet ads, movies, and music television videos are filled with exceptionally thin models who look very little like real women. For example, Kate Moss, model, is 5'7" and weighs only 105 lbs. American social mores derive women's worth and femininity in how good they look, and suggest that a woman with the perfect body and face will not have any problems in life (Wolf 1991). While it is difficult to say that this cultural context causes eating disorders, it certainly serves to promulgate and maintain women's poor body image and obsession with weight.

As a result, 45% of American women are dieting at any one time. In less than a decade, the dieting industry doubled its gross income to over $33 billion a year; today, it is over $60 billion. Sadly, the onset of dieting is occurring at earlier and earlier ages, as well. In fact, one study found that 50% of nine-year-old girls and 80% of 10-year-old girls had already dieted (even though only 15% of these girls were overweight) (National Eating Disorders Association 2010).

In an era when women's roles are rapidly changing, women receive conflicting messages about how they should behave in the home, school, or workplace, as well as in relationships and as individuals. As a result, the ability to manipulate and control what they do or do not eat is a comforting method of alleviating the feelings of powerlessness and confusion.

What is Emotional Eating?

Emotional eating refers to the use of food to alleviate negative feelings such as rejection, frustration, anxiety, disappointment, anger, sadness, or fear. Food can temporarily numb feelings and fulfill the need for intimacy and comfort. However, emotional eating results in a vicious cycle in which the temporary state of regaining control through bingeing or purging is followed by guilt, which only fuels more shame and feelings of failure.

What Are the Signs and Symptoms of Eating Disorders?

Only a qualified mental health professional can diagnose an eating disorder. The following guidelines are provided in order to facilitate early identification and intervention. Please note that many individuals who are thin do not have anorexia nervosa; conversely, individuals who are overweight are not necessarily compulsive overeaters. Rather, eating disorders are a complex combination of physical and psychological outcomes.

The following are general characteristics of people who have eating disorders:

- extreme preoccupation with weight and/or appearance;
- increased isolation from friends, partners, and family;
- increased irritability, tearfulness;
- compulsive neatness or cleanliness;
- compulsive exercising;
- hyperactive or restless;
- over-involvement in academic, extracurricular, or professional activities;
- perfectionistic;
- eats very slowly;
- cuts food into little pieces;
- avoids coming to the table for meals, seems tense at meals;
- leaves laxatives or diuretics lying around;
- hoards food in the room;
- glands look swollen;
- unusual eating habits: eats large amounts of food all at once in private, or takes little bits of many foods (e.g., takes out just the raisins from cookies); and/or
- collects recipes, likes to cook, and likes others to eat.

The following are more specific behavioral indicators of* anorexia nervosa *(self-starvation):

- thin to the point of emaciation (15% below healthy body weight);
- severe weight loss with no known medical reason;
- intense fear of gaining weight;
- believes she is fat even when she is at or below healthy body weight;
- reduction in food intake, denial of hunger, and decreased consumption of fat-containing foods;
- prolonged exercise despite fatigue, weakness, or illness;
- peculiar patterns and rituals associated with eating and handling food;
- may have episodes of binge eating followed by self-induced vomiting and/or abuse of laxatives or diuretics (water pills);
- hypothermia (cold hands and feet);
- dry or yellowish skin (increased blood levels of carotene);
- lanugo hair (a fine down all over the body);
- general weakness;
- constipation and digestive problems (feeling bloated, ulcers, etc.);
- insomnia (inability to sleep);
- amenorrhea (loss of menstrual periods);
- severe chemical imbalances;
- frequent illnesses and stress fractures; and/or
- heart failure.

The following are more specific behavioral indicators of* bulimia nervosa *(bingeing and purging):

- average to slightly above healthy body weight (10% below to 15% above healthy body weight);
- overly concerned with weight and body shape;
- attempts to control weight by dieting, over-exercising, self-induced vomiting, and/or laxative/diuretic/emetic abuse;
- eating patterns alternate between binges and fasts;
- bingeing on foods with high caloric content;
- secretiveness about binges and vomiting;
- unusual interest in food and cooking;
- feelings of lack of control when bingeing;
- depressive moods;
- frequent and rapid weight gains and losses;
- alcohol or other drug abuse;
- dehydration;
- ulcers, constipation, and digestive disorders;
- severe dental problems;
- muscle weakness; and/or
- heart irregularities.

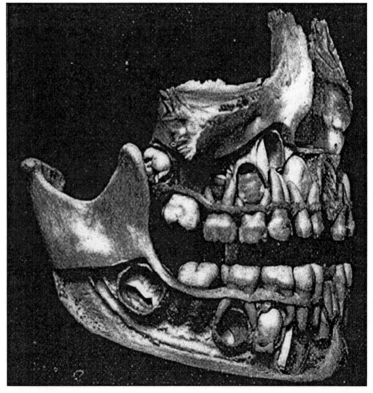

The following are more specific behavioral indicators and medical complications of compulsive overeating ***(bingeing):***

- overweight or obese (20% or more over healthy body weight);
- consumption of large amounts of food high in caloric and fat content;
- binges in secret;
- abuses alcohol or other drugs;
- shortness of breath;
- high blood pressure;
- joint problems;
- heart and gall bladder diseases;
- diabetes; and/or
- serious depression.

What are the Medical Complications of Eating Disorders?

Serious medical conditions can result from eating disorders. The extent of the damage is determined by the severity and longevity of the condition. Therefore, it is imperative that treatment be sought as early as possible for these conditions.

Anorexia. Anorexia takes as many as 1,000 lives every year, which is the highest mortality rate among any psychiatric disorder. It is essential an intervention take place at the first indication of the disorder (NEDA 2005). In Zerbe (1996), it is suggested that there is a 5% mortality rate for someone who has been suffering for five years and an 18% mortality rate for having anorexia for thirty years. These deaths are most often related to starving the body of essential nutrients needed for normal functioning. Only 17%–40% of people with anorexia are able to continue their lives without other mental disorders, but most will suffer with severe obsessive, compulsive, or depressive symptoms (Zerbe 1996). The following are the most common medical conditions associated with anorexia (NEDA 2010; Zerbe 1996).

- Abnormally slow heartbeat and low blood pressure
- Fatigue and weakness due to anemia and muscle loss
- Osteoporosis (dry, brittle bones and a reduction of bone mass)
- Heart failure due to electrolyte imbalance
- Dehydration and kidney failure
- Reproduction problems—loss of menstruation for women and decreased sperm motility for men
- Development of downy hair called lanugo and intolerance to cold due to low body temperature
- Dry hair and yellowed skin; hair loss
- Insomnia
- Constipation

Bulimia. Like anorexia, bulimia is often paired with other psychological disorders, such as depression, anxiety, and substance abuse. The most common conditions experienced by those with bulimia include (Zerbe 1996; NEDA 2010; NIMH 1994):

- dental problems due to tooth decay and staining as a result of constant exposure to stomach acids
- chronically inflamed esophagus, which can actually erupt; sore throat
- intestinal distress, constipation, and kidney problems as a result of laxative abuse
- heart failure caused by an electrolyte imbalance
- several dehydration as a result of purging liquids

- gastric eruption caused by excessive bingeing, which results in death 80% of the time
- substance abuse
- mineral deficiencies resulting in seizures and hair loss
- disrupted reproduction

How Are Eating Disorders Treated?

Individuals can engage in disordered eating over long periods, sometimes for many years. People with anorexia can hide their thinness under baggy clothes, while people with bulimia tend to have average body sizes. In addition, the obsession with dieting and thinness, as well as the extreme body dissatisfaction in someone with an eating disorder, are masked by the fact that so many women have these same issues.

When someone is diagnosed with an eating disorder, a treatment will usually require a multidisciplinary approach, with the collaboration of many health professionals, including physicians, psychologists/therapists, registered dietitians (RD), and health educators. First, the individuals must be medically stabilized. In some instances where severe weight loss, malnutrition and dehydration, serious metabolic disturbances, or extreme depression are present, the woman will need to be hospitalized. Evidence shows that antidepressants can be useful in the management of eating disorders, as well as the treatment of co-occurring depression (NIMH 1994).

To help cope with the eating disorder and its underlying emotional issues, as well as address body image perception, individuals will undergo both individual and group counseling. With the help of educators and RDs, a person with an eating disorder will relearn eating habits and develop a more healthful eating regimen (National Eating Disorders Association 2010).

How Can I Talk to Someone I Think Has an Eating Disorder?

1. Time your discussion to take place when the individual is not engaged in any of the unhealthy behaviors associated with eating disorders (eating, purging, exercising).
2. Respect the individual's privacy and right to control her own life. Talk to your friend in a confidential environment.
3. Be nonjudgmental and supportive. Remember, an eating disorder is a serious medical condition and mental health problem that requires treatment. Someone with an eating disorder is not any less capable or worthy; rather, their desire to be a better person is what drove them to disordered eating in the first place.
4. Begin by saying that you are concerned about her welfare. Use a lot of "I" statements. Share your feelings of anger, fear, and sadness that her behaviors generate and the eating disorder's effects on you as a friend, roommate, sister, etc.
5. Avoid generalized accusations or expressions of pity. Rather, cite specific examples of "red flag" behaviors you have observed (e.g., severe weight loss, vomiting in the bathroom after a lunch buffet, walking into the room when they are bingeing, finding laxatives or diuretics hidden in the kitchen cabinets, over-exercising, etc.).
6. Prepare for defensiveness or denial by keeping the confrontation focused on what is happening to her—the two of you can talk about you at a later time.
7. Recognize your limits; change occurs only if the person wants it and is willing to take care of herself. However, do refuse to condone or enable their unhealthy behaviors.
8. Communicate your willingness to help. Provide a list of campus and community resources.

So What is Healthy Eating?

Nutritional habits significantly impact on a person's risk for heart disease and cancer, the two leading killers of Americans. In general, the American Cancer Society recommends the following dietary and lifestyle guidelines: (1) eat a variety of foods; (2) maintain a healthy weight: (3) choose a diet low in fat, saturated fat, and cholesterol; (4) choose a diet with plenty of vegetables, fruits, and grain products; (5) use sugars only in moderation; (6) use salt and sodium only in moderation; and (7) avoid cigarettes and excessive alcohol use. In addition, everyone should become familiar with the food guide pyramid as a useful tool for grocery shopping, meal planning, and eating out.

What is Healthy Dieting?

In general, women's expectations for body weight are much too low, while their body composition goals do not reflect physical or genetic realities. Similarly, men oftentimes have unrealistic expectations about their body shape and size, as well. To calculate a rough estimate of a healthy body weight for a female, begin with 100 pounds for the first five feet, and add five pounds for each additional inch of height. For men, healthy body weight is determined by assigning 106 pounds for the first five feet and adding six pounds for each additional inch of height. However, with either sex, add 10% of this figure for a large frame, and subtract 10% for a small frame. To be healthy, women require a body fat composition of 20–30%, and men require 10–15%.

Our national obsession with dieting continues despite the wealth of data that say the majority of dieters regain their weight within one year. Most "fad diets" are doomed to fail, and are characterized by: (1) a rapid rise and fall in popularity; (2) social appeal or prestige (e.g., the "Madonna Diet"); (3) sounding incredibly easy (e.g., "eat all you want and still lose weight"); (4) relieving the dieter of all responsibilities and decisions; (5) promoting a particular food or special diet; (6) distorting or ignoring basic nutritional principles; and (7) seldom including a variety of foods.

By contrast successful weight loss programs are typified by a high level of social support, require exercise as part of the weight-loss routine, teach individuals ways to appropriately modify sedentary or stressful lifestyles, help dieters develop effective ways for coping with feelings associated with body image and weight loss, and foster gradual weight loss over time (no more than one or two pounds a week). That is, these programs provide strategies to change what, where, why, when, and how one eats.

Toward Healthier Body Image

Differential treatment of individuals based on their size remains the last socially acceptable form of discrimination in our society. The fashion industry and the media continually portray limiting and narrow definitions of beauty and attractiveness. Men and women expend considerable—sometimes exorbitant— amounts of energy and money to achieve an impossible ideal of physical perfection. These are human resources that could be better directed toward fostering size acceptance and self-love.

As college men and women, it is imperative that we generate a new culture that regards people of all shapes, sizes, and colors as beautiful and deserving of respect. We need to shed the assumptions and moral judgments we typically make in relation to someone's size (e.g., thin is good because it demonstrates self-discipline, fat is bad because it represents overindulgence). These stereotypes only serve to hurt and divide individuals. Rather, let us begin teaching children and young adults to nurture their inner souls and appreciate their outer bodies.

Suggestions for Further Reading

Brownmiller, S. (1984). *Femininity.* New York: Fawcett Columbine.

Chernin, K. (1982). *The Obsession: Reflections on the Tyranny of Slenderness.* New York: Harper & Row Publishers.

Hayes, D. (1996, October). *Basic Tenets of Health at Every Size: A Size Acceptance Approach to Health Promotion.* Paper presented at the American Dietetic Association Annual Meeting, San Antonio, TX.

Hirschmann, J. R., & Munter, C. H. (1995). When Women Stop Hating Their Bodies. New York: Fawcett Columbine.

Wolf, N. (1991). *The Beauty Myth: How Images of Beauty are Used Against Women.* New York: Doubleday Publishing.

Also visit the Alliance for Eating Disorders' website at www.eatingdisorderinfo.org for several other resources and suggested reading lists divided by topic.

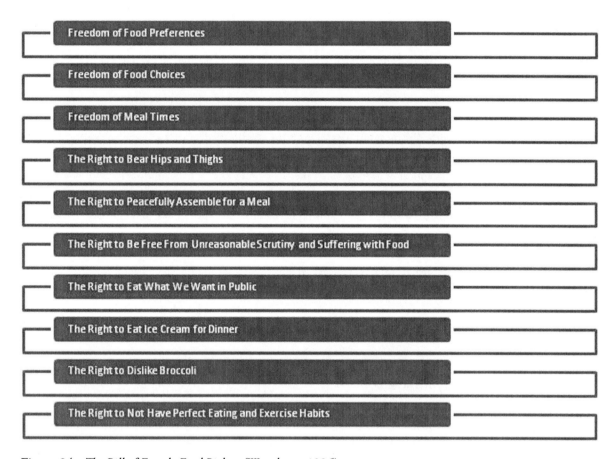

Figure 24: *The Bill of Female Food Rights. (Waterhouse 1996).*

Quick Facts about Figures

1–4%	Percentage of high school and college girls who have either anorexia or bulimia nervosa.
10%	Percentage of teenagers with eating disorders who are boys
25%	Percentage of men who have ever dieted
46%	Percentage of US men who are dissatisfied with their appearance
33%	Percentage of US women who wear a size 16 or larger
56%	Percentage of US women who are frequently dissatisfied with their appearance
50%	Percentage of US women on a diet at any given time
50%	Percentage of 9-year-old girls who have ever dieted
80%	Percentage of women who have ever dieted
33-23-33	Average measurements of a contemporary fashion model
36-18-33	Projected measurements of a Barbie doll, in inches, if she were a full-sized human being; she would also experience amenorrhea
5′4″, 145 lbs	The average height and weight of a woman in the US
5′9″, 110 lbs	The average height and weight of a model
$10 billion	Revenues of the diet industry in 1970
$68.7 billion	Estimates revenues of the diet industry in 2010

Phillips 2010; Schniede 1996; "US weight loss" 2007

Figure 25: *How Healthy Is Your Body Image?*

Instructions: For each of these statements below, rate the degree to which it applies to you. Circle only one number for each statement. After rating yourself on all statements, total your points to get your body-image score.

	Never	Sometimes	Often	Always
1. When I look in the mirror, I dislike what I see.	0	1	2	3
2. When I shop for clothing, I am more aware of my weight problem and consequently find shopping for clothes somewhat unpleasant.	0	1	2	3
3. I'm ashamed to be seen in public.	0	1	2	3
4. I prefer to avoid engaging in sports or exercise because of my appearance.	0	1	2	3
5. I feel friends and family are embarrassed to be seen with me.	0	1	2	3
6. I think my body is ugly.	0	1	2	3
7. I feel that people must think my body in unattractive.	0	1	2	3
8. Feeling guilty about my weight preoccupies my thinking.	0	1	2	3
9. My thoughts about my body and physical appearance are negative and self-critical.	0	1	2	3
10. I feel ashamed of my body in the presence of a special person.	0	1	2	3
11. I compare my body to others to see if they are heavier than I am.	0	1	2	3
12. Enjoying activities is difficult because I am self-conscious about my appearance.	0	1	2	3
Totals				

Now total the points you have circled in each column. The higher your body-image score, the more negative your body-image is. If your total points are 0, your body-image is very good; continue liking and valuing your inner and outer self. If your total points are 36 (you circled 3 for every statement), this may mean you place more value on appearances as an indicator of success than is healthy. Look for other ways to nurture and validate your self-worth.

Questions to Consider

1. What are the dangers of the word "diet"?
2. You recognize someone may have an eating disorder. How do you address this concern?
3. What is the difference between a person having a negative body image and an eating disorder?

References

The U.S. weight loss and diet control market. 2007. (9th ed.). Tampa, FL: Marketdata Enterprises Inc.

American College Health Association. (2009). *American College Health Association-National College Health Assessment: Reference group executive summary Fall 2009.* Baltimore: Author.

American Dietetic Association. (1992). *Manual of clinical dietetics (4th ed.).* Chicago: American Dietetic Association.

Douglas, Kathy A., et al. (1997). Results from the 1995 National College Health Risk Behavior Survey. *Journal of American College Health, 46,* p. 55–66.

Levine, M. P. (1987). Student eating disorders: Anorexia nervosa and bulimia. Washington, DC: National Education Association.

National Institute of Mental Health. (1994) Eating Disorders. (NIH Publication No. 94-3477).

National Eating Disorders Foundation. (2010). *Statistics: Eating disorders and their precursors. Retrieved from http://www.nationaleatingdisorders.org/uploads/statistics_tmp.pdf*

National Eating Disorders Association. (2010). *Treatment of eating disorders. Retrieved from http://www.nationaleatingdisorders.org/uploads/file/information-resources/Treatment%20of%20Eating%20Disorders.pdf*

Philips, K. A. (2010). Unhappy with you looks? Or is it a disorder? *The New York Times. Retrieved from* http://consults.blogs.nytimes.com/2010/04/16/unhappy-with-your-looks-or-is-it-a-disorder/

Powers, P. (1999). Athletes and eating disorders: Some ramification of the NCAA study. *Eating Disorders Review, 10(6).* Retrieved from http://www.bulimia.com/client/client_pages/printable_pages/newsletter5print.cfm

Zerbe, K. J. (1995). *The body betrayed: A deeper understanding of women, eating disorders, and treatments.* Carlsbad, CA: Gurze Books.

Chapter 18

National Nutrition and Fitness Guidelines

By Luoluo Hong and Julie Catanzarite

The Dietary Guidelines for Americans are published by the US Department of Agriculture (2005), and apply to all healthy Americans over the age of two. They reflect the recommendations of nutrition experts who agree that enough evidence exists to show that diet has a large effect on health.

Recommendation 1: Eat a Variety of Foods

The body needs over forty different nutrients. Most likely it needs nutrients that have not even been discovered yet but are contained in the foods we eat. Therefore, it is important to eat foods from each of the different food groups. Items have been placed into food groups based on the nutrients they contain.

The MyPyramid offers the following recommended daily servings from various food groups, which is based on a 2,000-calorie diet:

1. **Breads, cereals, pastas, and rice (6 oz)** for carbohydrates, B vitamins, iron, and fiber.
   Serving = 1 slice bread, 1 oz. dry cereal, ½ cup cooked cereal/pasta/rice.
2. **Vegetables (2½ cups or 5 servings)** for carbohydrates, vitamins A and C, minerals, and fiber.
   Serving = 6 oz. juice, 1 cup raw vegetable, ½ cup cooked vegetable.
3. **Fruits (2 cups or 4 servings)** for carbohydrates, vitamins A and C, minerals, and fiber.
   Serving = 6 oz. juice, ½ cup raw/canned/cooked fruit, 1 medium apple/orange, ½ banana/grapefruit.
4. **Milk, cheese, and yogurt (3 cups)** for protein, vitamins, and calcium.
   Serving = 1 cup milk/yogurt, 1.5 oz cheese, ½ cup ice cream.
5. **Meat, poultry, eggs, seafood, nuts, and dry beans (5½ oz)** for iron and protein.
   Serving = 2–3 oz. cooked meat/poultry/seafood, 1 egg, ½ cup cooked/dry beans.
6. **Fats, oils, and sweets (6 tsp.)** Use sparingly.

The specific number of servings an individual needs from each groups varies depending on height, weight, gender, and age. To find the appropriate amounts for you, go to MyPyramid.gov.

Recommendation 2: Balance The Food You Eat With Physical ACTIVITY

If you are overweight or underweight, your chances of developing health problems are much greater. In the US 33% of adults are obese by medical standards, and this is continually rising. In fact, obesity rates have grown 43% in the last 15 years (Stewart 2009). Consequences of obesity include high blood pressure, heart disease, stroke, and diabetes. These diseases represent the main killers of Americans.

Individuals who are too thin are at risk for osteoporosis. Also, older women who are underweight are at greater risk of early death.

Whether your weight is healthy or not depends on how much is fat, where fat is located in the body, and if you have other medical problems. Exact healthy weight has not been determined, and researchers are trying to develop precise guidelines.

Exercise plays an essential role in weight maintenance and overall health. All the diseases listed above as consequences of obesity are also the result of a sedentary lifestyle. No matter what an individual weighs, exercise will affect health positively. In addition, it is almost impossible for individuals who lose weight to keep it off if they do not exercise regularly. The CDC (2008) recommends that each American accumulate at least 2 hours and 30 minutes of moderate activity or 1 hour and 15 minutes of intense aerobic activity and at least two days of strength training every week.

Non-Nutritional Benefits of Exercise. Exercise has numerous physical and emotional health benefits. In addition to burning off calories to help you lose or maintain weight, exercise,

- raises metabolic rate;
- may increase HDL, "good cholesterol," level;
- improves heart and lung capacity;
- improves overall appearance and self-image;
- reduces stress, tension and anxiety, as well alleviates anxiety and depression;
- gives you more energy;
- increases resistance to fatigue;
- improves ability to fall asleep quickly and sleep well;

- tones muscles; and
- controls appetite.

Developing an Exercise Program. The key to a successful exercise program is selecting activities that you enjoy. However, exercises that improve the condition of your heart and lungs must be

Brisk: raising heart and breathing rates
Sustained: done at least 15–30 minutes without interruption
Regular: repeated several times per week

Each exercise session should consist of a warm-up, exercise within your THRZ (see below), and a cool-down.

Not all exercises give you the same cardiovascular conditioning benefits. Cross-country skiing, jogging, stationary cycling, and uphill hiking condition the heart and lungs. Bicycling, basketball, downhill skiing, swimming, tennis, and walking are excellent conditioners if done vigorously. Baseball, bowling, football, golf, and softball do not condition heart and lungs.

Proper Equipment and Attire. Proper equipment and exercise attire are important. Proper shoes minimize injury while walking, jogging, doing aerobics, or playing racquetball. If you cycle, wear a helmet to prevent head injuries, and use reflectors on the wheels at night.

Wearing layered clothing and a hooded sweatshirt or a hat in the winter if you are exercising outdoors will minimize body heat loss without being uncomfortable. Be sure to wear warm socks and gloves or mittens.

During the hot summer months, replenish fluids frequently when exercising; drink 8–12 ounces of water 10–15 minutes before exercising, and a few sips every 15 minutes during. In order to prevent heat exhaustion, avoid exercising between 3:00 and 5:00 PM—the hottest part of the day. Cooler times are early morning or later evening.

In both summer and winter, choose a material that is wicking (e.g., CoolMax and dri-fit). This type of material keeps you cool in the summer and warm in the winter.

Reaching the Target Heart Rate Zone (THRZ). To condition your heart and lungs, you must bring your heart rate, measured by taking your pulse (beats per minute), within a certain range called the target heart rate zone (THRZ). Your THRZ depends on your age and your maximum heart rate. Your maximum heart rate is determined by subtracting your age from 220. Your THRZ is 60%–75% of your maximum heart rate. When you begin exercising, aim for the lower part of your THRZ (60%); as you get into better condition, gradually build to the higher part of your THRZ (75%). After six months or more of regular exercise, you can exercise at up to 85% of your maximum.

To determine how hard you are exercising, at the end of a workout, quickly place the tips of your first two fingers lightly over one of the arteries (carotid) on your neck located to the right or left of your Adam's apple. Count your pulse for ten seconds and multiply by six.

Nutritional Needs. For athletes, nutritional requirements are not that different from recommendations for the general public:

Carbohydrates 45%–65% of daily calories
Protein 10%–35% of daily calories
Fat Less than 25%–30% of your daily calories
Fluids 8–9 glasses a day
Vitamins Supplied by eating at least nine servings of fruits or vegetables every day

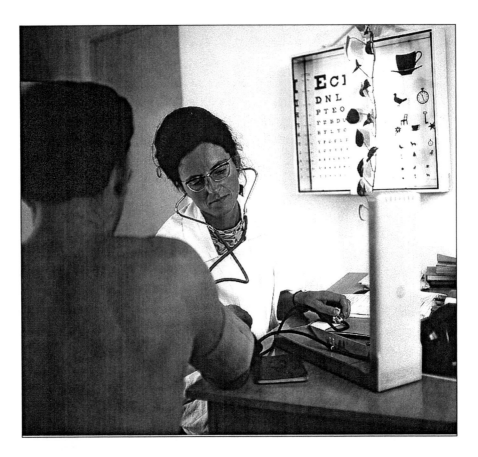

Healthy Body Weight. In a study at Washington State University, based on 1983 Metropolitan Life Height and Weight Table:

- 46% of the men perceived themselves to be overweight;
- 54% of them exceeded their recommended weight;
- 71% of the women perceived themselves to be overweight; and
- fewer than 23% of them exceeded their recommended weight (Beeman 1990).

A healthy body weight can be determined by using the following formulas:

Male	106 lbs. for the first five feet + 6 lbs. for each additional inch
Female	100 lbs. for the first five feet + 5 lbs. for each additional inch
Either sex	+ 10% for large frame; − 10% for small frame

Body Composition Goals. Both men and women should range between 20% and 25% body mass.

Recommendation 3: Choose a Diet With Plenty of Vegetables, Fruits, and Grain Products

These foods are important parts of the varied diet discussed in the first guideline, but are emphasized here for their complex carbohydrate, dietary fiber, and vitamin and mineral content. They are also low in fat. Complex carbohydrates are foods such as starches, breads, cereals, pasta, rice, dry beans and peas, potatoes, and corn.

Dietary fiber is a part of plants that cannot be digested by the human body. It is found in whole grain bread and cereal, dry beans and peas, vegetables and fruit. Too little fiber is related to constipation, diverticular disease, cancer, and hemorrhoids. Experts recommend that each American eat nine servings of fruits and vegetables daily to receive enough vitamins, minerals, and fiber to prevent disease.

Recommendation 4: Choose a Diet Low In Fat, Saturated Fat, and Cholesterol.

Populations like ours with high intakes of fat and saturated fat have more obesity, heart disease, and cancer. Also, research indicates that excess dietary fat is the culprit of most weight problems. Many find just by decreasing fat, weight is lost.

The American Heart Association recommends that no more than 30% of your caloric intake be from fat, and less than 10% (3%–7% is ideal) of caloric intake be from saturated fat. This is typically 50–60 grams of fat for a college female and 60–75 grams for a college male. Experts also recommend that total cholesterol be less than 200 mg/dl. Total cholesterol is composed of "good" cholesterol (high density lipoprotein, or HDL) and "bad" cholesterol (low density lipoprotein, or LDL).

To decrease fat intake, avoid or minimize alcohol, fast foods, condiments, late-night eating, and traditional dining out, and adopt fruits/vegetables and fiber. It is important to remember that fat is an essential nutrient. Too little fat can cause one to consume excess calories, because fat serves a purpose of satiety. It stays in the stomach much longer than the other nutrients, carbohydrate and fat. Therefore, most people should eat at least 20 grams of fat daily.

Calculating Percent Calories from Fat

number of fat grams x 9 calories per gram = calories from fat

calories from fat/total calories x 100 = percent calories from fat

Fats are composed of different types of fatty acids. Saturated fats are hard at room temperature and found in animal products and tropical oils (coconut and palm). Because the body uses saturated fat to manufacture blood cholesterol, a diet low in saturated fat can help maintain a desirable cholesterol level and lead to a reduced risk of heart disease.

Unsaturated fats are liquid at room temperature and are of two types, poly- and mono-unsaturated fats. Monounsaturated fats such as olive and canola oils have been found to have a favorable impact on blood cholesterol.

Recommendation 5: Choose a Diet Moderate In Sugar

Foods high in sugar often have no other nutrients needed by the body. This can lead to excess calories and weight gain. Per capita, Americans consume a pound of sugar every three days. This is not surprising—one 12 – oz. can of Coke has nine teaspoons of sugar!

Recommendation 6: Choose a Diet Moderate In Salt and Sodium

Sodium is an essential nutrient. But excess sodium can increase blood pressure in salt-sensitive individuals, leading to health problems. Sodium can also lead to water retention. The body only requires 200 mg. of sodium per day (1/10 tsp. of salt). It is recommended that Americans consume less than 3000 mg. per day. One teaspoon has 2300 mg.!

Recommendation 7: If You Drink Alcoholic Beverages, Do So In Moderation

Moderation is considered two drinks daily for men and one drink for women. Women who are pregnant or those trying to conceive should not drink under any circumstance. Alcohol can affect a fetus's growth adversely most significantly in the first trimester when a women may not know she is pregnant.

Alcohol may also increase the risk for cancer, cirrhosis, and pancreatitis. Research has indicated that red wine may have a protective effect on heart disease. However, due to the risks of other diseases, physicians do not generally recommend that those who do not drink begin to do so to prevent heart disease. For example, one study found that 3–9 drinks per day decreased heart disease risk in women by 40%. But as little as one drink per day increased risk for breast cancer.

Recommendation 8: Know Your Recommended Caloric Intake

Recommended caloric intake is roughly 2,000 for a typical college woman and 2,400 for typical college man. However, this figure increases with greater activity level, and also depends on height, weight, and age. To determine your specific caloric needs, visit the United States Department of Agriculture's (USDA) National Agricultural Library Website at www.nal.usda.gov. Go to the food and nutrition section and explore the interactive tools to help determine your specific nutritional needs.

The revised food label format must be present on all processed foods regulated by the Food and Drug Administration. What appears here is a sample of the kinds of information which are provided.

Note that serving sizes are standardized to reflect the amount of foods people actually eat. The list of nutrients includes those most important to the health of today's consumers. Percent daily values show how a food fits into the overall daily diet; they are based on a daily diet of 2,000 calories. Finally, the label tells the number of calories per gram of fat, carbohydrates, and protein (Tufts University 1993).

Figure 26: *Reading Food Labels*

Nutrition Facts

Serving Size 1/2 cup (114g)	Servings Per Container 4

Amount Per Serving

Calories 260	Calories from Fat 120

	% Daily Value*
Total Fat 13g	**20%**
Saturated Fat 5g	**25%**
Cholesterol 30mg	**10%**
Sodium 660mg	**28%**
Total Carbohydrate 31g	**11%**
Dietary Fiber 0g	**0%**
Sugars 5g	
Protein 5g	

Vitamin A 4%	Vitamin C 2%
Calcium 15%	Iron 4%

*Percent Daily Values are based on a 2,000-calorie diet.
Your daily values may be higher or lower depending on your calorie needs:

	Calories	2,000	2,500
Total Fat	Less than	65g	80g
Sat Fat	Less than	20g	25g
Cholesterol	Less than	300mg	300mg
Sodium	Less than	2,400mg	2,400mg
Total Carbohydrate		300g	375g
Fiber		25g	30g

Calories per gram:	Fat 9	Carbohydrates 4	Protein 4

Question to Consider:

Based on the information covered in this chapter, what theories addressed in Chapter 2 seem most appropriate to use? Design an activity to present to your peers.

References

Beeman, K. A., et al. (1990). The effects of student residence on food choice. *Journal of American College Health, 38,* p. 215–220.

CDC. (2008). *Physical activity for everyone.* Retrieved from http://www.cdc.gov/physicalactivity/everyone/guidelines/adults.html

Stewart, S. T. (2009). Forecasting the effects of obesity and smoking on U.S. life expectancy. *New England Journal of Medicine, 361*(23), p. 2252–2260.

Tufts University. (1993). *Tufts University Diet and Nutrition Letter, 10(12).*

US Department of Agriculture and US Department of Health and Human Services. (2005). *Dietary guidelines for American.* Retrieved from http://www.health.gov/dietaryguidelines/dga2005/document/pdf/DGA2005.pdf

Chapter 19

Cardiovascular Disease

By Luoluo Hong and Julie Catanzarite

Statistics

In 2006, 432,709 females died due to cardiovascular disease, which is the lowest number recorded since 1979. Yet, women represent 52% of those who have the disease, clearly suggesting heart disease isn't just a man's disease, which is a common belief among many Americans (American Heart Association [AHA], 2010). Every year about 1,255,000 people have a heart attack (Lloyd-Jones, Adams, and Brown 2010). Despite a decrease in the prevalence of coronary heart disease and stroke in the US, cardiovascular disease continues to kill nearly as many Americans as do all other diseases combined (CDC 2009a).

Definitions

Heart disease is a general, broad term that refers to all ailments of the heart, from heart attacks to congenital defects.

Cardiovascular disease is also a broad term that refers to disorders of the heart and circulatory system ("cardio" means heart, "vascular" means blood vessels). This includes hypertension, atherosclerosis, stroke, and rheumatic heart disease.

Coronary artery disease (CAD) refers to a condition that causes narrowing of the coronary arteries (atherosclerosis) so blood flow to the heart is reduced. This results in **coronary heart disease (CHD)**, in which damage to the heart muscle is caused by insufficient blood supply from obstructed coronary arteries. Permanent damage to or death of the heart muscle is called a **heart attack** (myocardial infarction). When there is an insufficient supply of blood to the brain, a **stroke** can result (CDC 2009b).

Major Modifiable Risk Factors for Cardiovascular Disease

Hypertension (High Blood Pressure). *Systolic pressure* (the top number) measures the pressure in the arteries when the heart is beating, while *diastolic pressure* (bottom number) measures the pressure in the arteries when the heart is resting. Blood pressure equal to or exceeding 140 mm Hg systolic and/or 90 mm Hg diastolic constitutes high blood pressure. Normal blood pressure is 120/80. Note that heavy drinking increases blood pressure. African Americans and Hispanics have a higher prevalence of hypertension. High salt and sodium intake is correlated with high blood pressure.

High Blood Cholesterol. HDL (high density lipoprotein) is "good" cholesterol; LDL (low density lipoprotein) is "bad" cholesterol. Desirable total cholesterol levels should be no more than 200 mg/dL. High cholesterol occurs at 240 mg/dL or more. Individuals should limit dietary cholesterol to 200–300 mg. or less per day.

Cigarette Smoking. Any amount of cigarette smoking increases the risk of both CHD and stroke.

Other Modifiable Risk Factors (USDA and HHS 2006; CDC 2009b)

Obesity. Obesity, or being overweight (30% or more above healthy body weight), raises blood pressure. Conversely, losing weight has the positive effect of increasing HDL levels.

Sedentary Lifestyle. Exercise helps reduce risk for heart disease by decreasing obesity and raising HDL levels. An effective exercise routine includes aerobic activity that elevates heart rate for 45–60 minutes at a time, at least four times a week.

High-Fat Diet. Diets high in fat, saturated fat, and *trans* fat (comes from hydrogenated vegetable oils), increase risk for heart disease, in large part because fat is a major source of LDL. Limit total fat intake to no more than 30% of calories consumed, although 10%–15% of calories consumed is ideal. Saturated fat should constitute no more than 7%–10% of calories consumed. Note that polyunsaturated fats (in vegetable oils such as corn, cottonseed, soybean, sunflower, and safflower oils) and monounsaturated fats (olive and canola oils) do not elevate blood cholesterol.

You can easily calculate the amount of fat grams you should be consuming daily. For example, if you're on a 2,000 calorie daily diet, no more than 600 calories, or 30% of 2,000 should come from fat. Divide 600 by 9 (each gram of fat has 9 calories), and you find that your diet should contain no more than 66–67 grams of fat per day.

Heavy Drinking. Moderate amounts of alcohol raise HDL levels and reduce the risk of high blood pressure. Moderate drinking is defined as *no more than* two alcoholic beverages (beer, wine, or liquor) per day for men and *no more than* one alcoholic beverage per day for women. Note that drinking at higher levels greatly elevates blood pressure, and increases CHD risk.

High-Sodium Diet. More than 2,300 mg. of sodium a day constitutes a high-sodium diet. Limit daily sodium intake to 1,500 mg. ideally, and increase potassium consumption.

Diet Low in Soluble Fiber. Be sure to have at least nine servings a day of vegetables and fruits, and 6 oz of breads/cereals/rice/pasta daily.

Diet High in Antioxidants. Growing evidence exists that vitamin E and other antioxidants reduce risk for heart disease. Take 400 mg. (400 IU) of vitamin E, 15 mg. (25,000 IU) of beta-carotene, and 250–500 mg. of vitamin C daily. Eat foods rich in these vitamins: vitamin C is found in grapefruit, oranges, papaya, kiwi, green peppers, cantaloupes, and broccoli; vitamin E is found in sunflower seeds, wheat germ, fortified cereals, assorted nuts, olive oil, and dried apricots; and beta carotene is found in carrots, sweet potatoes, yellow squash, spinach, and cantaloupe.

Excessive Stress. Undue physical, emotional, and/or psychological stress can increase high blood pressure. A variety of methods (behavior modification, relaxation techniques, cognitive restructuring, humor, etc.) can alleviate the negative impact of stress on your health.

Oral Contraceptive Use. Use of birth control pills has been shown to increase blood pressure in some women.

Unmodifiable Risk Factors (CDC 2009b)

Race. African Americans and Hispanics have a greater prevalence of high blood pressure.

Gender. Until age 45, men tend to have higher cholesterol levels than women. Women after menopause experience increased prevalence of high blood pressure, as well as a rise in total cholesterol levels, and a drop in HDL. Men typically experience the onset of high blood pressure between the ages of 35 and 50.

Age. Both blood pressure and LDL cholesterol levels increase with age.

Family History. If members of your family have experienced hypertension, heart attacks, strokes, etc., your own risk for heart disease increases.

Diabetes. Having diabetes increases triglyceride levels and decreases HDL.

Sources: Centers for Disease Control and Prevention, 2009b

Questions to Consider

Why do many college students not consider cardiovascular health a risk? What can peer educators do to debunk this myth?

References

AHA. (2010). *Women and cardiovascular disease: Statistics 2010.* Retrieved from http://www.americanheart.org/downloadable/heart/1260905040318FS10WM10.pdf

CDC. (2009). *FASTSTATS: Leading cause of death.* Retrieved from http://www.cdc.gov/nchs/fastats/lcod.htm

CDC. (2009). *Heart Diseases: Coronary Artery Disease.* Retrieved from http://www.cdc.gov/heartdisease/coronary_ad.htm

Lloyd-Jones, D., Adams, R. J., & Brown, T. M. (2010). Heart Disease and Stroke Statistics—2010 Update. A report from the American Heart Association Statistics Committee and Stroke Statistics Subcommittee. *Circulation.* Retrieved from http://circ.ahajournals.org/cgi/reprint/CIRCULATIONAHA.108.191261v1

US Department of Agriculture and US Department of Health and Human Services. (2005). *Dietary guidelines for American.* Retrieved from http://www.health.gov/dietaryguidelines/dga2005/document/pdf/DGA2005.pdf

Chapter 20

Increasing Campus Diversity Power

By Luoluo Hong and Jason Robertson

Important Definitions in Diversity Education

Prejudice is a set of beliefs, involving stereotypes and strong, often negative emotions about a group of people, which predisposes one to act in a certain manner toward that group (Hraba 1994). Any person can be prejudiced, and all people are; similarly, any group can be prejudiced against another group. Just because a group is typically the target of prejudice doesn't necessarily stop members of the group from being prejudiced against some other group.

Discrimination is an overt action directed toward an individual or group of individuals because of their perceived group membership, which has the effect of limiting the target group's access to opportunities in the larger society (Hraba 1994).

Stereotypes are preconceived or oversimplified generalizations about an entire group of people without regard for their individual differences. While often negative, stereotypes may also be complimentary, yet even positive stereotypes can have a negative impact and can feed into prejudice (Hetherington 1995).

Oppression involves the combination of prejudice and power. If Group A believes themselves superior to Group B (prejudice) and Group A has access to political, social, and/or economic power, Group A can systematically subjugate Group B (Hetherington 1995). Sexism, racism, and heterosexism are all forms of oppression.

Sexism is prejudice or discrimination based on the belief that gender is the primary factor determining human traits and abilities. Sexism holds that genetic or inherited differences make one gender inherently superior or inferior to another (Hetherington 1995).

Racism involves both prejudice against people of color and the political, social, and economic power to reinforce that prejudice. Racism always exists at individual, cultural, structural, and institutional levels, and it can be both conscious and unconscious, both subtle and overt (Reynolds and Pope 1994). Only those individuals or groups who are prejudiced against a racial group *and have and use the power to act on those prejudices* can be accurately labeled as racists.

Homophobia is the fear of gay, lesbian, and bisexual individuals. This fear, based on negative stereotypes and prejudices, results in denial of civil and legal protection, overt acts of violence, and exclusion of non-heterosexuals from the community (Hetherington 1995).

Heterosexism refers to the assumption of heterosexuals that everyone is heterosexual or ought to be (Hetherington 1995).

Cultural racism refers to forms of discrimination against a targeted group that are inherent in societal mores, community norms, educational practices, implicit or explicit messages in mass media, etc.

Institutional racism refers to forms of discrimination against a targeted group that are embedded in the socioeconomic policies and laws of a community.

Ethnocentrism is the tendency of members of a racial or ethnic group to consider their own physical appearance and way of life as superior and most desirable, while their respect for the styles of other groups is a function of how closely those styles approximate their own (Hraba 1994).

Power is defined as the ability to define reality and have other people believe it is their reality, as well.

A multicultural organizational environment is a community in which significant time, attention, and resources, both human and monetary, are dedicated to creating openness to all cultures and peoples and to eradicating social injustice (Reynolds and Pope 1994).

Culture is the body of learned beliefs, traditions, principles, and guides for behavior that are commonly shared among members of a particular group. Culture serves as a road map for both perceiving and interacting with the world (Locke 1992).

Defining "Diversity Power"

Diversity power refers to the extent to which an organization maximizes demographic variability and variety of thought and uses these elements to enhance organizational effectiveness.

Demographic diversity means including individuals from a wide array of backgrounds: sex, race, ethnicity, religion, age, socioeconomic status, sexual orientation, physical/emotional ability, political affiliation, geographic region, etc. into the decision-making core of an organization.

Diversity of thought means including individuals who have a variety of perspectives, life experiences, philosophical frameworks, disciplinary strengths, and value systems into the decision-making core of an organization. Note that increasing demographic diversity is correlated with greater diversity of thought.

Organizational Culture

Organizational culture is a pattern of basic assumptions—invented, discovered, or developed by a given group as it learns to cope with its problems of external adaptation and integration—that has worked well enough to be considered valid and, therefore has to be taught to new members as the "correct" way to perceive, think, and feel in relation to their problems (Schein 1985, 9).

Every organization develops distinctive patterns and assumptions over time. Many of these patterns and assumptions are unconscious, or taken for granted, and are reflected in myths, fairy tales, stories, rituals, ceremonies, and other symbolic forms. Managers and leaders who understand the power of these symbols have increased success in influencing their organization (Bolman and Deal 1991). When speaking of group distinctions, Bolman and Deal state:

> A family, group, organization or society with cohesion and a sense of itself rarely offers free admission to outsiders. The price is usually higher for people who are somehow different or who question or threaten existing values, norms, and patterns. Representatives of groups that have been excluded because of their gender, race, ethnicity, or religion cannot become full-fledged members of a group or organization unless they are initiated into the inner sanctum. [...] Yet, only a weak culture will accept newcomers with no initiation. The stronger a culture, the stronger the message to newcomers that, "you are different and not yet one of us." The initiation reinforces the existing culture at the same time that it tests the newcomer's ability to become a member (1991, 248).

Diversity power is a strategy to ensure that your organization's culture doesn't shut out opportunities for new members or for new ideas.

Why Strive for Diversity Power? (Border and Chism 1992)

1. **The Moral Argument.** There is a need to redress grievances of underrepresented social and cultural groups who have been unjustifiably denied access to higher education in the US.
2. **The Demographic Argument.** As the traditional pool of white applicants for higher education decreases and the pool of students of color increases (US population is estimated to be 24% Hispanic, 15% African American, and 12% Asian American by 2080), it is in the long-term, pragmatic self-interest of institutions of higher education to adjust the balance within their student populations.
3. **The Civic Argument.** The country's need for a skilled work force requires access to higher education for all citizens.
4. **The Enrichment Argument.** The intellectual enterprise is enhanced by the dialogue of multiple viewpoints and perspectives.
5. **The Political Argument.** Inaction in the face of increasing campus conflict and violence is untenable. Access for student from underrepresented groups must be increased and appropriate support furnished.

Advantages of Diversity Power

1. *Increases the organization's problem-solving capacity.*

Diversity helps an organization avoid the pitfall of single-scope vision. Individuals from a wide array of backgrounds or cultures offer different ways of understanding the challenges facing the organization, as well as provide a wide range of possible solutions. Differing perspectives help to reframe the question as well as the answers.

2. *Increases the organization's ability to adapt.*

One of the keys to organizational survival is the ability to change in response to new environments and contexts while minimizing the impact of change-related stress on its members. Diversity in the organization allows open-mindedness and flexibility to supersede singular thought and rigidity. Diversity prevents an organization from maintaining status quo.

3. *Ensures the organization's longevity.*

As society becomes increasingly multicultural, organizations must attempt to accommodate new demands and new interests. Diversity in an organization provides a wealth of resources for planning, programming, and self-evaluation processes that embrace diversity of experience, as well as assist with recruitment and retention of diverse individuals.

4. *Teaches important life skills.*

Organizational diversity provides a safe learning environment for members to interact respectfully and effectively with individuals who are different from themselves. Incorporating the various perspectives and strengths that each person brings to a group requires excellent communication abilities, mutual trust, and open-mindedness on the part of both leaders and followers. These are characteristics that are crucial to professional and personal success in today's increasingly international marketplace.

Consider this: If we shrank the world's population to a village of 100 people, it would look approximately like this:

- There would be 57 Asians, 21 Europeans, 8 Africans, and 14 would be from the Western Hemisphere (North and South America).
- 51 would be female, 49 male.
- 70 would be non-white and 30 would be white.
- 30 would be Christians, 18 Muslims, 13 Hindus, 6 Buddhists, 5 Animists, 1 Jewish and 27 would be other, (Atheist or no religion).
- 50% of the village's wealth would be in the hands of only 6 people, and all 6 people would be Unites States citizens.
- 70 would be unable to read.
- 50 would suffer from malnutrition.
- 80 would live in substandard housing.
- One would be near death, one would be near birth.
- Only one would have a college education.
- No one would own a computer.

When seeing the world from such an incredibly compressed perspective, the value of both tolerance and understanding becomes glaringly apparent (School for International Training Newsletter).

Strategies for Achieving Diversity Power

1. *Organizational Assessment.*
Determine organization's current status with regard to diversity. Examine leadership in the upper echelons of the organization with regard to commitment to diversity. Establish goals and timelines for achievement of those goals.

Examples of questions to ask include:
    a. What patterns and assumptions (myths, fairy tales, stories, rituals, ceremonies, etc.) are present in my organization?
    b. What is the process by which newcomers are initiated or accepted into this organization? Is the process similar or different for all newcomers? How so?
    c. As a newcomer to your organization, how did you learn about "the way things are done around here?"

2. *Organizational Mission Statement.*
Include explicit language that demonstrates that the organization seeks and values diversity. Include clear prohibitions against sexual and/or racial harassment. Clearly state that the organization does not tolerate discriminatory behavior by its members. Cite consequences for members who display prejudicial behavior. Describe appropriate grievance procedures in detail. Enumerate specific goals relative to achieving and maintaining diversity.

3. *Recruitment.*
Advertise though multiple venues and various media that target mainstream as well as alternative audiences and populations groups. Publicize without relying solely on "word of mouth." Include outreach to groups who are not currently represented in the organization. Have candidates provide a statement about their views regarding diversity as a condition of membership.

4. *Retention.*

Have an organization that includes a diversity of individuals into the decision-making core of the organization, whether through formal structures, informal structures, or both. Establish processes for decision-making that are sensitive to differing communication and language styles. Establish procedures and policies for promotion, pay raises, and other rewards that are fair and consistent. Sponsor social activities that are inclusive of a broad range of cultural interests and wants.

5. *Ad Hoc Committee or Task Force.*

Ensure that diversity is encouraged and valued. Assist with implementing suggestions for multicultural programming and diversity training. Review organizational leadership and membership for uncompromising adherence to the mission and goals for diversity. Hold the organization accountable with regard to diversity-related goals and activities.

6. *Community Action.*

Involve the organization's members in service activities that support and/or promote social and political diversity. Advocate on behalf of others who experience prejudice or discrimination. Capitalize on appropriate opportunities to take a public stand in support of diversity.

Suggestions for Further Reading

Adams, M. (1992). Promoting diversity in college classrooms: Innovative responses for the curriculum, faculty, and institutions. *New Directions for Teaching and Learning, No. 52. San Francisco: Jossey-Bass Inc.*

Brown, C.R. & Mazza, G. (1991). Peer training strategies for welcoming diversity. Washington, DC: National Coalition Building Institute.

Dalton, J. C. (1991). Racism on campus: Confronting racial bias through peer interventions. New Directions for Student Services, No. 56. San Francisco: Jossey Bass Inc.

Questions to Consider

1. What is the demographic make-up of the campus?
2. What steps, as peer educators, can you take to make your campus an open and welcoming environment for all students?

References

Bolman, L. G., & Deal, T. E. (1991). *Reframing organizations: Artistry, choice, and leadership.* San Francisco: Jossey-Bass Publishers.

Border, L. L. B., & Chism, N. V. N. (Eds.). (1992). *Teaching for Diversity.* San Francisco: Jossey-Bass Publishers.

Hetherington, C. (1995). *Working with groups in the workplace: Celebrating diversity.* Duluth, MN: Whole Person Associates.

Hraba, J. (1994). *American ethnicity.* Itasca, IL: F.E. Peacock Publishers, Inc.

Locke, D. C. (1992). *Increasing multicultural understanding: A comprehensive model.* Newbury Park, CA: Sage Publications.

Reynolds, A. L., & Pope, R. L. (1994). Perspectives on creating multicultural campuses. *Journal of American College Health,* 42, p. 229–233.

Schein, E. H. (1985). *Organizational culture and leadership: A dynamic view.* San Francisco: Jossey-Bass.

Chapter 21

Combating Homophobia and Transphobia

By Luoluo Hong, Jason Robertson, and Parker Hurley

Introduction

Everything we learn about relationships, romance, and yes, sex, we learn from a predominantly heterosexual society. From the very beginning, we are instilled with the heterosexual ideas that will shape the course of our lives. These are the ideals that are broadcast through every segment of society—families, schools, places of worship, and the media. Composing as much as 10% of our population, members of the gay, lesbian, and bisexual community have been isolated from these heterosexual norms and ideals. To them, the predominant heterosexist culture is meaningless, devoid of positive guidance and role models for love and sexuality enjoyed by the mainstream, heterosexual community.

Contrary to some beliefs, being gay is not a disease or the sign of a dysfunctional individual. Evidence suggests that sexual orientation is determined at an early age and that being gay is not a matter of choice—rather, it is biologically determined. Many misconceptions about gays and lesbians are the result of people confusing gender identity with sexual orientation. In other words, people mistakenly believe that gay men are somehow "feminine" and that lesbians are "masculine," when in reality, the range of masculine and feminine expression among gays and lesbians is just as varied as it is among heterosexuals. For example, one common myth is that men become gay because their mothers dressed them up as little girls, or that they had domineering mothers. Yet, many gay men play football, watch sports, lift weights, and participate in other stereotypically "masculine" activities.

There are many stereotypes about gay men and women that perpetuate ill-will toward the gay, lesbian, and bisexual communities. Images of effeminate males speaking with a lisp or the husky female who is sexually frustrated, the misconception that gay lovers enact "male" and "female" roles, the idea that gays and bisexuals seduce young children to convert them to "their ways," and the belief that AIDS is a form of God's judgment on homosexuals, are all examples of the discrimination and hatred aimed at the gay, lesbian, and bisexual communities. Such fallacies are bred from homophobia and a lack of understanding on the part of the heterosexual society. As a result, many gay people are driven to conceal their identities in a shroud of "normalcy," marrying members of the opposite sex, keeping friends and family members in the dark about their sexuality, and even seeking counseling in an effort to be "cured."

When we can break down the stereotypes and misconceptions about being gay, we will find that gays, lesbians, and bisexuals are not very different from heterosexuals. They have the same emotions, desires, goals, vices, and strengths. Gay men and women have been, and continue to be, productive members of society working toward a common goal of human kind.

Gay, Lesbian, and Bisexual Relationships

Research has found very little difference between gay and heterosexual relationships. Most resemble "best friendships" combined with romantic and erotic attraction. Gays, lesbians, and bisexuals exhibit the full spectrum of love and sexuality as do heterosexuals—some prefer intimacy, some seek sexual gratification; some are monogamous, some have multiple partners; some kiss on the first date, others do not. While gay couples cannot be married under the auspices of the law in most states, many gays celebrate unions complete with a full ceremony, the exchanging of vows, and lifetime commitment to their partners. These unions, though recognized by many religious affiliations and gaining acceptance in society, still lack the legal rights and privileges of heterosexual relationships such as holding joint insurance policies, being granted next-of-kin rights, sharing employment benefits such as medical and dental policies, the ability to maintain joint financial accounts, adopting children, and many others that heterosexuals take for granted.

Gay, Lesbian, and Bisexual Health Concerns

Gays, lesbians, and bisexuals experience the same health concerns as the rest of the society—cancer, couples violence, eating disorders, etc. But existing in a heterosexist society that is at best indifferent to gay lifestyles and at worst, hateful and prejudiced, can have adverse effects on their self-esteem and physical health. Internalized homophobia refers to a situation in which gay, lesbian, or bisexual individuals dislike or even hate themselves—in essence, they internalize the negative messages propagated by the media and society in general. Internalized homophobia may keep some gay, lesbian, and bisexual individuals "in the closet," for fear of being judged, ostracized, or discriminated against.

Because our society does not value gay men and women, gay men and women who are victims of physical and emotional abuse frequently don't receive the same amount of caring and support. In addition to bouts with depression, there is a high prevalence of substance abuse and drug dependence as well as suicide in the gay community; the stress of coping with a homophobic society can take its toll. Anyone experiencing these or similar problems should seek support through professional counseling and gay and lesbian organizations in the community.

Gays, lesbians, and bisexuals who are sexually active are also at risk for contracting sexually transmitted infections and HIV. While AIDS is not a "gay disease," gay men do account for a significant portion of those presently infected in the US, and the incidence of HIV infection is rising in adolescent and young gay men. Gays, lesbians, and bisexuals who are sexually active should practice safer sex, including the use of condoms with spermicide during anal intercourse, and condoms or dental dams during oral sex.

Coming Out

For gays and lesbians, "coming out of the closet," or revealing the truth about their sexual orientation, is a life-long process. Beginning from the time they first discover their homosexuality, gays and lesbians must make a decision to come out each and every time someone assumes that they are heterosexual. In a society that casts a negative shadow on being gay, this decision can be very difficult. Before deciding to come out to your friends, family, and others, you must first consider your own situation and needs. Here are some suggestions that might help you approach this task.

Coming Out to Yourself

Gays and lesbians report going through four general stages after the discovery that they are gay. A common first reaction is **denial**—gay persons, socialized in a predominately heterosexist society, will fight to repress any feelings or notions of their gayness. This often will create internal conflict and confusion as they resist the natural processes that they are experiencing. Eventually, they will come to **acknowledge** their gayness and begin to sort out the situation in their mind. It is then that they are likely to enter a stage of **exploration** in which they may seek sexual as well as nonsexual encounters with other gays and lesbians and begin to experiment with different looks, attitudes, and lifestyles in an effort to learn more about themselves. The final stage, acceptance is reached when these individuals become more comfortable with their gayness, achieving great ease of mind about who they are.

The road between discovery and acceptance is likely to be a bumpy one. Most gays and lesbians agree that coming out to themselves is the hardest part of the process, and they commonly experience bouts of depression and guilt associated with the denial mentioned above. On the upside, coming out and accepting your gayness can be very therapeutic and a tremendous relief from the agony of maintaining your secret. Once you have learned to accept your gayness and overcome your own reservations about being gay, you can be fairly certain that you have the confidence and strength necessary to face the road ahead of you. There are a couple of suggestions that you might find helpful when working things out internally:

- **Seek Support.** There are likely to be issues that you are having difficulty resolving, and counseling by a trained professional could prove to be very beneficial for you. Gay and lesbian groups on campus and in the community can also be an excellent source for additional information and support.
- **Be clear about your own feelings before coming out to others.** People will be able to sense any uncertainty that you may feel, and this might fuel any negative reactions that they might have.

Coming out to Friends and Family

Once you have come to terms with your sexuality, you may want to share your news with at least a selected few of the people who are close to you. Friends and family members, once they have accepted the fact that you are gay, can prove to be an excellent source of support. Before talking with them, consider the following suggestions that could help reduce friction in the process.

- **Choose an appropriate time and place.** Be aware of the listener's health, mood, and attitudes, as well as any other barriers that can affect the person's willingness and ability to accept your revelation. Never come out during an argument or at a time when tension in the relationship is high. When given proper consideration, timing can be an important ally to your efforts.
- **Reaffirm the relationship.** Emphasize that you are still the same person you have always been. If possible, try to affirm a mutual love and respect before you break the news.
- **Be prepared for their reaction.** While most friends and family members will be tolerant, some might take the news poorly. Parents may blame themselves for your "condition" and friends may feel betrayed and angry. Allow them time to absorb the news and get over the initial shock.
- **Remain open to questions.** You have dropped a major revelation on them and it is likely that they will want to know more. Be prepared to answer any reasonable questions and refer them to a local group for friends and families of gays and lesbians.
- **Recognize true friendship.** A true friend is one who accepts who you really are—not just who s/he thinks you are. Anyone who rejects your willingness to share a personal part of your life with them is not a friend worth having—cut your losses and move on. Never lose sight of your own self-worth.

Coming Out to Others

There may come times at which you deem it necessary or desirable to reveal your sexuality to those in your life—classmates, co-workers, distant relatives, neighbors, etc. The decision to do so is one that should be evaluated carefully in light of your personal situation and needs. Should you decide to do so, there are a couple of things that should be considered prior to revealing your sexuality to them:

- **Exercise caution.** Evaluate your reasons for coming out to people, and be aware of the level of homophobia and discrimination in your community.
- **You are under no obligation to do so.** Each individual has the right to decide to whom and to what extent s/he will reveal personal information. Your sexuality is nobody's business but your own and your partner's. Do not let external pressure from political groups or other interested people unduly influence your decision to come out.

When Someone You Know is Gay

Everyone knows someone who is gay—your best friend or a fellow classmate, a close family member or a distant relative, a co-worker, or one of the many acquaintances you come in contact with on a daily basis. It is highly probable that someone will come out to you at some point in time, and your willingness and ability to accept the news will have a profound effect on your relationship, whether it will be strengthened or destroyed.

If a friend comes out to you, there are several things you can do to ensure a smooth transition into the next chapter of your relationship:

- *Understand the full significance of your friend's decision to come out to you.* Society has not made it easy for gays to be open about their lives, and by coming out to you, your friend is bestowing a deep trust in your relationship.
- *Ask yourself how you honestly feel about the news and discuss your feelings openly as a caring friend.* Ask questions if you are confused about the news or need some clarification, but be considerate of his or her right to privacy and respect. Allow yourself time to absorb all of the information before you react hastily.
- *Be supportive and understanding.* Your friend will no doubt face some challenging times and has turned to you for support.
- *Don't buy into the negative stereotypes and myths about gay people that are bred from homophobia and prejudice.* Keep an open mind and try to see things from your friend's point of viewpoint—you owe it to your friend, you owe it to yourself.
- *Respect their confidentiality.* It is not your job to turn around and share their news with others. Ask who else knows, whom you may discuss it with, etc.

Remember, your friend is coming out to you, not *on* to you. New information that a friend is gay should have little effect on your relationship with the person. He or she is still the same friend you knew yesterday. There is, however, room for that friendship to grow, thanks to an energized level of mutual trust, understanding, and respect.

You will probably undergo various stages after someone comes out to you. The first reaction will be **denial.** With time, you will **acknowledge** that your friend is gay. Finally, **acceptance** sets in.

Oftentimes, gays will come out while they are in a heterosexual relationship. As a partner in such a situation, it will be particularly difficult for you to understand. Do not try to blame yourself; nothing you did "made" them gay, just as nothing "makes" someone heterosexual. Parents should be similarly advised; rather than blaming themselves, parents should instead seek to understand and support their child.

When trying to relate to a gay individual, try to consider the emotions you feel as you consider the questions listed in Figure 27. Often these are the types of feelings and questions gay individuals must deal with and experience in a society dominated by heterosexuals.

Figure 27: *How Do You Know You're Heterosexual?*

1. What do you think caused your heterosexuality?
2. When and how did you decide that you were heterosexual?
3. Is it possible that your heterosexuality is just a phase you might grow out of?
4. Is it possible your heterosexuality stems from a neurotic fear of others of the same sex?
5. If you've never slept with a person of the same sex and enjoyed it, is it possible that all you need is a good gay lover?
6. To whom have you disclosed your heterosexual tendencies? How did they react?
7. Why do you heterosexuals feel compelled to seduce others into your lifestyle?
8. Why do you insist on flaunting your heterosexuality? Can't you just be who you are and keep it quiet?
9. Would you want your children to be heterosexual, knowing the problems they'd face?
10. A disproportionate majority of child molesters are heterosexual. Do you feel it is safe to expose your child to heterosexual teachers?
11. Even with all the societal support marriage receives, the divorce rate is spiraling. Why are there so few stable relationships among heterosexuals?
12. Why do heterosexuals place so much emphasis on sex?
13. Considering the menace of overpopulation, how could the human race survive if everyone were heterosexual like you?
14. Could you trust a heterosexual therapist to be objective? Don't you feel s/he might be inclined to influence you in the direction of his or her learning?
15. How could you become a whole person if you limit yourself to compulsive, exclusive heterosexuality? Shouldn't you at least try to develop your natural healthy potential?
16. There seem to be very few happy heterosexuals. Techniques have been developed to help you change if you really want to. Have you tried aversion therapy?

Source: *Dimensions*, the newsletter of DIGNITY, San Diego, CA.

Transgender

Within our development we are confronted with the assignment of gender roles. Gender roles are the social and cultural expectations associated with a person's sex. These gender roles affect virtually every aspect of our lives, from our eating behavior and the type of neighbor we are likely to be, to how long we are going to live and the cause of our death (Thompson and Hickey 1999). In dominant Western cultures the gender expression is assumed at birth: pink for girls and blue for boys. Girls are expected to grow up and be feminine, boys masculine (Feinberg 1996). Anticipatory socialization does not include the little "boy" who wears a dress, or the little "girl" who wears her father's tie when playing dress-up. These children are often labeled as sissies and tomboys, and when some of these people grow up into members of transgender communities, their stories are more often than not omitted from the pages of our textbooks. Their bodies continue to be pathologized and criminalized, and their lives are illegitimated through the erasures of their contributions. More obvert discrimination such as bullying, violence, and murder of transgender individuals is sanctioned through unjust laws, policies, and political and religious beliefs.

The pervasive pink-for-girls-and-blue-for-boys science filters into our language, how we relate to each other and to ourselves as well as our daily practices. Stigmas that exist in society concerning transgender issues can be partly attributed to the sheer lack of words in the English language; a language that is not fully inclusive and cannot begin to summarize the myriad of ways that people express their genders and bodies. Even the English word "transgender" is fairly new and being continually expanded and redefined.

What does transgender mean?

Considering that transgender, gender non-conforming people, and individuals who transcended the parameters of gender have been present in many cultures since the beginning of recorded history, the term "transgender" is

relatively new. The word transgender emerged out of "trans" communities to combat more medicalized and therefore, pathologized identities such as "transsexuals," or "transvestites." Although homosexuality was stricken from the pages of the Diagnostic Statistic Manual (DSM) in 1973, gender non-conforming people and those often seeking gender-affirming treatment such as surgery and/or hormone therapy, are still often forced to take on a mental health diagnosis of Gender Identity Disorder (GID).

"Since about 1995, the meaning of transgender has begun to settle, and the term is now generally used to refer to individuals whose gender identity or expression does not conform to the social expectations for the assigned sex at birth," (Currah, Juang, and Price-Minter 2006, xiv). At the crux of defining what it means to be transgender is the necessity to explicate the difference between sex and gender. Table 1 includes a few key terms.

Table 1: *Terms Necessary to Understanding Transgender Concerns*

Sex	refers to an individual's anatomical, physiological, and biological make-up (words for sex can be male, female, intersex, etc.)
Gender	"the social construction of masculinity and femininity in a specific culture. It involves gender assignment (the gender designation of someone at birth), gender roles (the expectations imposed on someone based on their gender), gender attribution (how others perceive someone's gender), gender expression (how someone presents their gender), and gender identity (how someone defines their gender)."
Gender identity	"an individual's internal sense of being male, female, or something else. Since gender identity is internal, one's gender identity is not necessarily visible to others".
Sexual Orientation	"an individual's emotional, romantic, sexual, or affectional attraction." Examples of sexual orientations are gay, straight, bisexual, asexual, etc. Transgender individuals can be gay, straight, bisexual, lesbian, queer, or asexual. Like many of us, these identifications can be fluid and change over the course of one's life. Adapted from: Beemyn, B. G. (n.d.) Transgender terminology.

While a host of gender-affirming options is available, it is important to note that a transgender identity is not necessarily a precursor to pursuit of gender-affirming medical procedures, such as surgeries and/or hormone therapy. Many individuals cannot afford costly surgeries and often are victims of discrimination within the healthcare system. Some individuals choose not to undergo a medical transition and may change their name, style of clothing, or nothing at all to match societal expectations of their preferred gender.

Transgender communities are not one homogenous entity but are composed of a kaleidoscope of classes, races, abilities, nationalities, and ages. The intersectionality of these identities can be points of unity as well as causation of further discrimination and marginalization. Some transgender people live as "out" trans men, women, gender-queers, etc., while others do not. Transgender people are parents, neighbors, athletes, professionals, children, etc., and in the fight to remain a buoyant representation of the human reality, it is safe to surmise that for every person who identifies as transgender, there are just as many narratives and identification(s) to be recognized.

Transphobia

What do we do with the people who don't fit into their ascribed gender role? When applying Charles Horton Cooley's looking-glass self-theory to gender roles in this society, in particular in reference to the transgender community, the disproportionately high number of suicides and hate crimes committed against this section of the population can be perceived as ramifications of a larger transphobic society. Transphobia is "the fear, hatred, or intolerance of people who identify or are perceived as transgender." (Beemyn n.d.)

When asked about the umbrella term "transgender," most people are confronted with thoughts of sexual fetishes and social deviance, pedophilia, and side show exhibits. Even within the most obtuse analysis of how attitudes are developed, none of them are completely objective and do inevitably entail some sort of prejudice. One can surmise that the information made available to us about the lives and contributions of trans and gender non-conforming individuals has a profound effect on language and attitudes. A more subtle form of transphobia is the omission of transgender narratives within elementary and secondary school history curricula. The narratives encompassing trans histories, lives, and deaths are often found distorted in mainstream media. Trans people are often depicted as the sociopathic serial killers in science fiction movies or as the main attraction on daytime talk shows, featuring the audiences vying for an opportunity to guess, "Is 'it' a man or a woman?" never once mentioning the contributions made to society by trans people since the beginning of recorded history. Feinberg (1996, 22) states:

> In the tradition of the Native American people who assumed "roles of the opposite sex" from which they were born-called "berdaches"- not only existed but such individuals were held in high esteem by Native nations. It was only in the colonization of the Americas that such people were denounced. In fact, "berdache" was a derogatory term European colonizers used to label any Native person who did not fit into their narrow notions of woman and man. [...] Native nations had many respectful words in their own language to describe such people. However, cultural genocide has destroyed and altered the Native language and traditions. Native people have since restored the use of the term "Two-Spirit" in replace of the offensive colonial word.

Transgender studies promises to make critical radical interventions by excavating the truths and the stories of trans people throughout history otherwise masked or buried in post-colonial texts. The need to enforce binary language and thinking with the aspirations of producing binary people has permeated our society and consciousness and has manifested into bewildering rates of hate-motivated violence against trans folks (at least one transgender person per month is murdered in the United States) (Currah et al. 2006), disproportional disparities in health care and education, job discrimination, and unjust incarcerations. According to Currah et al.:

Many members of the transgender community struggle to access stable employment, housing, and health care, the essential triad that directly affects one's ability to maintain health and well-being. Most transgender people have experienced societal stigma, ridicule, and family rejection from the time they were small children, making it difficult to access basic educational opportunities. In addition, many have left home to flee family violence and harassment, only to encounter employers who refuse to hire them, throwing them into dire economic straits. All races and socioeconomic statuses are affected, though health risks increase considerably when compounded by other layers of marginalization (2006, 192).

These unmet needs in conjunction with low self-esteem and lack of support oftentimes result in higher rates of substance and alcohol abuse, "risky" sexual behavior, and elevated negative mental health concerns. These realities are both produced and exacerbated by the continuation of Gender Identity Disorder being listed as a mental illness diagnosis outlined in the DSM-IV. The use of reductionary language and praxis such as the diagnosis of GID continues to pathologize transgender individuals and conceptualize their identities and their bodies within the same framework, that simply reproduces in another mode the transphobia and heterosexism it was arguably designed to challenge. The language affiliated with GID including "pre-op" and "post-op" helps to replicate discourse that seeks to make clear distinctions between more authentic identities and those that are not authentic at all. Who gets to be a real man? Who gets to be a real woman? Does one get to be a successful "man" or "woman" after a certain amount of years in therapy or after a certain surgery? Problematic language and systemic inequalities in policies and practices work to maintain the power of the keepers of the status quo to defer trans people and trans-allies from uniting and achieving true gender equity.

For more information about gay, lesbian, bisexual, and transgender issues, contact the **National Gay and Lesbian Task Force**, 1734 14th St. NW, Washington, DC 20009.

Questions to Consider

1. How do homophobia and transphobia affect the college environment?
2. As a peer educator, why is understanding homophobia and transphobia important to your work?
3. What are ways you, as a peer educator, can address homophobia and transphobia on the campus?

References

Thompson, W. E. & Joseph Hickey. (1999). *Society in focus: Introduction to sociology.* New York: Addison-Wesley.

Currah, P., Juang, R. M., & Price Minter, S. (Eds). (2006). *Transgender rights. Minneapolis,* MN: University of Minnesota Press.

Feinberg, L. (1996). *Transgender warrior: Making a history from Joan of Arc to Dennis Rodman.* Boston: Beacon Press.

Beemyn, B. G. (n.d.) Transgender terminology. Retrieved from http://www.umass.edu/stonewall/uploads/listWidget/8758/trans%20terms.pdf

Chapter 22

Combating Racism

By Luoluo Hong

One of the dilemmas in promoting multicultural understanding is the failure of many individuals to identify and acknowledge their assumptions. Each person grows up receiving messages about various cultural groups; from these messages, that person develops a "record" of how s/he believes members of that group behave and believe. Unless the individual interacts extensively with many members from a particular group, his or her ideas about that group will tend to be inaccurate and stereotypical—often negative. However, if a person makes a concerted effort to learn about the experiences, challenges, and hopes of another cultural group from its perspective (rather than filtered through one's own biases), s/he develops an appreciation not only for the characteristics that are different, but also an awareness of those values, emotions, and goals that are similar between cultural groups.

Acknowledging and appreciating other cultures does not mean that an individual has to disavow or disparage his or her own culture. Often, people who are most afraid of reaching out to those who are different from themselves are insecure about who they are and their cultural heritage. Difference does not have to be better or worse. Rather, difference can enhance one's life experiences and world view. In addition, an awareness of and competence in cultural diversity enhances one's ability to communicate with a broad array of individuals in any number of settings—academic, social, professional, spiritual, etc. Race and culture mediate communication by impacting on all three aspects of communication: (1) the sender; (2) the receiver; and (3) the message. The sender's own culture determines how s/he will convey information; the receiver's background will determine how s/he will hear or interpret the information; and the message varies in meaning both for the sender and the receiver depending on the respective culture perspectives.

Certain aspects of Western philosophy tend to hinder the development of multicultural understanding. Epistemology refers to the branch of philosophy that studies the nature of knowledge and the process by which knowledge is acquired and validated. Modern Western societies in general, and institutions of higher learning specifically (until recently) have been dominated by an epistemological doctrine of positivism. In positivism, physical and social environments exist independently of the individuals who created them or who observe or study them. Observations of this reality, if unbiased, constitute objective, scientific knowledge. The quintessential example of positivism is the scientific method, predicated on controlled collection of data—preferably quantitative—to "prove" existence of or explain the mechanism of natural phenomena.

However, the assumption of an objective reality and the reliance on quantitative data become problematic when discussing issues of race or gender. Given a particular action, one individual may perceive prejudice or discrimination, while another may not. Disagreements across race and gender escalate because each "side" believes there can only be one truth, one objective reality. The "proof" typically is expected to take the form of quantitative, "hard" data—oftentimes inadequate for capturing a variable as intangible and complex as prejudice. Mistrust, suspicion, and resentment build up as each side argues its own case and tries to discount or dismiss the other's. In fact, both perceptions may be true—informed by differing experiences and backgrounds.

An opposing epistemological position, one that is more conducive and consistent with cultural competence, is known as postpositivism. Positivism is based on the assumption that social reality is constructed by the individuals who participate in it; these constructions take the form of interpretations, that is, the ascription of meaning to the social environment. Features of the social environment are not considered to have an existence apart from the meanings that individuals construct for them. Furthermore, social reality is constructed differently by different individuals. An extension of postpositivism is that individuals construct themselves—we do not have an objectively real self. Each of us constructs a self, sometimes multiple selves, for example, a created self that is totally private to us, and a social self that is created through our style of dress, mannerisms, and other devices displayed to others. This social self also forms multiple selves, because we dress and act differently for different groups and on different occasions.

Postpositivism, therefore, would acknowledge that one action could indeed be interpreted in varying ways. In addition, qualitative data—the "science" of intuition and meaning—are valued as much as quantitative in the postpositivist tradition as reliable and credible sources of information. A major goal in multicultural education is to assist individuals in developing skills—first for understanding, then respecting, and finally incorporating multiple perspectives without anger, fear, or resentment or loss of self-esteem.

Components of White Culture

Because Caucasians of Western European heritage have compsed the majority of individuals in the US, it is important to examine the values and beliefs associated with this culture, as well as to understand how groups outside the dominant white culture respond to those values, how the values and beliefs of other groups are frequently compared to (and usually judged inferior or deficient) those values, and to recognize that all groups do not necessarily hold similar values. Many of these values are positive, enriching ones that have contributed to the success of the US democracy. These values have only been damaging insomuch that they are adopted or deemed superior to the exclusion of others. Note that many of these values are more typical of a male-dominated and heterosexist society, as well. In addition, these values are not exclusive to white culture; other cultures share some of the same beliefs and values listed below (Hetherington 1995).

- **Rugged Individualism:** I, as an individual, am a primary unit. I, as an individual, have primary responsibility. I should be independent and autonomous. I, as an individual, can control the environment.
- **Competition:** I should win at everything I do. I either win or lose.
- **Action Orientation:** I must master and control nature. I must always do something about a situation. I should have a pragmatic and utilitarian view of life.
- **Decision Making:** I, as a White American, have power. I am at the top of the hierarchy. I am the peak of the pyramid structure.
- **Communication:** I speak standard English. I am the leader in the written tradition. I use direct eye contact. I maintain limited physical contact with others. I control my emotions.
- **Time:** I adhere to rigid time schedules. I think time is a commodity.
- **Holidays:** My holidays are based on Christianity. I count on holidays based on the birthdays of white male leaders.
- **History:** My history is based on European immigrants' experience in the US. My older relatives romanticize war.
- **Protestant Work Ethic:** I think it is bad not to work hard. I play only when my work is completed.
- **Progress and Future Orientation:** I plan for the future. I believe that delayed gratification is a positive goal. I value continual improvement and progress.

- **Emphasis on Scientific Method:** I use objective, rational, and linear thought. I believe in cause-and-effect relationships. I have quantitative emphasis in my life (more is better). I believe that right and wrong are clear (dualistic thinking).
- **Status and Power:** I think status and power are measured by economic possessions. It is important to have credentials, titles, and position. I believe my system is better than other systems. I think that owning goods, space, and property is important.

- **Family Structure:** I think the heterosexual nuclear family is an ideal social unit. I think of the male as the breadwinner and household head. I believe the female is the homemaker and the subordinate spouse. I live in a patriarchal structure where men are in charge of most parts of my life.
- **Health and Wellness:** Traditional medicine and technology are the best ways to cure myself of disease. The physician knows and is the most credible source of health information. When it comes to healing, treating the body is more important than the mind. I believe that most health problems are the result of individual lifestyle and behaviors.
- **Aesthetics:** I think important music and art are based on European culture. I think that the most beautiful women are blond, blue-eyed, thin, and young. I believe that men's attractiveness depends on power, economic status, and athletic ability.
- **Religion:** I believe in Christianity. I feel intolerant of others who do not believe in a single God.

Cross-Cultural Communication

The "white" or European American culture dominates the US, and most Americans take its elements for granted. African Americans, Hispanics, and Asian Americans often grow up using different verbal and nonverbal communication patterns. White Americans have assumed that all racial and ethnic groups will adapt their habits to those of the dominant culture. White individuals often cannot name the rules of their culture because they take them for granted. People of other groups may be more aware of the dominant culture's rules because they have been discriminated against for not following them. As the world becomes more and more multicultural, it is important for whites to understand the communication rules of other cultures.

Figure 28: *Possible Verbal and Nonverbal Sources of Miscommunication between Various Ethnic Groups and White Americans* (Hetherington 1995).

African Americans often ...	Whites often ...
1. Consider having one's hair touched by another person to be offensive.	1. Consider the touching of one's hair by another person a sign of affection.
2. Prefer indirect eye contact during listening and direct eye contact during speaking as signs of attentiveness and respect.	2. Consider direct eye contact during listening and indirect eye contact during speaking as signs of attention and respect.
3. May be emotionally intense, dynamic, and demonstrative in public.	3. Expect public behavior to be modest and restrained—emotional displays are seen as irresponsible or in bad taste.
4. Clearly distinguish between arguing and fighting—verbal abuse is not necessarily a precursor to violence.	4. Do not distinguish arguing from fighting—heated arguments suggest violence is imminent.
5. Consider asking personal questions of a new acquaintance improper and intrusive.	5. Consider asking a new acquaintance about jobs, family, etc., as friendly.
6. Usually tolerate interruption during a conversation—competition for the floor is granted to the most assertive person.	6. Usually do not tolerate interruptions during conversations—taking turns is the rule.
7. Regard conversations as private—butting in is seen as eavesdropping and is not tolerated.	7. Consider adding points of information and insights to a conversation one is not engaged in as helpful.
8. Consider the expression "you people" as pejorative and racist.	8. Tolerate the use of expression "you people."

Hispanics often ...	Whites often ...
1. Consider hissing to gain attention acceptable.	1. Consider hissing to be an impolite gesture that indicates contempt.
2. Touch one another during conversation.	2. Consider touching to be unacceptable—it may carry sexual overtones.
3. Consider avoidance of direct eye contact to be a sign of attentiveness and respect—sustained direct eye contact may be interpreted as a challenge to authority.	3. Consider direct eye contact a sign of attentiveness and respect.
4. Stand closer to one another in conversation than members of other cultures do.	4. Stand farther apart from one another in conversation than Hispanic speakers do.
5. Precede official or business conversations with lengthy greetings, pleasantries, and other talk unrelated to the point of business.	5. Value getting to the point quickly and directly.

Asians often ...	Whites often ...
1. Consider touching or handholding between males to be acceptable.	1. Consider touching or handholding between males to be unacceptable.
2. Consider handholding, hugging, and kissing between men and women in public to be unacceptable.	2. Consider handholding, hugging, and kissing between men and women in public to be acceptable.
3. Consider a slap on the back an insult.	3. Consider a slap on the back as a sign of friendliness.
4. Avoid outright verbal conflict at all costs—choosing to resolve disagreements indirectly and discreetly.	4. Engage in outright verbal conflict when necessary without hesitation.
5. Do not shake hands with a person of the opposite sex.	5. Customarily shake hands with persons of the opposite sex.

Question to Consider:

Develop a discussion for an ethnic group, other than your own, related to racism.

Reference

Hetherington, C. (1995). *Working with groups in the workplace: Celebrating diversity.* Duluth, MN: Whole Person Associates.

Chapter 23

College Student Mental Health

By Julie Catanzarite and Jason Robertson

What is Mental Health?

When people think of the term "*mental health*" they often have very different understandings and perspectives. Unfortunately, the term "mental health" is used by some to describe individuals who "can't deal with life" or "are crazy." Mental health is important during times of increased stress or traumatic life experiences, including a relationship break up, divorce, health problem, or death of a family member or friend. While these events certainly impact a person's life, it is important to understand that **everyone has mental health and mental health is important all the time.** In order to help people think of mental health in this manner, it is often helpful to think of mental health as existing on a continuum.

Mental Health Continuum

Positive Well-being   Elevated Stress   Less severe disorders   Severe/persistent disorders

The term "*mental illness*" is sometimes used interchangeably with mental health; however, mental illness is more of a medical term and refers to specific mental disorders that have been assigned a diagnosis in the *Diagnostic and Statistical Manual of Mental Disorders* (DSM-IV-TR). The term mental health is a more inclusive term than mental illness.

Talking About Mental Health

Finally, terminology is important when we consider how to describe someone who manages mental health problems or a mental disorder. It is not uncommon to hear someone state, "they are depressed" or "she has issues." You may even hear an individual self- identify as "I got issues" or "I'm bipolar." When considering the act of labeling others with mental health problems or mental disorders, it is critical to remember that **people are not their mental health problem or mental disorder.** For example, when we refer to people who are managing a physical health concern, such as diabetes or AIDS, we would never say, "She is diabetes" and might feel uncomfortable if the person self-identified as "I'm AIDS." For this reason, when serving as a peer educator, it is important to educate others about terminology and the inappropriate use of labels to describe individuals.

Common Mental Health Problems

Anxiety—Most common disorder in United States

Signs and symptoms include:

- racing thoughts with trouble quieting the mind
- catastrophic thinking patterns with thoughts on top of thoughts
- excessive worrying about life events
- fear of impending doom or loss of control
- feelings of panic in situations or anticipated situations
- physiological symptoms such as sweating, feeling faint, experiencing chills, becoming dizzy, tingling in the body, chest pain, tension in shoulders, shortness of breath or rapid breathing, increased heart rate, and nausea

Depression—Second most common mental disorder in the United States

Although an individual's cultural background impacts the particular presentation of depressive symptoms, the common symptoms include:

- persistent sadness
- crying spells
- agitation or anxiety
- fatigue or muscle weakness
- sleep problems
- feelings of guilt
- decreased motivation and interest in pleasurable activities, including sex
- significant changes in appetite and/or weight
- loss of concentration and attention
- memory problems
- thoughts of hopelessness or worthlessness, which for some can lead to thoughts of self-harm, death, or suicide

Eating Disorders—third most common mental health disorder in the United States. People are more likely to die from this disorder than any other mental health disorder.

Attention-Deficit Hyperactive Disorder—Fourth most frequently diagnosed mental disorder. Signs and symptoms include:

- significant trouble sitting still
- frequently talk while others are talking
- engage in impulsive decision making with drug/alcohol use, sexual activity, or money
- often daydream during class and in interpersonal situations

Bipolar Disorder—affects approximately 2 million individuals each year and is commonly referred to as **manic-depressive**. Because bipolar disorder includes rapid mood shifts, it is possible for an individual to feel "on top of the world" one day and facing profound depression the next day. The important piece to consider with Bipolar Disorder is that everyone experiences mood swings and what differentiates this condition from general ups and downs is the intensity and duration.

Schizophrenia—Among all the mental disorders described, schizophrenia is the most severe, persistent, and disabling over time. Schizophrenia affects close to one percent of all adults in the US; people with this condition often hear voices and may have frequent thoughts of hurting themselves. People also tend to exhibit a lack of trust, paranoia, and hear voices, and experience thoughts of hurting themselves.

Substance Use/Dependence Disorders—although it is not technically a mental disorder, it does severely impact people's lives and inhibits people as much as or more than mental disorders. This condition refers to addiction to and abuse of drugs or alcohol. The most frequently abused substances in college include:

- *Alcohol*
- *Marijuana (pot, weed, hash)*
- *Illicit stimulants (cocaine, methamphetamine)*
- *Stimulant medications (Adderall, Ritalin, Dexedrine)*
- *Pain-management medication (Hydrocodone, Loratab, Percocet, Oxycodone)*
- *Hallucinogens (mushrooms, LSD, PCP, ecstasy)*

See Chapters 8, 10, and 11 for more information on each of these topics.

Suicide

Suicide is the second leading cause of death among college students, and it is estimated that 1,088 college students die by suicide each year (National Mental Health Association and The Jed Foundation 2002). Estimates are that the rate of attempted suicide among youth is somewhere between one hundred and two hundred for every completed suicide (American Association of Suicidology 2004).

The Suicide Prevention Resource Center (SPRC) has called college suicide and attempted suicide only "the tip of the iceberg of a larger mental health and substance abuse problem among college students" (2004, 5). In fall 2006 American College Health Association conducted the National College Health Assessment in which, 83% of respondents reported "feeling overwhelmed by all I have to do"; 28% felt that way frequently. Similarly, almost 79% reporting feeling very sad and almost 60% reported feeling hopeless. Just over 42% at times felt so depressed it was difficult to function, and 9.4% seriously considered suicide (American College Health Association 2007). Likewise, directors of college counseling centers report an increase in the number of students with severe psychological problems (Gallagher 2006).

College can be a breeding ground for psychiatric problems. Poor eating habits, irregular sleeping patterns and experimentation with drugs and alcohol—especially combined with the academic stress of college life—may all play roles in triggering mental problems. Additionally, many of the major psychiatric illnesses, including depression, bipolar disorder, and schizophrenia, often do not manifest themselves until the late teens or early twenties (Kelly 2001, 51).

Many factors—stress, depression, anxiety, hopelessness, transition issues, loneliness—that put students at risk for suicide or attempted suicide (Kadison and DiGeronimo 2004) can be treated before the situation

reaches the stage of suicide if students can be connected with available mental health services (Kadison 2004). Unfortunately, 80%–90% of college students who die by suicide do not seek help from their college counseling centers (Kisch, Leino, and Silverman 2005), and only a minority of those at potential risk seek counseling services (Furr, Westefeld, McConnell, and Jenkins 2001; Kisch et al. 2005). A recent study (Eisenberg, Golberstein, and Gollust 2007), for example, found that, among college students who screened positive for depression or anxiety, between 37% and 84% (depending on the disorder) did not seek services.

There are a number of reasons that students do not seek the services available to them. Some students are unaware of the availability of counseling services on their campuses or do not know where to access the services (Eisenberg et al. 2007). Some students are skeptical about the efficacy of counseling (Eisenberg et al. 2007). Stigmas associated with seeking counseling also may prevent students from seeking help (Deane and Todd 1996). Additionally, even though students may have health insurance, they are uncertain if that insurance covers mental health services (Eisenberg et al. 2007). Other reasons include not seeing a need to seek services and lacking time to access services (Eisenberg et al. 2007).

Warning Signs of Suicide:
- Suicide threat or other statement of desire to die.
- Specific plan and method for suicide.
- Recent changes in mood and/or behavior (eating, sleeping, sexual patterns, etc.).
- Mental depression.
- Tends toward isolation.
- Getting affairs in order or giving away prized possessions when associated with several of the above signs.

High-Risk Groups:
- Persons who have made previous suicide attempts.
- Survivors of family member who have died by suicide.
- Mental health patients.
- College students, ethnic minorities, males, LGTB groups, creative artists, student athletes, veterans, graduate students, students taking class online/by correspondance, and international students.
- Chemically dependent persons.
- Survivors of violence (e.g., veterans, persons who've been raped).
- Individuals who have experienced a recent loss.

Why are college students not getting the help they need?

A large portion of college students do not access mental health services. Although student populations experience various forms of mental distress, only a small number of students needing services actually seek them out. Process evaluation data suggest that anywhere between 2% and 60% of college students nationwide use counseling facilities, with variation across regional, state, and institutional classification. Service utilization rates are even lower among minority, international, and male students. College students often do not seek help for the following reasons:

1. *Availability/accessibility:* Students may not be aware that the counseling center exists, how to access services, or what the counseling process is like.
2. *Devaluation of problems:* Students frequently do not perceive their problems to be appropriate or important enough to discuss with a counselor or are not aware that they should seek help.
3. *Confidentiality:* While most students are aware that counseling sessions are mostly confidential, many students are uncertain about when confidentiality can/will be broken, and are therefore still concerned about lack of confidentiality.
4. *Affordability:* Students may be concerned with cost of services or may not be aware that their insurance covers mental health services.
5. *Attitudes/beliefs:* Many students have negative views toward the counseling center, incorrect information regarding counseling services (i.e., mistaking psychological counseling for career guidance counseling), or may not think the services would help.
6. *Embarrassment:* Many students may be embarrassed to seek services for the first time or to talk to strangers.
7. Time: Students frequently cite lack of time as a primary reason for not using services.

Questions to Consider

1. What are the most common mental health concerns on the campus?
2. In what ways can peer educators work to end stigmas associated with mental health?
3. What are some potential campus resources and partners for the peer education program for referral and program development?

References

American Association of Suicidology (2004). *Youth Fact Sheet. Retrieved November 20, 2007* from http://www. suicidology.org

American College Health Association. (2007). *American College Health Association-National College Health Assessment: Reference group executive summary Fall 2006.* Baltimore: Author.

Deane, F. P., & Todd, D. M. (1996). *Attitudes and intentions to seek professional psychological help for personal problems or suicidal thinking. Journal of College Student Psychotherapy,* 10, p. 44–59.

Eisenberg, D., Golberstein, E., & Gollust, S. E. (2007). Help-seeking and access to mental health care in a university student population. Medical Care, 45, p. 594–601.

Furr, S. R., Westefeld, J. S., McConnell, G. N., & Jenkins, J. M. (2001). Suicide and depression among college students: A decade later. Professional Psychology: Research and Practice, 32, p. 97–100.

Gallagher, R. P. (2006). National survey of counseling center directors 2006. Alexandria, VA: International Association of Counseling Services.

Kadison, R. D. (2004, December 10). The mental-health crisis: What colleges must do. The Chronicle of Higher Education, p. B20.

Kadison, R. D., & DiGeronimo, T. F. (2004). College of the overwhelmed: The campus mental health crisis and what to do about it. San Francisco: Jossey-Bass.

Kelly, K. (2001, January 15). Lost on the campus. Time, p. 51–53.

Kisch, J., Leino, E. V., & Silverman, M. M. (2005). Aspects of suicidal behavior, depression, and treatment in college students: Results from the Spring 2000 National College Health Assessment Survey. Suicide and Life-Threatening Behavior, 35, p. 3–13.

National Mental Health Association and The Jed Foundation. (2002). Safeguarding your students against suicide: Expanding the safety network. Alexandria, VA: Author.

Suicide Prevention Resource Center. (2004). Promoting mental health and preventing suicide in college and university settings. Newton, MA: Education Development Center, Inc.

Chapter 24

Stress Management for the Peer Educator

By Luoluo Hong and Julie Catanzarite

Many peer educators find that doing such work, while oftentimes rewarding, can result in increased stress levels. Having to get up and speak in front of a group can arouse performance anxiety for many individuals. The pressure of having people count on you can be overwhelming and sometimes draining. Making time for meetings and workshops demands good time-management skills, and working with people so much requires assertiveness in order to set appropriate boundaries between one's personal life as a student and paraprofessional life as a peer educator. This section is designed to provide the peer educator with some essential tools for managing stress more effectively.

Defining Stress

Definition:

1. A state of dynamic tension created when one responds to demands and pressures from outside or within oneself;
2. Perception of a demand that exceeds one's ability to cope; and
3. Characterized by muscle tension, pounding heart, increased blood pressure, cold and clammy hands, and knotty stomach ("fight-or-flight" response).

Eustress (Positive Stress). This type of stress can help you concentrate and focus, but it can also literally help you to survive. Your physical stress (arousal) response helps you to meet challenging (or threatening) situations and is an automatic and essential fact of life. This stress is short-lived, for as soon as the challenge or threat has been addressed, your body relaxes and returns to normal.

Distress (Negative Stress). Your physical reaction to stress is always the same, but with negative stress your body stays geared up and doesn't relax. There is no true relaxation between one stress "crisis" and the next. When stress becomes chronic and ongoing, your physical and emotional health can suffer.

Types of Stressors. Aging. Body image. Change. Chemicals (external or internal). Commuting. Decisions. Disease, injury, and illness. Emotional. Environmental factors. Family obligations. Finances. Pain and physical exertion. Phobias. Prejudice and discrimination. Social situations. Technology. Work.

Overview of Stress Management Techniques:

- *Adaptive Behavioral Responses* (Time management; Assertiveness; Building and using support networks; Self-nurturance; Preventive maintenance of technology and appliances, including car; and Organization of home and work space)

- *Adaptive Physical Responses* (Adequate sleep; Balanced and nutritious diet; Regular exercise; Low-risk alcohol consumption; Abstinence from other drugs such as caffeine, nicotine, etc.; Relaxation and breathing techniques; and Massage therapy)
- *Adaptive Cognitive Responses* (Cognitive restructuring; Positive visualization; Stress inoculation; Self-guided imagery and meditation; and Internal locus of control)
- *Adaptive Emotional Responses* (Anger management; Crying; Humor; Intimacy; and Spirituality)

Figure 29: *Stress Exhaustion Symptoms*
_____

Emotional

anxiety • frustration • feeling out of control • mood swings • bad temper • nightmares • crying spells • irritability • "no one cares" • depression • nervous laughter • worrying • easily discouraged • little joy

Spiritual

emptiness • loss of meaning • doubt • unforgiving • martyrdom • looking for magic • loss of direction • cynicism • apathy • needing to "prove" self

Mental

forgetfulness • dull senses • low productivity • negative attitude • confusion • lethargy • distracted mind • no new ideas • boredom • negative self-talk • poor concentration

Relational

isolation • intolerance • resentment • loneliness • lashing out • hiding • clamming up • lowered sex drive • nagging • distrust • lack of intimacy • using people • fewer contacts with friends • physical aggression

Physical

appetite change • headaches • migraines • tension • fatigue • problems with sleeping • weight change • frequent colds • muscle aches • digestive upsets • pounding heart • accident-prone • teeth grinding • rash • restlessness • foot-tapping • finger-drumming • increased alcohol, tobacco, or other drug use

Time Management
_____

Time management is probably one of the basic tools to help you manage stress. It involves more than buying a calendar or keeping a virtual calendar. It requires a total management plan that establishes goals and objectives, prioritizing, daily planning, and periodic self-evaluation.

Consider this: *If you had a bank that credited your account each morning with $86,000, that carried over no balance from day to day, allowed you to keep no cash in your accounts and every evening canceled whatever part of the amount you had failed to use during the day, what would you do? Draw out every cent every day, of course, and use it to your advantage! Well, you have such a bank, and its name is TIME. Every morning, it credits you with 86,400 seconds. Every night, it writes off as lost whatever of this you have failed to invest to good purpose. It carries over no balances. It allows no overdrafts. Each day, it opens a new account with you. Each night, it burns the records of the day. If you fail to use the day's deposits, the loss is yours. There is no going back. There is no drawing against TOMORROW. It is up to each of us to invest this precious fund of hours, minutes and seconds in order to get from it the utmost in health, happiness and success!* (Source: **The Stress Examiner**, Aid Association for Lutherans, 1982)

Therefore, **plan every day.** Setting aside 5–10 minutes daily (either first thing in the morning or last thing before bed) to review the past day and prepare for the next will save hours in otherwise wasted time later. Write the plans down—in a notebook, in a diary or journal, or in a datebook that you always carry around with you.

Focus on goals. Ask yourself: what do you want to accomplish or have achieved over the next day? The next week? The next month? The next year? The next five years? Knowing what you want to achieve will help you eliminate the unnecessary activities that we clutter our days with but don't ultimately help us reach our ultimate goals—in fact may detract or hinder us from those goals.

Plan realistically. It's impossible to pack a forty-hour day into twenty-four hours. Many individuals are unaware of just how much time we spend on such things as gossiping, snacking, running a quick errand, making that one quick phone call, or stopping in the bathroom—those minutes add up. Yet, it's important to have a feel for how long it takes you to accomplish regular tasks, and then plan accordingly. For instance, if it usually takes thirty hours for you to research, write, and edit a ten-page paper, it wouldn't make sense to allot only fifteen for the task. Similarly, if you know it takes thirty minutes to drive from your home to work at off-peak times, allow at least an extra ten to fifteen minutes during rush hour traffic. By setting realistic expectations for yourself, you don't set yourself up for failure, disappointment, and added frustration. Remember, never double-book yourself. You'll constantly feel inadequate, and you'll earn a reputation for being unreliable.

Prioritize. Don't just write down "to do" lists; rank each item in order of importance. Differentiate between those that require urgent, immediate attention; those that require short-term attention (within one to two days); and those that require long-term attention (three or more days).

Be creative with your time-management system. Use wall calendars, color-coded pens, post-it notes, dry-erase boards, a Google calendar, email, and other items to supplement your memory and enhance your planning system. Need a reminder to call the doctor tomorrow morning? Write yourself a note on a post-it note and slap it on the bathroom mirror the night before. Have to run an errand when you get home? Email yourself from school or work and remind yourself to that effect.

Avoid the "hurrieder I go, the behinder I get" complex. Block out sufficient time to complete tasks and activities of daily living, and build in time cushions for flexibility and changeability. Some individuals pack their days so chock full that they don't even leave time for a bathroom break! Don't be afraid to leave some empty spaces in your calendar; that way you won't always feel like you're behind schedule. And if you should end up being early, take those free extra moments to read recreationally, do a quick homework review, check messages, etc. Don't forget to account for commuting time.

Follow the "D" Rule with every assignment, task, or responsibility you receive: *delegate* it immediately (but appropriately, or it will just end up back in your lap), *defer* (until a later time), *delete* (is it really necessary? besides, we can't do it all), or *do* (no procrastinating!).

To combat procrastination, divide large tasks into smaller ones, and complete one task at a time. You don't have to necessarily start at the "beginning," either (for example, when writing a paper). Sometimes, starting at the "end" can help get you motivated and focused. Set up a small reward system for your accomplishments.

Know your peak times. Work on high-priority or more challenging assignments and tasks during those times.

Control interruptions. Shut the door, take the phone off the hook, or let voice mail answer. Get out of the kitchen and away from the television. Politely excuse your friends or coworkers—unless you work effectively in study groups and committees. By eliminating distractions and maintaining focus, you will use your time more efficiently, minimize errors, and avoid having to redo or repeat a task.

Don't forget to plan time for yourself. If all you are doing is fulfilling your academic, professional, or civic responsibilities without any regard for your own wants and needs, you'll start to "burn out." Recreation time should not be a haphazard "catch as catch can" deal; plan in time for yourself on a regular basis, otherwise you'll continually be trying to "steal it" out of your work or study time. Also, remember to schedule in sleep (7–8 hours each night) and mealtimes. Knowing that you'll have time to spend for yourself at a later, prescheduled time will help you stay focused on the not-so-desirable responsibilities of life.

Assertiveness

Assertiveness is an important skill to develop for peer educators. In addition to enhancing your workshop facilitation skills, it helps you set appropriate boundaries with students, significant others, and family members—assisting you in keeping your personal life and paraprofessional life separate.

Difficulty with being assertive has stereotypically been a challenge ascribed to women. However, research on violence and men's roles demonstrated that many physical altercations result from poor communication that then escalates into larger conflicts. Many men feel powerless in the face of aggressive communication from men or women in their lives; conversely, passivity in some situations can arouse frustration and anger for many men. As such, assertiveness can be an effective tool for men who are seeking to proactively alleviate violence in their lives, as well as a tool for fostering healthier, more satisfying lives. Similarly, women who develop assertiveness will bolster their self-esteem, achieve more satisfying intimate relationships, and decrease their risks for sexual and physical victimization, as well.

Sociologists and mental health professionals are finding that assertiveness is usually displayed in certain circumstances. That is, assertiveness is not a personality trait that persists consistently across all situations. Different individuals exhibit varying degrees of assertive behavior depending on whether they are in a work, social, academic, recreational, or relationship context. Therefore, a goal for assertiveness training is to maximize the number of context in which an individual is able to communicate assertively.

A **non-assertive** person is one who is often taken advantage of, feels helpless, takes on everyone's problems, says yes to inappropriate demands and thoughtless requests, and allows others to choose for him or her. The basic message he/she sends is "I'm not OK." The non-assertive is emotionally dishonest, indirect, self-denying, and inhibited. He/she feels hurt, anxious, and possibly angry about his/her actions (Davis, Eshelman, and McKay 1980).

Non-Assertive Body Language:
1. Lack of eye contact; looking down or away.
2. Swaying and shifting of weight from one foot to the other.
3. Whining and hesitancy when speaking.

An **assertive** person is one who acts in his/her own best interests, stands up for self, expresses feelings honestly, is in charge of self in interpersonal relations, and chooses for self. The basic message sent from an assertive person is "I'm OK and you're OK." An assertive person is emotionally honest, direct, self-enhancing, and expressive. He/she feels confident, self-respecting at the time of his/her actions as well as later (Davis et al. 1980).

Assertive Body Language:
1. Stand straight, steady, and directly face the people to whom you are speaking while maintaining eye contact.
2. Speak in a clear, steady voice—loud enough for the people to whom you are speaking to hear you.
3. Speak fluently, without hesitation, and with assurance and confidence.

An **aggressive** person is one who wins by using power, hurts others, is intimidating, controls the environment to suit his/her needs, and chooses for others. An aggressive person says, "You're not OK." He/she is inappropriately expressive, emotionally honest, direct, and self-enhancing at the expense of another. An aggressive person feels righteous, superior, and deprecatory at the time of action and possibly guilty later (Davis et al. 1980).

Aggressive Body Language:
1. Leaning forward with glaring eyes.
2. Pointing a finger at the person to whom you are speaking.
3. Shouting.
4. Clenching the fists.
5. Putting hands on hips and shaking the head.

Communication is not only a matter of what you say, but also a function of how you say it!

How to Improve the Communication Process:
1. Active listening: reflecting back (paraphrasing) to the other person both words and feelings expressed by that person.
2. Identifying your position: stating your thoughts and feelings about the situation.
3. Exploring alternative solutions: brainstorming other possibilities; rating the pros and cons; ranking the possible solutions.

Making Simple Requests:
1. You have a right to make your wants known to others.
2. You deny your own importance when you do not ask for what you want.
3. The best way to get exactly what you want is to ask for it directly.
4. Indirect ways of asking for what you want may not be understood.
5. Your request is more likely to be understood when you use assertive body language.
6. Asking for what you want is a skill that can be learned.
7. Directly asking for what you want can become a habit with many pleasant rewards.

Refusing Requests:
1. You have a right to say NO!
2. You deny your own importance when you say yes and you really mean no.
3. Saying no does not imply that you reject another person; you are simply refusing a request.
4. When saying no, it is important to be direct, concise, and to the point.
5. If you really mean to say no, do not be swayed by pleading, begging, cajoling, compliments, or other forms of manipulation.
6. You may offer reasons for your refusal, but don't get carried away with numerous excuses.
7. A simple apology is adequate; excessive apologies can be offensive.
8. Demonstrate assertive body language.
9. Saying no is a skill that can be learned.
10. Saying no and not feeling guilty about it can become a habit that can be very growth enhancing.

Assertive Ways of Saying "No":

1. Basic principles to follow in answers: brevity, clarity, firmness, and honesty.
2. Begin your answer with the word "NO" so it is not ambiguous.
3. Make your answer short and to the point.
4. Don't give a long explanation.
5. Be honest, direct, and firm.
6. Don't say, "I'm sorry, but …"

Steps in Learning to Say "No":

1. Ask yourself, "Is the request reasonable?" Hedging, hesitating, feeling cornered, and nervousness or tightness in your body are all clues that you want to say NO or that you need more information before deciding to answer.
2. Assert your right to ask for more information and for clarification before you answer.
3. Once you understand the request and decide you do not want to do it, say NO firmly and calmly.
4. Learn to say NO without saying, "I'm sorry, but …"

Evaluating Your Assertions:

1. Did you say what you wanted to say?
2. Were you direct and unapologetic?
3. Did you stand up for your own rights without infringing on the rights of the other person?
4. Were you sitting or standing in an assertive posture?
5. Did your voice sound strong and calm? Were your gestures relaxed?
6. Did you feel good about yourself after you finished speaking?
7. Did you listen for feedback from the other person to understand what he/she was feeling?

Assertive Techniques:

1. *Broken Record*—Be persistent and keep saying what you want over and over again without getting angry, irritated, or loud. Stick to your point.
2. *Free Information*—Learn to listen to the other person and follow up on free information people offer about themselves. This free information gives you something to talk about.
3. *Self-Disclosure*—Assertively disclose information about yourself—how you think, feel, and react to the other person's information. This gives the other person information about you.
4. *Fogging*—An assertive coping skill is dealing with criticism. Do not deny any criticism and do not counter-attack with criticism of your own.
5. *Agree with the truth*—Find a statement in the criticism that is truthful and agree with that statement.
6. *Agree with the odds*—Agree with any possible truth in the critical statement.
7. *Agree in principle*—Agree with the general truth in a logical statement such as, "That makes sense."
8. *Negative Assertion*—Assertively accepting those things that are negative about yourself. Coping with your errors.
9. *Workable Compromise*—When your self-respect is not in question, offer a workable compromise.

Method of Conflict Resolution:

1. Both parties describe the facts of the situation.
2. Both parties express their feelings about the situation, and show empathy for the other person.
3. Both parties specify what behavior change they would like or can live with.
4. Consider the consequences. What will happen as a result of the behavior change? Compromise may be necessary, but compromise may not be possible.
5. Follow up with counseling if you need further assistance.

Every person's Bill of Rights:

1. The right to be treated with respect.
2. The right to have and express your own feelings and opinions.
3. The right to be listened to and taken seriously.
4. The right to set your own priorities.
5. The right to say NO without feeling guilty.
6. The right to get what you pay for.
7. The right to make mistakes.
8. The right to choose not to assert yourself (Davis et al. 1980).

Figure 30: *Comparison of Communication Styles*

Aggressive Style. In this style, opinions, feelings, and wants are honestly stated, but at the expense of someone else's feelings. The underlying message is, "I'm superior and right, and you're inferior and wrong." The advantage of aggressive behavior is that people often give aggressive individuals what they want in order to get rid of them. The disadvantage is that aggressive individuals make enemies, and people can't avoid them entirely and therefore may end up behaving dishonestly toward them in order to avoid confrontations.

Passive Style. In this style, feelings and wants are withheld altogether or expressed indirectly and only in part. The underlying message is, "I'm weak and inferior, and you're powerful and right." The advantage of passive communication is that it minimizes responsibility for making decisions and the risk of taking a personal stand on an issue. The disadvantages are a sense of impotence, lowered self-esteem, and having to live with the decisions of others.

Assertive Style. In this style, you clearly state your opinion, how you feel, and what you want without violating the rights of others. The underlying assumption is, "You and I may have our differences, but we are equally entitled to express ourselves to one another." The major advantages include active participation in making important decisions, getting what you want without alienating others, the emotional and intellectual satisfaction of respectfully exchanging feelings and ideas, and high self-esteem.

Figure 31: *Getting an Attitude Adjustment*

Maintaining a positive and healthy attitude is essential to developing self-esteem and reducing stress in your life. We commonly encounter two opposing types of attitudes, irrational and assertive, both of which have a direct effect on the satisfaction we experience with ourselves and in relationships. Accepting and using your assertive beliefs can profoundly enhance the quality of your life. Holding on to irrational beliefs, however, will ultimately increase the stress in your life, reducing your ability to achieve that quality. Therefore, it is important to recognize your irrational ideas and replace them with assertive beliefs. The following are examples of irrational and assertive beliefs.

Adapted from: *Stress Management for the College Student* by L.C. James & A. Ellis, and from R.;(Ellis and Grieger 1977)

Irrational Beliefs	Assertive Beliefs
1. It is a dire necessity for me to be loved or approved for everything by every significant person in my life.	1. I can judge my own behavior, thoughts, and emotions, and take responsibility for their initiation or consequences.
2. I should be thoroughly competent, adequate, and achieving in all possible respects.	2. I can offer no reasons or excuses for justifying my behavior.
3. Unhappiness is caused by outside circumstances, and I have little or no control over my sorrows and disturbances.	3. I can determine if I am responsible for finding solutions to other people's problems.
4. My past history is all important, and once something has strongly affected my life, it must continue to do so.	4. I can change my mind.
5. There is always a right, precise, and perfect solution to human problems, and it is catastrophic if this perfect solution is not found.	5. I can make mistakes and be responsible for them.
6. If something is dangerous or fearsome, I should be terribly concerned about it and should keep dwelling on the possibility that it might happen.	6. I can say, "I don't know."
7. There are bad, wicked, and evil people in the world, and they should be severely punished or blamed for their villainy.	7. My actions can be independent of others' opinions.
8. It is awful and catastrophic when things are not the way I would like them to be.	8. I can be illogical in making decisions.
9. It is easier to avoid than to face certain life difficulties and self-responsibilities.	9. I can say, "I don't understand."
10. I should get very upset over other people's problems and disturbances.	10. I can say, "I don't care."
11. If I could make the changes in my appearances that I want to, I know I would be happy.	11. I do not confuse my outer appearance with my inner self-worth.

Relaxation Techniques

Relaxation is valuable for the peer educator, both as a method for reducing performance anxiety prior to conducting a workshop, as well as a tool for dealing with stress in your everyday life. Relaxation training is designed to teach you skills to deal with anxiety and stress. After you practice these skills repeatedly, you will be able to use them anytime during the day to relieve you from overwhelming tension. Relaxation training is not designed to just help you go to sleep, nor is it designed to solve your problems. What is does do is relax you enough so that you are not so overwhelmed and are better able to think clearly. When you are thinking clearly, it is much easier to work on your problems.

Relaxation is a skill, and like any skill, it takes a great deal of serious practice to learn. Therefore, the different relaxation techniques you are about to learn will only begin to work effectively after repeated practice. There is a wide variety of relaxation techniques available, and some methods will work better for you than others. You will be exposed to four readily available and easily mastered techniques so that you can choose the technique(s) that will work best for you.

Guided Imagery. Guided imagery is a relaxation technique that uses the image of a relaxing place or situation to relieve you of stress and anxiety. In guided imagery, you imagine a haven, a safe place where there is no stress or

anxiety. Your body then will begin to react to the image as though it is actually true, and you will become relaxed. Practice in using guided imagery gradually results in being able to reach a point of deep relaxation in a relatively short period of time by simply recalling the relaxing image.

There are a wide variety of tapes that are available for guided imagery, or you can use your own image, such as the following example:

1. Select a comfortable sitting or reclining position.
2. Close your eyes, and think about a place that you have been before that represents your ideal place for physical and mental relaxation. (It should be a quiet environment, perhaps the seashore, the mountains, or even your own back yard. If you can't think of an ideal relaxation place, then create one in your mind.)
3. Now imagine that you are actually in your ideal relaxation place. Imagine that you are seeing all the colors, hearing the sounds, smelling the aromas. Just lie back, and enjoy your soothing, rejuvenating environment.
4. Feel the peacefulness, the calmness, and imagine your whole body and mind being renewed and refreshed.
5. After five to ten minutes, slowly open your eyes and stretch. You have the realization that you may instantly return to your relaxation place whenever you desire, and experience peacefulness and calmness in body and mind.

Note: Guided imagery can be best used by people who are able to vividly imagine places or situations and are able to concentrate on that image for five to ten minutes. If you have difficulty doing this after several sessions, another relaxation technique may be more effective for you.

Passive Relaxation. Passive relaxation is a relaxation technique that uses sights or sounds that naturally produce a sense of calm. In passive relaxation, you repeatedly see (e.g., watching fish in an aquarium, or a fire flickering) or hear (e.g., the ocean's waves, or the rain falling) stimuli that become the focus of your attention. As the stimuli repeat, you gradually begin to clear your mind of anxiety-producing thoughts and the repetition of the stimuli becomes the focus, allowing both your mind and body to relax.

It seems that certain sights and sounds are naturally relaxing, and each person has a favorite that can be readily available in their natural environment. There are also DVDs, MP3 downloads, and CDs available to provide this type of relaxing environment.

Deep-Breathing Exercises. Deep breathing is a relaxation exercise that focuses on full-depth breaths that allow the body to relax. When you are anxious, your breathing is shallow and irregular and your heartbeat quickens. When you are relaxed, your breathing deepens and your heart rate slows. By purposely practicing deep, slow breathing, you automatically trigger other bodily responses related to relaxation.

For any deep-breathing relaxation exercise, the key is proper breathing. To determine if you are breathing properly, place your hand directly under your rib cage. If your hand moves outward when you take a deep breath, then you are inhaling properly. If you exhale completely, then you are completing the breathing process properly.

There are a variety of deep breathing exercises available for relaxation purposes. An example of one such exercise follows:

1. Select a comfortable sitting position.
2. Close your eyes, and direct your attention to your own breathing process.
3. Think about nothing but your breath, as it flows in and out of your body.
4. Say to yourself something like this: "I am relaxing, breathing smoothly and rhythmically. Fresh oxygen flows in and out of my body. I feel calm, renewed and refreshed."
5. Continue to focus on your breath as it flows in and out, in and out, thinking of nothing by the smooth, rhythmical process of your own breathing.
6. After five minutes, stand up, stretch, smile, and continue with your daily activities.

Progressive Muscle Relaxation. Progressive muscle relaxation is a relaxation technique that uses the principle that you cannot be physiologically anxious and relaxed at the same time. The progressive relaxation of your muscles reduces pulse rate, blood pressure, respiration rate, and perspiration—all bodily responses to anxiety. Therefore, you can use this technique to literally let anxiety systematically flow out of your body.

Each person carries around tension in certain muscle groups of the body. However, most people are not aware of these muscle groups that are often tense. Progressive muscle relaxation teaches you to be aware of muscles that

are tense so that you can relax them. This is done by systematically tensing muscle groups so that you can become aware of how tension feels, and then releasing the tension to that you can achieve and be aware of relaxed muscles.

With practice, you will eventually be able to identify certain muscle groups that are tense and use this procedure only on that particular group. This will greatly shorten the time needed for relaxation.

There are a wide variety of sequences and methods available on audio tapes and in written form. An example of a typical muscle relaxation sequence is available in Figure 32.

Figure 32: *Progressive Muscle Relaxation Exercise (Davis et al. 1980; Zastrow 1981)*

Get in a comfortable position and relax. Now clench your right fist, tighter and tighter, studying the tension in your fist, hand, and forearm. Now relax. Feel the looseness in your right hand, and notice the contrast with the tension. Repeat the entire procedure with your left fist, then both fists at once.

Now bend your elbows and tense your biceps. Tense them as hard as you can and observe the feeling of tautness. Relax, straighten out your arms. Let the relaxation develop and feel that difference. Repeat this and all succeeding procedures at least once.

Turn attention to your head; wrinkle your forehead as tightly as you can. Now relax and smooth it out. Let yourself imagine your entire forehead and scalp becoming smooth and at rest. Now frown and notice the strain spreading throughout your forehead. Let go. Allow your brow to become smooth again. Close your eyes now, squint them tighter. Look for tension. Relax your eyes. Let them remain closed gently and comfortably. Now clench your jaw, bite hard, and notice the tension throughout your jaw. Relax your jaw. When the jaw is relaxed, your lips will be slightly apart. Let yourself really appreciate the contrast between tension and relaxation. Now press your tongue against the roof your mouth. Feel the ache in the back of your mouth. Relax. Press your lips now, purse them into an "O." Relax your lips. Notice that your forehead, scalp, eyes, jaw, tongue, and lips are all relaxed.

Press your head back as far as it can comfortably go and observe the tension in your neck. Roll it to the right and feel the changing locus of stress; roll it to the left. Straighten your head and bring it forward; press your chin against your chest. Feel the tension in your throat and in the back of your neck. Relax, allowing your head to return to a comfortable position. Let the relaxation deepen. Now shrug your shoulders. Keep the tension as you hunch your head down between your shoulders. Relax your shoulders. Drop them back and feel the relaxation spreading through your neck, throat, and shoulders; pure relaxation, deeper and deeper.

Give your entire body a chance to relax. Feel the comfort and the heaviness. Now breathe in and fill your lungs completely. Hold your breath. Notice the tension. Now exhale, let your chest become loose, and let the air hiss out. Continue relaxing, letting your breath come freely and gently. Repeat this several times, noticing the tension draining from your body as you exhale. Next, tighten your stomach. Breathe deeply into your stomach, pushing your hand up. Hold and relax. Feel the contrast of relaxation as the air rushes out. Now arch your back, without straining. Keep the rest of your body as relaxed as possible. Focus on the tension in your lower back. Now relax, deeper and deeper.

Tighten your buttocks and thighs. Flex your thighs by pressing down with your heels as hard as you can. Relax and feel the difference. Now curl your toes downward, making your calves tense. Study the tension. Relax. Now bend your toes toward your face, creating tension in your shins. Relax again.

Feel the heaviness throughout your lower body as the relaxation deepens. Relax your feet, ankles, calves, shins, knees, thighs, and buttocks. Now let the relaxation spread to your stomach, lower back and chest. Let go more and more. Experience the relaxation deepening in your shoulders, arms, and hands. Deeper and deeper. Notice the feeling of looseness and relaxation in your neck, jaw, and all your facial muscles.

Combating Insomnia

Everyone has trouble sleeping at times. In fact, over one third of all Americans say that they are constantly tired, with about 15% of adults claiming they suffer from insomnia regularly. Physicians say exhaustion is one of the most common patient complaints. Much of this exhaustion can be attributed to stress and people skimping on sleep in an attempt to get more hours out of an already long day. A recent government study found that the average American had added over 150 hours a year to his or her work schedule since 1969.

The amount of sleep we need each night varies from person to person. Some people can get by on only five hours a night, while others need as much as ten. A few "insomniacs" are people who are five- or six-hour sleepers who believe they need more. The average adult requires seven to nine hours a night in order to feel sufficiently rested. Americans average only six and a half (Fackelmann 2007). Sleep experts say you can tell if you're getting enough sleep if it takes you approximately 10–15 minutes to fall asleep, and you wake easily in the morning. Remember, also, if you stay up late one night (or even a few nights in a row), you don't have to make up the exact amount of sleep you lose. Studies have shown that, even after going without sleep for days, most people need only one long night's sleep to recover.

What is Insomnia? Everyone has trouble sleeping sometimes, particularly in times of stress. The length of time that insomnia has gone on is a key to treating it. Experts generally acknowledge three types of insomnia:

- *Transient insomnia:* Lasts no more than a few days and is often triggered by excitement, nervousness, or travel. Most people catch up on sleep after a few days.
- *Short-term insomnia:* May last as long as three weeks. Usually occurs in times of personal stress or serious medical illness.
- *Chronic insomnia:* May last for years. It can often be attributed to chronic stress. Some people become mired in a poor sleep cycle and develop "learned insomnia." Chronic insomniacs of all types usually require behavioral therapy.

Do Sleep Aids Help? "Compared with the few studies that suggest pills will make you feel better the next day, there's a huge body of studies that show you may feel worse," says Dr. Wallace Mendelson, head of the sleep study unit at the National Institute of Mental Health. Most sleep medications cause drowsiness, dizziness,

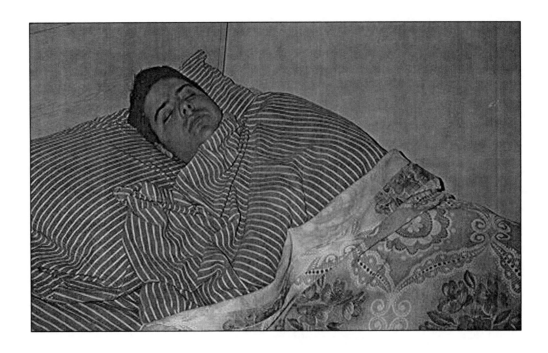

memory problems, and loss of coordination that can interfere with your ability to drive and manage complex mental tasks (like studying and test taking) the next day.

While sleeping pills may knock you out and help you sleep temporarily, they tend to disrupt the sleep cycle further. They typically lead to an increase in fragmented sleep, disturbing dreams, and daytime fatigue. Also, tolerance to the pills can become a problem. Taken nightly, some pills can lose their effectiveness in a week or two. After quitting use of the pills, several nights of "rebound insomnia" may follow, making the person think that the sleep problem has escalated.

Strategies for Getting the ZZZs

- If you are having trouble getting to sleep, these hints may help. Try different tricks (or combination of tricks) on different nights to see which work best for you.
- *Set an alarm clock and get up at about the same time seven days a week, no matter what time you go to bed.* Don't sleep in on weekends (at least, not more than an hour or two). This will help to keep your biological clock synchronized. Only go to bed when you are sleepy. If you are not asleep in fifteen or twenty minutes, go into another room and read or watch TV until you feel sleepy.
- *Reserve your bed and bedroom for sleep only.* Don't read, eat, watch TV, or talk on the phone in bed. This will help prevent the bedroom from becoming an anti-sleep stimulus.
- *Soundproof and lightproof your bedroom.* Noise disturbs sleep, even if you don't awaken completely. If necessary, mask sounds with "white" noise from a fan or air conditioner.
- *Try not to nap during the day.* Even if you're tired, tough it out until bedtime.
- *Avoid caffeinated drinks and chocolate after 4 PM, and don't smoke at bedtime*—nicotine is a stimulant, too.
- *Don't drink alcohol at bedtime.* Although it may relax you, alcohol is a depressant drug and provides poor-quality sleep. Because it is a short-acting drug, it causes frequent awakenings in the latter half of the night.
- *Exercise regularly to increase the quality and quantity of your sleep.* Avoid vigorous exercise just prior to bedtime (after about 7 PM), because it acts as a stimulant.
- *Eat with sleep in mind.* A supper high in carbohydrates, such as pasta, may foster sleepiness. Also, a light bedtime snack may keep hunger pangs from waking you up in the middle of the night.
- *Set up pre-sleep rituals and routines to psyche you into the sleeping mood.* If you have been experiencing trouble sleeping, you should start some fresh habits.

Mind-Relaxation Techniques. These methods help to relax your body and distract your mind from worries. Try a few of these tactics to see which ones help you get to sleep:
- *Use mental diversions to banish unwanted thoughts.* Focus on your physical surroundings or on an interesting task. Count ceiling tiles or examine the construction of a piece of furniture.
- *Focus on a train of thought that diverts your mind from thinking about going to sleep.* Recite a poem, do mental arithmetic, count sheep, list categories of things, alphabetize items, or compose a letter to a friend.
- *Focus on body sensations.* Where do you feel cold, warm, pressure, or tingling? Try to use mind power to induce calm, warmth, and heaviness in different body parts.
- *Practice deep breathing.* Slowly fill your lungs with air and exhale slowly and completely. Repeat slowly five to ten times.

- *Use monotonous stimulation.* Many people find the sound of ocean waves, raindrops, or a fan to be soothing. You can buy CDs with sounds on them, or you can use household items (fan, air conditioner, etc.).
- *Try progressive muscle relaxation.* Tense different muscle groups in your body, keep them tensed for 5–10 seconds, then release the tension and relax the muscles. Begin with the toes and work up to the head and neck. Go slowly and try to make your muscles as limp as possible after tensing them. Concentrate on the difference between the tense and relaxed muscle states.
- *Try imagery.* Conjure up a beach scene. Recall the warmth of the sun and the tranquil sound of the waves. Go for a mental stroll along the sand, remembering specific sights, sounds, smells, and touch. Try to be inside the scene rather than outside watching yourself.

Remember that relaxation training does not work for everyone, and may not work for those insomniacs who are already relaxed, but still cannot fall asleep. Other behavioral techniques may suit these persons better (Lamberg 1986).

Attitude Adjustments

Cognitive Restructuring. Changing how you perceive situations will result in different feelings about them. Use the "ABCDE" method: identify the *Activating* event, identify the irrational *Belief*, identify the emotional or stressful *Consequence*, *Dispute* your irrational belief, and create a less stressful *Emotion*.

A situation in which cognitive restructuring can be effective is when "wants" are erroneously labeled as "needs." For example, many college students believe that they need to work a certain number of hours in order to go to school; working is in fact a choice. Work becomes a stressor, especially when it interferes with study or class time. The consequences of not working might include having less money, not having nice clothes, not being able to have a car on campus, etc. Nevertheless, working is a choice to support other choices; it is not a need. A person may perceive a particular task or stressor as a "need," a must-do, when in fact it is a choice. The only true needs that any individual has are those require for subsistence—air, water, sleep, food, shelter, clothing, and intimacy. We often create other needs in our minds, when in fact we have choices. Each choice results in consequences—both positive and negative ones. Sometimes, when a person doesn't want to face negative, undesirable, or uncomfortable consequences, he or she will describe the choice as a need, when in fact s/he still has the ability to choose. To resolve the need-dilemma, determine what the potential consequences are for each of your options, decide what you can live with, then make a choice and take responsibility for it. In the example about work used above, the student who actively chooses to work and then accepts the corresponding consequences, will experience less stress.

Stress Inoculation. Identify your stressors. Identify those you can avoid, prevent, or eliminate. For stressors you can't change, control your reaction; anticipate, prepare, and accept. Have realistic expectations of yourself and others.

Positive Visualization. Turn off your inner "critical voice." Maintain positive thoughts and images. Use thought-stopping techniques to let go of negative thoughts such as guilt or self-doubt. Avoid perfectionism.

Healthy Relationships

Remaining in an unhealthy dating relationship can severely impair an individual's self-esteem and physical well-being, as well as add a constant stressor. There are distinct warning signals that can alert you to the possibility that a dating partner will prove to be violent or exploitive. The items below help both men and women recognize unhealthy patterns in either same-sex and heterosexual relationships. The more that an individual responds "yes" to these questions about his or her partner, the greater the likelihood of a problem. This checklist was developed by Alan McEvoy, Ph.D.

1. Has this person ever hit you, pushed you, thrown objects at you, or otherwise displayed violent outbursts directed toward you?
2. Has this person ever been violent toward former dating partners?
3. Does this person become verbally or physically abusive when under the influence of alcohol?
4. Is there a history of domestic violence in this person's family?
5. Does this person have a history of getting into frequent fights with others?
6. When there are disagreements between the two of you, does this person always have to "win" the argument? Does this person fail to respect your needs and views when there is a disagreement?
7. Does this person always make you feel guilty about the relationship, often by placing you in "no win" (i.e., "damned if you do, damned if you don't") situations?
8. Does this person often berate you or put you down (even in front of others) in order to feel superior?
9. Does this person make you feel incompetent to make your own decisions?
10. Does this person become extremely upset when you do things without his (or her) permission, or when you reject his (or her) presumed authority?
11. Does this person resent your having friends of your own?
12. Does this person try to control your friendships (e.g., place restrictions on whom you can see and when you can see them)?
13. Does this person threaten to harm your friends (especially those of the opposite sex) if you continue seeing them or if they try to help you?
14. Does this person threaten violence toward you or toward self (i.e., suicide threats) in order to make you stay in the relationship?
15. For male partners, is there excessive "male bonding" where only males seem to exert an influence on him? How do his male friends treat their partners?
16. Does this person hold in low regard members of the opposite sex (e.g., disregard their rights and abilities), but say that "you are special?"
17. For male partners, does he exhibit an obsession with pornography?
18. Does this person take pride in your achievements, or does he (or she) view your accomplishments as threatening? Does this person seem to feel better when you fail?
19. Does this person believe in an "adversarial" or game-like system of sexual conquest? Does this person boast of sexual intimacy as a victory or achievement, or define members of the opposite sex as sexual property?
20. Has this person ever forced you or manipulated you into having sex when it was against your wishes?

There are two basic principles to remember. First, under no circumstances should a person tolerate physical and sexual aggression, even in the context of dating. Second, successful relationships are based on equality and a fundamental respect for the rights and integrity of another.

In general, the elements that constitute a healthy and successful intimate relationship include:

1. *Mutual respect and acceptance* on the part of both partners (regarding religion, family upbringing, personality traits, etc.)
2. *Mutual trust* (without excessive jealousy)
3. *Honest, open communication* (without manipulation, domination, or passive-aggressiveness)
4. *"Fair fighting"* (wherein both partners are able to express grievances and have them heard)

5. *Equity* (not necessarily equality) of power and control (including financially, sexually, and emotionally)
6. *Compromise*
7. *Interdependence* (as opposed to codependence)
8. *Common values and goals* regarding the relationship itself, as well as for issues such as money management, childrearing, professional and life expectations, etc.)

Laughter Really Is the Best Medicine

Several studies have shown that laughter can reduce psychological stress. Laughing stimulates brain production of endorphins, the body's natural pain-relieving peptides. Laughter may also have healing and recuperative powers. Many people claim their recoveries from serious illness have been aided by laughter. In fact, laughter strengthens the immune system.

Laughing exercises the lungs, increases blood oxygen levels, and tones the entire cardiovascular system. Twenty seconds of laughter (or "inner jogging") gives the heart the same aerobic workout as three minutes of hard rowing. Adults average fifteen laughs a day. Laughter may be the elixir of your life.

People who are young in spite of their years share one thing in common—a sense of humor. Children laugh about four hundred times a day. Somewhere in between, we lose three hundred eighty-five laughs each day.

Comedian-pianist Victor Borge said, "The shortest distance between two people is a smile." So, know your humor style, seek out humor, make laughter last, surround yourself with humor, and laugh at yourself.

Other Stress-Management Strategies

Spirituality. *Spirituality* can be defined as a universal, generic, personal set of private beliefs that enhance one's life. The dimensions of the spiritual life task include:

- belief in a higher power;
- hope and optimism;
- worship, prayer, and meditation;
- purpose in life;
- self-giving love;
- moral values; and
- transcendence.

Creative Arts Therapy. If you enjoy dance, art, music, or drama as hobbies, such art forms can become powerful and cathartic outlets for expressing and unloading emotions: anger, joy, hope, fear, sadness, etc. Healthy emotion management requires the acknowledgment and appropriate expression of the entire range of human feelings. Art is a conduit for doing so. Sign up for a class on campus or at a local community center. You don't need to win an Oscar or Pulitzer Prize; do it for the sheer enjoyment of it.

Pet Therapy. If you are an animal lover, get a pet—fish, cat, dog, whatever. Watching them play, receiving their nonjudgmental affection, and interacting with the pet can provide stress release and relaxation. Research has also demonstrated a correlation between pet companionship and lowered blood pressure.

Questions to Consider

1. What are the six most common stressors on campus? How can these be addressed?
2. How does setting boundaries increase one's ability to handle stress?
3. How can relationships both cause and relieve stress?
4. Develop a personal action plan to manage your own stress.

References

American Psychiatric Association. (1994). *The diagnostic and statistical manual of mental disorders (DSM-IV) (Rev. 4th ed.).* Washington, DC: American Psychiatric Association.

Davis, M., Eshelman, E. R., & McKay, M. (1980). *The relaxation and stress reduction workbook.* Richmond, CA: New Harbinger Publications.

Ellis, A., & Grieger, R. (1977). *Handbook of Rational-Emotive Therapy. (1st ed).* New York: Springer.

Fackelmann, K. (2007). Americans skip sleep to make time for leisure activities. *USA Today. Retrieved from* http://www.usatoday.com/news/health/2007-08-29-sleep-study_N.htm

James, L. C., & Ellis, A., (1977). *Stress management for the college student.*

Lamberg, L. (1986, March). *A rescue kit for insomniacs. American Health.*

Zastrow, C. (1981). The practice of social work. Homewood, IL: The Dorsey Press.

Chapter 25

Conflict Resolution for Peer Educators

By Anne Keyworth

Over the course of your college career, conflict is undoubtedly something you will experience. This may be with your friends, family members, classmates, group mates, professors, students in your extracurricular activities, or even with yourself. This is a natural part of our growth as emerging professionals, and something we can all learn a great deal from. In order to effectively learn and move on from conflict, there are certain things you should be mindful of that may help you resolve conflict. This chapter aims to provide you with some ideas of how to think about conflict and how to effectively manage situations when you're in conflict.

Conflict isn't always a bad thing

What do you usually think of when you hear the word "conflict"? Many people would assimilate it to negative experiences in their lives, but in reality, conflict doesn't always have to be something negative (Wilmot and Wilmot 1967). Whether or not a conflict ends up as a completely negative experience is really up to how the situation is handled—whether the dispute is used to advance a situation, a relationship, or people's interests, or it is used to worsen it (Wilmot and Wilmot 1967). For example, you and a best friend have probably had disputes before, and you have probably found ways to work productively through some of them in order to positively influence your relationship with one another. Your relationship with that person has probably grown stronger because of those instances and you probably understand each other better as a result. The success of a conflict is reliant upon how each individual addresses the situation, and what strategies they use to determine the best possible solution for all parties involved (Wilmot and Wilmot 1967).

How do you handle conflict?

In facing a situation where there may be a conflict, it is important to recognize that not everyone fully understands how they react in a confrontational situation. Often, one's reaction depends on the person they're with, and how the other person handles the situation. How people react to conflict is typically determined by their background, experiences, issues they're sensitive to, self-esteem, what the social context is, their priorities, their perceptions and assumptions, and how people they grew up around handled conflict (Wilmot and Wilmot 1967). Knowing what these factors are in yourself (and perhaps for a person you're in conflict with) can help in figuring out how to best address a situation. Most of the time, conflict also arises from unmet needs regarding identity, security, control, recognition, and/or fairness (Perlstein and Thrall 1996). Some people may find that they end up in conflict more over some of these psychological needs than others. Think about how you handle conflict. Do you know what things make you upset or angry, and are you aware of the coping strategies you use that either do or do not work in a conflict? We'll talk more in another section about different styles of managing conflict.

It's also important to think about the different types of relationships where conflict can occur—do you work through conflict differently with a sibling, a parent, a friend, a co-worker, or an authority figure (National Association for Community Mediation [NAFCM] 1999)? In what ways does your arguing with a co-worker or boss differ from the ways you argue with a friend? Take a minute to think about why you approach conflict differently in different situations, how you approach them differently, and what you think does and does not work for you.

Similarly, think about whether or not you handle conflict the same way when you take a minute to think about things, compared to when you just react without thinking. Do you think your reaction is different when you stop and think about it compared to just reacting, or do you think you behave the same way regardless of how much time you take to think about it (Wilmot and Wilmot 1967). Many people tend to react without thinking about the potential consequences of their words or actions, and this can end up hurting a relationship and/or the potential outcomes for the situation. Hopefully this chapter will help you become more conscious of how you handle conflict.

Identifying a conflict

It's important to know how to identify a situation that either could lead to or currently is a conflict. Sometimes it's obvious; people may be visibly unhappy with something or someone and may have clearly expressed their feelings. Other times you may have to infer what a person is feeling based on their body language, tone, or a subtle remark they may make. Additionally, sometimes it may appear there is a conflict over one issue when in reality, a person may be more upset about a different issue but is taking it out on this smaller issue (Coltri 2004; Perlstein and Thrall 1996). For example, perhaps one partner in a serious relationship gets extremely upset about their partner going out with friends on a Friday night, but at a deeper level, they may actually fear that their partner is being unfaithful. Either way, it's critical that you are aware of what the issue at hand is so that you can begin to process it and think constructively about how to handle the situation.

Conflict styles

The National Association for Community Mediation (NAFCM) (1999) and Perlstein and Thrall (1996) describe five different conflict styles that represent the majority of ways in which people tend to handle a conflicting situation. These include:

- **Accommodation:** giving into someone else, either because you were wrong or because you value the relationship more than the argument.
- **Competing:** making sure you get what you want, regardless of whether or not it addresses the other person's needs and concerns. It shows that you value the argument more than the relationship.
- **Avoiding:** failing to not bring up the argument at all and remaining unhappy about the situation with no one's needs being met.
- **Compromising:** working with the other person so that you both get part of what you want or need, but not completely.
- **Collaboration:** where there is equal emphasis and value put on your needs, the other person's needs, and the issue at hand.

Do any of these sound familiar? Many people tend to consistently use a particular style depending on the relationship they have with a person, whether they're conscious of it or not. If you're not really sure what style you tend to lean toward, check out this quiz (Adkins 2006): http://www.ncsu.edu/grad/preparing-future-leaders/docs/conflict-management-styles-quiz.pdf.

Conflict resolution

There are many models for conflict resolution, but in this chapter we're going to use the NAFCM model (1999), which is an eight-step process to effectively handling conflict. The eight steps are as follows:

1. **Deal effectively with anger:** there are many feelings and emotions that can arise from a conflict. One feeling that is sometimes present in conflicts is anger, and anger can at times be overwhelming. People deal with anger in different ways, some of which are constructive and some of which are destructive (Wilmot and Wilmot 1967; Perlstein and Thrall 1996). First, it's important not to ignore your anger. Ignoring an emotion doesn't make it go away; it just makes your concerns and feelings unheard and therefore unmet and can be harmful in the future, as the situation may escalate. A good way to think of it is to act with thought instead of in reaction to whatever triggered your anger. It's helpful if you're aware of what kinds of things trigger you to get angry, so when those things occur, you can pause for a minute, realize you may be getting angry, and think constructively about how to handle the situation.

2. **Think before you approach:** both you and the other person in the conflict have something you want out of the situation (Perlstein and Thrall 1996; Wilmot and Wilmot 1967). In this sense, both parties involved are "interdependent; they have some degree of mutual interest" and the conflict exists because of the parties "[perceived] incompatible goals, scare rewards, and interference from the other party in achieving their goals" (Wilmot and Wilmot 1967, 9). It's important to understand what those interests are, and to think about how they affect you both. It's also important to think about what kinds of assumptions you may have toward the other person or toward their interests, and why you have made those assumptions. What assumptions do you think they've made about you, and why might that be? This is also the stage where you can begin to consider, based on the interests and the person you're with, what style of conflict resolution may be best for this situation.

3. **Set a positive tone:** make it clear that you are genuinely interested and invested in working things out. Here your body language and tone can be crucial (Perlstein and Thrall 1996); if you're yelling at someone telling them you want to work things out, or if you're not making eye contact with them, they may not take your comments seriously and might not want to bother taking the time and energy to work things out. Asking them (not telling them) if the two of you can sit down and work things out is a good start.

4. **Use ground rules:** sometimes these are stated, and sometimes they're not. If they're unstated, you each may have your own ground rules that may be misunderstood or unacknowledged. Some common rules to keep in mind are to let one person talk—uninterrupted—at a time, remain calm throughout, and to try and stay positive and work toward improvement throughout the conversation.

5. **Discuss and define the problem:** make sure you both understand what the problem is, and what each person wants from the situation. Each person should have equal opportunity to share their side of things. Communication is key here; the way you listen and the way you speak will make a significant difference. It's helpful to paraphrase what the other person says, to make sure you have a full understanding of what it is they're thinking and feeling. In the next section we will discuss good listening skills and paraphrasing more.

6. **Brainstorm possible solutions:** sometimes it might seem like there are only two answers to a solution: the way you want it, and the way the other person wants it. In some circumstances, this might be true, but in most, there are more solutions than a situation in which one person wins and the other loses. Brainstorming all possible solutions to a problem is crucial. More than likely you will be able to come up with something that meets some of the interests of both parties—perhaps not all, but some.

7. **Evaluate and choose solutions:** hopefully, a good solution will address both parties' interests. Ideally, the solution will be something that both parties agree on, and is realistic, specific, and balanced.

8. **Follow up:** this step is crucial to ensure that both parties are happy with the way things are going. Set up a time (perhaps a week or a month from the time of your initial conversation) that the two of you can check back in with each other and make sure both of you are still happy. If one or both of you isn't happy, you'll be better equipped now to ensure that you follow the steps again to reach another solution and give things another try.

Other helpful things to think about

A few other helpful tips are that it's a good idea to try and tone down your language, and use I/we-statements (Perlstein and Thrall 1996). When we're angry, we tend to use very powerful and dynamic language that can send very strong messages—perhaps stronger ones than we really intended. Making sure we keep cool and under control is important so we don't say things that are overly offensive. Additionally, making I-statements shows the person that you're in on this too—that it's not *just* them doing something wrong. For example, if someone has been making passive-aggressive remarks toward you, instead of saying something like "you've been really mean lately and I'm not sure why," you could say, "I've noticed that we haven't been hitting it off the best lately, and I was wondering if we could talk about what we could do to help each other understand one another a little bit better." This isn't putting blame on anyone, and the other person is more likely to infer that you realize there is a problem with the interpersonal dynamic, not specifically with that person. Most likely, they'll be more open to working things out than if you were to say something that put the blame on them.

Good listening is crucial in any relationship, but particularly during a time of conflict. There are a few key components to listening. First, it's important to let both people fully explain their side of things, without being interrupted. Each person should have a fair opportunity to do this, and while they are, the other should be listening to gather information—not automatically working to problem solve (NAFCM 1999). This can be a hard thing to do because it forces you to hear things fully from a different perspective—one that you may not agree with—and to give them the respect of hearing their full side. However, a significant part of resolving conflict is understanding where the other person comes from and why they feel the way they do, which can only come from listening (Perlstein and Thrall 1996).

Second, the listener should always try to paraphrase what they think they heard to check the accuracy of what it is they think the other person is saying (Perlstein and Thrall 1996). In paraphrasing, it's a good idea to identify the person's interests in the position as well as what they want out of the conflict. If the listener heard it wrong, it will give the other person a chance to clarify what they mean so both people fully understand the needs of all parties involved. It might also be helpful to ask open-ended questions (Perlstein and Thrall 1996), which gives the other person an opportunity to give you a full explanation for what they're feeling, instead of just a simple one-word answer to a question you posed. It can help for both you and the other person to make sure you're on the same page after someone explains what they're feeling.

Sometimes you may find that, while you're willing to be an active listener and give the other person your respect during a conflict, sometimes the other person isn't. At this point, you'll need to make a choice: do you want to continue to be proactive in the argument (NAFCM 1999)? It can be hard to be proactive when the other person isn't doing the same. Still, you will probably find that you will benefit from remaining proactive, and that remaining proactive won't do you any harm.

Finally, be cautious (and conscious) of your nonverbal communication (Perlstein and Thrall 1996). This is something that can be hard to control, but nonverbal communication sends some very strong messages to others in conversation with you. Here are some of the most common things you or someone else may say with your body language (Lewis 1998):

Gesture	Meaning
Chewing/biting lips	Uncertainty, hesitancy, nervousness
Pursed lips	Defensive position; will likely not open up
Wide open eyes with the corner of the eyebrows being turned down	Aggression toward someone
Relaxed mouth, natural smile, and chin projected forward	Considering a suggestion
Lowered eyebrows and tense lips pushed forward (teeth not visible)	Rejection or disagreement
Tilted head with hand at the chin	Positive response/interest
Head tilted down	Negative or judgmental
Palm facing up	Positive ideas
Palm facing down	Negative ideas/authority
Crossed arms	Protection against an expected attack
Crossed arms—hands holding on to upper arms tightly	Negative and/or suppressed attitude
Arms behind back; one and holding the other by the wrist with a clenched fist	Restraining oneself
Mouth covered with hand and thumb at cheek; fingers to mouth; or closed fist at/in the mouth	Lying or suspecting someone else of lying
Putting index finger up to mouth	Wants the speaker to stop speaking
Stroking the front of the neck	Doesn't fully believe the speaker
Rubbing the back of the neck	Trying to get someone to acknowledge a fact, or lying
Resting the palm on the back of the neck	Admitting defeat
Rubbing eyes	Attempting to deceive someone
Bending ear forward	Wants to have a turn talking
Finger inside an ear	Person doesn't want to listen to the speaker any more because they're too offensive or loud
Rubbing the nose	Rejection or doubt
Hand held flat against forehead	Feels harassed
Locking feet together	Defensive and/or tension
Sitting on the edge of a chair	Openness and a positive attitude
Sitting at the back of the chair, leaning forward and arms holding on to the chair	Closed and negative; not willing to openly communicate
Sitting/standing straight up with good posture	Confidence

When listening to someone who is clearly angry, try your best to stay calm (Perlstein and Thrall 1996). This will help both you and the other person. Listen to what they're saying. Essentially, they're venting to you, and they've most likely got some pent-up emotions that are coming out at you. After they're done, try paraphrasing what they've told you, and then ask them if the two of you can talk it out in a way that meets the wants and needs of you both. For example, if the conflict is with a roommate about the television being on, you could say something like, "Let's try to figure this out so that we're both getting what we want. How can we make it so that I can still have the television on without bothering you?" Then the two of you can come up with several potential solutions—having defined hours and/or days where the TV will be on/off, setting volume limits, or specifying a certain amount of time after which the TV will be turned off. Just make sure to arrange a way to check in with one another to make sure both of your needs and interests are being met.

Before you start on conflict resolution, it's essential to value resolution in the first place (Levine 1998). You can know all the strategies to effective communication and conflict resolution in the world, but if you don't actually care and value the person and the problem, you're not likely to have a truly successful and genuine conversation. It's also helpful and constructive to think of resolving conflict from a long-term perspective (Levine 1998), where you are thinking about the person as a whole and not just as what they mean to you in this incident. This will make it more likely that you will have a long-lasting and healthy relationship where you both are able to communicate your needs to one another.

Be creative! There may be other ways to arrive at the same solution without someone having to give up what they're originally thinking. This is where the brainstorming suggestion comes into play—try to think outside the box and build off one another's ideas for the best possible solution for your circumstances. As Stewart Levine puts it, "The trick is framing the situation as an opportunity to demonstrate your creativity" (1998, 54).

Tell them everything that's relevant to the conversation—withholding information can only lead to negative consequences, unless you really think that it's doing the person some genuine good by not telling them something. Being totally open demonstrates trust and that you have good faith in them to work together toward resolution (Levine 1998).

Mediation

There might be times when you feel like a situation has gotten to the point where you need some assistance from outside help in a conflict with another person. In times like this, it may be helpful look to a mediator, or a third party who is "typically impartial with respect to the disputants and neutral as to the settlement reached" (Coltri 2004, 306). Levine suggests finding a person who will partner *with* you but who won't do all the work *for* you, as well as a person who is a good listener and has autonomous opinions (1998). A formal mediator may be a trained professional in conflict resolution or a judge or lawyer in legal cases, and an informal mediator may be someone you look to as a role model, a friend, or some other person. Sometimes people may not even notice that they're acting as a mediator in a dispute. Mediators can help to guide effective communication and negotiation, and they can also attempt to "narrow the gap" (Coltri 2004, 307) between the parties' interests.

Keep in mind that as a peer educator, you may find yourself being a mediator among other people's conflicts. If this is the case, there are some questions you may want to ask yourself to get a better idea of your role in the dispute (Wilmot and Wilmot 1967):

- Is someone actively seeking your help?
- Do you feel that you have the appropriate skills to help them? You may feel comfortable handling some situations and not others; that's okay, and it's important to have an idea of what you can handle.
- What options do you have in your role as the negotiator? Are you assumed to be taking one side over the other because of loyalties, or are you in a position where you may come to be seen as one

of the parties rather than a neutral third party? How involved will you become with the emotional aspects of the dispute?

Wilmot and Wilmot (1967) also recommend the following when you find yourself being a mediator:
- Try to be descriptive of each side instead of judging sides
- Have both parties make an effort to be as specific as possible in describing their frustrations
- Work through things that can actually be changed
- Encourage both parties to give feedback when it's encouraged
- Make it clear that when you describe what you're hearing and seeing, you're only speaking for yourself and either party can provide clarification
- Encourage the quieter party, if there is one, to vocalize their thoughts more by showing interest in what they think. This will make them more comfortable to open up.
- Keep on track in the discussion. Having an agenda can help guide the discussion and ensure that people will stay focused.
- Paraphrase to make sure both parties understand one another's positions
- Recognize the limitations you have as the mediator and the fact that you cannot fix all of their problems
- Try to diffuse as much tension in the room as you can before the conversation has ended

Conclusion

Hopefully this chapter has given you some helpful ideas for how to think about and approach conflict. Every situation is different, but you will probably find that you use some of the same techniques in many cases to help resolve the issue at hand. The important thing is to find what works for you and that you feel confident in your conflict resolution knowledge and skills. Just remember that conflict is a normal part of life, and the outcome is dependent upon how the situation is handled. If you're interested in any further reading regarding conflict resolution, check out some of the books in the reference section.

Questions to Consider

1. In what ways can conflict be good?
2. How can peer educators act as mediators in conflict?
3. Outline a time in which you have had to handle a conflict. In what ways did it go well and in what ways did it go badly? How would you change the way you handled it knowing what you know now and based on the reading of this chapter?

References

Adkins, R. (2006). *Elemental truths.* Retrieved from http://elementaltruths.blogspot.com/2006/11/conflict-management-quiz.html

Coltri, L. S. (2004). *Conflict diagnosis and alternative dispute resolution.* Upper Saddle River, NJ: Pearson Education, Inc.

Filley, A. C. (1975). *Interpersonal conflict resolution.* Glenview, IL: Scott, Foresman and Company.

Guilar, J. D. (2001). *The Interpersonal communication skills workshop: a trainer's guide.* AMACOM.

Levine, S. (1998). *Getting to resolution: Turning conflict into collaboration.* San Francisco, CA: Berrett-Koehler Publishers, Inc.

Lewis, H. (1998). *Body language: A guide for professionals.* Thousand Oaks, CA: New Delhi/Thousand Oaks/London.

Mayer, B. S. (2004). Beyond neutrality: Confronting the crisis in conflict resolution. San Francisco, CA: Jossey-Bass.

National Association for Community Mediation. Face to face: A presenter's manual on conflict resolution and communication skills. 1999.

Perlstein, R., & Thrall, G. (1996). Ready-to-use conflict resolution activities for secondary students: strategies for dealing with conflict in real-life situations plus guidelines for creating a peer mediation program. San Francisco, CA: Jossey-Bass.

Ross, O. (2003). Situational mediation: Sensible conflict resolution. Ravensdale, WA: Issues Press.

Wilmot, J. H., & Wilmot, W. W. (1978). Interpersonal conflict. Dubuque, IA: WM C. Brown Company Publishers.

Chapter 26

Peer Intervention Strategies

By Luoluo Hong and Julie Catanzarite

Given the prevalence of substance abuse, gambling addiction, depression, eating disorders, and sexual assault on the college campus, there is a high likelihood that someone you care about—a friend, a relative, a partner, or a roommate—will at some point in the future confront a health problem that requires the attention of a trained professional. Helping a friend in need is accompanied by a lot of confusing feelings and thoughts. You may wonder how to approach that person or what exactly you should say. You may believe that you are overreacting, perhaps reading too much into a situation that eventually will pass. This individual may be doing things that interfere with your own life—perhaps he or she is even hurting you physically or emotionally. This checklist is designed to assist you in understanding when and how to intervene with a friend who is in need.

1. **Take the time to learn about the common signs and symptoms that might indicate a problem.** There are a lot of misconceptions about who develops certain health problems and what causes those problems. Students who are experiencing difficulties with alcohol, depression, sexuality, or food typically exhibit a predictable range of behaviors and emotions. Learning about these behaviors and emotions will increase the likelihood of detecting problems that your friends are facing in the early stages. For example, withdrawal from hobbies and friends, a sudden change from typical daily routine, or disruptions in usual sleep, eating, or sexual habits are common indicators that something may not be right. Becoming informed about the various health issues increases your ability to take care of yourself and those closest to you.

2. **Don't wait until the consequences have escalated to a serious level before you confront the person.** In general, it is easier to address a health problem in its earlier stages. Often, we are frightened of confronting those we care about when their behaviors appear to be unhealthy or hurtful to themselves and others. We don't want to lose the friendship, nor do we want to make false accusations or find that our suspicions were mistaken. True friends, however, believe that confronting a problem directly is worth the risk, because the benefits include honest, open communication and the potential for early intervention should a problem indeed exist. Our culture typically emphasizes independence over interpersonal accountability. Ultimately, if a friend is having a problem, it is your responsibility to confront them and help them address the problem. If you're thinking that perhaps it's not your business to step in, perhaps you aren't the friend you thought you were.

3. **Respect the individual's confidentiality.** Nothing can put a rift in a relationship more quickly than irresponsible gossip. If someone you care about is experiencing difficulties, the only person you should be talking to about those difficulties is the person you are concerned about. Calling his or her parents to "tattle," spreading rumors based on conjecture and speculation, or otherwise disrespecting the person's privacy may distance the individual from you and damage your credibility as a true friend.

4. **Demonstrate your genuine caring.** Nobody wants to feel as though they are being judged or patronized for their choices or actions. Focusing on your fears, disappointment, confusion, anger,

and other feelings about this person's behavior will emphasize your concern but not come across as accusatory. Begin the conversation by saying that you are concerned about this person's well-being and health.

5. **Focus your intervention on specific behaviors, not about the individual as a whole.** Avoid generalizations about that individual's character (e.g., you're a liar, you're too perfectionistic, you're not trustworthy, you're a failure, etc.). Such generalizations only cause the listener to become defensive and stop listening. Instead, cite specific examples of past actions and statements, and recall the negative consequences of those actions and statements, both for the individual and for those closest to him or her.

6. **Be prepared for defensiveness and denial.** A person with a health problem rarely is willing to admit to it on the first confrontation. Many health problems such as eating disorders or alcohol abuse serve a purpose; they may help the individual in coping with other life stressors, or they may create a temporary semblance of order and control over their lives. In addition, it requires a lot of courage for any individual to admit that he or she has a problem or needs help. As a result, the person you confront may, in turn, attack you and your choices. Be persistent, keep the confrontation focused on the individual (and off you), patiently validate then diffuse the person's anger. Don't give up. You may have to confront a countless number of times before the message is heard.

7. **Establish boundaries.** Most individuals with health problems are unable to recognize that they have one until they have to face the negative, inescapable consequences of their actions and choices. However, many of us have strong caretaking and caregiving instincts. When we see a friend in need, we want to be able to give them whatever is necessary to alleviate the pain or distress; we want to "fix" the problem for them. However, many individuals with health problems can be very manipulative of their significant others—whether intentionally so or not. They will have a constant stream of excuses for why things are going badly, and frequently blame others for their difficulties without owning any personal responsibility. Be sure that you don't inadvertently enable unhealthful behaviors by giving in to the person's demands, pleas, or arguments. For example, if a roommate is missing a lot of classes due to excessive drinking hangovers, volunteering to take notes for him or her will only prolong the problem.

8. **"Become familiar with campus and community resources.** Remember, you are a friend who is concerned, but you do not possess the knowledge or skills to solve your friend's problem for him or her. Ultimately, the responsibility for change lies within the individual who has the problem. No one else can do the work or healing for him or her. Therefore, the goal of your confrontation is to encourage your friend to seek assistance from a trained professional with counseling expertise and accurate health information. By becoming aware of the vast array of resources available now, you will save time later when you really need to make some quick referrals.

In Figure 33, make a list of campus and community contacts, and resources and numbers for each issue presented. National resources have been added for you.

Figure 33: *Health Resources On and Around Campus*

	Campus	Local	National
For depression and suicide			National Suicide Prevention Lifeline **800-273-TALK**
For sexual assault/rape			Sexual Assault Hotline **800-656-4673**
			RAPE (People Against Rape) **800-877-7252**
For domestic violence			National Domestic Violence Hotline **800-799-7233**
For eating disorders			Eating Disorders Center **888-236-1188**
For HIV and other sexually transmitted infections			National AIDS Hotline **800-232-4636**
			STI Hotline **800-227-8922**
For alcohol and other drug abuse			Drug and Alcohol Treatment Hotline **800-622-HELP**
For unwanted pregnancy			Option Line **800-395-HELP**
For gambling addiction			FIRSTEP **877-338-9911**
For sexual/racial harassment			

Questions to Consider

1. How can you use the resources identified above in your peer education efforts?
2. Develop a peer education Website demo (does not have to be online) to showcase resources, overall resources, and services by your program.
3. Develop three personal goals you will use as you grow and develop as a peer educator and when working with your peers.

CPSIA information can be obtained at www.ICGtesting.com
Printed in the USA
BVOW05s0044270116

434295BV00005B/96/P